Isbn 978-0-88146-154-1   MUP/H789

Selected Spiritual Writings of Anne Dutton,
Eighteenth-Century, British-Baptist, Woman Theologian
Volume 6: *Various Works*
Copyright ©2010
Mercer University Press
All rights reserved
Printed in the United States of America
First edition

Mercer University Press is a member of Green Press Initiative
<greenpressinitiatige.org>, a nonprofit orgaization working to help
publishers and printers increase their use of recycled paper
and decrease their use of fiber derived from endangered forests.
This book is printed on recycled paper and meets the minimum
requirements of American National Standard for Information Sciences—
Permanence of Paper for Printed Library Materials, ANSI Z39.48-1984.

Library of Congress Cataloging-in-Publication Data

[CIP data is available from the Library of Congress.]

[See at the end of this volume the list of titles in the Baptist series.]

CONTENTS

ANNE DUTTON
from the frontispiece to
Selections from Letters on Spiritual Subjects /etc./ (1884)

PREFACE

I am grateful to Dr. Russell Morton, Research Librarian, Ashland Theological Seminary and Ms. Sylvia Locher, Head Librarian, Ashland Theological Seminary for helping to acquire the following manuscripts.

I want to thank Mr. Seth Kasten, Head of Reference and Research, Special Collections, The Burke Library at Union Theological Seminary, Columbia University Libraries, New York, for permission to publish the following in rekeyed format:

> *A Postscript To A Letter lately published, on the Duty and Privilege of a Believer, To Live by Faith, and to improve his Faith unto Holiness. Directed To The Society at the Tabernacle in London. To make The Author's Sense of some Words and Phrases in that Letter, more plain to the Persons to whom That was sent, and This is addressed. To which is added, A Caution against Error, when it springs up together with Truth. In a Letter to a Friend. As also, some of the Mistakes of the Moravian Brethren. In a Letter to another Friend. With Postscripts to the Letters added.* London: J. Hart, 1746.

I also want to thank Margaret Sherry Rich, Reference Librarian/Archivist of the Rare Books Division, Department of Rare Books and Special Collections, Princeton University Library for permission to publish the following in rekeyed format: *Letter Sent to an Honourable Gentleman, For the Encouragement of Faith.* London: J. Hart 1743. The last page of this manuscript was acquired from a transcription sent by Kathy M. Flynn, Head of Reference Services, Phillips Library Division of Peabody Essex Museum, Salem, Massachusetts, to whom I express my appreciation.

Also, I wish to thank the Duke University Divinity School Library for permission to publish in rekeyed format the *Letters on Spiritual Subjects: Sent to Relations and Friends.* Parts I and II. 2nd ed. revised. London: Printed for the editor, by T. Bensley; sold by R. Baynes, 1823, 1824.

A special thanks to Kathleen Slusser and Leah Pippen of Ashland Theological Seminary for typing and preparing the manuscripts. My appreciation is also due to Drs. Russell and Dawn Morton for assistance in compiling the index. My thanks to my husband, Dr. Duane F. Watson, for his editorial assistance, and my daughter, Christina Lucille Watson, for her support.

Appreciation is expressed to Mercer University Press for undertaking the entire project.

The manuscripts have been rekeyed, but the original spelling has been retained, expect for the Old and Middle English *f* routinely becomes "s" and the long s (β) has become "ss." Page references to Anne Dutton's works in the introduction refer to the original manuscripts, not as reprinted in this volume.

* * *

In memory of my father,
Laurence W. Ford (1920–2006).

* * *

INTRODUCTION

Letters Sent to an Honourable Gentleman

Letters Sent to an Honourable Gentleman, for the Encouragement of the
Faith. By One who has Tasted that the Lord Is Gracious. London: Printed
by J. Hart, in Poppings-Court, Fleet-Street: And sold by J. Lewis, in
Bartholomew-Close, near West-Smithfield; and E. Gardner, at Milton's
Head, in Gracechurch-Street. 1743.[1]

Anne Dutton's autobiographical work—*A Brief Account of the Gracious Dealings
of God, with a Poor, Sinful, Unworthy Creature*[2]—records in her list of publications
in part III, "Letters sent to an Honourable Gentleman for the Encouragement of
Faith, Vol. I."[3] There once existed two other volumes of letters to this Honourable
Gentleman. The appendix after part III records a volume II of nine *Letters Sent to
an Honourable Gentleman, for the Encouragement of the Faith*."[4] Dutton also
records in the appendix the date on which she wrote this second volume, June 29,
1749.[5]

---

[1]The original manuscript title reads "Letter Sent . . . ," but the first page of the
actual letter reads "Letters sent" (p. 11) and the latter is how the manuscript is
typically referenced and will be so in this volume.

[2]*A Brief Account of the Gracious Dealings of God, with a Poor, Sinful, Unworthy Creature, Relating to Some Particular Experiences of the Lord's Goodness,
in Bringing Out Several Little Tracts, to the Furtherance and Joy of Faith. With an
Appendix, and a Letter Prefixed on the Lawfulness of a Woman's Appearing in
Print.* Part III by A. D. London: Printed by J. Hart, Sold by J. Lewis, 1750.

[3]*A Brief Account of the Gracious Dealings of God*, part III, 93.

[4]*A Brief Account of the Gracious Dealings of God*, appendix, 149.

[5]*A Brief Account of the Gracious Dealings of God*, appendix, 140. Edward C.
Starr, ed., *A Baptist Bibliography* (Rochester NY: American Baptist Historical
Society, 1959) sec. D, 202, records volume III of Dutton's *Letters Sent to an
Honourable Gentleman, for the Encouragement of Faith*. W. T. Whitley , *A Baptist
Bibliography*, 2 vols. (London: Kingsgate Press, 1916, 1922) 1:212, also lists three
volumes, dating vol. II about 1749 and vol. III at 1761. John Cudworth Whitebrook,
Ann Dutton: A Life and Bibliography (London: A. W. Cannon and Co., 1921) p. 16,
no. 10, also notes three volumes, but does not have a date for vol. III.

In the first volume of these letters as printed in this volume, Dutton addresses, "The Author to the Worthy Gentleman, to whom the following Letters were sent."[6] After an amplified address to this gentleman, she adds an "Epistle to the Reader.[7] She writes, "*Dear Reader,* if thou art born from above, if as a *Newborn Babe,* thou *desirest the sincere Milk of the Word that though mayest grow thereby* . . . And for this End, if the Lord please, I have publish'd these letters. And with the same Desire, after the Glory of GOD, and the Service of Souls, the worthy *Gentleman* to whom they were written, most heartily joins with me in their Publication."[8]

The eighteen letters to the Honourable Gentleman follow, ending with, "In the sweet, strong, encircling arms of his unchangeable, everlasting LOVE, I leave you.—And requesting your Prayers, with the utmost Gratitude for all your exceeding great Favours, and particularly for your last kind Visit; permit me to subscribe, dear Sir. Your Honour's most obliged, And most obedient humble Servant.[9] Dutton's letters are for the encouragement and upbuilding of the faithful in situations of trial and persecution. She writes in letter VI, "I rejoice Sir, that your Soul longs to serve your dear Lord Jesus, and that you count it your Honour, your Glory to follow him whithersoever he goeth, notwithstanding the Persecution and Reproaches which may attend it."[10]

In letter VII, Dutton continues that the trials of life are meant to be used for the benefit of greater growth in God, moving the Christian away from reliance upon pleasures. She writes, "Indeed Sir, you meet with Ingratitude, Treachery, Losses and Crosses from the Creatures:—But *these* are to *endear* the Creator, and his infinite Excellencies the more to you. GOD is weaning you from the Breasts of *Creature-Enjoyments,* to solace your Soul with the River of *his* Pleasures. Emptying you of *Creatures,* to fill you with *himself.* And is not HE *better,* infinitely *better* than *all!*"[11]

She continues to discuss the nature of suffering in letter IX, raising up the strength of the Almighty as a shelter in times of trial. She admonishes the Honourable Gentleman, "Wherefore, *trust in the* LORD *at all Times,* and especially, when you are *afraid,* and *pursu'd* by Enemies, *flee unto Him to hide you. Get,* my dear

---

[6]*Letter Sent to an Honourable Gentleman,* iii.

[7]*Letter Sent to an Honourable Gentleman,* vi-ix.

[8]*Letter Sent to an Honourable Gentleman,* vi.

[9]*Letter Sent to an Honourable Gentleman,* 126. The manuscript used for this volume ends abruptly at "And requesting your." The remainder of the quotation was provided by Kathy M. Flynn, Phillips Library, Peabody Essex Museum, Salem MA.

[10]*Letter Sent to an Honourable Gentleman,* 36.

[11]*Letter Sent to an Honourable Gentleman,* 45.

Brother, get by *Faith* into CHRIST afresh; his Heart and Arms are always *open* to embrace you."[12]

In letter XII, Dutton gives the reader her understanding of the significance of her correspondence:

> And I love to hear your Complaints, and the Causes of your Grief. Not that I take pleasure in your *Grief,* but in your pouring out the same into *my Bosom.* Oh that our dear Lord Jesus would give me a *large Heart,* like his *own,* that may have *room* enough in it for all your sorrows, and a *quick Sensation* of all your Griefs! And oh, that while I *suffer* together with *you,* as a dear Fellow-Member in the Body of Christ, my Lord would pour his *Spirit* upon me, that like *him,* in my *little Measure,* I might know how to *speak a Word in Season to your weary Soul!*[13]

Letters on Spiritual Subjects

Letters on Spiritual Subjects; Sent to Relations and Friends. By the Late Mrs. Anne Dutton. Parts I & II. Edited by Christopher Goulding. Second edition, revised. London: T.Bensley, 1823, 1824.[14]

The editor, Christopher Goulding, prepared these letters of Anne Dutton for publication with the help of the then current pastor of her former congregation, Rev. Mr. Skilliter of the Great Gransden Baptist Church, and a Mrs. Tippet who was personally acquainted with Anne Dutton.[15] Goulding published her works "so that ANNE DUTTON may no longer remain a stranger to the church of Christ; but her memory be rescued from oblivion. . . . "[16] He praised Dutton's literary and spiritual ability, writing:

> It is unnecessary for me to say any thing in commendation of these letters, as both the style and matter of them sufficiently declare the Authoress to have been an extraordinary woman, eminently taught of the Spirit, and

---

[12]*Letter Sent to an Honourable Gentleman,* 66.

[13]*Letter Sent to an Honourable Gentleman,* 78.

[14]Goulding's edition probably gleaned letters from Anne Dutton's, *Letters on Spiritual Subjects and Divers Occasions, Sent to Relatives and Friends,* 7 vols. (London: Printed and Sold by John Oswald and Ebenezer Gardner, 1740–1749). See Whitebrook, *Ann Dutton,* 16n.5.

[15]*Letters on Spiritual Subjects Sent to Relations and Friends* 1:v.

[16]*Letters on Spiritual Subjects* 1:v.

possessing a depth of knowledge of the mysteries of the kingdom of God (Luke viii.13) far beyond what his children in general are favoured with.[17]

Goulding contended that the major contribution of these letters was as an encouragement for the weak of the flock. He writes, "The Authoress considered herself called upon to labour in behalf of the young and weak of the flock, more particularly than to old established Christians."[18] Goulding supports his contention by quoting from one of Dutton's letters to a minister:

I thank you, Sir, for your kind desire of my weak correspondence: but I humbly think that it is not my work to write much to the eminent servants of my Lord; but rather, as he has called and enabled me, to feed his Lambs; and towards the *young and weak of the flock* he gives me yearning bowels."[19]

Summarizing the significance of Dutton's letters, Goulding declares, "Her letters, therefore, are in general very encouraging to such as are quickened by the Holy Spirit to feel their lost estate, and are earnestly seeking after the knowledge of their interest in the Saviour. . . ."[20]

Part I of *Letters on Spiritual Subjects* begins with Dutton bearing testimony that her writing was due to her intimate relationship with Jesus Christ for over thirty years: "As for Christ, my Jesus, my friend, my bridegroom, my life, my all; this is the testimony I bear of him, from more than thirty years' acquaintance with him—that he is altogether lovely, the chiefest among ten thousand."[21] For Dutton the fullness of Christ's grace was a boundless ocean in her life: "But the fulness of Christ is a boundless ocean that has neither shore nor bottom! . . . And yet my Lord's fulness will for ever abide an inexhaustible, undiminished ocean; a sea of life for me to swim in, that to the days of eternity I can never swim over."[22]

Part I contains letters I-XIX addressed to men and women. letter XI is of particular note as it defines her doctrines of election according to Reformed theology, expounded with the use of such references as Genesis 25:22-23; Deuteronomy 14:2; Psalms 85:4; Malachi 1:2; Romans 5:5; 8:29-31; 9:6, 29; 11:5,7; Ephesians 1:1-11; 3:11; Hebrews 10:23; and I John 4:16,19; 5:3. She defends the doctrine of God's choosing the elect, writing, "But, as election is a secret hid in God, and can only be known, as to the persons interested therein, by their being called by special grace,

---

[17]*Letters on Spiritual Subjects* 1:vi.
[18]*Letters on Spiritual Subjects* 1:iii.
[19]*Letters on Spiritual Subjects* 1:iv.
[20]*Letters on Spiritual Subjects* 1:iv.
[21]*Letters on Spiritual Subjects* 1:1-2.
[22]*Letters on Spiritual Subjects* 1:2.

according to God's purpose, fix your mind rather upon the general call of the gospel unto faith in Christ, and repentance towards God. . . . "[23] She concludes with a plea to come to Christ: "If then, dear Sir, the cry of your soul is, 'What must I do to be saved?' hear what the answer of God to you is, 'Believe on the Lord Jesus Christ, and thou shalt be saved,' Acts xvi.31."[24]

Part II contains letters XX-XXXII addressed to men, women, and clergy. The first one, letter XX, is to a "Mr. W." which could be Mr. George Whitefield to whom she corresponded, but it is uncertain.[25] Letter XXXII is addressed to a "Mrs. T"[26] which might be Dutton's acquaintance, Mrs. Tippet that Goulding refers to in his preface, [27]but that is uncertain. Like Part I, these are letters of encouragement for the seeking soul and the weak in faith. Of particular note is letter XXIII entitled, *"On the Lord's being the Portion of his People,"*[28] which is the longest letter in Part II. It is a letter addressed to a "Dear Sir" and speaks of God as the hope of his people using Lamentations 3:24.

> *Dear Sir,* My heart rejoiceth in your consolation, by that sweet persuasion which the Lord gave you, that he was your portion. And, as to the word you want me to hint something from, alas, I am a child, and cannot speak! nevertheless, if the Lord by unworthy me will please to give you any hints for your furtherance and joy of faith, I would gladly bring what he sends from the words you request my thoughts upon, as they stand recorded, Lam, iii. 24, "The Lord is my portion, saith my soul, therefore will I hope in him."[29]

A Postscript to a Letter

A Postscript to a Letter lately published on the Duty and Privilege of a Believer, To live by Faith, and to improve his Faith unto Holiness. Directed To the Society at the Tabernacle in London. To Make The Author's Sense of some Words and Phrases in that Letter, more plain to the Persons to whom That was sent, and This is addresseed. To which is added, A Caution against Error, when it springs up Together with Truth. In a Letter to a Friend. As Also, Some of the Mistakes of the Moravian

---

[23]*Letters on Spiritual Subjects* 1:68.

[24]*Letters on Spiritual Subjects* 1:69.

[25]*Letters on Spiritual Subjects* 2:3.

[26]*Letters on Spiritual Subjects* 2:115.

[27]*Letters on Spiritual Subjects* 1:5.

[28]*Letters on Spiritual Subjects* 2:14.

[29]*Letters on Spiritual Subjects* 2:14.

Brethren. In a Letter to another Friend. With Postscripts to the Letters added. By One who has tasted that the Lord is Gracious. London: Printed by J. Hart, in Popping's-Court, Fleet-Street, 1746.

Anne Dutton wrote to George Whitefield's Society at the Tabernacle in London about the influence of the Moravian Brethren there. She articulates mistakes of the Moravian Brethren as she saw them from her Calvinist perspective. She is writing at the time when many of the people are leaving Whitefield's Tabernacle and joining the Moravians.

Whitefield began the Tabernacle in 1741 in Moorfields in London. By 1742, he had nearly 1100 members. John Cennick (1718-1755), a lay evangelist was Whitefield's assistant at the Tabernacle. Whitefield and Cennick began visiting the Moravians in England in 1741 and 1742. Moravian influence grew at the Tabernacle thereafter. By 1744, when Whitefield left Cennick in charge of the Tabernacle when he traveled to America, the Tabernacle was strongly influenced by the Moravians. In January 1745, Howell Harris, Welsh revivalist and associate of Whitefield, warned Whitefield that many of his followers would become Moravian Brethren. Harris later became in charge of Whitefield's work at the Tabernacle. Harris was most prophetic, for on November 20, 1745, Cennick wrote and asked to become Moravian Brethren. Many others from the Tabernacle followed Cennick to join the Moravian Brethren By 1746, Whitefield stated that he had lost 400 of his 1100 members approximately to the Moravians.

Harris reported that followers from the Tabernacle who wanted to become Moravians, but were rejected, eventually joined William Cudworth (1717/18–1763). He was the former school supervisor at Whitefield's Tabernacle who had become antinomian. Cudworth believed that faith exempted one from the moral law. For this belief, he was expelled from Whitefield's Tabernacle and the English Calvinist Methodist Association. On November 13, 1745 Cudworth asked to be involved with the Moravians, but they declined. Thereafter, he established his own meeting houses.[30]

Dutton wrote at this crucial time after John Cennick left Whitefield for the Moravian Brethren. She writes this pamphlet of several letters in refutation of the doctrine of the Moravian Brethren. She begins with a postscript to a letter which she had written previously to William Cudworth. She then adds two more letters with postscripts addressed to friends refuting Moravian Brethren doctrine. Wesley disagreed on similar issues with the Moravians as did Dutton, for example, the doctrine of Stillness.[31]

---

[30]Colin Podmore, *The Moravian Church in England, 1728–1760*, Oxford Historical Monographs (Oxford UK: Clarendon Press, 1998) 88-94.

[31]JoAnn Ford Watson, comp., *Selected Spiritual Writings of Anne Dutton:*

Beginning with the postscript, Dutton wrote Cudworth in 1747 in a letter entitled, *A Letter to Mr. William Cudworth, In Vindication of the Truth from his Misrepresentations: with Respect to the Work of the Spirit in Faith, Holiness, The New Birth & c. Being a Reply to his Answer to the Postscript of a Letter Lately Published, and c.* Cudworth replied with a dialogue entitled, *Truth Defended and Cleared from Mistakes and Misrepresentations.* This work is found in Cudworth's collected works entitled *Christ Alone Exalted* (London, 1747) which includes various Moravian sources and works that Dutton refutes in her letters; sources by such Moravian theologians as John Eaton (1574/75–1641), John Simpson, and Samuel Richardson who emphasized justification by faith alone and Christ's grace and righteousness to the exclusion of sanctifying works.

The first letter is entitled, "A Postscript to a Letter lately published on the Duty and Privilege of a *Believer*, To live by Faith, and to improve his Faith unto Holiness. Directed *To the Society at the* Tabernacle *in* London. To Make The Author's Sense of some Words and Phrases in that Letter, more *plain* to the Persons to whom *That* was sent, and *This* is addressed." Dutton is writing this letter to clarify some of her thoughts about the Moravian Brethren she had written in a previous letter. Dutton pens, "Permit me then, my dear Brethren and Sisters, to prevent Mistakes about some Words and Phrases in my Letter, to give you a few Hints. . . . "[32] Dutton offers five hints which are also as follows:

> I. of my Intendment in such Words, as *Sight,* Inward *Feelings,* and Spiritual *Sense.* II. of what I *intend* by Believing *without* and *upon* These. III. Of some of those *Notions* which have been advanc'd of late, which I take to be *Anti-Scriptural,* and *Anti-evangelical.* IV. Concerning some Things which have been said by Those who advance These Notions. And to close the Whole, V. With a Word to you, my dear Brethren and Sisters, who Thro' the *Power of Christ resting upon you,* are enabled to *hold fast the faithful Word as you have been taught.* . . .[33]

Dutton writes again about such practices, "And to say, That a *Christian* hath true *Faith* in Christ, or *believes* on Him, without *Sight,* without an internal Revelation of his Glory by the Holy Ghost thro' the Word of the Gospel; without the *Feeling* of the Love and Power of Christ upon his Soul, and of his own Acts of Faith towards this blessed Object; and without any *Sense,* or Experience of his Faith

---

Eighteenth-Century, British-Baptist, Woman Theologian, vol. 1: *Letters* (Macon GA: Mercer University Press, 2003) xxiv-xxx, xxxiv-xxxv.

[32]*A Postscript to a Letter*, 1.

[33]*A Postscript to a Letter*, 1-2.

working by Love, unto Holiness of Heart and Life: Is *Anti-Scriptural*, and *Anti-evangelical*."[34]

Dutton critiques Moravians again regarding a limited understanding of sanctification by the Holy Spirit, particularly their denial of personal holiness: "Another *Notion* advanc'd, which I take to be *Anti-Scriptural* and *Anti-evangelical*, is, That the Holy Ghost's *revealing* of Christ's perfect personal Holiness, as our Representing-Head, and *shewing* us, our mystical Completeness in Him; is all that is intended by *The Sanctification of the Spirit*. . . . "[35] She points out the Moravian Brethrens' conflict of denying personal holiness and yet affirming areas of spiritual growth: "That tho' They *deny* inherent and personal *Holiness*; they do *not* deny the *Fruits of the Spirit*, and a *Conversation becoming the Gospel*.[36] She insists that sanctification is expected by the very nature of Christianity, especially as taught by Whitefield:

> "Was not the Doctrine of the *New Birth*, of Heart-Holiness, of a Change of Nature, or a Man's being a *new Creature* in Christ Jesus; one of the great Doctrines *preach'd* by the Rev. Mr. *Whitefield* and his *Assistants*, as absolutely necessary to be experienc'd by every Man, in order to his spiritual and eternal Happiness, in the present and everlasting Enjoyment of God?"[37]

Dutton concludes the letter with a call to faithful witness: "And, *Blessed* are *they*, who are honour'd of the Lord, to be his faithful *Witnesses*. With Him. *The faithful and true* Witness, they shall *live and reign forever*! Even so then, *Stand fast in the Lord, my beloved Brethren*; contending *for*, and living up *to the Truths* of his *holy Gospel*."[38]

The second letter is entitled, "*A Caution Against Error, when it springs up Together with, Truth. In a Letter to a Friend.*" Here Dutton again addresses Moravian Brethren controversy. She particularly mentions divisions mentioning the divisions between Brother Cennick and Brother Harris. She writes, "My Concern for *you*, in an especial Manner; for dear Brother *Cennick,* and the rest of the Brethren, which appear on one Side, against Brother *Harris*, and others of the Brethren, since I heard that there was a Division among you; has been great."[39]

Dutton distinguishes faith and works, clarifying that faith is for justification and works show sanctification. Dutton writes, "But, my dear Brother, the

---

[34]*A Postscript to a Letter*, 6.

[35]*A Postscript to a Letter*, 11.

[36]*A Postscript to a Letter*, 18.

[37]*A Postscript to a Letter*, 18.

[38]*A Postscript to a Letter*, 50.

[39]*A Caution Against Error*, 51.

Acceptance of our *Works*, as I humbly think, belongs rather to *Sanctification* than to *Justification*; to that Sanctification of our *Services*, which we have in and thro' Christ, than to the Justification of our *Persons*.[40] Dutton assets Reformed theology to correct the Moravian Brethren misunderstanding of the relationship between faith and works. At the end of this letter is a postscript with a letter to Whitefield showing her sympathies with his Reformed theology.[41]

Dutton's third letter is entitled, "*Some of the Mistakes of the Moravian Brethren. In a Letter to a Friend.*" Dutton was asked to write a letter about the mistakes of the Moravian Brethren and she responds by focusing on four points: "I take the *Moravian Brethren* to be mistaken in the four following Points: In That, I. They assert *Universal Redemption.* II. They are against a *Doctrinal Knowledge* of the *Truths of God in his Word.* III. Are against the *Use* of the *Means of Grace*, by *unconverted Sinners*, and *weak Believers.* And IV. Against the *Law* of *God,* as to its being a *Rule of Life* to a *Believer* under the *Gospel.*"[42]

Dutton writes against the Moravian Brethren doctrine of universal redemption or atonement that Christ died for all. She advocates the Calvinist doctrine of particular atonement that Christ died for the elect. She advocates predestination unto election in Christ for salvation.

> *First.* In that they assert *Universal Redemption:* or, the Redemption of all, and every Individual of the Human Race. Whereas our Lord faith, That he laid down his Life for *his Sheep*, John X. 15. For the Elect of God, appointed to Salvation thro' Jesus Christ, before the World began. For these, given by God the Father to Christ, to be his *Sheep*, did HE as the *good Shepherd*, lay down his *Life.* And not for the *Goats*, who shall stand at the last Day on his *Left-Hand*, and be sent away from him, as *cursed,* into *everlasting Fire, prepar'd for the Devil and his angels*, Mat. XXV. 33, 41.[43]

Dutton continues to critique the Moravian Brethren, particularly her understanding that they wanted only heart knowledge and not head knowledge of the Bible. They did not advocate learning doctrinal knowledge of the truths of God's Word found in the Bible. She writes, "This they slight, as if it was nothing Worth. Whereas, one great Design of God, in the Revelation of his Truths in the Holy Scriptures, is, that we should *acquaint ourselves* therewith. And a *Head-Knowledge* thereof, the Lord hath appointed, in order to an *Heart-Acquaintance* there with."[44]

---

[40]*A Caution against Error*, 65.

[41]*A Caution against Error*, 69-70.

[42]*Some of the Mistakes of the Moravian Brethren*, 72.

[43]*Some of the Mistakes of the Moravian Brethren*, 72-73.

[44]*Some of the Mistakes of the Moravian Brethren*, 74.

Responding to Moravian Brethren practices toward unbelievers or weak believers on the practice of the Lord's Supper, she believes that all Christians should partake. She writes, "Again, the *Moravians* say, That it is not the Duty of weak Believers, of such that have not the full Assurance of Faith, to partake of the *Lord's Supper*. Whereas the weakest Believer, hath an equal Interest in Christ, and Right to this Ordinance, with the strongest."[45] Dutton continues, "The *Moravians* therefore, by saying that those who have not the full Assurance of Faith, ought not to partake of the Lord's Supper: Do *err* from the Truth, and hinder the Faith of weak Believers."[46]

Dutton also states that the Moravian Brethren are against preaching the Word of God, the Law, to people about their sinful nature and ways. She writes, "Once more, under this Head, the *Moravian Brethren*, are against *preaching*, or *expounding* of the Word of God. They are against preaching of the *Law*, to shew Sinners their Misery by Nature: And say, we have nothing to do with the *Law*, in this Regard, under the *Gospel*."[47]

Dutton further objects to the Moravian Brethren understanding of the Law of God. She asserts that they do not understand the Law of God as a rule of life for a believer under the gospel, writing, "In that they are against the *Law of God*, as to its being a *Rule of Life* to a *Believer* under the *Gospel*."[48] Dutton states, "That henceforth, we should perform good Works, not to *ourselves*, under the Influence of the Law of Works, for our Justification; but unto God, under the Influence of the Love of Christ, and for the Glory of Him who hath saved us."[49]

At the end of this letter Dutton adds a postscript which provides another rebuttal of the Moravian Brethren notion of universal redemption or atonement. She again asserts particular atonement that Christ's grace is for the elect. She also emphasizes faith in Christ. It is election unto salvation. She writes:

> And as to the Attribute of Divine *Mercy*, that is and will be glorify'd in a Way of absolute *Sovereignty*. The Lord will *have* Mercy, *on whom he* will *have* Mercy. And not a *Dram* of Mercy, will the *God* of Mercy, shew unto *any out* of *Christ*. There is no *Salvation* by *Christ* for *any*, but for those who *believe* in him. And *All* will be found *out* of Christ at last, who don't enter *into him* by Faith now."[50]

---

[45]*Some of the Mistakes of the Moravian Brethren*, 78.
[46]*Some of the Mistakes of the Moravian Brethren*, 78.
[47]*Some of the Mistakes of the Moravian Brethren*, 78.
[48]*Some of the Mistakes of the Moravian Brethren*, 81.
[49]*Some of the Mistakes of the Moravian Brethren*, 82.
[50]*Some of the Mistakes of the Moravian Brethren*, 102.

BIBLIOGRAPHY

Primary Sources: Anne Dutton[51]

A Brief Account of the Gracious Dealings of God, with a Poor, Sinful, Unworthy Creature, in Three Parts . . . With an Appendix. And a Letter Prefixed, on the Lawfulness of a Woman's Appearing in Print. London: John Hart, 1750.
This autobiography was published in three parts over a period of years. Part 1 and part 2 were originally published together with separate titles as *A Brief Account of the Gracious Dealings of God, with a Poor, Sinful, Unworthy Creature, Relating to the Work of Divine Grace on the Heart, in a Saving Conversion to Christ, and to Some Establishment in Him* and *A Brief Account of the Gracious Dealings of God, with a Poor, Sinful, Unworthy Creature, Relating to a Train of Special Providences Attending Life, by which the Work of Faith was Carried on with Power.* London: John Hart, 1743. Part 3 and the "Letter" were included with the 1750 publication (see above). Part 3 is entitled *A Brief Account of the Gracious Dealings of God, with a Poor, Sinful, Unworthy Creature, Relating to Some Particular Experiences of the Lord's Goodness, in Bringing Out Several Little Tracts, to the Furtherance and Joy of Faith.*
The publications referred to in the title ("Several Little Tracts") are pamphlets published by John Hart before 1750.
(Parts 1 and 2 [1743] are available in the United States at Harvard University and Baylor University. The complete work [1750] is in the British Library, London.)

Brief Hints Concerning Baptism. London, 1746. May be identical to *Letters on the Ordinance of Baptism* (1746). (Whitebrook, 18 no. 25.)

Brief Hints on God's Fatherly Chastisements, Showing Their Nature, Necessity and Usefulness, and the Saints' Duty to Wait upon God for Deliverance When under His Fatherly Corrections. 1743. (Whitebrook, 17 no. 14.)

A Caution against Error When It Springs Up together with the Truth, in a Letter to a Friend. 1746. (Whitebrook, 17 no. 24.)

---

[51]"Whitebrook" refers to the bibliography of John Cudworth Whitebrook, in his *Ann Dutton: A Life and Bibliography*, 15-20, as offprinted from "The Life and Works of Mrs. Ann Dutton," in *Transactions of the Baptist Historical Society* 7:129-46.

A Discourse Concerning God's Act of Adoption. To Which is Added a Discourse upon the Inheritance of the Adopted Sons of God. London: E. Gardner, 1737. (British Library, London.)

A Discourse Concerning the New-Birth: To Which Are Added Sixty-Four Hymns; Compos'd on Several Subjects; with an Epistle Recommendatory, by the Reverend Mr. Jacob Rogers, B.A. London: John Hart, 1743. (Yale University Beinecke Rare Books Library.)

A Discourse Concerning the New-Birth: To Which Are Added Two Poems: The One on Salvation in Christ, by Free-Grace, for the Chief of Sinners: The Other on a Believer's Safety and Duty: with an Epistle Recommendatory, by the Reverend Mr. Jacob Rogers, B.A. London: John Oswald and Ebenezer Gardner, 1740. (British Library, London.)

A Discourse upon Justification: Shewing the Matter, Manner, Time and Effects of it. To Which are Added Three Poems: I. On the Special Work of the Spirit in the Hearts of the Elect. . . . III. On a Believer's Safety and Duty. London: printed by John Hart and sold by J. Lewis and E. Gardner, 1740, 1743. (The 1743 edition is at Harvard University Libraries.)

A Discourse upon Walking with God: In a Letter to a Friend. Together with Some Hints upon Joseph's Blessing, Deut. 33.13, &c. As Also a Brief Account How the Author Was Brought into Gospel-Liberty. London: printed for the author and sold by E. Gardner, 1735. (Gale Group.)

Divine, Moral, and Historical Miscellanies in Prose and Verse. Edited by A. Dutton. 1761. (British Library.)

Five Letters to a Newly Married Pair. 1759. (Whitebrook, 18 no. 33.)

Hints of the Glory of Christ: As the Friend and Bridgroom of the Church: From the Seven Last Verses of the Fifth Chaper of Solomon's Song: In a Letter to a Friend. London: printed by John Hart and sold by J. Lewis, 1748. (British Library, London.)

Originally published as *Meditations and Observations upon the Eleventh and Twelfth Verses of the Sixth Chapter of Solomon's Song.* 1743. (Whitebrook, 16 no. 13; 18 no. 27.)

The Hurt that Sin Doth to Believers, etc. 1733. Second edition, 1749. (Whitebrook, 18 no. 30.)

A Letter from Mrs. Anne Dutton to the Reverend Mr. G. Whitefield. Philadelphia: printed and sold by William Bradford, 1743. (Library Company of Philadelphia.)

A Letter on the Application of the Holy Scriptures. Poppings Court: printed by John Hart and sold by J. Lewis, 1754. (Whitebrook, 18 no. 31.)

A Letter on the Divine Eternal Sonship of Jesus Christ: . . . Occasioned by the Perusal of Mr. Romaine's Sermon . . . Entitled, A Discourse Upon the Self-Existence of Jesus Christ. With Three Letters on Assurance of Interest in Christ: . . . Written as the Author's Thoughts, on Part of Mr. Marshal's . . . The

Gospel-Mystery of Sanctification. And Two Letters on the Gift of the Holy Spirit to Believers . . . By One Who Has Tasted that the Lord is Gracious. London: printed by John Hart and sold by G. Keith, 1757. (Oxford University Bodleian Library.)

A Letter on the Duty and Privilege of a Believer to Live by Faith, and to Improve His Faith unto Holiness. 1745. (Whitebrook, 17 n. 21.)

A Letter on Perseverance, against Mr. Wesley. 1747. (Whitebrook, 18 no. 38.)

A Letter to All Men on the General Duty of Love among Christians. 1742. (Whitebrook, 16 no. 7.)

A Letter to all the Saints on the General Duty of Love: Humbly Presented, by One That is Less Than the Least of Them All, and Unworthy to be of Their Happy Number. London: printed by John Hart and sold by Samuel Mason, 1742; printed by John Hart and sold by J. Lewis and E. Gardner, 1743. Philadelphia: Joseph Crukshank, 1774. (Harvard University Andover; Harvard Theological Library has the 1743 edition.)

A Letter to All Those That Love Christ in Philadelphia. To Excite Them to Adhere to, and Appear for, the Truths of the Gospel. 1743(?). (Whitebrook, 17 no. 19.)

A Letter to the Believing Negroes, lately Converted to Christ in America. 1742. (Whitebrook, 16 no. 9.)

A Letter to Christians at the Tabernacle. 1744(?). (Whitebrook, 18 no. 37.)

A Letter to Mr. William Cudworth, In Vindication of the Truth from his Misrepresentations: With Respect to the Work of the Spirit in Faith, Holiness, The New Birth &c. Being a Reply to his Answer to the Postscript of a Letter Lately Published, &c. 1747. (Whitebrook, 18 no. 26.)

A Letter to the Reverend Mr. John Wesley. In Vindication of the Doctrines of Absolute, Unconditional Election, Particular Redemption, Special Vocation, and Final Perseverance. Occasioned Chiefly by Some Things in His Dialogue between a Predestinarian and His Friend; and In His Hymns on God's Everlasting Love. London: printed by John Hart and sold by Samuel Mason, 1742. (Pitts Theology Library, Emory University.)

A Letter to Such of the Servants of Christ Who May Have Any Scruple about the Lawfulness of Printing Anything Written by a Woman. 1743. (Whitebrook, 17 no. 18.)

Letters against Sanddemanianism and with a Letter on Reconciliation. (Whitebrook, 18 no. 36.)

Letters on the Being and Working of Sin in a Justified Man. 1745. (Whitebrook, 17 no. 20.)

Letters on the Ordinance of Baptism. 1746. May be identical to *Brief Hints Concerning Baptism.* London, 1746. (Whitebrook, 18 no. 25.)

Letters to the Reverend Mr. John Westley [sic] *against Perfection as Not Attainable in This Life.* London: John Hart, 1743. (Pitts Theological Library, Emory University; John Rylands Library, University of Manchester.)

Letters on Spiritual and Divers Occasions. London: G. Keith, 1749. (Whitebrook, 18 no. 29.)

Letters on Spiritual Subjects, and Divers Occasions, Sent to Relatives and Friends. London: printed and sold by John Oswald and Ebenenzer Gardner, 1740. London: printed by John Hart and sold by J. Lewis, 1748.

Letters on Spiritual Subjects and Divers Occasions, Sent to the Reverend Mr. George Whitefield And others of his Friends and Acquaintance. To Which is Added, A Letter on the Being and Working of Sin, in the Soul of justify'd Man, as Consistent with His State of Justification in Christ, and Sanctification Through Him: With the Nature of His Obedience, and of His Comfort, Consider'd: As the One is from God, and the other to Him; notwithstanding his Corruptions may be great, and His Graces Small in His Own Sight. As Also, A Letter on the Duty and Privilege of a Believer, To Live by Faith, and to Improve his Faith unto Holiness. By One Who Has Tasted that the Lord is Gracious. London: John Hart, 1745. (Pitts Theology Library, Emory University. Incomplete copy.)

Letters on Spiritual Subjects Sent to Relations and Friends. Two parts. Second revised edition. Edited by Christopher Goulding. London: T. Bensley, 1823–1824. (Duke University Library.)

Letters Sent to an Honourable Gentleman, for the Encouragement of Faith. By One Who Has Tasted that the Lord is Gracious. London: printed by John Hart and sold by J. Lewis and E. Gardner, 1743. (Boston Athenaeum.)

Meditations and Observations upon the Eleventh and Twelfth Verses of the Sixth Chapter of Solomon's Song. 1743. Published later as a pamphlet entitled *Hints of the Glory of Christ as the Friend and Bridegroom of the Church: From the Seven Last Verses of the Fifth Chapter of Solomon's Song, &c*. 1748. (Whitebrook, 16 no. 13; 18 no. 27.)

Mr. Sanddeman Refuted by an Old Woman: or Thoughts on His Letters to the Author of Theron and Aspasio. In a Letter from a Friend in the Country to a Friend in Town. London: John Hart, 1761. (Brown University Library.)

A Narration of the Wonders of Grace, in Six Parts. I. Of Christ the Mediator, as Set Up from Everlasting in All the Glory of Headship. II. Of God's Election and Covenant—Transactions Concerning a Remnant in His Son. III. Of Christ's Incarnation and Redemption. IV. Of the Work of the Spirit, Respecting the Church in General, throughout the New Testament Dispensation, from Christ's Ascension to His Second Coming. V. Of Christ's Glorious Appearing and Kingdom. VI. Of Gog and Magog; Together with the Last Judgment. To Which Is Added, A Poem on the Special Work of the Spirit in the Hearts of the Elect, also, Sixty One Hymns Composed on Several Subjects. A new edition. Revised, with a preface and collected memoir of the author, by John Andrews Jones. London: John Bennett, 1833. Pages xxxii + 115. (Covenant Theological Seminary, St. Louis.)

Second edition. "Corrected by the author, with additions." London: printed for the author and sold by John Oswald, 1734. Pages viii + [9-]143.

First edition. London: printed for and sold by the author, 1734. Pages viii + 139.

Occasional Letters on Spiritual Subjects. Seven volumes. Popping's Court: John Hart and Bartholomew Close: J. Lewis, 1740–1749.

A Postcript to a Letter Lately Published, on the Duty and Privilege of a Believer to Live by Faith, &c . . . Directed to the Society at the Tabernacle in London. . . . As Also, Some of the Mistakes of the Moravian Brethren. . . . By One Who Has Tasted that the Lord is Gracious. London: printed by John Hart and sold by J. Lewis and E. Gardner, 1746. (Union Theological Seminary, New York.)

Selections from [Occasional] Letters on Spiritual Subjects: Addressed to Relatives and Friends. Compiled by James Knight. London: John Gadsby, 1884. (Turpin Library, Dallas Theological Seminary.)

A Sight of Christ Necessary for All True Christians and Gospel Ministers. 1743. (Whitebrook, 16 no. 11.)

Thoughts on the Lord's Supper. London, 1748. (Whitebrook, 18 no. 28.)

Three Letters on I. The Marks of a Child of God. II. The Soul-Diseases of God's Children; . . . III. God's Prohibition of His Peoples Unbelieving Fear: . . . By One Who Has Tasted that the Lord is Gracious. London: printed by John Hart and sold by G. Keith and J. Fuller, 1761. (Oxford University Bodleian Library.)

A Treatise on Justification: Showing the Matter, Manner, Time, and Effects of It. Third edition. Glasgow: printed by William Smith for Archibald Coubrough, 1778. The author is listed as "the Rev. Mr. Thomas Dutton," presumably one of Anne Dutton's pseudonymns. (British Library, London.)

Primary Sources: Dutton's Contemporaries

B. D. [Benjamin Dutton]. *The Superaboundings of the Exceeding Riches of God's Free Grace, towards the Chief of the Chief of Sinners, &c.* No publisher, no date.

Baker, Frank, ed. *The Works of John Wesley.* Volume 26. *Letters II (1740–1755).* Oxford: Clarendon Press, 1982.

Bunyan, John. *The Holy War.* London: printed for Dorman Newman and Benjamin Alsop, 1682.

__________. *Pilgrim's Progress.* 1678. Repr.: Ulrichsville OH: Barbour Publishing, 1985.

__________. *The Works of John Bunyan: With an Introduction to Each Treatise, Notes, and a Sketch of His Life, Times, and Contemporaries.* Three volumes.

Edited by George Offor. Repr.: Edinburgh and Carlisle PA: Banner of Truth Trust, 1991. Original: Glasgow: W. G. Blackie and Son, 1854.

Cudworth, William, *Truth Defended and Cleared from Mistakes and Misrepresentations*. See Arthur Wallington, "Wesley and Ann Dutton," 48.

Middleton, Erasmus. *A Letter from the Reverend Mr. [Erasmus Middleton] to A[nne] D[utton]*. 1735. (British Library, London.)

Wesley, John. *A Dialogue Between a Predestinarian and His Friend*. London: W. Stratan, 1741.

__________. *Wesley's Standard Sermons*. Two volumes. Edited by Edward H. Sugden. Fifth edition. London: Epworth, 1961.

__________. *The Works of John Wesley*. Fourteen volumes. Third edition. Edited by Thomas Jackson et al. London: Wesleyan Conference Office, 1873–1893. Repr.: Grand Rapids: Zondervan, 1958-1959.

__________. *The Works of John Wesley*. Volume 19. *Journal and Diaries II (1738–1743)*. Edited by W. Reginald Ward and Richard P. Heitzenrater. Nashville: Abingdon Press, 1990.

Wesley, John and Charles. *Hymns of God's Everlasting Love*. Bristol: S. and F. Farley, 1741.

__________. *The Poetical Works of John and Charles Wesley*. Thirteen volumes. Edited by George Osborn. London: Wesleyan-Methodist Conference Office, 1868–1872.

Whitefield, George. "A Letter to the Rev. Mr. John Wesley in Answer to His Sermon Entitled 'Free Grace' " (24 December 1740). In [Whitefield's] *Journals*, 571-88. London: Banner of Truth Trust, 1960.

__________. *The Works of the Reverend George Whitefield*. Six volumes. London: Edward and Charles Dilley, 1771–1772.

Secondary Sources

Austin, Roland. "The Weekly History." *Proceedings of the Wesley Historical Society* 11/2 (June 1917): 239-43.

Burder, Samuel. See under Thomas Gibbons.

Dana, Daniel. See under Thomas Gibbons.

A Dictionary of Hymnology. Edited by John Julian. New York: Scribner's, 1892.

Gibbons, Thomas. *Memoirs of Eminently Pious Women, Who Were Ornaments to Their Sex, Blessings to Their Families, and Edifying Examples to the Church and World*. Two volumes. London: printed for J. Buckland, 1777.

  (2) Dana's abridged edition: "Abridged from the large work of Dr. Gibbons, London, by Daniel Dana." Women and the Church in America 9. Newburyport MA: printed for the subscribers by Angier March, 1803.

  (3) Jerment's expanded edition: "Republished [with some omissions] in 1804, with an additional volume by George Jerment." Two volumes. (Volume

1 contained all of Gibbons's material, originally in two volumes; volume 2 contained additional material by Jerment.) London: printed by W. Nicholson for R. Ogles, 1804.

(4) Burder's new and further expanded edition: "A new edition, embellished with eighteen portraits, corrected and enlarged by Samuel Burder." Three volumes. (Volume 1 comprises the original material of Gibbons; volume 2 is Jerment's 1804 addition; volume 3 adds Burder's new material.) London: Ogles, Duncan, and Cochran, 1815.

(Gibbons's *Memoirs* is most readily available today in the following Burder edition. Consequently, *Memoirs* is routinely cited in the literature under "Burder" as author.)

(5) Reprint of the Burder expanded edition: "From a late London edition, in three volumes; now complete in one volume." One volume. Philadelphia: J. J. Woodward, 1834ff. (This is the edition routinely cited herein, and that in its 1836 reprinting.)

Green, Richard. *Anti-Methodist Publications: Issued during the Eighteenth Century: A Chronologically Arranged and Annotated Bibliography of All Known Books and Pamphlets Written in Opposition to the Methodist Revival during the Life of Wesley; Together with an Account of Replies to Them, and of Some Other Publications. A Contribution to Methodist History*. London: C. H. Kelly, 1902. Repr.: New York: Burt Franklin, 1973.

Haykin, Michael. "The Celebrated Mrs. Anne Dutton." *Evangelical Times* (April 2001). (The third in an extended series of articles under the general title "A Cloud of Witnesses.")

Heitzenrater, Richard P. *Wesley and the People Called Methodists*. Nashville: Abingdon, 1995.

Herbert, George. *The English Poems of George Herbert*. Edited by C. A. Patrides. London: S. M. Dent and Sons, 1991.

Jerment, George. See under Thomas Gibbons.

Johnson, Dale A. *Women and Religion in Britain and Ireland: An Annotated Bibliography from The Reformation to 1993*. ATLA Bibliography Series 39. Lanham MD: Scarecrow Press, 1995.

MacHaffie, Barbara J. *Her Story: Women in Christian Tradition*. Philadelphia: Fortress, 1986.

The Oxford Dictionary of the Christian Church. Second edition. Edited by F. L. Cross and E. A. Livingstone. Oxford: Oxford University Press, 1974. Third edition. 1997.

Robinson, H. Wheeler. *The Life and Faith of the Baptists*. Revised edition. London: Kingsgate Press, 1946; first edition, 1927; repr.: Wake Forest NC: Chanticleer, 1985. The section on Anne Dutton appears on pp. 50-56: "Studies in Baptist Personality: (6) A Baptist Writer (Ann Dutton)."

Starr, Edward, editor. *A Baptist Bibliography*. Rochester NY: American Baptist Historical Society, 1959. (Section D, 201-204, lists about seventy works by Anne Dutton.)

Stein, Stephen. "A Note on Anne Dutton, Eighteenth-Century Evangelical." *Church History* 44 (1975): 485-91.

Wallington, Arthur. "Wesley and Anne Dutton." *Proceedings of the Wesley Historical Society* 11/2 (June 1917): 43-48.

Watson, JoAnn Ford, "Anne Dutton: An 18th Century British Evangelical Woman." *Ashland Theological Journal* 30 (1998): 51-56.

Whitebrook, John Cudworth. *Ann Dutton: A Life and Bibliography*. London: A. W. Cannon and Co., 1921. Also appears as "The Life and Works of Mrs. Ann Dutton," *Transactions of the Baptist Historical Society* 7 (1920–1921): 129-46. (*Transactions*, 1908–1921, became the *Baptist Quarterly*, 1922 to date.)

Whitley, William Thomas. *A Baptist Bibliography: Being a Register of the Chief Materials for Baptist History, Whether in Manuscript or in Print, Preserved in Great Britain, Ireland, and the Colonies*. Two volumes. London: Kingsgate Press, 1916, 1922. Repr.: Two volumes in one: Hildesheim: Georg Olms, 1984.

LETTER

SENT TO AN

Honourable GENTLEMAN,

FOR THE

Encouragement of FAITH.

By ONE *who has Tasted that the* LORD *is* GRACIOUS.

Wherefore comfort yourselves together, and edify one another, even as also ye do, I Thes. v. 11.

L O N D O N:
Printed by J. HART, in *Poppings-Court, Fleet-Street:* And sold by J. LEWIS, in *Bartholomew-Close,* near *West-Smithfield;* and E. GARDNER, at *Milton's-Head,* in *Gracechurch-Street.* 1743.
[Price One-Shilling.]

THE

A U T H O R,

TO THE

Worthy GENTLEMAN,

TO WHOM

The following LETTERS were sent.

Honoured Sir,

GRACE and Peace be multiplied unto you, through the Knowledge of *GOD*, and of *JESUS* our *LORD.—As you have been pleased, Sir, to signify your kind Acceptance of my poor Letters in* Manuscript, *and that the GOD of all Grace has made them of Use, to help your Faith and Joy: May I beg Leave, most humbly to present them to your Honour in* Print. *Most heartily praying, that the* same Letters, *under fresh Influences of Divine Grace, may be made* new Blessings *to your Heaven-born-Soul!—My humble Thanks are* due, Sir, *for that Freedom of Mind, which most kindly you have intimated, as to their Publication: That, if the Lord please, what He first sent to* you, *might be of Use to* others *of his dear Children. Oh may these poor Letters be blest to Thousands of the Lord's People! And* your Love *to them, and* Desire *to serve them hereby, be richly* rewarded *by the GOD of Love, both* now *and in the Day of CHRIST! Indeed, Sir, your Royal MASTER, will note down this your Service, in the* Book of his Remembrance, *and of his Royal Grace,* you shall receive your own Reward, according to your own Labour.—*In these Letters, Sir, the Lord enabled me to give you some little* Hints *of the Glory of CHRIST, and of our Duty and Privilege of abiding in Him by Faith, and living unto Him in Love. And tho'* my Words *may soon be run through; the* Things *in them* cannot. And by a weak Word, *a Word formerly spoken, the God and Father of our Lord Jesus Christ can break in upon your Soul, with* Almighty Energy, *and a* fresh Ray of Divine Glory, *unto your* further *Knowledge of Him, and Conformity to Him. CHRIST, Sir,* your *JESUS, is such a* Mass of Treasure, *that his* Riches are unsearchable! *Such a* Sea of Glory, *that can neither be* founded, *nor* sail'd over! *Let us follow on to* know *CHRIST, whose Love and Glory* passeth *KNOWLEDGE! To live in, to dive into, and adore this boundless, bottomless SEA of BLISS, should be our Work thro' Time, and will be our delightful Employment to Eternity. Oh for more* Faith, *to possess our great LORD JESUS, that unspeakable GIFT of the Father's Love, as our* own! *And for more* Love, *to give up ourselves in all holy*

Obedience, unto HIM that hath loved us, in Heart, Lip and Life, to his Glory*!—Yet a little while, Sir, and* that which is perfect shall come: Then that which is in Part shall be done away. *We shall see JESUS as HE is, be made perfectly like HIM, and* appear with him in Glory!—*And now, That* you, *Sir, may* increase with all the Increases of GOD, *unto all Faith, Joy and Holiness in* this World, *and a weighty Crown of Glory in* that to come: *is the earnest Desire and Prayer of, Dear Sir,*

Your Honour's most obliged,

And most Humble Servant,

In our glorious LORD,

------ ------

E P I S T L E

TO THE

R E A D E R.

Dear Reader,

IF thou art born from above, if as a *New-born Babe,* thou *desirest the sincere Milk of the Word that thou mayest grow thereby;* thou art one of those that have my *Heart,* and whose Edification in Faith and Love I much desire. And for this End, if the Lord please, I have publish'd these letters. And with the same Desire, after the Glory of GOD, and the Service of Souls, the worthy *Gentleman* to whom they were written, most heartily joins with me in their Publication. So that, dear Reader, if thou reapest any *Advantage* hereby, thou hast *our Hearts* herein, and the *Profit* of thy Soul will by our present and future *Joy.* Yea, let me say, in all the *Good* thou mayest gain hereby, thou hast CHRIST's *Heart:* With *Desire* hath HE *desired* to bring it unto *Thee,* and while thou enjoy'st it, over thee HE will *rejoice* with an Infinite *Joy;* from his infinite, unchangeable, everlasting *Love!* There is ne'er a *Gift* bestow'd on thee by thy SAVIOUR's *Hand,* be it ever so *small,* but thou hast his *Heart, Himself,* his *great* SELF in it! And this makes all our Blessings sweet and great. And if we believ'd the infinite Grace of CHRIST towards us, in every Degree of Refreshment given us, great would be our Joy and Thankfulness. Yea, dear

Reader, thou Heaven-born Soul, *the Father himself loveth thee:* In all the *Good* thou mayest receive by the following letters, GOD the *Father* will *rejoice* over thee with an infinite *Joy,* from *his* infinite, unchangeable, everlasting *Love* to thee in CHRIST! Aye, and GOD the *Holy Ghost* too: For Father, Son and Spirit, these *Three are One.* One in Essence, one in Will, and one in Love to all the Vessels of Mercy, in all the Dispensations of Grace towards them. Oh *Believer,* there is not the *least Comfort* thou receivest, the *least Help* of thy Faith and Joy, but what springs from the *great Love* of GOD, of Father, Son and Spirit, who sat in *Counsel* about it from Everlasting. All those Refreshments which come to *thee* from the gracious Presence of the LORD here, as well as all those Refreshments thou shalt have from his glorious Presence hereafter, were Matters of Appointment, and so many Gifts and Donations of Grace to thee, in GOD's everlasting Covenant with his SON. Infinite Wisdom drew the Line of thy Inheritance, and infinite Grace gave every Inch of Ground, every Piece of thy Enjoyment, particularly, and all thy Enjoyments, collectively, out of its own Riches; its immense and inexhaustible Riches! Thy GOD, in the Infinity of his *Grace,* hath *abounded towards thee, in all Wisdom and Prudence!* And thus every Favour comes streaming down to *thee,* from the Love of God thy Father, from the Love of the Lord thy Redeemer, and from the Love of the Holy Ghost thy Comforter, thro' the Channel of thy Saviour's Blood, in all the Ways and Means of Divine Appointment. And among the Rest, thy GOD can *ordain Strength,* strong Consolation for thee, even *out of the Mouth of a Babe;* while *his Strength* is made *perfect,* appears to be *so,* with glorious Evidence, unto glorious Effects, in the *Weakness* of the feeblest Worm. Ask HIM therefore for this Blessing, in thy reading the following Lines. And may the LORD grant *thy,* and *my* Request herein: To the Glory of his Grace by *us,* and all *His, World without End!* Amen.

And to Thee, Reader, whoever thou art, into whose Hands these letters may fall, that mayest see no Excellency in the Things contain'd in them, but look upon them as Matter of Banter and Ridicule, to *thee,* let me say, that thou art at present in a most miserable wretched State. If the Things of CHRIST are *strange Things* unto thee, *thou* art a *Stranger* unto HIM, wast never *born again,* but *art in the Gall of Bitterness, and in the Bond of Iniquity.* If heavenly Things are *disagreeable* to thee, thou art *unprepar'd* for Heaven, the Spirit of CHRIST doth not dwell in thee, but thou art under the Power of Sin and Satan; and if thou *die* in this Condition, thou canst not escape the *Damnation of Hell. What meanest thou* then, *O Sleeper? Arise, call upon thy God, if so be that God will think upon thee,* have Mercy on thee, *that thou perish not.* There is but an Hair's Breadth, as it were, between *thee,* and *eternal Ruin.* The Pit of Hell opens her Mouth wide to receive thee. Satan drives thee on in the Ways of Sin. And thou, foolish Sinner, Satan's willing Prey, runnest Blindfold towards the Lake of Fire, the Abyss of endless Misery, with all the *Haste* thou canst make.—But oh, *Hark!* There's a Voice *behind thee,* a glorious *Sound of Grace,* which calls after thee, to *return! Let the Wicked* (says GOD) *forsake his Way, and the unrighteous Man his Thoughts: And let him return unto the*

LORD, *and He will have Mercy upon him, and to our* GOD, *for He will abundantly pardon,* Isa. lv. 7. Oh *Sinner,* GOD has given his SON to *die* for *Transgressors,* the *just* for the *unjust,* that they might *live!* And HE calls upon thee to return, and has promis'd thou shalt find Mercy. What *sayst thou?* Wilt thou run into his open Arms! Believe it, *Fury is not in* GOD, towards any poor *Sinner that comes unto* HIM *by* JESUS CHRIST. If thou return *now,* thou *shalt* find Mercy. And tho' *thou hast done as evil Things as thou couldest,* the rich, free, reigning Grace of God will *superabound* over all thy *abounding Sin,* to thy *eternal Life, thro' Jesus Christ our Lord.*—That *thy Heart,* by the omnipotent Power of Divine *Love,* may be sweetly and strongly *drawn* unto CHRIST, and to GOD by HIM: Unto thy full Deliverance from *all Misery,* and Salvation unto *all Glory:* is the earnest Desire of

Thy Soul's Well-wisher,

L E T T E R S

SENT TO AN

Honourable GENTLEMAN,

LETTER I.

Worthy Sir,

As by Mr. *W----d's* Direction the enclos'd was to be sent to *you,* in order to its Conveyance to *Him*; I conclude, Sir, That you are one of *those* that love the Lord Jesus, his Servants and Cause in the Earth. A distinguishing Favour, *This!* That *you,* Sir, a Person of *your Rank and Quality,* should be on the *Lamb's Side*; while *Thousands* of the Great and Mighty, the Rich and Noble of the Earth, are making *War* with the Lamb, *opposing* his Cause, and *oppressing* his Servants in the World! oh surely, it is a special Revelation of the *Lamb's Glory*, and an experimental Acquaintance with his *Love*; in the Forgiveness of your Sins through his Blood; that has fir'd your Soul with Love to his Person, and *Zeal* for his Glory. And as you have *begun* to love and serve the Lord Jesus, *go on*, Right Noble Sir, *always abounding in the Work of the Lord, forasmuch as you know that your Labour is not in vain in the Lord. Death* and *Eternity* hasten. *Christ comes quickly;* in his *own*, and in his *Father's* Glory, and in the Glory of his holy *Angels*, attended with all his *Saints:* To be *glorify'd* in *them*, and *admir'd* in all that *believe;* and to take *Vengeance* upon all that *Know not God, and that obey not the Gospel.* And *happy*, unspeakably *happy* are the Men, who are now *prepar'd* to meet the LORD, in that glorious, awful, delightful, dreadful DAY! That have *run into Christ by Faith*, as the glorious *Refuge*, the *Hiding-Place* prepar'd of *God*, for the everlasting *Salvation*, the endless *Glory* of Law-condemned *Sinners*. And that being *quickned* from the Death of Sin, unto a Life of Holiness, have laid out their *Time, Strength* and *All* for GOD. For lo, *Eye hath not seen, nor Ear heard, neither hath it entred into the Heart of Man to* conceive those *great Things,* those *bright Glories*, which GOD hath *prepared* for them, and will bestow upon them in that bright DAY! Those that *serve* CHRIST, and *suffer* with Him here, shall be *glorify'd* with Him hereafter. CHRIST, Sir, is such a rich and glorious, such a sweet and delightful MASTER, that it is the highest *Honour*, the greatest *Pleasure* to *serve* Him, and to *suffer* for Him! Such is the infinite Glory, and sweetness of his *Person*, that He makes, both his *Work*, and his *Cross, sweet* to all his happy Favourites, whom he *employs* in the one, and *honours* to bear the other! And such, Sir, is the *Bounty*, the Royal *Grace* of this great LORD, to his *Servants*, his *Sufferers*, that there's *none like him!* He Rewards them of the freest Grace, every Way like his Great SELF! Yea, HIMSELF will be their *exceeding great* REWARD!

That this, Sir, may be your happy Lot, to have CHRIST for your Time-Portion, and your eternal ALL, in the hearty Desire of,

> *Honour'd Sir,*
> *Your most Obedient, and*
> *Humble Servant in the Lord,*

——— ———

L E T T E R   II.

Honoured Sir,

YOUR acceptable Favour—I receiv'd, and return most humble Thanks for *that*, and your kind *Intention* to give us a Visit. As for *me*, Sir, I am utterly *unworthy* of your Notice, *less than the least of all Saints*, and *the chief of Sinners.*

But from the free, sovereign Pleasure of the great JEHOVAH, vile, unworthy I, have *found Grace in his Sight!* And from his infinite, free *Favour* towards me through Jesus Christ, He has given me *Favour* with many of his dear Children. And I wonder, Sir, at the *Grace of God*, that he should put vile *me*, into *your Heart*. Oh may *his* Name have *all* the Glory! And the *Converse* we may have with each other on Earth, whether personal, or by Writing, be a blessed *Mean* of helping us *forward* in our Way to Heaven!

Your Letter, Sir, as it gives Account of the wonderful Work of God in *S----d*, in the Advancement of the Redeemer's Kingdom; was very delightful to me. And glad am I, that as a Subject of *Sion's* King, you rejoice in his *Victories*, and pray for the Spreading of his *Glories* over all the Earth. Be of good chear, Sir, *God has set his King upon his holy Hill of Zion:* And he must *reign* until all his People are *saved to the uttermost*, and all his Enemies made his *Footstool*. And the *great Things* which we of late have been blest to see and hear, are but the *Dawn* of *that Day's Glory*, which hastens on upon us, when the *Knowledge of the* LORD *shall cover the Earth, as the Waters do the Sea!*

I rejoice, Dear Sir, that you not only *love* the LORD JESUS, but have been long *acquainted* with Him. And much *Heart-Union* with you, and *Esteem* of you, the Lord hath rais'd in my Soul. I trust, I shall frequently be enabled to bring *you* and *your* Case before his Throne. And verily, our GOD, *hath not said unto the Seed of Jacob, seek ye me in vain.* No, such is his infinite Grace, to us his Favourites, that he will not only hear us for *ourselves*, but for *others* also! And such his condescension, that He takes it *kindly*, as if done to *Himself*, when in the Bowels of Jesus Christ we *compassionate* each other, and *bear* each other's Persons and Cases upon our Hearts before Him! Our heavenly Father loves his *Children* so, that He would have us lay out our Love to *Him* in loving *them*; and therein he accounts *himself* beloved. Oh infinite Grace! How *near* are we made unto *God*, and to *each other*, by the *Lamb's Blood*; And What a *Debt of Love*, do we owe to the *God of Love*, and to his *beloved Children!*

I am glad, Sir, that God's free, rich, superabounding *Grace* in Christ, humbles you in the *Dust* before Him, and makes you look upon *yourself* to be one of the Chief of Sinners. That is true *Humility,* which flows from, and is nourish'd by the *Faith* of God's great *Love,* and tender *Mercy* in Christ. And with such *humble Souls*, the God of all Grace will *dwell*. Glad am I, that you can say, *My* JESUS! *My* LORD, and *my* GOD! And is JESUS *Yours*, Sir: What can you *want more!* CHRIST is *full of Grace and Truth! In him dwelleth all the Fulness of the* GODHEAD *bodily!* CHRIST is *made of* GOD *unto you, Wisdom, Righteousness, Sanctification and Redemption!* See you not how *full* your *Beloved* is? Oh, come into CHRIST by *Faith*; the infinite *Love* of the Three One GOD, has set open all his Stores unto *you!* Be *free* with the Fulness of JESUS; it is all *your own!* Your Right, your Portion, your Inheritance, for Time; and for Eternity! God the *Father* will account himself *honour'd*, in the exceeding Riches of *his* Grace towards you, if you come in by

Condescension in *him,* to notice the Services of the upper World; of perfect Saints and holy Angels in all the flaming Glories of that Love and Duty, with which they bow before his Throne! Much more then, is it a Stoop, an amazing Stoop of infinite Grace, that the *Lord of all* should cast a favourable Eye upon the imperfect Services of mortal, sinful Worms, in this low Land!—But the Truth is, our JESUS, acts like *himself,* his great SELF, whose *Grace* knows no Limits, Change, or End! And lo, he is a *Lover!* and *Love* delights to *condescend.* But, that the Son of God should love *Creatures,* should love *Sinners,* should love *you,* and love *me,* notwithstanding all our Vileness, by Nature and Practice, both before and since he call'd us into Fellowship with him; is *astonishing;* And that the Son of God should *so* love us, to be born, to live, to die, to rise, and live for evermore for *us!* If CHRIST *loves,* he will love like HIMSELF! And meet it is, that all created Love should *disappear,* when uncreated Love *displays its Glory! Herein is* Love, *not that we loved God, but that he loved us, and gave his Son,* and the Son gave himself *to be the Propitiation for our Sins!* Oh what a mere *Trifle,* or rather a nameless *Nothing* is the *Love of Creatures,* of Men, of Angels, if compar'd with the *Love* of CHRIST, which hath in it *all the Fulness of* GOD! Here's *Love,* that in itself and Fruits, hath Heights, Depths, Lengths and Breadths, which far surpass *Knowledge!* Never was such a *Love* as the Love of CHRIST! Such a great, free, and fruitful Love! Such a doing, suffering Love! such a forgiving, All-conquering Love!—Oh Sir, *Words* fail me! My poor pained Soul wants a *Tongue* to lisp out the *Love* of JESUS! And had I the Tongues of Men and Angels, and were they employ'd to an eternal Space, in telling out the Glories of CHRIST's *Love,* they would be far from *declaring the Thing as it is!* Here's Love to be *ador'd,* rather than express'd! to be *enjoy'd,* rather than declar'd! Only then let me say, come *taste and see,* what immense Glories, what ineffable Sweetnesses there are in the *Love* of JESUS, in his infinite, free, unchangeable, and everlasting Love! In which he delights in your Person, regards your Services, and will reward them, both here and hereafter! And, *O Man greatly beloved!* Give up yourself, your whole self, in Heart, Lip and Life, as a holy, living Sacrifice to the God of Love! So shall *the Name of our Lord be glorify'd in you, and you in him, according to the Will of God and our Father.*

You see, Sir, I have prevented myself from answering your last sweet kind letter. I humbly thank you for it. The Lord made it refreshing and delightful to my Soul, both at its Reception, and since. I see thereby, that the *Love* of Christ, that *Christ* in Love, in what he did for you below, and doth for you above, is *your Life.* That your humble Soul is willing to be *nothing;* and that CHRIST should be ALL! And that your Heart *mourns* within you, that you can love and serve JESUS no more, that you forget him so much, or remember him so coldly and faintly.—But be of good Cheer, your JESUS doth never forget you, but earnestly remembers you still. His invariable Love to *you* is always in an infinite Flame, amidst all the Variations of your Love to *him.* And Christ's *perfect Love* will pardon the *Imperfection* of yours, and make it *perfect* in his own Time.—And mean-while, that

Love which your mourn over, as *black,* Christ will call *fair,* rejoice in it, yea, admire it with an *How fair is thy Love, my Sister, my Spouse! How much better is thy Love than Wine! And the Smell of thine Ointments than all Spices!*

Glad am I, that "the Advancement of Christ's Kingdom, and gaining of Hearts and Souls unto him, is sweet above all Things to you in this World; and a most refreshing Comfort, amidst all the Troubles and Perplexities you meet with therein." Thrice *happy Soul!* You are *born from above!* A *Child,* an *Heir* of that Kingdom, that immortal Crown, which the Lord hath promis'd to them that *love him!* You that rejoice in Christ's Kingdom of *Grace,* shall reign with him in his Kingdom of *Glory;* and drink for ever of the River of *his Pleasures,* of that *pure River of Water of Life, which proceedeth from the Throne of God, and of the Lamb!* Your dear Soul, which now delights in the Communion of *Saints below,* and finds such a sensible Pleasure in hearing some few Stories of Divine Grace, tho' but lisped out by Babes and Sucklings; shall ere long be bless'd with the Communion of *Saints above,* and fill'd with Joy unknown, while you hear all the Saved of the Lord, met together in one general Assembly, declare all the Wonders of his Grace, toward all the Vessels of Mercy, thro' all the Ages of Time! Oh Sir, those will be *bless'd Days indeed!* Blessed beyond Expression! and blessed to an endless Duration! Your Joy then will be *full;* and into the Fulness of your Lord's *Joy,* that boundless, bottomless *Ocean,* your capacious Soul shall be cast there to bath itself in Pleasures, in a vast Variety of new Delights, to the *Days of Eternity!*

Mr. *G----d's* Sermon, Sir, I have perus'd. I think it a very suitable Discourse for the Times; and that it strongly militates against the prevailing Errors of the Day; whereby the Doctrines of the Gospel, and of the Reformation, have so generally been banish'd out of the *establish'd Church.* The manifest Tendency of Mr. *G----d's* Discourse is, to lay a *crucify'd Jesus* as the *only Foundation* of a Sinner's Happiness and Salvation; and to turn *topsy turvy* the Babel-building of those, who, refusing the *chief Corner-stone,* would climb up to Heaven without him.—May the Lord raise and spirit up many, to preach CHRIST *crucify'd;* who, tho' *to the Jews a stumbling Block, and to the Greeks, Foolishness; is to them which are called, both Jews and Greeks,* CHRIST *the Power of GOD, and the Wisdom of GOD!* And may the whole Earth be filled with the MEDIATOR's Glory! *Amen,* and *Amen!*

I crave a Remembrance by you, Sir, at the Divine Throne; and wishing all Grace unto all Glory: beg Leave to subscribe myself,

    Honoured Sir,

        Your most obliged humble Servant in the Lord,

<hr>

LETTER IV.

Worthy, and very Dear Sir,

PLEASE to accept my humble Thanks for the Favour of your last very kind letter. I rejoice to see such a Spirit of *Love* upon your dear Soul. The Lord *increase* it more and more! Truly, Sir, I love you much, because you love my dear Lord Jesus, and his dear People for his Sake. That you love them, because *he* loves them, and in your Measure, *as* he loves them, *viz.* Notwithstanding their imperfections, their Spots and Deformities by Sin. It refresh'd, and delighted my Soul much to hear you say, of Christ's Redeemed, even of the most spotted of them, That "they shall be presented Spotless, and are the more astonishing Instances of blessed redeeming Love." Oh Sir, *my* Spots and Blemishes in myself, while I see myself *spotless* in my Lord, make me loath myself in my own Sight. My Heart *breaks* under the sweet Influence of *God's Love,* that I am so *unlovely,* so *unlike him,* that I have done, and can do so *little* for him, and have done so *much* against him! But I rejoice, that God's *Free Grace,* in its exceeding *Riches,* will have the more abundant *Glory,* in saving such a *great Sinner!* Yet doth not *Free Grace* make me *love Sin,* or have *light Thoughts* of it; but sets on my Soul the keenest *Edge* against it. I am sure that the Gospel of Christ, tho' it gives the strongest Consolation to the *Chief of Sinners,* that are willing to be saved by him, gives no *Liberty to Sin,* either in its Doctrine or Influence. No; the Love of God to saved Sinners, sweetly *constrains* them to love the Saviour, so *far* as his Love is shed abroad in the Heart, and while its Influence *abides* on the Soul.

But, Sir, sad it is to see, how *far* the Influence of Sin and Satan prevails at his Day, even over those that *love the Lord,* to make them act the Part of them that *have him.* And in nothing is this more apparent, than in that general *Decay* of Love, and *Bitterness* of Spirit which is found amongst Christians. Lamentable indeed it is, To see Brethren in Christ, persecuting each other; and our Lord's great Command, *of Love,* so much despised! And glad am I, that you have a Heart given you to *mourn* for these Things. God will set a *Mark,* for Deliverance and Honour, upon those that *sigh* and *mourn* for the *Abominations* which are among them, when he comes forth in his tremendous Judgments against his own People for Sin—And such is the dreadful Degeneracy of God's People at *this Day,* that I can't but think, He will bring us thro' the *Fires,* to purge away our *Dross,* and take away our *Tin.* And as the *Deadness* of old Christians, so the extraordinary *Zeal* of new Converts, especially for *suffering,* seems to portend, *trying Times at hand.* I have oft thought, with dear Mr. R----*be,* "That there is something very remarkable, in that Spirit for suffering, which is pour'd out upon new Converts at this Day:" And was glad to see him express the same Thing in *your letter.*—This may be our Comfort, That if our Way is rough and thorny, our *Shoes shall be Iron and Brass, and as our Days, our*

Strength: That if we are call'd to pass thro' the *Fires,* CHRIST will be *with* us there, and bring us thence, as *Gold seven Times refined.* Our Lord will have a *glorious Church* in his own Time! The Hearts of *divided Saints,* shall be *united;* and all the Members of Christ's Body, wrought up by his almighty Hand, into the strictest *Unity* with *Him,* and with *each other.* This is what our Lord has pray'd for, That *all His,* may be *One.* This is the Work which his Father gave him to do: And this is the Glory He will put upon the Church. And then, *Zion* will be the *Perfection of Beauty* indeed! And out of her, The Glory of GOD will *shine,* as the burning *Lamp,* thro' the *crystal Glass!*

Mean time, It is some Relief, That thro' the grievous Differences and Animosities which are among the Brethren of our Lord, the Children of his Family are such, which make their Carriage towards each other, look like *That,* which our Lord foretold would be the Carriage of the *ungodly World* towards *them;* yet that there is a vast Difference between the *Principle,* from which the Saints oppose each other, and *that,* from which the World make Opposition against them. All that are *Born of God, love one another,* they pray for and wish well to each other: and they cannot but do so, according to the *New Nature.* Saints, don't oppose Saints, as *such,* nor hate them because they bear *Christ's Image.* Which is the *grand Reason* of the World's Hatred to, and Opposition against them. And tho' this may'nt be reflected upon by wicked Men, as *such;* yet no unregenerate Soul, can *love* the Image of Christ in one that is born of God, but has an *Aversion* to it, and more or less *opposes* and *persecutes* the Person where it is. It must needs be so, from that *Enmity* which is put between the *Seed of the Woman,* and the *Seed of the Serpent.* Whereas the Opposition that Saints make against each other, springs chiefly from the *Difference* of their *Judgments,* about Things of lesser Moment. Which thro' the Subtilty of Satan, and the Prevalency of Corruption, greatly breaks that *Love* which *ought* to be between them.—But let differing Saints *talk* together of the *Things which have happened,* with respect to the Dealings of God with their Souls, by which the Image of Christ is formed in them; and presently they see *Christ* in each other, and *their Hearts burn within them* in love to *him,* and to *one another*; they sweetly *unite,* in the *uniting Head:* Because there is a Principle of *Love* in their Souls, to *Christ,* and those that are *His.* And our Lord, who has *begun* to unite us to himself, and to each other in Love, will *compleat* the Work; *His Hands that laid the Foundation,* will *lay the Top-Stone:* and then, *Farewel Division, for ever!*

The Grace of our Lord Jesus Christ be with your Spirit. Amen!
Pray for, Dear Sir,

Your Honour's,

at all Obedience in the Lord

L E T T E R V.

Honour'd Sir,

MOST thankfully I acknowledge the Reception of the last very kind letter you was pleas'd to favour me with.—The Accounts, Sir, which you gave me, of our Lord's carrying on his Work in *S----d,* were most acceptable and joyful. I am highly oblig'd to you for the same.—You see, Sir, that the LORD can, and will *Work* by whom *He pleaseth.* And in infinite Wisdom and Goodness, orders Things *so* by his permissive, or effective Will, relating to his Servants whom He designs to Honour, as shall most *advance* the Glory of his great Name, and *exclude* all Creature-boasting. And *well* is it for us, that He doth so. Such is the *Greatness* of our GOD, that it's meet his infinite *Glories* should shine *Radiant,* and reign *Triumphant,* in and over all his Works! And such is the *Nearness* of his Relation to *us,* and the Fulness of *our Bliss* in the display of *his Glory,* that it's meet his dearest Favourites should be NOTHING, and the LORD *alone exalted in All,* as *their* ALL! We shall never give unto the LORD the *Glory* due his Name, nor possess a full and lasting *Happiness,* till we come wholly out of our *little selves,* into the *great* GOD! Till we love HIM *in* All, *above* All, and *as* our ALL! And *ourselves* and every *Thing else,* all Creatures and Things for *his sake.* Then casting our *Beings,* and our *Joys,* as a *Drop* into *his vast Ocean,* we shall most delightfully *lose* and *find* ourselves in GOD; and an immense andendless Fulness of Bliss, in the Self-existent, and All-sufficient JEHOVAH, the everlasting I AM! And the more of this excellent Spirit we attain, the more holy and happy shall we be in this World. Oh how much Dishonour do we bring to GOD, and how much Happiness do we rob our Souls of, by abiding at Home in *ourselves!* by setting up, and bowing down to, this grand Idol SELF, in all its Forms. Whereas, if we pass'd out of ourselves, into GOD, and made *Him,* as indeed He *is,* the first Cause, and last End of all Things; how much Glory should we bring to his Name? what full and solid Happiness should we enjoy? and how noble, free and brave would be all our Actions? And in a Word, in what glorious Liberty should we walk, as the Sons of GOD here! And how great would be our Preparation for, and how weighty our Crown of Glory hereafter!—

I rejoice, Sir, in those great Things which the LORD hath done for your Soul; and to see such a Spirit upon you for GOD. Such an Esteem of CHRIST and his Service, and such Mourning, and Humiliation that you can love and serve him no more. Your Lord, Sir, looks at your *Desire* to serve him; and will call *that, your Kindness.* We must be carried in to *Glory* in the Arms of *Free-Grace;* Reigning thro' Righteousness by *Jesus Christ,* unto our eternal Life, as poor miserable *Sinners* in ourselves. If God's Love had not been free, infinitely free, and independent upon *our Goodness;* it had never been fix'd upon *us.* And that same

Free Love, which at first took us up in its Arms, will never cast us out thence, for our Unworthiness and Provocations: No, not for *all that we have done!* GOD's *Love* to us in CHRIST, is as *immutable* as his BEING: and the *Love-passage* of his Heart being *opened* thro' his crucify'd Son, it is become an All-conquering, eternal *Flow,* that riseth higher than the pointed Mountains of our *Sins,* And reigns triumphant over all, unto the everlasting Salvation of our *Persons,* as the Beloved of the LORD! Of this adorable Love, Sir, you have had precious Experience hitherto. It has follow'd you in its infinite All-prevailings until *this Day;* and it will follow you *still* even to the *last Moment* of your Life, till by infinite Love in the Stream, you are wafted into its immense and endless Ocean! God will go on to love you, Sir, till all Enmity against Him, is utterly *destroy'd* from out of your Nature, and you are perfectly *changed* into his Love-Image. And then, being fully *fitted for,* you shall be *solac'd* with, the Glories of his infinite LOVE, of HIMSELF in Love, unto *Ages without End!* And such great Things will the GOD of LOVE do for you, that are both *ineffable* and *inconceiveable!*

They would indeed far surpass our *Belief,* had they the least Dependance upon *our Goodness,* as the moving Cause. But Faith has to do with a *great* GOD, with a *great* SAVIOUR, and with *great, exceeding great and precious Promises;* all irreversibly confirmed by the *great* Sacrifice of Attonement, and for their Fulfilment, in the Hand of the *great* and *almighty* COMFORTER! And therefore, we may well have *great* Confidence in GOD, and Expectations from him, under the *greatest* Discouragements that can possibly arise from *ourselves.* And a great Part of the Wisdom of Faith it is to *seek for,* and *fix upon,* its true and proper Ground, *viz.* upon the GOD *of all Grace* without us; and not upon *ourselves,* and the *Grace* that is in us. Gracious Experiences *within us,* belong rather to spiritual Sense than Faith. Our Faith is always most pure and strong, when we *consider not* our own Deadness, nor *stagger* at he Promise of God because of it; but take the God of Truth at his *Word,* in his Promise of Grace without us; and hold this *fast,* in the Face of a thousand Difficulties, and seeming Improbabilities within us. This is the Faith that gives Glory to God, and brings Comfort to the Soul. And the *stronger* our Faith is, the *more* it will work by Love, and *hearten us on* in our Conflict with the Powers of Darkness. Whereas, if we give *Way* to Unbelief (to which Satan tempts us, upon every new Failure in our Obedience) we become *weak* to every good Work, and an *easy Prey* to our spiritual Enemies.

I rejoice, Sir, that the Lord is instructing and leading you more to look to, and live upon CHRIST for *Holiness,* and Supplies of Grace out of his Fulness, to enable you to walk with him daily. A constant abiding in Christ by *Faith,* is God's appointed *Means* of our bringing forth much Fruit. It is the most *direct Course* we can take, to get the Victory over Sin, Satan and *the* World, and to become *burning and shining Lights, in the midst of a crooked and perverse Generation.*

Briars and *Thorns,* Sir, are common to the Saints, during their Abode in the *Wilderness.* Grieve you they *may;* but hurt you they *shall not.* None of them can *touch you,* without a special Permission from Heaven. And all of them, under the supreme Direction, and All-wise, and All-gracious Dispose of the LORD your own GOD, shall *together work for Good, and turn to your Salvation.*

Yield not, dear Sir, to such Suggestions, that the Lord's Work upon your Soul is but a *common Work;* and that *your Spots* are not the Spots of *God's Children.* The Design of the Enemy hereby, is to weaken your *Heart* and *Hands,* and to draw you off from *God:* And so, into a willing Subjection to *himself,* and *Service. Wherefore cast not away your Confidence, which hath great Recompence of Reward.* A common Work, how high soever it may rise, never makes CHRIST *precious,* in his Person and Office, as a *compleat* SAVIOUR, to any one Soul. *Unto you therefore which believe,* saith the Apostle, *He is precious.* They are all bless'd with *precious Faith,* to whom the CHRIST *of* GOD *is precious;* as the only *Foundation* which he has laid in *Zion,* for the Salvation of Sinners, from all Misery unto all Glory. And however great their *Weaknesses* are, the strong, the living Foundation on which they rest, and to which they are inseperably united, will hold them *unshaken* in a State of Grace, and *strengthen* and *brighten* them to eternal Glory, notwithstanding the utmost Efforts of the Gates of Hell against them.—

You are pleas'd, Sir, with *my retired Life:* And I am glad to see you resign'd to the divine Dispose in the publick Manner of *your own.* Infinite Wisdom, cast the *Lot* for us both. Yours is best for *you,* and mine for *me.* Our GOD in the Infinity of his Wisdom and Grace, has dispos'd of our *Time-Circumstances,* as shall most subserve his own Glory in our *eternal Salvation:* and nothing, for each of us, could be *better than it is.* If I in Solitude should have a greater Advantage of *Communion with God; You,* Sir, in publick Life, have richer Opportunities to *glorify him before Men.* Let us therefore love and bless the Lord, for *all the Way* He leads us thro' the *Wilderness,* and labour to glorify Him in all; and when he has brought us to the *City of Habitation,* we shall see it was all *right:* to our eternal Joy, and his eternal Praise. I beg leave to subscribe, Sir,

Your Honour's,
At all Obedience in the Lord,

————— —————

L E T T E R   VI.

Honoured Sir,

MOST humbly I thank you for the Favour of your last.—Such is the *Greatness* of our GOD, and the *Wisdom* of his Providence, that He supremely *governs* all his Creatures, and all their Actions, to subserve his own most holy, wise, and gracious *Designs.* The *Wisdom* and *Power* of GOD, over-rules all the *Weakness* and *Folly* of his Creatures, for his own *Glory* and the *Good* of his People. And the most *casual Events,* and *minute Circumstances,* to bring about Matters of *Appointment,* and Things of the *greatest Moment,* continually pass on in the Round of Divine Providence, in the State and Majesty of GOD! JEHOVAH passeth by before us, in every thing we see or hear, *working all Things* in Providence, *according to the Counsel of his Will.* And had we more *Faith,* to behold his *Glory,* we should bow down and worship, love and adore, and with joyful Wonder cry out, *O the Depths of the Riches both of the Wisdom and Knowledge of* GOD! *how unsearchable are his Judgments, and his Ways past finding out!*

I rejoice Sir, that your Soul longs to serve your dear Lord Jesus, and that you count it your Honour, your Glory to follow him whithersoever he goeth, notwithstanding the Persecution and Reproaches which may attend it. Indeed Sir, The LAMB that has bought us with his Blood, is well *worthy* of our Persons and Services. And such is the Greatness of our REDEEMER's *Person,* and the Excellency of his *Work,* that it is the *Honour* of all the Saints, both in Heaven and Earth, and of Angels and Arch-angels to *serve Him.* It is their *Bliss,* their *Glory,* to prostrate themselves at his *Feet;* to wait his *Orders,* and obey his *Commands.* The great Apostles of the LAMB, glory'd in their Character, as *Servants of* JESUS CHRIST. And *David* the Man after GOD's own Heart, said, *I will speak of the Testimonies before Kings, and will not be ashamed.* And happy are those Saints, who in their Lord's Name and Work, appear before Sinners *now,* in their private Conversation, as array'd with that holy Boldness, that majestick Greatness of Spirit, with which they shall be openly clothed, when advanced to *sit with* CHRIST *on his Throne,* to judge the World, wicked Men and Devils at the great decisive DAY! Oh had we a due Sense of the *Greatness* of GOD; and of the *Littleness* of the Creature, we should esteem it our *Glory* to appear for him before the greatest of earthly Monarchs, without *Fear or Shame.* Nothing debaseth us, but *Sin,* or makes us truly noble, but *Holiness.* The more we are *like* GOD, and the more we *appear for,* and *serve him,* the more *Glorious* we are. The brighter *Lights* we are in *this* World, and the more *radiant* shall we shine in *that to come.* Holiness, clothes the Man where it is, so far as it appears with Majesty *here;* and with Glory, shall the holy Man be clothed *hereafter,* with a *proportionable Glory* to every of his *holy Actions.* Not an holy Word or Deed, that we speak or do, but as GOD is *delighted* with it, and *honour'd* by it, so he will put a *Glory upon it,* and upon *us* according to it; not only a present Glory, but an eternal Crown of Glory! And had we these Things more in *View,* how *Covetous* should we be, continually to walk so as to please GOD, and to abound therein *more and more;* that so we might glorify his great Name, have the Honour of being his Servants in the present Time, and receive that exceeding great and eternal Weight of Glory, which of his Free-Grace, he hath reserved for his Servants in the World to come! Oh how *watchful* should we be, to improve every Opportunity to speak or act for GOD, if we really *believ'd,* actually thought in Faith, that we could *lose* no Season for either, but with the *Loss* of eternal Glory! Of those additional Glories, which our Lord will confer upon his Servants in the *future*

World, according to their Improvements, their Works and Labours in the *present State!* A believing *Converse* with eternal Glory, would make us *prize* every Moment of Time to prepare for it. *We run for a Crown,* says the Apostle, *an incorruptible Crown!* Oh had we the Crown more in *view,* how would it *hearten us on* in our spiritual Race! The great Things of *Eternity,* would make *Time-Things* appear *little* in our Sight. Especially, if we liv'd as we ought, as Persons just ready to *leave* this little Spot of Time, and to *launch forth* into the vast Ocean of an endless Eternity! How sweetly would the Faith of *Eternity,* model our Apprehensions about the *Things of Time?* And what just *Ideas* would appear *little,* or *great* to us, but what is *so* with regard to Eternity. The World with its flattering Glories would not get our *Hearts,* nor would its angry Frowns *terrify us.* In a constant Course of *active Obedience,* we should delightfully follow our dear Lord, and rejoice to be counted *worthy to suffer Shame for his Name.* The more the Lord's People are *holy Men unto him,* the more of the *Majesty of* GOD is upon them, and the greater *Terror* they strike into the wicked.—And tho' the more they *appear* for God, the more they may be expos'd to Reproach, from the World that lieth in Wickedness, yet the greater our Reproaches for CHRIST's Sake are, the greater is our *Honour* now, and will be our *Glory* for ever. We may well esteem the *Reproach of* CHRIST *greater Riches than the Treasures* of the Universe! That's a *compleat Christian* indeed, a *glorious Soul,* that is honour'd both to *do,* and *suffer* much for CHRIST!—And whenever, dear Sir, the Captain of our Salvation calls us unto *either,* let us chearfully *follow him,* and fight our way thro' all Difficulties, Enemies and Oppositions, as valiant Soldiers under his glorious Banner; for *we are* and shall be *more than Conquerors thro' Him that hath loved us!* wishing daily Fellowship with the Three-One GOD, unto a rich Increase of all Grace *here,* and a weighty Crown of Glory at CHRIST's *Appearing:* I beg leave to subscribe myself,

 Honour'd Sir,

  Your most Obedient,

   and most humble Servant,

    in our Glorious Lord,

L E T T E R   VII.

Worthy and very dear Sir,

YOUR exceeding great Favours to so worthless a Worm, call for the most grateful Acknowledgments. Most humbly I thank you, and most richly will my Lord reward you. The most acceptable Favour of your last, was very delightful and profitable to me. I wonder at *your* Kindness, dear Sir, that you should so tenderly regard, and so familiarly correspond with poor sinful *me.* And much more do I wonder at the Kindness of my *God,* in making *vile me,* of any *use* to your dear Soul. May *his* infinite Grace have *all* the Glory! Truly the Account you gave me of it, did very much *affect me;* as herein I saw the Lord's fulfilling of his *Promise* to me, and granting the *Petitions* which I asked of him; not only the *Things,* but as it were according to the very *Words* in which I had requested them. Upon which I fell down before the LORD, and gave him Thanks; I ador'd his infinite Kindness, and bewail'd my own Ingratitude. I saw that GOD in CHRIST was *mine,* that *he* had given me his great SELF in Love; I mourn'd that I could love him *no more,* and being afresh overcome with his Kindness, I gave him my *little self.* And I thought, if I had a *thousand Souls,* and a *thousand Lives,* I would give them all to *him,* and for the Advancement of *his Glory.* But the Lord only knows, how *little* I love and serve him, with the *one Soul,* the *one Life* which me hath given me! If his Grace was not *Infinite,* he could not *bear* with my little Love, and my great Ingratitude! And as for *me,* I should utterly *sink* under the Weight of them. But I *feel* the Rock beneath me: I have to *do* with a GOD of boundless Perfections, of immense and unchangeable Love, of never-failing Mercy, and glorious Faithfulness! And thro' a crucify'd JESUS, thro' the infinite Merit of my Redeemer's Blood and Righteousness, and his all-prevailing Advocacy with the Father, I rejoice to *live* under the bright Displays of divine Glory, and to *feel* the Heat, the Soul-quickning Energy of this *Infinite Shine!*

Most humbly I thank you dear Sir, for the Perusal of those letters which you was pleas'd to favour me with, and for the Account you have given me of your present Trials. The Lord made the same a Means of my further Sympathy with you, and Concern for you at the Throne of Grace.

But Sir, before I say any thing to your Exercises, permit me to rejoice with you, and to congratulate your Happiness, in that Honour which God's Free-Grace hath put upon you in making you one of his New-Covenant Children and Servants. Since *not many Mighty, not many Noble are called;* how is it, dear Sir, that *you* should be *one* of those *few!* What distinguishing Grace is *This!* How has the sovereign Lord of all, pass'd by *thousands* and took *you!* Oh why was not *your Lot,* cast among those of this World's wise, great and mighty Men, who have their *good things here, their Portion in this Life!* That are awfully estranged from God, and Enemies to him, his Cause and People in this World, and shall be the Objects of his eternal Vengeance! What Grace was *this,* that your honour'd Mother should be a *chosen Vessel* unto Christ, and honour'd to promote his Gospel and Cause in the Earth! And that the same *Faith* which dwelt in your honour'd *Mother,* should be wrought in *your dear Soul,* such *Love* also given *you* to the glorious Redeemer, and such a Concern for the Propagation of his Kingdom and Interest! And in a word, that *you* should *not be appointed unto Wrath; but to obtain Salvation thro' Jesus Christ!* I know, dear Sir, you say, *Even so Father, for so it seemed good in thy Sight!* Oh thrice *happy Soul! What great Things hath the LORD done for* you! He has set his Heart upon you, and has given you nothing less than his great SELF, for your Time-

Portion, and your everlasting ALL! he hath call'd you out of Darkness, into his marvellous Light, and into Fellowship with his Son, Jesus Christ our Lord; both in Grace, and in Glory! he hath put his Holy Spirit within you and upon you, and honour'd you as an Instrument to advance his Glory, and for the good of his dear Children! Yea, he hath given you such an intense Desire to honour him, that makes you forget the Things which are behind, and eagerly reach forth, after a more perfect loving and serving of him than ever! And to say no more, GOD in CHRIST, hath separated *YOU* unto *Himself:* And *neither Death, nor Life, nor Angels, nor Principalities, nor Powers, nor Things present, nor Things to come, nor Height, nor Depth, nor any other Creature, shall be able to seperate you from his* LOVE!

Indeed Sir, I am glad to see the *Nobleness* of your Spirit, in your Desires to serve the Lord Jesus, that at times you would even *forget* those great Things which he has prepared for them that love him, and reserve for his Servants in the World to come, and in all your Obedience, have a single Eye to *his* Exaltation and Glory! And that you count it Honour and Happiness enough, to get *leave* to love and adore HIM thro' all Eternity.—It is the true Spirit of *the Bride the* LAMB's *Wife,* to love her Bridegroom's *Person,* above and beyond all his *Benefits:* and to delight more in his *Service,* as *his* manifestative Glory is advanc'd thereby, than in all that *Happiness* which she enjoys in it, or that Glory which shall result from it. There is *this,* in that Principle of Love to Christ, which is wrought in the Heart of every true Believer; altho' it may'nt be *discernible* to them, doth not always *work* in them, nor ordinarily appear, so as to be sensibly *reflected on* by them, until the Life of Grace in their Souls, is arriv'd to some *Strength* and *Maturity.* And not the least *Spark* of this Spirit is to be found in any Soul, but in those who are *married unto the Lord.* We shall love GOD for HIMSELF, and his *own* infinite Excellencies, when we get to Heaven; and rejoice more in *his Glory,* than in our *own Salvation:* and in our own Salvation, *first* and *principally,* as his Glory is so exceedingly advanced there-by. And the greater *Advances* we make towards a Fulness of Stature in Christ, the more *pure* and *disinterested* will our Love to him be.—But such is the infinite Kindness of our Lord, that from the overflowing Fulness of his Heart-Love, he has promis'd us a *free,* and *exceeding great Reward!* And gives us leave to have respect unto it, to encourage our Obedience! And doubtless we may and ought to rejoyce in hope of the *Glory to be revealed,* and in all manner of holy Conversation and Godliness, to seek for *rising Degrees* thereof, inasmuch as thereby, the infinite *Grace of Christ* will shine the more conspicuously. The more fruitful we are *now,* the more is our Lord glorify'd in us *here;* and as he'll put the more Glory upon us *hereafter,* so in every Degree of *our Glory,* will he be the *more Glorified.* And thus the Redeemed, may *seek* the Redeemer's *Glory,* in *running* for their promis'd Crown.

But, dear Sir, you'll think I forget you. You are on the *Waters:* But *sink* into them, you shall not, so long as *everlasting Arms are underneath.* Indeed Sir, you meet with Ingratitude, Treachery, Losses and Crosses from the Creatures:—But *these* are to *endear* the Creator, and his infinite Excellencies the more to you. GOD is weaning you from the Breast of *Creature-Enjoyments,* to solace your Soul with the River of *his* Pleasures. Emptying you of *Creatures,* to fill you with *himself.* And is not HE *better,* infinitely *better* than *all!* And is not HE *enough* in the *Want* of all? Do Friends *fail you?* Care not much for it: You have a *Friend that loveth at all Times, that Sticketh closer than a Brother.* CHRIST will *never fail you, nor forsake you.* And by the *Failing* of Creatures, the more will HE commend his all-sufficient Fulness, and neverfailing Kindness to your dear Soul. Wherefore, dear Sir, permit me as it were to forget my *Distance* from you in the World, to assume my *Nearness* in the Church, to use a *Freedom* I am exceeding *unworthy of,* and say, *My dear and honour'd Brother in CHRIST, walk worthy of GOD!* of your entire *Interest* in him, and *Dedication* to him!—To be *happy in* GOD, and *holy to him,* is the proper Life of a *Christian.* Make GOD your ALL: and you can *lose nothing.* Give him your *All,* and you'll stand *prepar'd,* submissively and thankfully, to *part with any thing* that he calls for. Our God will have us to be *practical* Believers. He will have us to know *his* infinite All-Sufficiency, and *our* entire Dependency, not only *doctrinally,* but *practically.* He will have us to learn practically, that HE is our ALL, *to make him so* in the Estimation of our Souls, as we *Believe him to be so* doctrinally: And to give him our *All,* as we profess his Sovereign Right to *every thing* that HE hath given us.—And in order hereto, the Lord hath his *Times,* wherein he either *imbitters* the Creatures to us while we possess them, or *takes* them from us, or *threatens* so to do: To bring us out of *them,* into *himself,* and cause us to rejoyce in HIM as our ALL, in the *want of all.* And much is *his* Glory, and *our* Happiness concern'd herein.—Let me intreat you therefore, dear Sir, to be *careful for nothing,* under the present Dispensations, but only to *Glorify* GOD therein, and to *answer* the Voice of them. GOD will take care of *your Glory;* be you concern'd only about *his.* Doth the Lord's Hand seem to be lifted up to strike your Comforts, your Joys of *Sense dead?* He calls you hereby, to take a mighty *Leap* of *Faith,* over all your dying Comforts, into his own Bosom, as the *everliving* GOD, who is and will be *your exceeding Joy!* your *everlasting* ALL!—Oh give him *yourself,* your *Relations,* your *Honour,* your Riches, resign up *all* to his sovereign, all-wise, and all-gracious Dispose! Say, "Lord, *here am I,* and *all* that thou hast given me: do with me and mine as *thou pleaseth:* only get thyself Glory; and I have enough." This, dear Sir, will *glorify God,* and *please him* exceedingly.—And verily God will *glorify you:* he'll *commend* your Faith and Love before Men and Angels; and either give you *again* the Creature-Comforts you resign, or that which is *better* in the room of them: Yea, he will bless you with the sensible Possession of *himself* more than ever.—You know how it far'd with *Abraham,* when he offer'd up his *Son: By myself, says the LORD, have I sworn, that in blessing I will bless thee, and in multiplying I will multiply thee,* Gen. Xxii.16, 17. And *Abraham's* Children, in the Exercise of the same Faith, are *blessed with faithful Abraham,* Gal. iii. 9.

Oh dear Sir, do you say, "I know not what will become of me and mine?" Permit me to reply: For *yours,* commit them to the Lord; and he will deal well with them for your Sake.—And for *yourself,* let me say: Whatever befalls, you cannot be any other than a *blessed Man!* For *Blessed is the Man whose Transgression is forgiven, and whose Sin is covered, unto whom the LORD doth not impute Iniquity.* Blessed is that Man at *all* Times, in *all* Conditions: he can be no otherwise than *blessed,* it can go no otherwise than *well* with *him,* who hath an entire, and eternal Interest in GOD; the *Sum* and *Fountain* of *Blessedness!* who doth and will make every changing *Providence,* a new and increasing *Blessing* to him! Oh, *that Man,* that has an Interest in the Blessed JESUS, shall *Increase* in Blessedness, thro' Time, and to Eternity! Whatever the Blessed GOD takes from him here, he will never take away *himself;* nor take away any Creature-Comfort, but to give him *more* of himself: and so he can be no other than a *Blessed Man!*

Return therefore, dear Sir, *return unto your Rest: For the* LORD *hath dealt bountifully with you!* If like the *Bush,* you should be all on *Fire;* GOD is *in you,* and you shall not be *consumed.* If you *pass thro' the Fires,* you shall not be *burnt, neither shall the Flame kindle upon you.* And when you *pass thro' the Waters,* the LORD will be *with you, and the Rivers shall not overflow you.* Lie at Anchor therefore in the *Bosom of* GOD, however *stormy* and *tempestuous* the Sea may be round about you. For GOD *is your Refuge and Strength, a very present Help in Trouble.* Therefore *fear you not, though the Earth be removed, and though the Mountains be carried into the Midst of the Sea. Though the Waters thereof roar and be troubled, though the Mountains shake with the Swelling thereof.* Selah. *There is a River, the Streams whereof shall make glad the City of God, the holy Place of the Tabernacles of the most High.* GOD *is in the Midst of you; you shall not be moved:* GOD *shall help you, and that right early,* Ps. xlvi. 1, &c.

I rejoice Sir, to see such a Concern wrought in your Soul, for the Advancement of the Redeemer's Interest in those *Places* which you mention: Such Mourning for the Decay of it, and such a Desire after the Revival of it *there.* May the LORD give you the *Desire* of your Soul, and make those Places as a *water'd Garden!* That *when you see this, your Heart may rejoice, and your Bones flourish as an Herb!*—The Lord inclines me to seek him with you for this Favour.

And as, dear Sir, you are sensible that you have not acted so vigorously as you ought for your dear Lord while he continu'd your Interest in those Places; and as you apprehend, that he may be now about to shake you out of them as a Rebuke; *humble yourself under the mighty Hand of God; and he will exalt you in due Time. Faint not,* dear Sir, *in this Day of Adversity.* Remember, that *whom the Lord loveth, he chasteneth, and scourgeth every Son whom he receiveth.* You have not to do with God, as an angry Judge, that will condemn you for your Sins. No; in this Regard, he hath *blotted out your Transgressions as a thick Cloud, and will remember your Sins no more.* He only chastiseth you as a *Father,* from an Infinity of Bowels, to make you a *Partaker of his Holiness* thereby. He designs to make you a better Child by his Rod. And he will not deal *severely* with you as a Father. *He knows our Frame, and remembers that we are Dust.* He will not *contend for ever, nor be always wroth; lest the Spirit fail before Him, and the Soul which he has made.* Oh, if he was strict to *mark* our Iniquity, as a *Father,* we could not *stand* in his Service: *But there* is *Forgiveness with* him, *that he may be feared.*

Come then, my dear Brother, get by Faith to the Foot of the *Cross;* and there see your Sins piercing and wounding your dear *Lord Jesus;* and there mourn and be in Bitterness for *him;* and there view all his Wounds, as so many Channels of boundless Grace to *you!* Lay your Hand of Faith upon the Head of the *great Sacrifice,* and confess over him all your Iniquities. Be open-hearted with God, hide nothing from him, but pour out your whole Soul, and all your Griefs into the Bosom of your merciful Father. And he will hear your Moan; his *Bowels will be troubled for you,* and most *surely will he have Mercy on you.* He will speak Peace afresh to your Conscience, and cause his Grace to superabound over all the Aboundings of your Sin. For *he is a God ready to pardon; that passeth by the Transgression of the Remnant of his Heritage: Because he delighteth in Mercy!*

And having a fresh Peace with God thro' Jesus Christ, all Things shall go well with you as to his outward Dispensations. Either he will *continue* your Interest in those Places which you are concern'd for, and enable you to use it to his Glory; or if he shuts up *those* Ways of serving him, he will open *others,* which shall be more for his Honour and your Advantage. The Lord will go on to make you *fruitful,* even to *old Age;* and *most* fruitful after the *greatest* Barrenness. Our Extremity is GOD's Opportunity. And he frequently makes it manifest, that he has reserved the *greatest* Trials, and the *greatest* Blessings for his dear Children 'till the *last:* The more to display his infinite Wisdom, unchanging Love and Faithfulness; and to ripen their Graces, to perfect their Obedience, and to prepare them for their Crown.

Wherefore, dear Sir, as you would be *perfect and entire, wanting nothing, let Patience have its perfect Work.* And count it *all Joy* when you fall into divers Temptations. For they are *happy* which endure. And, *blessed* is the Man that endureth Temptations: For when he is *tried,* he shall receive the *Crown of Life* which the Lord hath promis'd to them that love him. Oh could you take it in by Faith, how *rich* in Grace, and how *great* in Glory, you are to be made by these Trials; your Heart would even *leap for Joy,* altho' you should be cast, as it were, into the Midst of a *burning fiery Furnace!* And since your *light Affliction which is but for a Moment, worketh for you a far more exceeding and eternal Weight of Glory;* Labour, dear Sir, to behave under it, with such a true *Greatness* of Spirit, as becomes an Heir of GOD! *Faith* can *tread* the Waters: It is our *Unbelief* that *sinks* us. And if we would *believe,* let us look directly to Faith's *Object,* to our Almighty SAVIOUR, and keep our Eye steadily fix'd upon *him;* and then with Joy we shall make our Way thro the roughest Sea, and Storms and Tempests will not greatly move us. Let us leave it to *them* who have no Interest in God, to be at their *Wit's End,* when Losses and Crosses of all Kinds surround them. But as for *us* that have

firm and *resolv'd* for our Lord's Interest, and less under the *Power* of those Fears, which painfully restrain'd you from appearing so openly for CHRIST, as your Soul desir'd. Praise to our almighty LORD, who in these Respects *hath brought you out of Darkness, and the Shadows of Death, and brake your Bands in sunder!*—I joy that your Faith of *Interest* in CHRIST is strengthened; and that you feel the sweet and powerful *Influence* of GOD's *Love,* so far as it is *shed abroad in your Heart by the Holy Ghost.*

And be not startled, dear Sir, and driven back from your Joy and Confidence in GOD, by the *Power of Sin,* and the various *workings* thereof which you experience. For *what will ye see in the Shulamite? as it were the Company of two Armies:* i.e. of Sin and Grace, set in Battle-Array against each other.—*Negligence* in the Things of Christ, is the sad Experience of all the Saints, when *Sin* prevails.—A Mercy it is, when our dear Lord, looks us again into *Repentance,* gives us Delight in himself, and a fresh Earnestness of Soul, to follow after him.—And when *Grace* has the Ascendant, and the Intention of the Soul is fixt upon *spiritual Things,* it's no wonder that *worldly Affairs* become in some Measure irksome to us.—Not that the Soul lothes any piece of Service for *Christ,* be it ever so low and mean. But when we are *near to* GOD, we must feel a kind of *Pain,* in being call'd from his *Bosom,* from the more immediate Enjoyment and Worship of him, altho' it be to serve him in some *remoter Work.* And we do not enough at such Times take into our Thoughts, the *Service of* GOD in worldly Affairs, to draw out that *Delight* which we ought to have in *them* for *his Sake.*—Like *Peter* in the *Mount,* we say, *It is good to be here.*—None but the *Man of Christ,* ever glorify'd God *universally* and *perfectly,* in *all* the Paths of Obedience, with *all* that Diligence and Delight which are called for. And well it is for *us,* that *Christ* obey'd *perfectly,* to make us *compleatly Righteous* before God. *Our* Duty it is, to copy after *his* bright Example. But alas! how many are *our Blots!* But *the Blood of JESUS cleanseth us from all Sin.* And his *Spirit* which hath *begun* to sanctify us, will *perfect* the Work, and make us *compleatly Holy.*—Mean time, let us call Things by their right Names, and say of ourselves, when *negligent* about spiritual Things, that *Sin* prevails; and when *earnest* about them, that *Grace* prevails. And tho' by reason of that Sin which *mixeth* with the highest Actings of our Graces, and *cleaves to us* in our Walk with God, we may not always, when *intense* about Spirituals, give that *due Attendance* unto Temporals, which is call'd for; yet is it *Faith,* and not *Fancy,* that gives us *Delight* in *Christ* and *his Things.*—They are all *New-born, and have precious Faith,* who *taste that the Lord is Gracious;* who have an Appetite to *relish* the Sweetness of the *Grace* of CHRIST, and to delight themselves in *Him.*—And think not, dear Sir, that you are not *a new Creature,* because the new Creation-Work in your Soul is so far from *Perfection in Degrees.*

"Degrees are wanting still;
"It's yet our Infant-State:

"But lo, we can Spell out the Man,
  "In Limbs that are not great."
  Would you, dear Sir, have *full Assurance of Faith?* Seek it in the unchangeable *Faithfulness, Word* and *Oath* of a GOD *that cannot Lie;* and not in your fleeting, changeable *Frames.*—Grace be with you,
  I am, dear Sir,
   Yours most Obediently in CHRIST,

L E T T E R   IX.

Honour'd Sir,

PLEASE to excuse my Freedom, in attempting to give you my Thoughts more *largely* on what I *hinted* in my last: *viz.* Of your seeking *full Assurance of Faith,* in the *Faithfulness* of GOD, and not in your own *Frames,* or the gracious, faithful *Carriage* of your Soul towards HIM.

  In your last, Dear Sir, you told me, "That where real Grace, really is, it gets the Victory over Sin and the World. And that as Sin had so much Strength in your Soul, you was kept back thereby from the full Assurance of Faith." Permit me to reply:

  Sin, a *whole Body* of Sin and Death, dwells and works, in *every true Believer,* in every Soul, where true real *Grace* is. And tho' it be a Truth, That Grace gets the *Prevalency* over Sin, in the Soul where it is; yet this can be said of it, only when it *works,* or is duly and fully *exercis'd.*—That the inherent Grace of the Saints, did not *always* get the Victory over their indwelling Sin; is abundantly evident, by the Account given us of their Lives and Actions in the sacred Records.—So far from *this,* that on the *contrary,* in how many Instances did Sin get the *Victory* over Grace! The Apostle *Paul, Romans* the Seventh, spake his *own,* and the sad *Experience* of *all* the Saints, when he cry'd out of his *Wretchedness,* as a most miserable Man, on account of the Strength and Prevalency of indwelling *Sin;* which not only *warred* against the Law of his Mind, but also brought him into *Captivity* to the Law of Sin and Death. And it must needs be, Dear Sir, that he Being and Working, the Power and Prevalency of *Sin,* should be one of the *Miseries* which the Saints groan under in the present State, unless Perfection was attainable in this Life, which God in his Word plainly declares is *not.*

  Should you not then, Sir, rather argue, from that *painful Feeling* which you have of the *Power of Sin,* that you are *a new Creature in Christ Jesus,* and have a *Principle of Grace* wrought in your Soul; than that you are in a *State of Sin,* and *devoid* of special Grace? For no *unregenerate Man, has* any *painful Sensation* of *Sin,* as it is a direct Contrariety to God, to his infinite Purity, a despising of his Authority, an Abuse of his Grace, a Hindrance of Conformity to Him, and of the Service and Enjoyment of Him.—The two Principles of *Grace* and *Sin,* wherever they are, *continually* oppose and *alternately* prevail against each other. Grace inclines strongly towards *Perfection,* and Sin seeks its *Destruction.*—And therefore, when *aspiring* Grace, is *supprest* by Sin, the *piritual Man,* the *new Creature in Christ,* must needs *groan,* under the *Weakness* of his Grace, and the *Power* of his Sin, of his *carnal Mind,* of his corrupt, old *Adam*-Nature; as he *joys,* when Grace gets the *Victory* over Sin. But an *unregenerate Man* is all of *a Piece,* and an utter *Stranger* to this Conflict.—And therefore, Sir, you may draw some Conclusion about your *State,* from your *Experience* in this regard.

But Sir, when you have the Joy, to see *Grace* get the Ascendant over *Sin,* and to feel yourself strengthned, by the Power of Christ resting upon you, to *deny Ungodliness and worldly Lusts, and to live soberly, righteously, and godly in this present World;* the *Evidence* which ariseth from hence, of your being chosen, called, and justifi'd, and so, that you shall be glorify'd; is rather as Assurance of *Sense,* than of *Faith.* There is a certain *Knowledge* of our Justification, and so, of our being Heirs of eternal Life, which ariseth from our Sanctification; the one being an Evidence of the other. As 1 *John* iii. 14. *We know that we have passed from Death unto Life, because we love the Brethren.* But *this* Knowledge, is rather an Assurance of spiritual *Sense,* than of pure, sheer *Faith.* The Knowledge of the *Thing* doctrinally, indeed, as it relates to the Revelation made of it in the divine Word, That God hath given eternal Life to those that love Him, is a Knowledge of *Faith;* but the *Application* of this unto ourselves, arising from the inward Evidence of our Love to God, is a Knowledge of *Sense. Faith,* always hath for its *Object,* the Grace and Promise of God without us; but *Sense,* the Grace wrought in us, and the visible Effects of promis'd Goodness wrought for us.

And tho' there is a *Knowledge* of our being passed from Death unto Life, of our being justify'd by Grace, and made Heirs of eternal Life, to be gather'd from our *Sanctification;* yet *this* is not the first and principal Way of the Soul's coming at *that* Satisfaction.—There is a *Knowledge* of our Salvation to be had by *Faith,* pure, sheer Faith, in *Believing the Record* which God hath given in the Word of Promise, and *crediting* his Testimony therein, *merely* because of his infinite Truth and Veracity. And *this,* the Lord hath ordain'd to be the *first* and *principal* Way of knowing our Interest in Christ; and that other Knowledge of *Sense,* to be *subordinate* to it, and *attendent* upon it. The Knowledge of *Faith,* may, and should, be *full* and *abiding* at all Times; as the Ground of it is the *Faithfulness* of GOD, which is *unchangeably* the same. But the Knowledge of *Sense,* will be *greater,* or *lesser,* more *constant,* or *inconstent,* according to the Ground of it, our *different* Experiences, *variable* Frames, and the *changeable* Dispensations we are under. The first, Assurance of Faith, we should labour to hold *fast,* at all Times, and follow after as *much* of the other, Assurance of Sense, as can be attain'd. Inasmuch as the Lord hath ordain'd *Sense,* to be an Handmaid to *Faith,* to corroborate and strengthen it.

But we, alas! by reason of that legal Spirit which remains in us, strongly incline to break the Order which God hath fix'd; to put that *first,* which is and ought to be *second.* We would fain *see,* to believe, instead of *believing* to *see.* And by our *Unbelief,* we woefully rob GOD of the Glory due unto his Name; and ourselves of that Pcacc and Joy, which are only to be had in *Believing.*

Pursue then, my dear honour'd Brother, *the Assurance of Faith.* For the more of it you *attain,* the more *Glory* will you give to GOD in believing; the more you will *honor Him* by a holy Conversation; the more *useful* will you be to your Brethren; the greater will be your own *Peace* and *Joy of Faith,* and the more abundant will be your *Joy of Sense* too. In a Word, the more you attain of Assurance of Faith, the greater will be your *Grace* in this World, and your *Glory* in that to come.

And in order to this great Blessing, *Ask it of the Lord;* and seek it by a steady *Adherence* to the *Faithfulness* of GOD *in his Promise,* where only it is to be *found.*—Come daily, as a miserable, perishing Sinner in yourself, unto CHRIST the great SAVIOUR, and commit your Soul into his Hands, to be *saved* from all Misery, unto all Glory. And then labour to take him at his Word, *That you shall be saved!* and hold fast this your Confidence in *Him,* in the Face of ten thousand Difficulties, and seeming Contradictions in *yourself.* For, *hath* HE *said it, and shall he not do it? or hath* HE *spoken, and will he not make it good?*—Oh stand not reasoning with Satan and Unbelief, whether you are a *Believer,* or *not;* lose no Time *that Way,* but believe *afresh* on the Son of God, let this be your *every Day's Work.* And when you can't come to Christ as a *Believer,* you may come as a *Sinner; that Door* is *always open.* And I can tell you, Dear Sir, from my own Experience, that you'll sooner get Satisfaction about your *former Acts of Faith,* by *one fresh Look to* JESUS, than by a *thousand Looks* into your own *Heart,* when the Spirit of the LORD doth not *shine* upon his own Work, and make it *visible* to your spiritual Sense.—*They looked unto* HIM, *and were lightned, and their Faces were not ashamed.* It is the Appointment of GOD, that *Sin-benighted-Souls,* should *look* to the given SAVIOUR, that LIGHT *to lighten the Gentiles,* who is GOD's *Salvation unto the Ends of the Earth.* And not a *Soul* that obeys it, let the *Darkness and Shadow of Death* in which he fits, be ever so great, but shall find by blessed Experience, that upon *Him* the *Light* hath shined: The Light of GOD's *Salvation,* and the *Joy* of it too; if the Soul doth, as it ought, not only obey the Divine *Command* of looking unto JESUS, but also take Him at his *Word,* in the Grant of Salvation which he hath made thereon, and thereby *set to his Seal that* GOD *is true.*

Oh Sir, Do you *look* to CHRIST for *Salvation?* If you question it, look and look *again,* till you *know* that you do. Do you *look to the Saviour?* and shall you not be *saved?* HE, that is GOD, and cannot *lie,* hath *said it:* And who, or what shall *gainsay* it? Or rather, who, or what shall *hinder it?* What are all your potent Enemies, within and without, to *stand* against the Captain of your Salvation? Are they a *Match* for *Almightiness?* What are *they,* what shall they *be,* before the omnipotent Grace of CHRIST, to save *you,* and his almighty Wrath, to destroy *them!* Are you surrounded with Thousands, with Millions of Enemies, with an innumerable Host, that proudly *Refuse to let you go,* into that glorious Liberty of the Sons of GOD, which CHRIST hath purchas'd for, and granted to you? Fear not; your REDEEMER is *strong; HE will thoroughly plead your Cause,* and with glorious Triumph, rescue your Soul as a Prey from the Jaws and Paws of these devouring Lions; to your present and eternal *Rest,* and to their present and everlasting *Destruction!* Wherefore, *trust in the* LORD *at all Times,* and especially, when you are *afraid,* and *pursu'd* by Enemies, *flee unto Him to hide you. Get,* my dear Brother, get by *Faith* into CHRIST afresh; his Heart and Arms are always *open* to embrace you. You will be always *Welcome* to your dear SAVIOUR, it will be his *Joy,* to see you make *your Refuge under the Shadow of his Wings, until your Calamities are overpast.* Abide not *without,* stay not among *Enemies,* haste you to the LORD your strong Rock, your City of Defence, your quiet, glorious Habitation; and *there dwell in Peace.*—And know, that whenever you enter into CHRIST by *Faith,* the LORD *shuts you in,* by his infinite *Faithfulness!* He surrounds you with, and for ever secures you by, his *exceeding great and precious Promises,* which are all YEA and AMEN, which have all the YEA and AMEN of GOD upon them, in CHRIST!

See then how *safe* you are! how *richly* the LORD hath provided for your *strong Consolation!* HE has given you his *Word,* and his *Oath;* and because HE could sware by no *greater,* HE hath sworn by HIMSELF; HE hath as it were laid his own BEING, and all his infinite *Glories* at stake, for *your Salvation?* And He hath done *this* on purpose that *you* might have *strong Consolation.*—And will you not *receive it?* will you not *believe Him?* will you not *credit* his Truth and Faithfulness? You shall *know* them, my dear Brother, whether you *believe* them, or *not.* Your *Unbelief,* shall not make the *Faith of* GOD *of none Effect.* But oh, for *his Honour,* and your *own Joy,* rest for ever upon this eternal *Rock,* which can never *fail* or *sink* beneath you, so long as GOD *stands!* whose Name is JEHOVAH, the everlasting I AM!—The Lord *warm your Heart* by what he hath given me to write! *Mine* has been all on *Fire* while writing it!—I commit you into the Arms of CHRIST; request your Prayers and Thanksgivings for me; and beg Leave to subscribe, worthy Sir,

Your most obedient humble Servant,
In your LORD, and mine,

———   ———

L E T T E R   X.

Worthy and very dear Sir,

Gladly I embrace the first Opportunity, most thankfully to acknowledge the acceptable Favour of your last. The Lord made it very sweet and savoury to my Taste, a Means of affecting my Heart with his great Goodness, and of enlarging my Soul to praise him, both for *you* and *me*. I read it with Tears of Joy, and to all your *Petitions,* my Soul said *Amen!* Oh my honour'd Brother, what am I, that the God of all Grace should so mercifully regard me, to make me of any *Use* to your dear Soul! Ten thousand Praises to his adored Name! Blessed be our own GOD, who was pleas'd to *point* the Eye of your Faith to its true and proper *Object,* his own Grace, Truth and Faithfulness in CHRIST, by the short *Note* at the Close of my last but one, and to shew it you more fully by my last. Oh, how *much* is there in a single Sentence, when GOD *fills it!* And how *little* is there in whole Volumes, when GOD is not sensibly *there!*—This shews us that the Instrument is *nothing,* and GOD the great is ALL, in all that he effects by instruments; and that to *him* alone all the *Glory* is due. I am glad, Sir, that you ascribe it wholly to him; and even *so* we will bless him for *ever,* for giving us any Fellowship with *himself,* by and thro' Fellowship with *each other* in our Way to Heaven. This, Sir, is a *Mercy,* which our own GOD hath kept for us 'till *now,* among the *Thousands* in his well-order'd Covenant. And oh, my dear Brother, if the Lord would further *instruct* your Soul into the Life of *Faith,* and bring you more out of *Self* into *Christ,* by what he sent you by me, how *rich* would be my Reward! And how *full* my Joy!

Indeed, Sir, I look upon *Assurance of Faith,* to be a Thing of very great *Moment* in the *Christian Life.* And that one *Means* of attaining it, is a due Conscience-Information about the great Duty of *taking* GOD *at his Word,* in the Promise of *Life* thro' his *Son,* which is given to every poor Sinner that *looks* to JESUS. If the Conscience is duly *inform'd* of this Duty, it will excite the Soul to *attempt it.* And while Strength from Christ, enables the Soul to *believe,* upon GOD's bare *Word,* his great, unchangeable, and all-producing *Word,* Faith finds its *solid Basis,* and the Heart is at *rest,* amidst the *greatest Shakings.* And much of the *Wisdom* of Faith, lies in a constant, steady *Adherence* to its immoveable *Rock,* the all-sufficient, unchangeable, and Covenant-engaged *Grace* of GOD in CHRIST, amidst all the *Wants* and *Changes,* which continually attend, and frequently pass over saved Sinners. Our Wants are *great;* but the Fulness of JEHOVAH, engag'd by Word and Oath to supply them is *infinite!* Our Changes, inward and outward, are *many;* but our God and Father, our Lord and Saviour, our blessed Comforter, the LORD our GOD *changeth not!* HE *is in one Mind;—and who,* or what can *turn him?* Let us then, my dear Brother, abide *with* GOD, abide *in* GOD, and stir not *out* of HIM, to seek *another* Foundation for our Faith. Whenever we attempt to make gracious Dispositions and Actions, our *prime* Evidence for Life, and lay the main Stress of our Persuasion thereof upon *these;* we do as it were build our House upon the *Sand.* Ah where will our *Faith of Interest be,* if it rests upon *our Frames,* which are as *variable* as the *Wind!* It cannot *stand the Storms,* the *Shock* that will come against it, when the *Rain descends,* and the *Winds blow,* when Corruptions and Temptations beat vehemently against us, and our *own Goodness,* like the *Morning Cloud,* and the *early Dew, quickly passeth away.* But if our Faith rests upon the *Rock* of Immutability, it will abide *unshaken,* when *we, feeble Reeds,* as to our Frames, are *bow'd* this Way or that. Let us then, as the *Psalmist,* say of the LORD, HE *is our Rock,* and *we shall not be greatly moved.*

And while our *Faith* rests in GOD, and *his* unchanging Grace and Faithfulness, let us most earnestly seek the *Fruits* of it in all Goodness, both in Heart and Life, to the Glory of him that hath loved us, and the Praise of that Grace which hath saved us. So far as we *discern them,* let us be thankful, and labour to improve them as a *subordinate* Evidence of our happy State. And so far as we *want them,* let us humble ourselves before the Lord, ask for fresh Supplies of the Spirit of Grace, *forget the Things which are behind, and press forward towards the Mark, for the Prize* of perfect Conformity to Christ, in Holiness and Glory. No Christians are so *fit* to examine their own Hearts and Lives, their inward and outward Walk before *him,* as those who have least Dependance upon these, as the *prime* Evidence of their State.

But alas! thro' the Subtilty of Satan, and the secret Workings of Unbelief, God's dear Children are frequently tempted, either to be always poring upon the *Grace* in their own Hearts, Words and Ways, to spell out the *Evidence* of their *State* in Christ; or else to *neglect these,* which are and ought to be the Evidence of our *Walk* with him. Both Ways the Glory of our Lord is *eclipsed,* and our Faith, Joy and Holiness *hindred.* Happy is the Soul that discerns the *Snare* which on *either Side* is laid for his *taking,* and avoids it. That *considers not its own Deadness,* when solicited thereto, as that which may nullify the Promise, but is *strong in Faith, giving Glory to* GOD; and that while he is *fully persuaded that what* GOD *hath promised, he is able also to perform,* is exceeding *careful* to walk before him in *Love,* as an Heir of Promise, and an Expectant of promis'd Grace and Glory. *That's a Christian indeed,* he *is* so, he *appears* to be so, that is *strong* in Faith, *servant* in Love, and *increasing* in Obedience. *He hath his Fruit unto Holiness, and the End* shall be *everlasting Life.*—Then, Lord Jesus, *increase our Faith,* inflame our *Love,* and enlarge our *Hearts* to run the *Way of thy Commandments.* that thou mayst be *glorify'd in us,* and *we in thee, according to the Will of God and our Father!*

You will please to excuse me, dear Sir, that I have added this, to what I wrote in my last. I know somewhat thro' Grace, how sweetly and strongly Assurance of Faith, doth *influence* the Soul to Holiness. And I know somewhat likewise of that great *Need* which we have, to maintain a strict and constant *Watch* over our own lazy, sluggish Hearts, that we yield not to spiritual Sloth, that when we have attain'd Assurance of Faith, we sit not down, as if all our Work was done, and our Race run. We had need seek to be strong in *Faith,* that so we may *glorify* GOD, have *full* Joy, and wax *valiant* in Fight against all our spiritual Enemies; and to increase in *Love* and every *Grace* of the Spirit, that we be not *barren nor unfruitful in the Knowledge of our Lord and Saviour Jesus Christ,* and that *an Entrance may be ministred unto us abundantly into his everlasting Kingdom.* And well it is for us, that our dear Lord Jesus is the *Author,* and will be the *Finisher* of both our Faith and Holiness: That HE that calls us to the Exercise of *Faith* and Performance of *Duty,* will strengthen us for our *Work,* and crown all our *Graces* with *endless Glory!*

Glad am I, honour'd Sir, that you *value* your Relation to CHRIST, our glorious elder Brother, and to his junior Brethren, so far *above* all worldly Relations and Titles whatsoever. The *Pleasure* you take in being familiar with *me,* and in my familiar addressing of *you,* as my dear Brother in Christ, gives me a great deal of *Freedom* so to do.—I am glad that some Hopes of the Lord's reviving his Work at P----n, is so joyous to you; and that the Thought, that it is even possible, that *you* should be honour'd as an Instrument thereof, some Way or other, makes your Heart to leap in your Breast. Well, my dear Brother, do I know what you experience. And I am persuaded that the Lord has great Mercy in Store for you. It *is* possible, that you should work successfully for Christ, under the Influences of the Holy Ghost. *If you can believe, all Things are possible.* Come then, cast your hungry, thirsty Soul upon the *boundless Grace* of CHRIST, to be *dealt with* according to it. And the Prince of Grace will abundantly *satisfy* your longing Soul, and say unto you, *Be it unto thee even as thou wilt.*—Oh Sir, do you long for Christ's coming quickly? Surely he is preparing your Heart to receive joyfully that gracious Visit which he intends to give you speedily.—Blessed be our Lord, who has given you such a practical Proof of his Almighty Power and Grace, in causing your Enemies to submit to you. And that thereby he has given you a Glimpse of some open Doors to serve him, which to your Grief, you fear'd might have been shut. Indeed, my Brother, the Lord never wants *Ways* to shew us Kindness, to own and honour his People, when he *resolves* to be *gracious.*—I am glad to hear you say, "That the Lord will do that which is *fit* to be done." *Rest* then in his All-wise, and All-gracious Dispose; *believing* that an Immensity of Grace, guided by an Infinity of Wisdom, stands *engag'd* to usher in upon you all the Blessings of the new Covenant, both for Time, and for Eternity.—As to the Trials and Afflictions which may abide you, they are among the *all Things* which shall *work for your Good,* and *turn to your Salvation.* Wherefore be meek and patient, joyful and thankful in all.—And if in some Respects you *never* was at so great a Plunge in your whole Life; then, dear Sir, you have an Opportunity, put into your Hands to glorify GOD herein, such an one, that you *never* had, or *may* have the like. Oh let not *this slip!* Flow into the Will of GOD, love, adore, and bless him in this *great Strait,* and delightfully commit yourself and All into his Hands. *For great are his Mercies,* great is the *Salvation* which his Almighty Arm will work for you, and great is the *Glory* which he will put upon your *tried Graces.*—Indeed, Sir, I am persuaded that the Lord himself gave me what I wrote to you, and all that concern for, and sympathy with you, which I have experienc'd. And if *you* bless the Lord for an Acquaintance with *me,* much more have I reason to bless him for an Acquaintance with *you.* I wonder at his Grace, that should permit it and effect it, unto mutual Usefulness! Verily I think, that if my God and Father was to look over *all his Children,* he could find *none* so vile, base and unworthy to be put *among them,* or made of any *Use,* to them, as poor sinful *me.* And yet he delights to be gracious to such a *chief Sinner!*—You say, dear Sir, "That you are a Babe, that you cannot requite me in the same Way, and hope that our Lord will requite me." It is good, my dear Brother, to have low Thoughts of *ourselves.* The *lower* we are in our own Esteem, the *fitter* we are made for *high* Communications from GOD.—As to your requiting *me,* Sir, in the same Way, God has made your letters *sweet* and *precious* to my Soul, and several of your Expressions repeatedly of *Use,* for which I bless him. And whenever the Lord is pleas'd to make any Thing of *Use* to *you,* that he sends by me, I esteem it a *rich Reward.* If I may, Sir, be of any Use to your dear Soul, to *help* your Faith and Joy, and to *promote* the Glory of our Lord thereby; Oh what a *rich Return* would it be of my *poor Labours!* Indeed, my dear Brother, my glorious LORD, is a rich and bountiful MASTER unto *me.* He loves and employs me to do *something* for him, makes his *Work* a little Heaven to me, *blesseth* my weak Labours, and *pours in upon me* strong Consolations, full Measure, heap'd up, and running over! And yet there is a Reward to *come,* that far surpasseth all *Thought!* HIMSELF will be *my exceeding great* REWARD! Oh infinite, free, rich, reigning *Grace,* to such a *Hell-deserving Sinner!*—Indeed, Sir, I can do but *little* to *praise* this Grace, to *love* the GOD of LOVE!—But it has been much upon my Heart of late, to ask him to make me *a Servant of all,* to run about his House, with a little *Refreshment,* with suitable Supplies, put into my Hand by his, for his dear Servant here and there, while they are at *Work* for him. And oh how *Happy* should I be, if the God of all Grace would *grant me that which I have requested!*—Unto his tender Mercies I commit you to be satisfy'd and solac'd with the Bounties of his Love, thro' Time, and to Eternity!—I humbly request your Prayers, and Leave to subscribe, Dear Sir,

 Your Honour's, at all Obedience in the Lord,

L E T T E R   XI.

Honour'd and very dear Sir,

Abundant Thanks for the most acceptable Favour of your last.—I rejoice, Sir, that you can say, "The Lord hath not altogether forsaken *me*." And be of good Chear; for HE hath said, I will *never* leave thee, nor forsake thee. I am glad, dear Sir, you feel, what you call, "any *Semblance* of his Life in your Heart." Call it, dear Sir, as it is, CHRIST's *Life in you.* For in you HE doth and will *live,* until all the present *Death,* under which you groan, is swallow'd up in the Joy and Victory of *Life eternal.* And tho' you say, "I creep on but poorly:" Yet be not *dismay'd;* For the LORD is *your* GOD. Tho' in yourself you are as weak as a *Worm;* yet *Worm Jacob,* hath a *mighty* GOD. Or, the *mighty* GOD is the GOD of *Jacob;* and has said to the *Worm Jacob, Fear thou not, for I am with thee,—I will strengthen thee, yea, I will help thee, yea, I will uphold thee with the right Hand of my Righteousness. Worm Jacob,* shall never *fail,* so long as *Jacob's* GOD *endures.* Because the everlasting Strength of JEHOVAH, is *engag'd* for *Jacob,* in his utmost Weakness. *Jacob,* that feeble, despicable, slow-pac'd *Worm,* shall never be deserted, despised, or disregarded, by his Almighty, and All-gracious GOD. HE *sees,* my dear Brother, with infinite Pleasure, all the little Motions and faint Struggles of your Soul after HIM, with your Loads of Earth upon your Back. And HE *compassionates* you under your *Weakness,* will *put Strength in you,* and defend you from all Harms. No Foot shall crush you to *Death,* so long as GOD *lives.* For *your Life is hid with* CHRIST *in* GOD.

> *Honoured Sir,*
>   *Yours most Humbly,*
>   *In our own LORD JESUS,*

L E T T E R   XII.

Worthy and very dear Sir,

IBless the Lord, that made my last poor letter acceptable to you, and any Expression therein of use. My most humble Thanks for the most acceptable Favour of your last. You need not, dear Sir, apologize for the Length of your letters to me. For the longer the letter is that I receive from you, the greater Indication of your Kindness I esteem it. And I love to hear your Complaints, and the Causes of your Grief. Not that I take Pleasure in your *Grief,* but in your pouring out the same into *my Bosom.* Oh that our dear Lord Jesus would give me a *large Heart,* like his *own,* that may have *room* enough in it for all your sorrows, and a *quick Sensation* of all your Griefs! And oh, that while *I suffer* together with *you,* as a dear Fellow-Member in the Body of Christ, my Lord would pour his *Spirit* upon me, that like *him,* in my *little Measure,* I might know how to *speak a Word in Season to your weary Soul!* Or rather, oh that my dear Lord, in whom the *Fulness* of the *Spirit* dwells, would pour out *gracious Words,* from his own Life-giving lips, thro' poor *me,* upon your dear Soul! Oh how glad should I be, if the opening of my Lips *might* asswage your Grief! But, my Brother, the opening of Christ's Lips *shall* do it. CHRIST will *speak Peace* to your dear Soul in Trouble, Joy in Sorrow, Light in Darkness; and with an infinite Efficacy, and almighty Energy, *apply* what he says, and *produce* what he calls for. It gives me much Pleasure and Satisfaction, that you are CHRIST's *Care:* That your Faith, Joy and Holiness, and the Whole of what concerns you, relating to your inward and outward Trials, are in *his Hands.* And therefore all Things to *you,* must needs *Issue well.* Oh my Brother, All is *Peace,* between GOD and *you,* in CHRIST! The LORD is carrying on your Salvation, with strong Hand gloriously. HE puts you into the Furnace! but he is and will *be with* you there; and *out* he will bring you thence, *as Gold seven Times refined.—Fear* neither Men nor Devils, with a *slavish, dismaying* Fear. For they are all in GOD's *Hand,* and cannot *Touch an Hair of your Head* without his Permission. They can proceed no further against you, than the LORD your own GOD permits them. And all that your Enemies may do *against* you, shall be over-ruled by the LORD your Friend, *for* you. The greatest Unkindness you meet with from them, the more Kindness will the LORD shew you. GOD will so richly *clothe* all their Unkindness, with his own infinite Kindness, that it shall not *hurt* you. Yea, HE will make the one to serve as a *Means* of conveying the other, and as a *Foil* to illustrate and set forth its Glory.—Wherefore *Fear not,* tho' in the *Furnace.* For the LORD sits by as the *Refiner,* and will not suffer the Fire to be too *hot,* nor to continue too *long* upon you. HE best knows, what Degree of fiery Trial is *needful* to purge away your Dross. And no more than what is absolutely *so,* will he suffer you to pass thro'. It is but if *need be,* that for a Season you are in Heaviness thro' manifold Temptations. I know you long to have *Sin* destroy'd, and seperated from you. And this is the blessed Work which the LORD is now about, by all the Trials which pass over you. This is all the *Fruit,* to purge away your Iniquity, to take away your Sin, to refine you from your *Dross.* And as for your *Gold,* your Faith, your Grace, GOD will take Care of *that,* that it sustain no Damage, that the least Grain of it be not lost, by the most fiery Trial that passeth over it. No; your Faith and Holiness are to be brightned and increased, not diminish'd by your Trials. Your *Gracious* GOD, designs to make you *very Glorious,* or HE would not bestow so *many Trials* upon you. HE designs to make your Faith and Holiness so bright and shining, that they shall be found unto *Praise, and Honour, and Glory at the Appearing of* JESUS CHRIST. Trials to *you,* Sir, don't come as Afflictions to the *Ungodly;* as so many Curses, but as so many Blessings. You have GOD's *Heart,* as a *Father* to you in CHRIST, in every Stroke of his *Hand;* as *Infinity of Grace,* in every *Affliction* that befalls you. And could your Faith take in but a thousandth *Part* of GOD's Loving-kindness towards you in every Trial, it would *sweeten* the most bitter Cup, that your wise and gracious Father, puts into your Hand; and make you say, with your Lord, "The Cup which my Father giveth me, shall I not Drink it?"—Oh Sir, would you be *willing* to have any Part or Degree of your Trials abated, upon this *Condition,* that GOD should lose any part of his Glory, his manifestative Glory, thereby? Or that *you* should lose any part of that Grace and Holiness, design'd for you by your Trials here, or any part of your Crown of Glory hereafter? If *not;* be at *rest* in your heavenly Father's *Will:* For it is founded on his *Counsel,* as that which is most for his own Glory, and your Advantage. And you could not be without the *least* Trial, or the *least* Degree of any Trial you meet with, but GOD would have *less* Glory in your Salvation, and you *less* Happiness as a saved Soul. And as your Trials shall be no more, no greater, nor last any longer than the Glory of GOD, and *your* Good are concern'd herein; from henceforth, be patient and joyful in all your Tribulation: And count it your *Happiness* to endure, and *all Joy,* when you fall into divers Temptations. *Moses endur'd, as seeing HIM who is Invisible.* And Christians must *count* at another rate, than the Men of the World do; or to what *End* serveth our *Faith?* When we esteem a Variety, Multiplicity, and Perpetuity of Trials, to be *all Sorrow;* we are Unbelieving, Carnal, and walk as *Men:* Not as *Christians,* not as Men of another Country, that are Strangers, and Pilgrims on Earth, that have their Conversation in Heaven, their ALL, in the All-Sufficient, and Unchangeable GOD, and this empty, nothing, changeable World under their Feet.—And no Trial, my dear Brother, can take you *unprovided* for it. The LORD your own GOD, that ordain'd the Trial, had laid up a Sufficiency of Grace and Strength in CHRIST, to carry you thro' it, and to bring you out of it, to *his* and *your* Glory and Joy. "When Trials are a coming, Grace is a coming:" as a dear deceased Servant of Christ, once said. If our Way be rough; our *Shoes shall be Iron and Brass; and as our Days our Strength.* It is all one to *Omnipotence,* to carry us thro' great or small, many or few, short or long Trials. We must be arm'd along by *Almightiness,* or *we,* feeble Worms, cannot get thro' the *least;* and *everlasting Arms* being underneath us, we shall be carried safely, comfortably, and advantageously thro' the *greatest.*—Then may we say with the *Psalmist, O* LORD *of Hosts, Blessed is the Man whose Strength is in thee!*

Dear Sir, so far as your Trials, or any Part of them, as you apprehend, are brought upon you as a Rebuke for your *Sins;* I know they are *heavy.* But let not your Heart *fail* and be *discourag'd,* even in *this* Case. For the Lord doth not visit you for your Iniquities, in a Way of fierce Wrath, and vindictive Justice, No; as a just *Judge,* for the Sake of Christ's Satisfaction, HE forgives all your Iniquities, and remembers your Sins no moire. He only chastiseth you as a *Father,* from, the *Love* of a Father, in the *Bowels* of a Father, from the *Care* of a Father, and with the gracious *Designs* of a Father, to make you *a Partaker of his Holiness* thereby. By his *Rod,* HE points us to our Follies, humbles us for them, and brings us to confess and forsake them. And when we are sufficiently humbled, and have receiv'd all the Good design'd us by the Chastisement; HE will burn his Rod, take us up in his Arms, and kiss and embrace us as his dear Children. When He speaks *against* us in his Providential Dispensations, He earnestly *remembers* us still, in the Infinity of his Bowels, in the Multitude of his tender Mercies. And when we *bemoan* ourselves, and our Peevishness, Frowardness, and Untractableness under his chastising Hand, HE will surely *hear* us, and say concerning us, *Is Ephraim my dear Son? Is he a pleasant Child? For since I spake against him, I do earnestly remember him still: therefore my Bowels are troubled for him; I will surely have Mercy upon him, saith the LORD.*

When God's People, his *Jerusalem,* had finished, and would not otherwise be reclaimed, He suffer'd their Enemies to prevail against them, and to bring them into Captivity. And tho' this was brought upon them as a Rebuke for their *Sin,* yet the Lord design'd it for their *Good.* He said expressly, That the *good Figs,* his own Children, should go into Captivity for their *Good.*—And when God's People are in Captivity for their *Sin,* Enemies make a great *Stir* about it, triumph over, and would bear them down, as if God had *forsaken them,* and they had no *Room* to hope and trust in Him *now,* because they have *sinn'd* against Him.—But *mistaken* they are: For *if Heaven above can be measur'd, and the Foundations of the Deep searched out beneath, then will the LORD also cast off the Seed of Israel, for all that they have done!* No; God's People, are too near and dear to HIM, ever to be forsaken of him, or forgotten by him, in the worst Circumstances they can possibly be brought into. He strictly *Regards* every Kind and Degree of their Affliction, whether brought upon them immediately by his own Hand, or mediately, thro' the Instrumentality of Creatures. And in his *Heart* they have a Fulness of Pity and Sympathy, that shall usher in full Deliverance, and glorious Salvation upon them.—And as for their *Enemies,* when they have got leave from GOD to afflict his Children, HE *sees* how far they go, to their Chain's End, and with what *despiteful Minds* they act against them; and he is much *displeased,* and will have a severe Reckoning with them for all their evil Treatment. They can't *touch* any of his dear Children, no, tho' they have sinn'd against him, but they *touch the Apple of his Eye.* And as HE takes *our Wrongs* as done to himself, he will most surely Revenge them. He hath styl'd himself a GOD *that pleadeth the Cause of his People.* And the Church when in Captivity could say, *I will bear the Indignation of the LORD, because I have Sinned against him; until he plead my Cause, and execute Judgment for me: HE will bring me forth to the Light, and I shall behold his Righteousness. Then she that is mine Enemy shall see it, and Shame shall cover her who said unto me, where is the LORD thy God? My Eyes shall behold her: now shall she be trodden down as the Mire of the Streets,* Mic. vi. 9, 10. And when GOD ariseth to Judgment, *for* his People, and *against* their Enemies, he will plead their Cause thoroughly; and say to them who have afflicted them, thus and thus have ye done unto *mine:* And what will ye Recompense ME? *Thus saith the LORD of Hosts, I am jealous for Jerusalem and for Zion with a great Jealousy. And I am very sore displeased with the Heathen that are at Ease: for I was but a little displeased, and they helped forward the Affliction. Therefore thus saith the LORD, I am returned to Jerusalem with Mercies,* Zech. i. 14, &c. And tho' the *Assyrian* was the Rod of

God's *Anger* against his sinful People; yet they were not to be *afraid* of them. *Therefore thus saith the LORD of Hosts, O my People that dwelleth in Zion, be not afraid of the Assyrian.* What, not afraid of a *cruel Enemy,* stirred up by *God himself* against his People, on account of their *Sin? No:* Because the *Enemy* was but a Rod in the Hand of their *Friend:* And there was Grace enough in the Heart of GOD, and Power enough in his Arm, to save his People, and to destroy their Enemies, when by them he had *performed all his Work upon Mount Zion. He shall smite thee with the Rod.* (saith the Lord) *and lift up his Staff against thee after the Manner of Egypt.* And yet God's People was not to be *afraid* of him. *For yet a little while,* (says he) *and the Indignation shall cease, and mine Anger, in their Destruction,* Isa. x. 24, 25. Thus GOD will burn his Rod, when he has *chastis'd* his Child. *The Rod of the Wicked shall not always rest upon the Lot of the Righteous; lest he put forth his Hand unto Iniquity.* God hath *other Thoughts* in chastising his Children, than the Enemies have. *His Thoughts* are Thoughts of *Peace* towards them, and not of *evil,* in all the Wars and Devastations which they make upon them. And says the *Psalmist, I will incline mine Ear unto a Parable; I will open my dark Saying upon the Harp. Wherefore should I fear in the Days of Evil, when the Iniquity of my Heels shall compass me about?* Ps. xlix. 4, 5. A *Parable,* a *dark Saying* indeed. What not *fear* in the Days of Evil, when the Iniquity of our Heels, our Walk in the World, compasseth us about? Faith must open the Mystery; for here, *Sense* is nonplust. But so it is, we that have believ'd in JESUS, need not *fear* in evil Days, when our *Iniquities* compass us about. Because GOD doth not *impute* them to us, nor will *deal* with us in Wrath; according to them. We are under *Grace;* and *Mercy* compasseth us about: So that no Evil, no Misery can *touch us,* but what comes *thro' these,* and is thereby made a Mercy, and a Blessing unto us. Surely in the *Floods of great Waters,* when the Waves and Billows of Affliction rise high, and pass over our Souls, *they,* our *Sins,* in the Imputation of their Guilt, and Execution of their Curse, shall not come *nigh us,* Psa. xxxiv. 6. And if Sin be removed, if all is *Peace,* as to our State, between God and us; what can *hurt* us? Surely if our GOD brings thro' Fire and thro' Water, He will be with us there, and bring us thence into a wealthy Place.—Wherefore, my honour'd Brother, let not your Faith and Confidence in GOD, be *marred* because of your *Sins;* nor harken to the Suggestions of your Enemies, as if you might not hope and trust in HIM for full Salvation, *because* of them. For tho' a Time of Affliction for *Sin,* when our Sin is brought to Remembrance by the *Rod,* is a very *evil* Time; yet even at *such* a Time, our GOD is *so good,* that he compassionates us according to the Measure of our Distress, and so much the *more,* as the *greater* the Evil is that we are tried with: And in the Infinity of his Grace, he will stretch out his Almighty Hand, to help and save us to the uttermost. And the *greater* the Evil is that we are under, (as it is always great in a Time of Affliction, when Sin presseth in upon the Conscience) the *more* will our God account Himself glorify'd, if at *such* a Time, we put our Trust under the Shadow of his Wings. And verily, *His Mercy shall be upon us, according as we*

Salvation from Him. And therefore it is our *Duty* to believe on CHRIST, that we *may be saved,* under every and all our Views of Want and Necessity. Nor shall we be *ashamed* of our Faith in CHRIST, nor Hope in GOD, *World without End!*

Indeed Sir, I have enjoy'd the great Blessing of outward *Tranquility* for some Time. But I have been inur'd to *Trials* of various Kinds: Nor do I expect to be long free from them while in this World. If *you* are in *Trouble* now, and I in some Measure of *Peace;* by and by, you and I may *change Places.* But since our *unchangeable* GOD will be with us, we need not be anxiously careful about any *Change* that doth or may pass over us.—But what mean you, my dear and honour'd Brother, by your being "in a crazy, leaky *Skiff,* toss'd in the Dark on the raging Ocean, amidst Banks and Rocks, by fierce Winds and cross Tides?" Is your *Faith* this crazy, leaky Skiff? You have a better Bark than *that,* to ride out the Storm in. At God's Call, you are entred into *Christ;* and the LORD hath *shut you in.* And CHRIST is such a *firm, strong Bark,* that not a *Drop* of the Waters of GOD's Indignation can *pierce thro'* to touch you, amidst the greatest Affliction-Storms that can possibly arise against you. What mean you, my dear, dear Brother, by your being *out of Sight of Land?* Is it that you can see no *End of your Time-Troubles?* Oh, open your Eye of Faith, and look to your *eternal Rest. What is your Life,* your troublesome Life? *It is even as a Vapour,* and as it were but for a Moment. You are almost got home. Look; *Yonder is the Land of Rest!* See you not how *near* you are to it? A few more *Storms,* and then, *Farewell Tempests for ever!* You will soon be *wafted,* dear Sir, into your *desired Haven. The LORD which hath shewed you great and sore Troubles, will quicken you again, and bring you up again from the Depths of Earth and Sea:* HE *will increase your Greatness, and comfort you on every Side.*

I leave you in the Arms of JESUS, your best, your everlasting Friend: In whom you are always safe and happy, and shall be eternally glorious! His Grace be with your Spirit! In HIM,

I am,

Honoured Sir,
Your most obedient Humble Servant,

------   ------

L E T T E R   XIII.

Honour'd Sir,

YOUR surprisingly kind and affectionate letter, I most thankfully receiv'd.—As to our Affliction, Sir, the Lord has been exceeding good to us in bounding and mitigating of it.—I hope the Lord will rebuke it, and put more Strength into me and my dear Yokefellow, in a little Time. We are his *Own:* And let him do with us as he pleaseth. He is worthy to be loved and blessed in all his Dispensations. They are wise and holy, just and good. I love and adore him in all.

As to that Advice, Sir, about our Case, and those Medicines for our Cure, which most kindly you propose to get for us; with the utmost Gratitude, we acknowledge and accept of your very great Favour therein.—

But Sir, from your kind Proposal, with the Incitements given to accept of the same, as, "That it would be exceeding obliging to you, using you as a Friend and shewing Confidence in you as such:" Let me say, JESUS is *your Friend:* Use, and trust in HIM as such. Are you sick and diseased, poor and needy, hungry and thirsty, *&c.* CHRIST hath all Fulness, of Meat and Medicine, of Life and Strength, and whatever you can possibly want. And he calls you to make your Application to HIM, in every Time of your Need. And such is his Love and Pity towards you, that it will infinitely delight his Heart, if with the greatest Freedom, you continually *use,* and *confide* in HIM as your *Friend.* The more you do so, the more you will please, the more you will honour HIM. If you love JESUS therefore, and would set his Glory high, and rejoice his Soul; be *free* with Him. And with his *whole Heart,* and with his *whole Soul,* will HE do you good. All the Love and Sympathy of a *Friend,* towards his dearest *Favourite* when afflicted, is but a faint *Shadow* of that Infinity of Grace, that Immensity of Bowels, which is in CHRIST's Heart towards *you,* his dear, his tried *Friend!* Encourage therefore, flee into his Bosom: With Joy He will let you in, to succour and defend you.

What you said, Sir, "of CHRIST's everlasting Love, and uninterrupted Care and Power, of his turning our Beds for us in Affliction:" was sweet to my Soul. And from many Years Experience, I can witness to this Truth, That JESUS *will make his People's Bed in their Sickness.* And oh how sweetly did HE open his Heart-Love towards, and sympathy with me, in one of my Afflictions, in that Word, *I was sick!* Truly I laid my *pained Head* in my *Lord's Bosom;* and sweetly it *eas'd* my Griefs, to have such a *Friend* bearing together with me, yea, bearing *me,* and all my *Load,* supplying me with Cordials, and wiping away all my Tears, with his own sweet, soft Hand! Wonderful it is to think of, but so it is, JESUS has been my *Nurse* when afflicted!—I read it with Surprize, Sir, "that with Pleasure *you* could perform the Office! I am glad you have an Heart like my *Lord's:* May HE reward your Kindness to us, every Way like HIMSELF! and succour and comfort you in every and all of your Distresses!

With surprising Pleasure, I view'd the infinite Grace of GOD, in making so weak, so vile a *Worm,* of use to *you,* Sir: And saw such particular Answers to my poor Prayers, in several of your Expressions, that appear'd very glorious in my Eyes. Oh what am I, vile *me,* that GOD should make me of any *Use* to his dear Servant! And if *I was offered on the Sacrifice and Service of your Faith, I should joy and rejoice with you.* My dear Brother, you have my *Soul,* in every little Hint my *Hand* fends you. And when you tell me, that the Lord doth *bless it* to help your *Faith,* it is my *Life. I live, if you stand fast in the Lord.* Oh how my Soul loves you as CHRIST's! And how do I compassionate and tender you, and fain would succour you as *his!* I know you are glad that my Lord puts you in my *Heart;* as I, that HE gives me a Place in *yours.* Let us both praise HIM, and love HIMSELF for, in, and above all. Let us not cast a Glance at *creature-Love,* without viewing it as CHRIST's Love to us in *that Creature.* And then our Hearts will be duly affected towards HIM, and *it.*—The LORD Jesus be with, and bless you abundantly! In HIM,

> *Honour'd Sir, I am*
> *Your most humble Servant,*

——— ———

L E T T E R   XIV.

Honour'd Sir,

WHAT Thanks shall I render for all the abundant Favours which you are pleas'd to heap upon me? Please to accept of all that I can give. And *a full Reward be given you of the* LORD *God of Israel!*—You was on the *Mount,* Sir, when you wrote last, and had begun *Heaven* in your Soul. I join'd the *Worship,* and to all your Prayers and praises, most heartily said *Amen!* This your exceeding kind, sweet letter, was most delightful to me. All Glory to the GOD of Love! Oh my dear Brother, by and by, you and I shall drop our Tenements of Clay, and our poor imprison'd Souls, brought into the full and glorious Liberty of the Sons of GOD, shall incessantly and unweariedly join the Choir of perfect Saints, and glorious Angels, who sing Praise to GOD and the LAMB for evermore! *That Day* hastens. Oh to serve CHRIST in the *mean Time!* That for us to *live* may be CHRIST! Then, what ineffable *Gain* will *Death* bring us!

I am glad that the Lord, by the Hint I gave you of his encouraging me to take the Copies of my letters last publish'd, excited your Joy and Praise. For this End, if the LORD please, I send for your Perusal, some Notes of what pass'd between God and my Soul, relating to some of my other Books.—My End in writing these Notes, was, that I might the better remember GOD's Promises, that so when I saw them fulfill'd in Providences, I might praise him the more. And if thereby you see the LORD's wonderful Kindness to *me;* Oh watch to give HIM all the Praise! And pray that such a favour'd Sinner, might be deeply struck with infinite Kindness, and chang'd into the Image of it! Oh Sir, I am so deeply *indebted* to Free Grace, that I owe *ten Thousand Talents* of Praise! And alas for me! I am so insolvent, in myself, I have not a *Mite* to pay! Oh my Stupidity, Ingratitude and Unthankfulness! Pray to the Lord to pardon such a great Sinner, and make me a Saint indeed! I have such an Hell of Iniquity in me, that if the Grace of GOD was not *infinite,* and his Long-suffering his *own,* HE would dash me into the Pit! But his LOVE *holds* his Hand! Oh help me to praise him, now and for evermore! And strive together in your

Prayers to GOD for me, that a poor, pained, Love-sick Sinner may some Way or other be honour'd to *serve* the SAVIOUR! I long to serve CHRIST, that I may *honour* him, that I may pour out a Soul full of *Love* to him and his. But oh my narrow Heart, my pinion'd Soul! GOD *be merciful to me a Sinner!*

There was one Thing, Sir, in yours—that I would just glance at: You said, "I hope your Persuasion, that the Lord has great Mercy in Reserve for me, springs from himself, and not from your Favour and Good-Will to me." Indeed, Sir, my Persuasion was from the LORD; not by Way of immediate Impulse, but from his *Word,* his Way of *dealing* with others of his *Children,* and with poor sinful *me.*—The LORD has made you a *sorrowful Soul,* for your Sins against him, for your past Neglect of his Service, and has enflam'd you with *Desire* to do more for him than ever! And what says his *Word* concerning those which he thus *works* upon?—I will *satiate* the longing Soul, and *replenish* every sorrowful Soul. He *satisfieth* the longing Soul, and *filleth* the Hungry with good Things. *Blessed* are they which hunger and thirst after Righteousness: For they shall be *filled, &c.* And his Children, in all Ages, have set their Seal to the *Truth* hereof. And among them, I that am least and last of all, will cast in my Mite: And say, from GOD's faithful Word, and my own Experience, That as sure as GOD is unchangeably true, and infinitely gracious, HE will have *Mercy, great* Mercy, upon your dear Soul. HE will fill every Corner of your Soul *brimful,* my Brother, unto *running-over* Praises for evermore!

I *felt* what you said, when your Heart leap'd in your Breast, at a *Possibility* of serving CHRIST. Truly you are my *Brother;* and our *Father* will be *gracious* to you.—You will see a little of such-like Working of Heart, in the short Notes of the few Things which I have sent. The LORD encourage your Heart thereby! Remember that I in myself, as you said of yourself, am *vile and worthless;* and give all the Glory to that infinite *Grace,* which casts such abundant Favours upon the *Chief of Sinners!*—You admire, Sir, that GOD *in very Deed should dwell with Men on Earth!* I join the Wonder and Praise. Ten thousand Glories to *the high and lofty* ONE, *who dwells with humble Souls, to revive their humble Spirits and contrite Hearts!*—Indeed, Sir, you well say, "That the Glory of Princes disappears, when the SUN of Righteousness ariseth." Oh what a little, low, worthless Thing, is all the *Court Grandeur* of the greatest of earthly Monarchs; when compar'd with the Royalties, the Glories, the State of that Court, which *our King,* JESUS, keeps in *Sion,* and in the *Heart* of every Believer! And *you,* Sir, had never had the least Glimpse of the Majesty, the super-excelling Glory of CHRIST's Reign, to delight your Soul, and attract your Desire, if you had not been *one* of happy Subjects thereof. Rejoice therefore, as one of *Sion's* Children, that the LORD shall *reign for ever,* in and over *you,* as *your* GOD, as the GOD of *Sion!*—

I rejoice, Sir, in our Lord's Victories. Oh may HE still triumph glorioiusly, and *ride on conquering, and to conquer;* until his Kingdom is extended, and exalted over All! Blessed for ever be his adored Name, that HE is coming! Come sweet

LORD JESUS into the open Arms of thy longing Bride! *Come, oh come quickly! Amen and Amen.*

It is *Time, high* Time indeed, my dear Brother, for the LAMB's Company to *unite,* now there are so many on every Side that make *War* against HIM, The LORD unite us *all* in Love, fire us with Zeal, fill us with Wisdom, and arm us with Strength to the Battle! That so, under the glorious Captain of our Salvation, we may behave as valiant Soldiers: To his Honour, and to our Joy, both here, and in the Day of CHRIST!—May great Grace be upon you! I remain,

>*Honour'd Sir,*
>>*Your very humble Servant,*
>>>*In our high and glorious LORD,*

L E T T E R XV.

Worthy Sir,

YOURS I most gladly received, and thankfully acknowledge your very great Favour therein. It much rejoyceth me, that our gracious GOD was pleas'd to make the Hint which he enabled me to give you, about being *free with* CHRIST *as your Friend,* acceptable and sweet to your dear Soul. Oh my Brother, *prove* CHRIST's Friendship to you more and more daily, by casting all your Care upon him, and confiding in him for every Thing you want; and you shall *see,* that he will be infinitely gracious!—It refresh'd me, that you said, "Glorious JESUS was *mine.*" Oh, for ever adored be Free Grace, HE *is* mine, inseperably and eternally mine! and I *know* him to be so! But griev'd I am at my very Heart, that I that am *his* by Gift and Purchase, by Possession and Love-Complacency, should be no more *his* by Resignation and Dedication! My new-born Soul is so pain'd and burden'd with my old corrupt Nature, that dwells and works in me, that I frequently long to drop my earthly Tabernacle, to be dissolved, and to be with CHRIST, that I might Sin against my Lord no more.—It glads my Heart, Sir, to hear you say for yourself, "And I, notwithstanding all Objections and Difficulties, venture to hope that CHRIST is *mine,* and vile wretched I am *his.*" And so *do,* my Brother. The more you believe in *Hope,* even *against* Hope, or in the Face of ten Thousand Difficulties and seeming Contrarieties; the more you will please and honour CHRIST, and the stronger will your Faith and Hope grow. *Acts* strengthen *Habits.* And the more *frequent* your Acts of Faith and Hope are, the *stronger* will these Graces be in your Soul. And it is for your Lord's Honour, that you trust your Soul in his Hands daily; and thereupon, believe that HE is *yours,* and *you* are *his.* You will hereby honour his infinite Grace, Truth, and Faithfulness. And if it was only for CHRIST's *Honour,* it is well worth our while to fight our Way thro' Armies of unbelieving Thoughts, to put forth an Act of Faith. We cannot draw back, without *wounding* our Lord's Honour, and *stabbing* him as it were to the Heart, both with Respect to his manifestative *Glory,* and the *Joy* which he takes in his People's Faith. Oh, could we think, how much our Lord is glorify'd, and how much it delights his Heart, when we *trust* in him, and especially when every Thing to the View of Sense, looks as if he would *slay* us; we should be more *valiant* in the good Fight of Faith, that we might please and honour him. And much it would animate our Spirits to the Exercise of Faith in the darkest Seasons, if we consider'd, that the *greater* the Fears, Discouragements, and Difficulties are, which lie in the Way of our Believing, the *more* it would glorify our Lord, and delight his Heart, to see us *press* thro' the Crowd, by a fresh Act of Faith: To see us *cut our Way* thro' the Enemy's Host, Sword in Hand, with this brave Resolve, this Venture of Faith, *I will go in unto the King,—and if I perish, I perish.* And much every Way would this be for our Soul's Advantage.

Much I bless the LORD dear Sir, that by poor, weak *me,* HE hath *helped your Faith.* My Reward herein is *full!* The Reward of my feeble *Attempts* to perform this Service, when my Lord sets his *Seal* to the Work, and doth any *Good* to your precious Soul thereby, is indeed *great!* And yet, as you pray, HE will bless *me,* even *vile me,* in the Performance of this Service, to all Eternity! Oh infinite Grace! Who would not love and serve our dear LORD JESUS! Blessed be our own GOD, that made any Thing in my Notes, exceeding sweet and good to *you!* Then have I not wrote them in vain. I am persuaded I shall bless the Lord for ever, for his giving of *you* to *me,* for this short Space. And I begin the Work now, and have a Foretaste of that Fulness of Joy, of that River of Pleasures, which I shall have in his Presence, at his right Hand for Evermore!

I was much pleas'd, Sir, with what you wrote in your former letter, "That you apprehend Faith is the Evidence of itself, as well as of our Justification and Salvation. And that you did not conceive Sanctification to be the prime Mark of our Interest in CHRIST." The LORD establish your Judgment in *this,* and strengthen your Soul to *act* accordingly! And then, holding fast your *Confidence* in CHRIST, with Respect to your *Justification* thro' him, tho' an ungodly Sinner in yourself, as to the whole of what you are from old *Adam;* you may safely and comfortably *look* at your *Sanctification,* as a lower Evidence of your happy State. But whether this can be *seen* or *not,* never let go of your Confidence and Joy of Faith.

And when you look for Sanctification, seek it rather in *Generals* than *Particulars:* In the general *Bent* of your Soul towards GOD, and the *Desire* of your Mind to be Holiness unto the LORD in the *whole* of your *Conversation,* than in *particular Actions:* Wherein a holy Man may *fail,* and slip aside into *sinful Ones,* and find his best Actions so sadly *mix'd* with Sin, that he may be at a Loss what to call them, whether *holy Ones,* or *not.*—Is it the *Desire* of your Soul, when you have any Persuasion of GOD's Love towards you, to *live to him?* Is *Sin* at such Times *hateful* to you? And do you desire above all Things to have it *destroy'd,* that you might *love* and *serve* the LORD? If so; GOD will call you, a *holy Man,* a *godly Man,* that he hath set apart for himself: Notwithstanding all that *Unholiness,* that

Ungodliness, which intermingles with all your Thoughts, Words and Actions. GOD will call the *Desire* of your Soul, your *Kindness* to him, and the *Labours* of your *Heart* to serve *him,* your *serving* of him with the *Mind;* altho' by Reason of the *Flesh,* the corrupt Nature that dwelleth in you, you are sometimes brought into *Captivity* to the Law of *Sin,* and continually *hindered* from doing the Things that you *would:* That is, from loving and serving the LORD, so universally, intensely, and constantly, as your Heaven-born Soul *desires.*—Thus look at the Holiness of your Heart and Life in the *General,* and count as GOD counts concerning it. For most certainly, you are one of that *Seed* that *serve* CHRIST, that are *counted* to the LORD for a *Generation.*

And if you would see your Sanctification in some *Particulars,* look for it at *such Times* when the LORD works up your Heart into an holy Frame, or moves upon your Soul in a special Manner, from Love to him, to serve him. I can give you an Instance or two.

You told me, Sir, "That what I wrote to you about the present Difficulty you was in, as being the greatest you ever met with, that it was as such the greatest Opportunity, in this Regard, you ever had put into your Hands to glorify GOD in: That the Consideration of this did much *move you.*" And in another letter you signify'd to me, "your earnest Desire to see the Kingdom and Glory of CHRIST *advanc'd,* whatever he did with *you.*"

Now, Sir, from hence let me say, There is not a Soul in the World, that is *mov'd* by the *Glory of* GOD, by a Prospect of *glorifying of* HIM, either to do or suffer any Thing for him; but *loves* the LORD, and is *holy* from him and to him; or hath a Principle of Holiness imparted from him, and acting towards him. There is not a Man upon Earth that desires the *Advancement* of the Redeemer's *Kingdom,* whatever becomes of *him,* tho' he may be frown'd away from his Royal Favour; there is not such a Man, I say, to be found on Earth, but *loves our Lord Jesus Christ in Sincerity,* and is one of his *sanctify'd Ones.* And tho' this Principle of Love in his Soul towards CHRIST, may not be always *visible* to his spiritual Sense; yet it always *abides* in his Heart, and more or less *works,* throughout the whole Course of his Life, in Hatred of Sin, in turning from it to GOD, and in seeking of his Glory, and rejoicing in the Display of it, all Manner of Ways. And so the Man is a *holy Man,* a *sanctify'd Man;* whether he can so far *reflect* upon his own gracious Experience, as to conclude Himself from *thence,* to be so, or not.

And now Sir, I would just give you a Hint of some late Experience of mine: I was thinking on some Part of the Providence of GOD towards me, which look'd as if he had no Delight in me, and did not regard my Prayers: And it was suggested to my Mind thus: "That in *this* I had an Opportunity to *glorify* GOD *more,* in some sort, than if Things had been as I desired." I thought there was but *few* that would love and bless him when He frown'd upon them, disregarded and smote them. And this sweetly drew my Heart to be *one* of those few; and enlarg'd the Powers of my Soul to love and bless the LORD for what he had done, as being most for his *own*

Glory, altho' He had not glorify'd Himself, nor favour'd me, in *that Way* which I desir'd. And with much Delight, I lov'd, ador'd and blest my GOD, and took a sort of holy Pleasure in the *Trials,* that hereby I had *room* to love him in such a *Way,* as I should not otherwise have had, and to give Him such a *kind* of Glory, which is not so frequently offer'd to him.—Upon which, my Father kiss'd me: and told me, that I should be *his, in the Day when He made up his Jewels; and that He would spare me, as a Man spareth his own Son that serveth Him.*

From hence, Sir, let me intreat you to *look about you:* See wherein the LORD has appear'd against you in any Providence, wherein He has seem'd to shut out your Prayers, to take no Notice of you, yea, to fight against you; and *be sure* to love and bless him *therein:* And you will render a Tribute of Praise, that is more *rarely* given him, and see reason to rejoice in your particular *Trials,* in that hereby you may in a particular *Manner* glorify GOD.—When he *smiles* upon us, and indulgeth us with his *Favour,* we ought indeed greatly to *bless Him.* His Loving-kindness towards us, *calls* for it. But in this, there is somewhat of Self-love. And indeed we may and ought to love *ourselves,* so as to rejoice in our *own Happiness,* in a due Subordination to GOD's *Glory,* when he casts upon us the bright Beams of his manifestative Favour: Then he expects, that, *touch'd* with his Kindness to us, we should *sound* his lofty Praise. But if we bless him when he seems to *disregard us,* we shew a more *disinterested Love* to him.—Let us therefore, dear Sir, love and bless our GOD at *all* Times. For well worthy is HE of this Glory from us, in *all* his Dispensations towards us; which are so good and gracious, great and glorious! And when we want a Sense of his Kindness towards *us,* to strike our Strings, and tune our Hearts for Praise; let us be touch'd with the Greatness and Glory of his Works in *themselves,* to raise our Hallelujah's: And we shall be called, *The Friends of* GOD.

You said, Sir, in one of your letters, "That a Man must be *sanctify'd,* or he is not *justify'd.*" I grant it. But it will not follow from hence, that a Man must *know* that he is sanctify'd, before he *believes* that he is justify'd. Because it is one Thing to *have* an holy Nature from GOD, and holy Actings of Soul towards him; and another Thing to be able to *reflect* upon them as such. And as I said before, when we come to God thro' Christ for *Justification,* we must come in the Views of our *Ungodliness,* and not of our *Holiness.* And take up our Faith of Salvation, *first,* and *principally,* from the Promise of GOD *without us.*

And tho' in this letter, Sir, I have pointed you a little to the Work of GOD *within us;* yet *beware* that you don't so strictly *adhere* to your Sanctification, as to *doubt* of your Justification, when you can't see it; or such *Fruits* of your Faith, which will evidence from your *Holiness,* that you are a *justify'd Man.* For if *Faith* is the Evidence of *itself,* as well as of our *Justification* and *Salvation;* we need not stay for the after Evidence of *Sanctification,* before we receive the first Evidence of our Justification.

I am glad that you view the Hand of GOD in afflicting Creatures, so as to restrain your natural Resentment against them. There is nothing like a believing *Converse* with the Heart and Hand of GOD in afflicting Creatures, to make us behave *well* towards HIM and them, in such kind of Afflictions.—Wishing all the blessed Teachings and Consolations of the Holy Ghost; and requesting your Prayers: Permit me to subscribe,

    Honour'd Sir,

        Your most Affectionate Humble Servant

        In our own LORD JESUS, &c.

L E T T E R   XVI.

Worthy and very dear Sir,

YOUR most kind Favour I gladly receiv'd, and thankfully acknowledge that, and all the many Instances of your tender Regard to a worthless Worm. I pray my Lord to *reward you an hundred-fold in this present Time,* and that, according to your Service herein, in additional Glories, you may *inherit everlasting Life in the World to come.*

In your former letter, Sir, the Lord made you an instrument of strengthning my Hands in GOD and his Work, while you hinted to me, "That what I now *publish,* may be of greater *Use* than I know of; and found unto the Comfort of some that may *need it,* who are yet *unborn.*" This delighted me much. *Blessed be you of the LORD,* dear Sir, in that you have thus *comforted, and spoken kindly to* such a poor, little, despicable *Worm,* the *least* of all that desire to serve the LORD and his People in the Earth!

The LORD gives me peculiar Bowels to his *needy Children.* And sometimes I have pray'd Him, "That if any of *His* were sick and weak, pained and wounded, He would send them to *me;* and out of his own infinite Fulness, minister Relief to them by me." And blessed for ever be his glorious Name, the LORD has sent *some* of his dear, tried Children unto *me;* and taking the *Chief of Sinners* into his own all-gracious, almighty Hand, he has comforted their Hearts, and bound up their Sorrows by me!—Praise Him, O ye Angels, on this Account! Let Heaven and Earth praise Him, now and for ever, *Amen!* And when, in the Infinity of his Grace He honours his vile Worm, to do but the least of *this Service,* my *Joy* is *unspeakable!* Some of GOD's Children seem to be *rich* and *full,* and to have *need of nothing.* And so far as they *are so,* I joy and rejoice with *them,* and would further seek their *Good.*—But others there are, that see themselves to be *miserable, poor, wretched, blind and naked, and to want all Things.* And *these,* oh *these,* have my *Heart.*

Towards *these,* my *Bowels yern,* and all the *Compassions* of my Soul *flow.* And therefore my Joy must needs be *full,* when the LORD by me, doth strengthen and comfort any of his *Weaklings.*

And from the inward workings of *my Heart* towards the Weak of the Flock, when I *compassionate* them in the Bowels of Jesus Christ, and *rejoyce* to succour them; I have thought with Pleasure, upon the infinite *Tenderness* of CHRIST's *Heart* towards his Sheep and Lambs, and especially towards the *weak* and *diseased* of his Flock, as they are his OWN, infinitely beloved of, and pitied by him, under all their Miseries and Distresses; and from hence, upon that *Joy* which he hath in Relieving them. Alas, when we have wounded our Souls, by Sinning against the LORD, we are ready to run away from our great Shepherd, as if now we were so sick and diseased, we should find *no Favour* with him. Whereas, such is his infinite Love to us, that *then,* in an especial Manner, his *Heart* is all on a *Flow,* in boundless *Compassion,* and infinite *Readiness* to help us; and with his *whole Soul will he Rejoyce over us to do us Good!*—Oh, what could keep us from CHRIST's Bosom, if we *Believ'd,* that the *greater* our Sins and Miseries are, the *more* he will Compassionate us, and take the *greater* Delight to save us! *Fury* is not in our JESUS, towards *Sin-burden'd Souls,* that flee to *him* for Relief. But on the Contrary, a Fulness, and Infinity, an Eternity of *Mercy!* Which is so *Great,* that if all the Bowels and Compassions that ever fill'd the Hearts of *all the Creatures,* were to meet in *one,* they would be no more than a *Drop,* to *his* immense *Ocean!* We have such a *merciful High Priest over the House of God,* that hath an *All-Fulness* of Bowels in HIMSELF, both *Created* and *Uncreated!* That hath all the *Mercies* of the Creature, and of the Creator, joined in his *Great Person,* as GOD-MAN!—*Having therefore such a great High-Priest, JESUS the SON of GOD, that is passed into the Heavens for us,* that is in Office to save us, and *Faithful to him that appointed him; let us hold fast our Confidence,* and *come with Boldness to the Throne of Grace to find Mercy, and Grace to help, in every of our Times of Need.*

In your last kind letter, Sir, you compare yourself to a "weakly Child, learning to walk, and stumbling, and ready to fall every Step." If you should Sir, be but a *weak Child,* I am glad you are a *living Child,* a *willing Child,* to foot it in the Way of *Faith,* to your Blessed Lord, amidst all your *felt Weakness.* And be not dismayed at your Weakness, for you have a *tender Father,* a *tender Nurse,* that hath *Omnipotence* in *himself,* and will *put Strength into you.* That never has his Eye *off* from you, nor lets you *go* out of his Hand.—Some of GOD's Children are long ere they learn to *go alone,* by *Faith,* without the *Prop* of spiritual *Sense.* And such is his infinite Condescension, that at times, He indulgeth us with Sense, to *help* our Faith. But as our Walking by Faith, is most for his Glory, and our Good: He calls us to Walk by Faith *alone,* and delights in every little, weak Step we take therein, while *his Strength* is made perfect in *our Weakness.*—And when we first begin to leave our *round-about-Way,* our *Props* of spiritual *Sense,* by which we us'd to *creep* to our Father, and venture to *foot it* to him directly by *Faith;* it is no Wonder that we are on a Totter, a Tremble, and just ready to Fall with *Fear* at every Straw in our *Way,* when we thus set out in such an *unaccustomed* Path and Exercise.—But my dear Brother, for your Lord's Honour, *venture* to foot it to Him by *Faith,* altho' you should sometimes *stagger,* and now and then get a *Fall.* You shan't fall to endanger your *Life,* to be mortally wounded thereby. Because *everlasting Arms* are round about you; and when you Fall, it is *into* and not *out if,* these sweet soft Arms, which are still *underneath you.* The Arms of JESUS, my Brother, are ready to *catch you,* whenever you *slip,* and to *set you up again.* They are before, behind, and on either Side of you, to secure you from all Harms, Deaths, and Dangers. Nor shall you ever get a *Slip,* but by *His* Wisdom and Grace shall be over-ruled for your *Good,* to make you more skilful and expert in the *Use of your Feet.*—Wherefore set your dear LORD *JESUS,* always before you, and in his Strength, *make directly to him;* and you will Honour and Delight him much. And the *more* you exercise Faith, the *stronger* and nor *regular* will be your Steps. From staggering, to walking, from walking, to running, with an holy Ease, and heavenly Agility shall your Course be. And thus, under fresh Influences, and renewed Exercises, you shall *go on from Strength to Strength, until you appear before GOD in Zion.*—Glad am I, that you would keep fast hold of your Blessed JESUS." And so *do,* my Brother. CHRIST is such a mighty *prop,* that if you lay but your *Hand of Faith* upon HIM, while your Soul is in *Motion* towards him, you can nevr *fall,* whatever inward Weakness, and Heart-Tremblings you may Experience. I know that Sin and Satan will do all they can, to *beat off* your Hold of CHRIST, the mighty SAVIOUR, the mighty *Staff* which the LORD hath given for your Support, while passing thro' this weary Wilderness, this Land of Pits and Snares, towards the Land of Rest. But endure *Hardness,* bear *Blows,* and the more the Enemies strive to beat off your *Hand-hold* of CHRIST, the faster let your Faith *clasp about him.* Oh let not go your *Life,* your *Strength,* your ALL!—I know, our Lord's *own Hand,* his Hand of great Grace, and omnipotent Strength, must *hold* the little Hand of *your Faith,* or you will soon *let go* your Hold of HIM. And that, your grand *Security* lies, in your LORD's strong and everlasting *Hold of you;* and not in your weak, inconstant *Hold of* HIM. Yet in the LORD's *Strength,* would I encourage your Soul, to be *valiant* in the Exercise of Faith: that so the *Glory* you give to GOD in Believing, may be *Great,* and your *own Joy, Full.*

I rejoice, that you can say, "The Word or two dropt about CHRIST, in my last, were sweet Words." A little of CHRIST, my Brother, is *sweet.* HE is such a *Mass,* such a *Bundle* of SWEETNESS, that exceedingly *Delights* our spiritual Senses, when but the least Part of his infinite Glory and Fulness is brought *near us!* The Bridegroom's *Name, is like Ointment poured forth,* which fills the Heart of the Bride with the most precious *Savour!* And *therefore do the Virgins,* Heaven-born Souls, and none but *they, Love* HIM!

I Joy with *you,* to hear, that our LORD's Name and Fame is spread abroad. *And let the whole Earth be filled with his Glory! Amen, and Amen.*—To the Heart and

Arms of your own LORD JESUS, I commit you. His Grace be with your Spirit! In HIM, I am,

> *Honoured Sir,*
>> *Yours at all Obedience,*

——— ———

L E T T E R   XVII.

Honour'd and very dear Sir,

Permit a Creature that is most unworthy of the Honour and Privilege of your Acquaintance, to give all the Thanks my narrow stupid Heart is capable of, for all your exceeding great and undeserved Goodness towards *us,* the very *least* of CHRIST's—We, Sir, *can't* repay you; but JESUS *will.* I'm glad you serve such a *great* MASTER, so *great* in Grace, that will *reward you like his great* SELF! I pray for you *Hundred-fold in this World, and Life everlasting in that to come.*

Meet you I can't, dear Sir, at *E----h,* personally, to *welcome* your Return to *S----d.* May *this* supply *my Place,* and say to *you, Come in thou blessed of the LORD! Blessed wast thou in thy going out; and blessed shalt thou be in thy coming in!* Oh may your dear Soul, see more of the Glory of CHRIST in *S----d,* than ever! And in particular, at those *Places* where you have so much *desired it!*

And tho' in some respects, dear Sir, you may be come into *Trouble;* yet your dear LORD JESUS will be with you in it, and make it the Matter of your *eternal Joy.* If you was to go into Trouble *alone;* you might count it *all Sorrow.* But since your JESUS is *with you;* count your divers Temptations, *all Joy.* And come up from the thorny *Wilderness,* resting in the Bosom, and leaning on the Arm of your Almighty, and All-gracious *Beloved.* For if HE brings you thro' Fire, and thro' Water, HE will bring you thence, into a wealthy Place.—Then Sir, for your LORD's *Honour,* behave with a true *Greatness of Spirit,* as a *Favourite of Heaven.* Let not *little Things,* the little Things of *this World,* move you: Since the *great* GOD is with you and for you, and so nothing can be *against you.* If you *love* JESUS, *cast all your Care upon* HIM. The *greater* your Burdens are, HE will account HIMSELF the *more* glorify'd, if you will cast them upon his *mighty Shoulders:* Which are well able to bear *you,* and all *your Weights.* CHRIST *loves* you so, that you will *delight* HIM exceedingly, if you will be *free* with HIM, and as *careless* (as free from anxious Care) about your own Concerns, as *Children are,* that have a *tender Father* to supply all their Wants. Only *by Prayer and Supplication with Thanksgiving, make your Requests known unto HIM;* and HE, your own GOD, will *supply all your Wants.* Why should *you care,* and CHRIST *care too?* You by taking *Thought, cannot add one Cubit to your Stature:* CHRIST's *thinking upon you* in all your *Need,* will be productive of all that *Supply* which HE, in infinite wisdom and Grace sees *best* for you. Wherefore *rest by Faith,* in the *Bosom of* JESUS, your ever-living, and everloving *Friend.* There's always *Room* for you. And the most sweet, refreshing *Resting-Place,* you will find it in *Trouble.* JESUS, your *Brother,* was *born for your Adversity:* And is *a Friend that loveth you at all Times,* with an infinite, free, invariable Love, amidst all the Changes, inward and outward, which pass over you. And HE will *stick closer unto you, than a Brother,* than any Brother, either in Nature or Grace. Wherefore in *all the Places* (Cases and Circumstances which attend your Travels thro' the Wilderness) whither CHRIST and *you* shall *come,* let this be the *Kindness* you shew unto HIM, say of HIM, HE *is my Brother.* For it will chear *his Heart,* and be the Strength of *your Spirit.* You well know, dear Sir, the *Heart of a Friend:* That from an inward Love to, and Sympathy with the Person which he calls, which he esteems his *Friend,* however unworthy that Person may be, He will use his *Interest* to serve him; and *rejoice* in every Favour he procures for his *Friend,* as if done to *Himself.* And if such is the Kindness of *Creatures* towards each other; oh, with what a superior Brightness, doth the CREATOR's Kindness shine, when HE resolves to *love,* and *deal* with a *Creature* as *his Friend!* JESUS is *your Friend,* my Brother, and calls *you his.* His *Love* towards you, is like HIMSELF; It is every way answerable to the Greatness of his Person, as GOD-MAN! To the Nearness of his Relations to you, and to the Greatness of his Office to save you! His *Bowels* towards you are *infinite!* And from an Infinity of Love and Bowels, HE will *rejoice* to use all his *Interest* with his and your Father, for *your good.*—Think then, my dear Brother, how *greatly* CHRIST loves you! How *great* his Interest is with the Father! And, how *great* that Deliverance, that Salvation must be, that shall flow to *you,* from so great a *Love!* From so great an *Interest!* In which the *Glory* of both, is for ever to *shine!* And expect *great Things* from your own *great* LORD JESUS, and from GOD your FATHER, who loveth you in HIM!—Only beware of *limiting* the high and lofty ONE, as to the Way, Manner and Time of his working for you; and you shall *see greater Things* than ever you have yet seen.—And if the LORD your *Friend,* will take away a little of the *Earth* which he hath given you, to give you a greater Possession of *Heaven;* will not *that* be *better?* If HE takes away any *Part* of your earthly Riches, Honour, Interest, to give you *more* Grace and Glory, and a more *sensible* and *full Possession of* HIMSELF; will not your *Gain* be *Immense,* by your *little Loss?*—Wherefore, *lose* your *own* Wisdom, in *infinite* Understanding, and delightfully be *swallow'd up* in GOD's *good Pleasure.* For lo, an Infinity of Love in his *Heart,* in every Thing his *Hand* bestows, shall flow out upon you, to your full Salvation, and eternal Glory! And let *this* be the Matter of your present Joy and Thanksgiving.

I have already made this letter longer than I design'd, and have been diverted from telling you what I purpos'd. But suffer me, dear Sir, just to give you a Hint. Yesterday, I had a refreshing View of CHRIST's *Design* to make me *perfectly holy:* From Phil. iii. 12. *I follow after, if that I may apprehend that for which also I am apprehended of Christ Jesus.* CHRIST, my dear Brother, has apprehended, took hold of *you* and I, by special Grace, to make us perfectly *like* HIMSELF, both in holiness and Glory. And on HE will go with his *Design,* maugre all *Opposition.* You and I, shall shortly be made as *holy to* GOD, and as *happy in* HIM, as if *Sin had never entered.* And have a *superior Glory,* with Respect to both, put upon us.—This Day, that Word was precious to me,*And my Delights were with the Sons of Men,* Prov. viii. 31. Oh, my Brother, were CHRIST's Delights with *us,* with *you,* with *me, before the Mountains were brought forth!* Then was his Love *free* and *ancient.* HE did not set his Heart on us, because of our *foreseen Goodness:* For we had *none,* nor ever could have *any,* but what *his free Love* must *give.* Nor did all our *foreview'd Badness,* prevent his loving and chusing *us,* to delight in us as his *own* for ever. Before *Time commenc'd,* or *Earth* had its *Being,* CHRIST's *Delights* were with *us.* HE *loved the Church,* (and us, our individual Persons, among the happy, blessed Number) and took Pleasure so long before-hand in giving HIMSELF to live and die for it: *That HE might sanctify and cleanse it with the washing of Water, by the Word, that* HE *might present it to* HIMSELF *a glorious Church, not having Spot or Wrinkle, or any such Thing; but that it should be holy, and without Blemish,* Eph. v. 25, 26, 27. And did CHRIST delight in the Thoughts of giving *himself,* his *great* SELF for *us,* my Brother, even from *Everlasting!* And shan't *we* delight to give up our *little selves* to HIM, in the *present Time?* Did CHRIST delight in *us;* and shan't *we* delight in HIM? Did HE love us *so,* as to give HIMSELF to make us *holy,* and shan't *his Love constrain us* to give up ourselves to HIM, *in all Manner of holy Conversation and Godliness,* in which *his Glory* and *our Happiness* is so much Concern'd?

I know, dear Sir, that this letter will be unexpected to you. But I deisr'd to bring a little *Refreshment* to your Spirit, if the LORD would send by *me,* after the *Fatigue* of your long Journey. And for my Encouragement, your LORD said, *I will repay thee.*—

 Honour'd Sir,
  Ever Yours, most Humbly,
   In our own LORD JESUS.

L E T T E R   XVIII.

Worthy and very dear Sir,
------IT is well for us, that our JESUS *lives;* that he lives for *us,* that he lives as *our* LIFE! Ah how soon would the little Grace in us be *lost,* was it not in *Union* to the *Life of* JESUS! To JESUS our LIFE! But since there is an Immensity, and Eternity of *Life in* CHRIST, since HE is our LIFE, and our *Union* to him cannot be *broken;* our Communion with him is *secur'd:* Unto a Continuation, and Increase

THE

EDITOR'S PREFACE.

--------■--------

Christian Reader.

Having already published a new edition of "A Poem on the special work of the Spirit on the hearts of the Elect;" written by the late Mrs. ANNE DUTTON; and also "An account of her Experience, in being brought to know her interest in Christ;" at the earnest solicitation of many persons, whom I much esteem, I now present you with some of her letters, which were written to her relations and friends; and, if they are well received, I mean to continue publishing more, being in possession of the greater part of what she wrote; assuring the reader that he will have a faithful transcript of the originals.

The Authoress considered herself called upon to labour in behalf of the young and weak of the flock, more particularly than to old established Christians. Her own words however will best express her ideas on this point; where, in a letter to a minister, she thus writes: "I thank you, Sir, for your kind desire of my weak correspondence: but I humbly think that it is not my work to write much to the eminent servants of my Lord; but rather, as he has called and enabled me, to feed his Lambs; and towards the *young and weak of the flock* he gives me yearning bowels."—Her letters, therefore, are in general very encouraging to such as are quickened by the Holy Spirit to feel their lost estate, and are earnestly seeking after the knowledge of their interest in the Saviour: also to such of the Lord's family as are in trying circumstances, whether of a temporal or spiritual nature, there is much wholesome instruction and good counsel given. And, lastly, to those who are singing in the heights of Zion, she will also be found a pleasant companion.

This first part of her letters is sent forth at a moderate price, hoping thereby they may be the more generally read; and I purpose to continue this plan, should it be approved of and called for by my friends.

At the conclusion of the account of her experience, I mentioned it as my intention to publish her interesting Memoirs; which intention I still retain; and, being in consequence anxious to obtain every particular respecting her, I have been twice at Great Gransden, in Huntingdonshire, where she lived thirty-four years. And I feel a sincere pleasure in availing myself of this opportunity of acknowledging the kind attentions of the Rev. Mr. SKILLITER, the present Pastor of that congregation; by whose assistance, as well as that of other friends, and more especially by the information of Mrs. TIPPET, who was personally acquainted with Mrs. DUTTON, and followed her to her grave; I have been enabled to collect some particulars respecting her that will I trust make the work more interesting, and enable me to present my reader with her Memoirs as complete as possible, so that ANNE DUTTON may no longer remain a stranger to the church of Christ; but her memory be rescued from oblivion, as a Christian of the brightest experience, and a faithful servant of Christ, and of his church—such being worthy of double honour. And I think it a kind providence that I should be the instrument, in any degree, of accomplishing so desirable an object. What the wise man says is applicable to her: "Many daughters have done virtuously, but thou excellest them all. Favour is deceitful, and beauty is vain: but a woman that feareth the Lord, she shall be praised. Give her of the fruit of her hands, and let her own works praise her in the gates," Prov. xxxi. 29—31.

It is unnecessary for me to say any thing in commendation of these letters, as both the style and matter of them sufficiently declares the Authoress to have been an extraordinary woman, eminently taught of the Spirit, and possessing a depth of knowledge of the mysteries of the kingdom of God (Luke viii. 13) far beyond what his children in general are favoured with.

Her letters have evidently been blessed to many already; wherefore I anticipate with pleasure that the Lord will still condescend to make them more extensively useful: that his grace, his Spirit, his power, and his presence, will be so enjoyed in the perusal of them, that many of his family will be instructed, established, and comforted, with that love that is from everlasting to everlasting, and therefore can never fail the happy subjects of it (Jer. xxxi. 3. Rom. viii. 35—39). It was this that made Paul's letters weighty and powerful (2 Cor. x. 10)—made others rejoice with joy unspeakable and full of glory (1 Peter i. 8)—and that caused the disciples' hearts to burn within them while on their journey to Emmaus (Luke xxiv. 32.)—That the same glorious enjoyment, and blessed effects, may be experienced in the perusal of the present, and of any future edition of Mrs. DUTTON'S LETTERS, is, and shall be, the prayer of,

Christian Reader,

Thy willing servant for the truth's sake,

CHRISTOPHER GOULDING.

London,
Northampton Square,
    Jan. 1, 1823.

LETTERS, &c.

--------■-------

Great Gransden, near Caxton, Huntingdonshire, January 16, 1741-42.

My dear and honoured Friend,

ACCEPT my humble thanks for your kind remembrance of us, and all the favours shewn us. May the God of love abundantly reward you, and pour down blessings upon you and yours, even the blessings of the everlasting hills! I ask your pardon for my long silence. I have had so much writing upon hand for this twelvemonth past, that I have had no leisure for any thing but what was absolutely necessary.

As to the dealings of God with my soul, he has been exceeding good to me, ever since the first manifestation of his love, and especially this last year. Oh, what ineffable delights have I found in the Lord and his work! little do the slaves of sin and Satan know what wonderful privileges and unspeakable pleasures the servants of Christ enjoy.

As for Christ, my Jesus, my friend, my bridegroom, my life, my all; this is the testimony I bear of him, from more than thirty years' acquaintance with him—that he is altogether lovely, the Chiefest among ten thousand. Whom have I in heaven but him? and upon earth there is none that I desire in comparison with him. O, my friend, dearest, everlasting and ever-loving Jesus! What a fountain of life, what a well-spring of bliss is he to me! Time, and all the creatures and things of it, are subject to change, full of changes; but my Jesus is yesterday, to-day, and for ever the same! his name is Jehovah, the Lord that changeth not. I behold his glory, as the only begotten of the Father, full of grace and truth! as full as my soul can desire him to be! Ah, what did I say? my Lord's fullness not only answers all my desires, but infinitely exceeds them! What are the desires of a creature, in their utmost perfection? what is creature capacity if stretched to its utmost height? They are limited and finite. But the fullness of Christ is a boundless ocean that has neither shore nor bottom! and of his fullness I have hitherto received, and shall receive through time and to eternity, and grace for grace; even all grace, according to the gift of it to me in Christ, unto all glory through him. And yet my Lord's fullness will for ever abide an inexhaustible, undiminished ocean; a sea of life for me to swim in, that to the days of eternity I can never swim over. In a word, in the Son of God I have an immensity, an eternity of life, to fill me as a vessel of mercy with a life of grace, and a life of glory! And, oh, how abundantly satisfied is my soul herewith! My Jesus is to me all desires, all delights! and, as for his service, this is the witness I bear concerning it, that it is perfect freedom, pleasure, profit; the most glorious, delightful, and advantageous work that the most noble creatures can be employed in. What reason then have we to lament, that we should ever go out of Christ for delights, and step aside from his service, his work, whose ways are pleasantness and all his paths peace. Oh how happy would our life be, if in the whole of it for us to live was Christ; and what gain is death to them that live such a life!

Wishing full joy in daily fellowship with God, until grace and joy imperfect are swallowed up in perfect joy and glory,

I am, my dear Sister,

Your most obliged, humble servant,

in our dearest Lord Jesus,

ANNE DUTTON.

LETTER II. To Mr. F.

Dear Sir,

I FIND you are at times attended with fears about your interest in Jesus. Remember that, so long as we are in this body, we are called to be combatants, to fight the good fight of faith, until we lay hold on eternal life. Until faith gets the victory over fear, to our full joy; until we can lay fast hold on God's promise of life in Christ, given to every poor sinner that looks, that comes to, that rests on him for salvation; and until we receive the end of our faith, the salvation of our souls, and enter into the full enjoyment of life eternal, we are called to fight this good fight of faith against that God-dishonouring, that soul-distressing, that easily-besetting sin of unbelief. For, in one shape or other, this cruel enemy, while we are in the body, will attack our faith, hinder us in our great work of believing, and so in running the race which is set before us. It will rob our Lord of that glory which we ought to give him, and us of that joy which we should otherwise have in him. The life we are called to live while in the flesh is "a life of faith on the Son of God;" of looking to him, as God's salvation to the ends of the earth; of coming to him, the great Saviour, whose arms are wide open, to receive the very chief of sinners; and of resting upon him, as that precious foundation which God hath laid in Sion; upon whom, whosoever thus believeth, shall never be confounded. And not only are we called continually thus to believe on the Son of God, but also to believe the record which God hath given of his Son; that "believing, we shall have life through his name:" that God hath given to us eternal life, by the promise of the Gospel, and that this life is in his Son. God gives his Son, as his salvation, to every poor sinner that looks for life to him the only Saviour. And, in and with his Son, he gives life to that soul. Yea, God gives his Son to be that soul's life. So that "he that hath the Son of God hath life." Life of justification, of sanctification, of consolation, and of glorification, in and with Christ: "who of God is made unto us wisdom, and righteousness, and sanctification, and redemption."

And, has God the Father given his Son for and to us? Has God the Son thus given himself for and to us? And has God the Holy Ghost revealed and applied the great Saviour, and his great salvation, unto us perishing sinners? O what thanks shall we render to our Three-one God for his unspeakable gift, of life in Christ! Let us believe this salvation-grace, and give glory to God our Saviour, in heart, lip, and life; by all holy obedience, continually and increasingly; until we shall see, and love, and serve the Lord perfectly, to his everlasting praise, through the endless ages of a blessed eternity.

God the Father so loved the world, that he gave his only begotten Son, to take our nature into personal union with himself, to obey and die for us; that, believing in him, we should not perish, but have everlasting life! God the Son so loved simmers, that he thus gave himself for us, to redeem us from all misery, and unto all glory! And God the Holy Ghost so loved us, as to set the joy of the Father's glory in our salvation before the Lord the Saviour, for which he endured the cross, and despised the shame; and so loved us, as to reveal and apply the salvation contrived and appointed by the Father, and engaged for and procured by the Son, in all its greatness and glory unto us, by his own illuminating grace and saving power! And God, Father, Son, and Spirit, as the one great Jehovah, hath loved, doth love, and will love us with an everlasting love, from everlasting death unto everlasting life!

And, if we are so beloved of God, so freely, greatly, immutably, and eternally; even us, when thousands were passed by; O let us love, let us give up ourselves in love to Him, who hath first, who hath thus, loved us! The heart of our Immanuel, God with us, was a flame of love to his Father's glory. And thence, what labours, what sorrows, did he undergo, that he might do and suffer his Father's will! When called of God, he engaged for us as our Surety in the everlasting covenant, with a "Lo, I come: I delight to do thy will, O my God." And, when he had actually assumed our nature, had lived a life of obedience, through a course of sufferings, and was just entering upon his last agonies, being called to give his life a ransom for many, to give a practical proof of his vehement love to his Father's glory in our salvation, he said, "But, that the world may know that I love the Father; and as the Father gave me commandment, even so I do. Arise, let us go hence," John xiv. 31. Well may we know that Christ loved the Father, when with such an amazing cheerfulness he went forth into the last part of his obedience unto death, to meet the bands of wicked men, which were just coming out against him; the powers of hell, which were soon to be let loose upon him; and the terrors of God's revenging wrath, which were to smite him, as made sin and a curse for us, even unto death. And, if the son of God, "learned obedience by the things which he suffered," in love to his Father; and if we are "predestinated to be conformed unto the image of his Son;" O let us love the Father too; and, to give a practical proof of it unto all, in zeal for his honour, let us comply with this call, whether it be to obey or suffer; and, with the deepest submission and the most cheerful acquiescence, let us arise, and go forth into every part of required obedience. For our dear Lord hath left us an example, that we should tread in his steps. And, if we "suffer with him, we shall reign with him, and be glorified together."

In Him, dear Sir, I am, yours for ever,

LETTER III.   To --------

My dear Sister in Christ,

I REJOICE that the ministry of dear Mr. D. has been made of such great use to your soul, that you can say concerning it—

'While I hear the word preached, I hope I feel it reach my case: I hope it has been blest, in making the way of salvation by Christ more glorious and acceptable to me a sinner, than ever I saw it before: and I hope that by his preaching I have been more established in the great truths of the Gospel, so that I could venture my soul in the belief of it.'

It is your great mercy, my dear friend, that you feel the word of the gospel reach your case. If you was not quickened to the new life, you would be insensible of your own misery as a sinner, and of the excellency of Christ as the great Saviour. Oh, to have the word reach the heart, to find out our very case, and to feel its power and suitableness unto any further direction and gracious relief, is a choice mercy.— To have the way of salvation by Christ made more glorious in your view, and acceptable to your soul than ever, this is a blessed fruit of the ministry you sit under. When the sinner and the Saviour are brought together by the preaching of the gospel, the preached gospel hath its designed end in the salvation of the soul. And, if you as a poor sinner, and Christ as the rich Saviour, had not been brought together by the ministry of the gospel, the way of salvation by Christ would never be glorious in your eye, nor acceptable to your heart. "Flesh and blood hath not revealed Christ unto you, (as God's way of salvation for lost sinners,) but his Father which is in Heaven:" and blessed are you in that revelation. The glory you see in salvation by Christ is from God's shining into your heart with a supernatural light, unto new-creation life. Christ, as the only Saviour, as the way to the Father, is a path that no vulture's eye, no natural man with his brightest speculations, hath seen. The glory you see in Christ, as God's salvation to the ends of the earth, as it is an effect of supernatural revelation, or the saving illumination of your mind; so likewise is it an effect of discerning faith in the understanding; which hath its influence on your will, and sweetly draws your heart to cleave in love to the Saviour beheld. Hence it is that the way of salvation by Christ is not only glorious in your view, but acceptable to your soul. While you behold Christ as the only Saviour, you see the fullness, freeness, and the greatness of his salvation; which, with the exceeding suitableness thereof to your case as a miserable sinner, makes the Saviour, and his salvation, most acceptable, or above all things desirable to your heart. So that you can say of Christ, in respect of choice, "Whom have I in heaven but thee? And there is none upon earth that I desire besides thee." Thus acceptable in the Saviour to your soul, when you get a glimpse of his glory. And in those happy moments, when you have a little hope of interest, O how your heart accepts of Christ, how gladly doth it open to receive him! Nothing gives you so high a joy as a glimpse that your beloved is yours, and that you are his; nor any thing so deep a grief, as a fear that you have no special relation to, nor interest in, this altogether-lovely Lord. And, wherever Christ is thus the chiefest among ten thousand to any soul, that soul is undoubtedly a believer in Jesus, is espoused to him, hath a conjugal relation, with conjugal affection, and shall never, never, be separated from him and his love.— Again, as you find this blessed fruit of the ministry you sit under, 'that you are thereby more established in the doctrines of the gospel, as such that you can venture your soul in the belief of;' it is hence evident that, as an effect of the arm of the Lord being revealed in you, the report of the gospel is savingly believed by you. Historical faith is seated only in the head; it never reacheth the heart. None venture their souls on the great doctrines of the gospel which they believe, and so on Christ revealed thereby, but those who have true, precious faith, the faith of God's elect; to which the salvation of the soul is inseparably connected.—You add, 'I desire to praise God, I hope he hath shewn me my own wretched state by nature, liable to the eternal wrath of God; that I am not capable of keeping one of his commands, but daily break them in thought and word; and I hope I have been helped to see an utter insufficiency in my own righteousness to justify me before God; and would count it my greatest mercy to be interested in Christ's perfect righteousness.'

And has the Lord shewn you your sin and misery by nature, your danger of the wrath to come, and the utter insufficiency of your own righteousness, that you can do nothing to help or save yourself? Be assured that this is a saving conviction of sin and misery; and you will see more of heart-sin daily, to your grief, (Ezek. viii. 6. &c.) But the blood of Christ cleanseth from all sin.— And has the Lord shewn you the all-sufficiency of Christ's righteousness, and would you count it your greatest mercy to be interested therein? O, be persuaded that, unto and upon you that believe, this righteousness is, unto justification of life. For it is unto and upon all them which believe, without difference, whether their faith of interest therein be strong or weak. It is the faith of submission to Christ's righteousness, as the righteousness of God, of his appointing for our justification before him, that is first required of us naked sinners. And wherever this faith is given, interest in this righteousness is declared and confirmed in the gospel, by the word of a God that cannot lie. It is "unto and upon all them that thus believe," without difference, Romans iii. 22. And as God has said it, has given this assurance of interest to a believer, upon his faith of submission to Christ's righteousness, he shall be brought to know his interest, his eternal interest, in this everlasting righteousness.—What, stript of all your own righteousness, and desirous above all things to be found in

Christ's perfect righteousness, and yet doubt your interest therein! Oh, fear not your interest this righteousness of God, since submission to it is given you. Who do you think this righteousness of Christ is for, if it is not for them, for all, and every of them, who desire to be found in it? Your desire to be clothed with this glorious robe is your submission to it, your shrouding your naked soul under the covert of it: and upon you it is and shall be of the freest grace, unto your eternal glory. Remember that the righteousness of Christ is a gift, a free gift, held forth by the gospel, to be received by every poor soul that is made willing to accept it. O that you may be able to stretch out the hand of faith, to receive this freely-given righteousness, and hold it fast with steadfastness, notwithstanding all your own unworthiness!

As to your fear, 'that you are not in the right path:' since you desire and endeavour to follow the Lamb, even whithersoever he goeth, you know that in this you go in a right way, as the Israelites did when they followed the pillar of cloud and fire. 'But so prevalent is your unbelief, that you fear you are not a true follower of Christ, or one that truly follows him.' But, since you are willing to receive a whole Christ in all his offices, as Prophet, Priest, and King, to be taught of him, atoned for by him, and governed by his laws; fear not, you are in Christ the way, on the King's high-way, travelling right on, under the conduct of your leader, the Captain of your salvation, to the "city which hath foundations, whose builder and maker is God." What though the howlings of the beasts of prey, and the hissings of the serpents of the wilderness, greatly terrify you, they shall not destroy you; for the Lord is and will be "a wall of fire round about you, and the glory in the midst of you."

> "A thousand savage beasts of prey
>   Around the forest roam:
> But Judah's Lion guards the way,
>   And guides the strangers home."

I and glad that you aim at stretching out the hand of faith, to lay hold on Christ, as the man with the withered hand attempted his duty, at Christ's command, to stretch forth his hand. But you say, 'I think he sensibly felt when he was healed; but when I am at stretching out my hand I do not sensibly feel that I am healed; but unbelief prevails, and still I fear I do not come aright.'—I reply, his was a bodily cure, and performed at once, and his sensation of it at once complete; but the soul's cure of the deadly disease of sin is not performed at once, and so the sense of it is not at once complete. As to the guilt of sin, the soul's cure is at once, upon its first act of faith in Christ, so far as respects a relative change of state; but the sensation of a pardoned state admits of various degrees and times. When God in his word does not charge sin upon the person, through remaining unbelief the conscience may not be discharged, to the soul's joy; and when it is, it may be again charged, till peace is spoken through faith in Christ afresh. And as to salvation from the power of sin, that is a progressive work, and therefore the sensation of it cannot be at once complete.— But, my dear friend, whenever you are afraid that you do not come to Christ aright, come afresh; for every act of faith on Christ is healing, and gives some sense of cure unto rest and refreshment; although perhaps that rest by faith is the next moment turned into trouble by unbelief.— Grace be with you.

I am yours in Christ,

LETTER IV.   To Mrs. H ----

My very dear Sister in Christ,

IT makes me very glad to hear of our Lord's infinite kindness to you. Those bright displays of his special favour, with which he is pleased to bless you, and those great desires to glorify him, which his own hand hath wrought in your heart, are tokens plain to me that he designs eminently to love you; either in using you as an instrument of his glory here on earth, or in receiving you soon up to heaven, to sound forth the praise of the glory of his grace for ever. And whether to abide in the flesh a while longer, to serve the Lord and his people, as he enables you in the church below; or to depart, and be with Christ, to serve and praise him in the church above; being in a strait betwixt two, I suppose you know not which to chuse. Then, my dear Sister, let the Prince of grace chuse for you. He will bless you with that which is most for his and your joy and glory.—You say,

'I think my Lord loves me as if he had no other to love.'— Thanks to the God of love that he so highly favours you! A privilege unspeakable it is to any of his people to be thus loved at any time. But O what a rising display of infinite grace is it to those, who are thus loved at this time, wherein so few of Christ's people live under the shine of his manifestative favour! Happy, thrice happy are you, to be thus the favourite of Heaven! to be thus called in to the King, and feasted with him in his banqueting house!

But, my dear Sister, when our great Lord, thus greatly, thus distinguishingly, loves any of his children, he is not thereby straitened in his ability to love the rest; for, though the objects of Christ's delight are innumerable, yet, because his love is infinite, there is enough in it to satisfy and solace, to ravish and surprise them all. Enough, did I say? Aye, and infinitely more than enough. It is no more for Christ to fill all the innumerable multitude of his favourites brimful, running-over-full, with his manifestative favour, than it is for the sea to fill a cockle-shell. Nor is it so much, neither; for the difference, though great, between the filling capacity of the sea, and the receiving capacity of the shell, is but as between created and created, one finite and another; but the love of Christ, the filling ocean, is in itself properly infinite; and the objects of his love, though an innumerable multitude, with the utmost of their receiving capacity, are but finite, and as so many small recipients, cast from an abundant fill into a fullness, a vast sea of grace, that is unfathomable, inexhaustible, and eternal! So that our great Lord, who is Lord of his own grace, and dispenseth the same according to his infinite wisdom in a sovereign way, as pleaseth him, is not in the least the poorer, when he communicates of his love-riches the most profusely to any one of his favourites; but hath then as much for the rest, for one and all of them, as if he had yet given out to none of them: because the riches of Christ are unsearchable, and unwasteable; a mine of infinite treasure, that cannot be bottomed, nor sunk one hair's breadth! His person, and his love, are yesterday, to-day, and for-ever the same! He is the Lord that changeth not, in his nature, nor in his love riches.— Thus, in the love of Christ's heart there is enough, and more than enough, to fill all the vessels of mercy with present and eternal glory; and one hath not, shall not have, the less for what another abundantly receives.

And, as all the objects of Christ's love are jointly interested in this infinite ocean, so every one for himself is entirely interested in a whole Christ, and in the vast infinity of his heart-love, as much as if he had no other object of his delight, or had no one else to love. For, though there is a vast variety in the dispensations of our Lord's manifestative favour towards the objects of his heart-love; yet every one of his favourites, in every kind and degree of displayed favour, hath the vast infinity of the love of his heart, as the source and spring of that flow, which much heightens the great blessings of his communion love, and should answerably advance our praises: while each of us enjoys as much of infinite love as infinite wisdom sees best, and in every kind and degree of our enjoyment an infinity of divine favour!

Hence then, my dear Sister, you see how it is that our great Lord can and doth love you thus freely and fully, as if he had no one else to love; in that in your abundant measure of manifestative favour you have the whole infinity of the love of his heart.

Hence also we may see, that those who have less enjoyment have no cause to complain, but rather to rejoice and give thanks, in that though they have not so large a share of manifestative favour as others, yet in what they enjoy they have the same infinity of love; and in that all our various enjoyments, whether greater or lesser, are dispensed favours, as infinite wisdom sees best for us, and as is most conductive to the glory of God, and the great designs of his infinite kindness towards us, in our glory, in and with him, in the present and future world.

Hence, likewise, we may learn what abundant room there is for the objects of Christ's delight to open their mouths wide, for the choicest manifestations and the richest fruits of his favour; in that there is such a vast infinity of love in his heart towards them.—Again,

Hence let us think, how full and glorious the enjoyment of Christ's love, to all the happy objects thereof, will be in heaven; in that this vast infinity of love, which is in his heart towards one and all of us, when all impediments in us are removed out of its way, will be set upon a full and endless flow, to our eternal joy, and his eternal praise.— Again,

Hence we may see our duty to love one another, to love all the saints, whom Christ so greatly loves; in that they are equally interested in the vast infinity of his love, and therefore ought to share in ours.— And,

Hence let us learn what high obligations we are under to give up ourselves to be entirely the Lord's, and to be devoted to his fear, to the filial reverence of him and his goodness, in a walk with, and before him, to his honour; in that, if our Lord in his royal bounty gives us his heart, it is meet that we in humble duty should give him ours; that we should cast all the love of our hearts into the vast infinity of his heart-love, as a finite drop into that infinite ocean!— Great grace be with you! Pray for me.

I am yours in the Lord for ever,

LETTER V.   To Mr. S ------

Honoured and dear Sir,

THE Lord made what you wrote of use to me. To say to every thing that would oppose us in the Lord's work, "Get thee behind me, for thou savourest not the things which be of God," we need great spiritual wisdom to discern, and strength to stand against, the subtle insinuations of Satan, when he gets into the arguments of brethren and friends, as well as when he joins with unbelief in suggestions to the heart. The voice of sin and Satan in both, with respect to the Lord's work, is, Spare thyself.—But happy, thrice happy, are they who, in the wisdom and strength of the Captain of their salvation, resist the enemy, endure hardness as good soldiers of Jesus Christ, bear blows, stand their ground in the hottest battle, and are brought from the field victorious! Distinguished crowns, and glittering robes of immortal glory, await such followers of the Lord the Lamb. To them who thus overcome will he grant, "to sit with him in his throne, even as he also overcame, and is set down with his Father in his yhrone." And this, O this, is our mercy, that, in all the work we are to do for God in the world, we shall receive strength for it, from the sufficient grace of Christ. When temptations to neglect it, and discouragements to attempt it, from within and without, beset us, the Lord our wisdom will give us counsel, and the Lord our strength will hold our right-hand, and so sweetly allure us to and carry us through it, that we shall not fail, nor be discouraged, until it is finished. One sweet inviting word, dropt into our hearts by our gracious Lord, assuring us that he will be glorified by this or that service he calls us to, will draw us more strongly to engage in it than the force of a thousand discouragements can dissuade us from it. And one accepting smile from the Prince of grace is an abundant recompense for a thousand difficulties run through in his service. If our Lord is pleased with us, it matters not much who is displeased. One glance of his infinite favour, one hint of his gracious approbation of our weak service, in a "well done, good and faithful servant, thou hast been faithful over a few things," will put such life and spirit into us for God, that will make us cheerfully face the storm of opposition, and run and not be weary, and walk and not faint in his work.

And not because our Lord loves us not, but because he loves us, doth he permit difficulties to attend us in his service: 1. To keep us from being lifted up in pride, to our destruction. 2. To humble us deeply, to make us meek and lowly in heart, and thereby to fit us for his work, and his delight. 3. To make bare his glorious arm, in supporting us under burdens, and in carrying us cheerfully through his service, though we shall be at times called to work, as it were, with weights on our back. 4. To prove the truth, and increase the strength, of our graces, to his honour and our joy. And, 5. To exalt his infinite grace, in bestowing on us a more weighty crown of glory, when he will find the trial of our faith, by his owning and commending it before men and angels, unto praise and honour and glory at his appearing.

And, if these are the gracious ends of our Lord's wise love, in permitting difficulties to attend us in his work, methinks, if we counted right, we should "reckon that the sufferings of this present time are not worthy to be compared with the glory which shall be revealed in us:" and be rather excited to diligence in our Lord's service, than hindered from it by any difficulty or discouragement which may stand in our way. And especially if we consider that, if we proceed in our Lord's strength to do our duty with but little encouragement, and through much discouragement, we shall show the more love to him, and single-heartedness for him, which he will account his glory. Our dear Lord looks not only at the matter, or bulk, of what we do for him, but also at the manner of our doing it. And, though we can do but little for him, yet, if we love him much in that little, and do what he calls for because he commands it, though others gainsay it, as we thereby give him honour as our great Lord and master, this is exceedingly pleasing to, and acceptable with him.

But ah, what are we! What are the greatest of his servants among mortal sinful men, the greatest of their services, and the highest strains of their love to his person and work, and zeal for his glory in their little attempts of duty, that the Prince of grace should cast a favourable eye, a kind thought, upon such little inconsiderable persons and doings, or rather nothings, and but mintings and aimings, when this great Lord of glory is loved, adored, and served, perfectly by the general assembly and church of the first-born, who bow before his throne with ceaseless praises and loudest Hallelujahs; when the innumerable company of holy, glorious angels, the whole host of seraphims, those winged flames for his glory, are swift as lightnings in his work, and excel in strength, to sound his lofty praise; and when all the joint worship in heaven, in their most profound reverence of his person and works, and their fervent zeal for his praise and honour, can never, never, reach the transcendent heights of his infinite glory, who is exalted far above all blessing and praise! If this great Lord, in his great grace, humbleth himself to behold the things which are done in heaven, the perfect love and service of perfect saints and angels, O what an amazing stoop of infinite condescension must it needs be in Him, to extend his kind regards to the best of his servants. and the best of their services, which at their best are attended with much imperfection on this earth! And yet the infinite grace of our Lord and master, our infinite lover, stops not here; but extends its benign influence, its cheering rays, to the very least and last of all his servants in this low land, and to the very least and last of all their services! Not the least babe in Christ escapes the gracious notice of our great Lord; nor the smallest attempt of duty, in love to his glory, small be unregarded, nor unrewarded of the Prince of grace.—Who then would not love such an infinite lover? And serve such an all-gracious, and all-endearing Lord and master? Allured by him, let us follow on to glorify him, until that which is perfect shall come.—Pray for me. Great grace be with you! Go on in the Lord's strength, to feed and guide the flock of God which is committed to your care, and when the chief Shepherd shall appear, you shall receive a crown of glory which fadeth not away. Farewell in the Lord.

I am very affectionately, dear Sir,

your most humble servant,

Letter VI. To --------

Dear Madam, beloved and honoured in the Lord,

I REJOICE to see that you love the Lord and hate evil; and that your faith is directed to its solid basis, viz. the unchangeableness of God in Christ, amidst all the shaking changes which pass upon your mind.

You mourn, Madam, that you cannot see into the covenant of grace as you desire. Praise to the Lord! though your sight of that covenant of full, free, and eternal blessings, is imperfect, your interest therein is perfect. Your God hath made with you "an everlasting covenant, which is ordered in all things, and sure;" and in this is "all your salvation, and all your desire, although he make it not to grow;" or the blessings thereof to flow down upon you at present, unto that full measure of growth in grace which your new-born soul aspires after.— It is your unspeakable blessing, that your heart cleaves unto that covenant; an evidence this that you are under it, not under the law, as a covenant of works, doing for life, but under grace. And grace, new covenant grace, hath a rich supply for your every want, and hath well provided for an exuberant fill of all your desires. O, dear Madam, was it not for God's rich, free, reigning grace, through the blood and righteousness of Christ, we sinners were undone! Our sins have been so great and abundant, and still, even still, iniquity aboundeth so much in our hearts and lives, to God's dishonour and our soul's grief, that, were we to be dealt with according to the law, the hottest hell must be our portion. But, O adorable grace, sinner-suiting, and soul-saving grace, "where sin hath abounded, grace doth much more abound! that, as sin hath reigned unto death, even so grace might reign through righteousness unto eternal life, by Jesus Christ our Lord!" Grace reigns over sin, in the abundant pardon of it, in given strength against it, for its present suppression; and will reign to its utter destruction, and our eternal salvation, to the endless praise of its immense glory. O, my dear Sister, the Lord our Father knew beforehand what rebellious, ungrateful children we should prove, and yet he took us into his family; and to make sure the great design of his heart-love, in conveying the vast inheritance of our eternal glory, he put us under, and resolved to deal with us according to, his free, sovereign, and immutable grace! And this makes our salvation and glory sure indeed, inviolably and immutably sure! For grace is bottomless, boundless, endless; an inexhaustible and all-overflowing ocean! and hosts of sins sink as lead in these mighty waters! Grace is a sin-drowning and a soul-exalting ocean; and in this triumphant grace let us triumph, as vessels of mercy, who soon by grace shall be filled with immortal glory!

You lament, dear Madam, that you have made so small a proficiency in grace, since you made a profession of the Lord's name. And who, O who is there, that has tasted the Lord is gracious, but may, and must, join with you herein! Alas, we are poor proficients in the school of Christ! And, I doubt not, those who have learned most think they want to begin again. But a privilege unspeakable it is, that we have a Master who is infinitely tender, that abounds in compassion, that can bear with our dullness, that loves us as his own, that can teach us to profit, and will shortly make us scholars of the highest form, and masters of the heavenly arts of perfect love and ceaseless praise, to his immortal honour and our eternal joy!

You add, Madam, 'My soul hath many dry and sapless seasons, many drowsy, fainting qualms, through the deceit of my own heart.' But remember, my dear Sister, that when you, as a branch of Christ the true vine, in your winter seasons, are dry and sapless, the Lord, your glorious root, your eternal life, is then for you as full of sap as ever: an immeasureable fullness of the Holy Spirit, and of all grace, dwells in him for you; and in the next spring of divine favour communications will be full and free. And mean time suspensions of influence are to learn you dependence, and the constant need you have to abide in Christ by faith, in order to your bearing much fruit.—As to your drowsy fits, the spouse of Jesus mournfully said, "I sleep!" but then her "heart waked;" the Lord, the strength of her heart, was vigorous when she was inactive: he lived as the fullness of her life, lived to God for her, and lived by his Spirit in her, to give a painful sensation of her own deadness, as preparatory to her after-joyful experience, of renewed quickenings, under his efficacious influence. Though you have fainting qualms, Madam, in drowsy fits, which proceed from unbelieving fears, the Lord, your physician, will minister spiritual cordials, to hold your soul in life, even in the midst of death. His matchless love, care, and skill, are all engaged to support and perfect your new life, which his precious blood procured, and his Holy Spirit hath wrought in your heart; and because Jesus lives you shall live also.

I was much pleased, Madam, with what you said, recollecting yourself, as it were, from the suggestions of your spiritual enemies in trying seasons: 'When I set reason and sense to work, I find it to be dangerous to dispute with that only which faith should take hold of, i. e. the promise of God. But O this dreadful hard heart of unbelief, when I cherish it, as I too often do, I find it makes as much mischief in the soul, as a wolf doth among a flock of sheep.' This, Madam, is a precious piece of experience. For surely in vain is the snare laid in the sight of any bird. If God has given his great unchanging word, and confirmed it by his inviolable oath, "that by two immutable things, wherein it was impossible for God to lie, the heirs of promise might have a strong consolation, who have fled for refuge to lay hold on the hope that is set before them;" shall they not receive it by faith, in the face of a thousand oppositions from unbelief? Yes, my dear Sister, let us come to Christ daily as poor sinners, and cast ourselves at the feet, and into the open arms, of this almighty Saviour; and let us take God at his word, that, believing in his sent Son, we shall not perish, but have everlasting life. Wishing great grace, until you are exalted to the heavenly glory,

I am with affectionate esteem, dear
Madam, your most obliged humble Servant,

————————

LETTER VII.   To --------

Dear Sir,

I SYMPATHIZE with you in your inward and outward trials; be of good cheer, you are the Lord's care; and he will see and provide a full supply for all your wants, in manner, measure, and time, as in his infinite wisdom and goodness he sees best. "Cast your care upon the Lord, for he careth for you;" and take no anxious thought for the morrow; for your Father, that knows what ye have need of before you ask him, will day by day give you your daily bread. Never fear perishing for want, since all the fullness of Christ is yours, both as to nature, grace and glory; and the Lord will give that which is good. Be diligent in appointed means, believe the grace of the promise, and doubt not the bounty of Providence. Godliness hath "the promise of the life that now is, and of that which is to come." He that feeds the sparrows, and the young ravens that cry, will never let his own children want any good thing. He may try them for a while, but will never forsake them. He brings us into trials, to exercise our graces; to learn us to trust him in the dark, to follow hard after him when he seems to go from us, and to wait patiently for him when he seems to take no notice of us; and when he hath tried us he will bring us forth as gold refined, brightened, and enriched with grace, as a further preparation for eternal glory, unto his endless praise, and our immortal joy. "He that spared not his own Son, but delivered him up for us all; how shall he not with him also freely give us all things?" Riches and honours, kingdoms and empires, the Lord gives to the men of the world, whose portion is in this life, time-things being their all: thus he gives them portions, and sends them away from himself for ever. But the inheritance he reserves for Isaac, for us that believe in Jesus, who are the children of promise. Unto us, the Lord-Jehovah gives Himself, as our present and everlasting portion; and in Him, by faith, let us possess all things, even when, to sense, we seem to have nothing. "For all things are ours; whether Paul, or Apollos, or Cephas, or the world, or life, or death, or things present, or things to come, all are ours; and we are Christ's, and Christ is God's." Strange! what the world ours, and many of us have so little of it? Yes: because poverty and riches, crosses and comforts, successively dispensed, or wisely intermixed, are bestowed on us, as gifts of infinite love, of that same everlasting kindness, which gave us Christ. And given us they are, and overruled they shall be, by infinite wisdom and grace, for our further conformity to his image; to the image of his holiness here, and to the image of his glory hereafter. If fullness and plenty, ease and rest, are best for us, they shall not be withheld; and, if penury and straits, pain and trouble, are best for us, these shall be bestowed; for "no good thing will the Lord withhold from them that walk uprightly." And well it is for us that our God and Father knows what we have need of, and will give us that which is best, in the best way and time. Our bitterest potions to sense and nature's taste are well sweetened by divine grace, and well relished by faith's palate. Our greatest afflictions, from the love of God's heart, through the blood of Christ, and under the influence of the Spirit of grace, divested of the curse, come streaming down to us, as so many choice blessings. What reason then have we to be patient, yea, joyful in all our tribulations, and in every thing to give thanks! Lord, forgive our unbelief, and increase our faith, that we may sing in sorrow, and give thee the praise of all thy grace! Since "our light affliction, which is but for a moment, worketh for us a far more exceeding and eternal weight of glory!" Be of good comfort, Brother, for our worst is better than the world's best; and, since "the day of our redemption draweth nigh," let us lift up our head, and "rejoice in hope of the glory of God."

I am, dear Sir, yours in Christ,

———————

LETTER VIII.   To ————

My dear Sister in Christ,

BE of good cheer; all is well between God and you in Christ. Grace and peace from God our Father, and the Lord Jesus Christ, shall be multiplied unto you by the Holy Ghost. You complain that your faith is so weak, that you can but just say, 'Lord, undertake for me; for I have no might, strength, nor righteousness of my own!'

And is it so? Are you stript quite naked; have you no righteousness of your own, in which you can or dare appear before a God of infinite holiness and strict justice? And have you no strength of your own, to help or save yourself? Are you so poor in spirit, that you have nothing, and can do nothing? O happy, thrice happy soul! so great is your blessedness, that "yours is the kingdom of heaven." (Mat. v. 3.) The kingdom of grace here, and the kingdom of glory hereafter, is yours! God's free, rich, grace, reigning through the righteousness of Christ, and so in a way consistent with the infinite righteousness of his pure nature, and the justice of his holy law, will do all for you in point of salvation, now you can do nothing; will bestow all upon you freely, now to buy you have not so much as a penny of your own money. The kingdom of grace is erected on purpose for such souls; and all those, who are thus poor in spirit, are the happy subjects of it. It is the reign of grace that hath made them thus poor; and that grace, which hath emptied them, will fill them; which hath humbled them, will exalt them; which hath made them needy, will enrich them gloriously. Alas, by nature we go forth in our own supposed strength, and pride ourselves in our own apprehended righteousness; and, while the soul is thus rich and strong in its own conceit, and hath need of nothing, there is no room for grace to glorify its riches, in bestowing upon it all things; and therefore, when God designs mercy for any soul, down he casts these high, towering imaginations, and shews the soul that it is miserable, poor, blind and naked, and hath need of all things. And, when the soul is thus blest with a sight of its own wretchedness, it sees itself plunged into such a gulph of misery, that, through the temptations of Satan, and the power of unbelief, it can hardly think that there is any help for it in God; that for such a miserable wretch he hath any designs of mercy; but, in anguish of spirit, it cries out, "Wo is me, for I am undone!" Whereas the soul is then new-made, hath a new principle of life given it, and from thence a quick sensation if its own misery, that with an hearty welcome it may be glad to receive saving mercy. And, when grace hath thus prepared its own way, there it will reign gloriously, in its freeness, greatness, and exceeding riches, to the full and eternal salvation of that poor soul.

Come then, my dear friend, lift up your head: the sight you have of your own misery is a precious fruit of saving mercy begun, and a preparation for saving mercy complete, in your full salvation from all misery, and unto all glory. Do not think, because you have no righteousness of your own, that you shall be found naked, and stand exposed to the wrath of a sin-revenging God. No, no, free grace hath a righteousness for you, that is unto and upon you, as a believer in Jesus, who approve of, submit to, and shroud your soul under it; a righteousness that covers you all over; that hides all your deformity, and makes you a spotless, glorious, beauty in the eyes of infinite purity. And do not think, because because your spiritual enemies are numerous and potent, and your own strength mere impotence, that therefore you shall one day perish by their cruel hands. No, no, free grace hath provided strength for you, an omnipotence of power in Him who is the Lord your strength; as well as a perfection of righteousness in Him who is the Lord your righteousness. You are, you shall be, "more than a conquerer, through him that hath loved you." The almighty strength of Jehovah-Jesus is engaged on your side, and in his strength you are well able to overcome them. Their defence is departed from them; justice is satisfied, the law is fulfilled, Satan is vanquished, and sin is condemned, by the dying of the Lord Jesus. The prince of darkness is cast out from his reigning power over you, and out he shall be cast from his molesting power. "The lawful captive shall be delivered, and the prey of the terrible shall be taken away;" for God the Father will contend with those that contend with the Lord the Saviour, and will save his children. And sin, that in its reign over you is destroyed by the reign of grace, even all your innumerable sins, are and shall be forgiven, your iniquities shall be subdued, and the very being of sin excluded from your nature in the Lord's time. For stronger is He that is in you than he that is in them; and, lo, your spiritual enemies are bread for you; their innumerable host, their mighty strength, shall serve as a foil to set off the more illustriously the unsearchable riches, the omnipotent power, of that superabundant and all-overcoming grace, which saveth you, to God's eternal praise, and to your eternal joy. And know that, as surely as stript of self-righteousness and strength, you flee unto Christ for both, with a 'Lord, undertake for me!' so surely will be the great Saviour undertake for you, a poor sinner, to relieve and deliver your oppressed and distressed soul; for "whosoever shall thus call upon the name of the Lord shall be saved," Rom. x. 13.

You ask, my dear friend, 'How may we know that the Spirit of God dwells in us?' I answer, by his work upon us. For, as the Holy Ghost is promised, to "convince the world of sin, of righteousness, and of judgment," (John xvi. 8,) so, whenever any person is thus convinced, it is a certain demonstration that the Holy Ghost is come to dwell in that heart; for when he is come he shall thus reprove; his work is the consequent of his coming and indwelling. If the Spirit of God had not been given to dwell in your heart, you had not been so convinced of sin, as to see your lost and perishing state by nature, and that you must perish for ever, were you to abide in unbelief, to die without the faith of submission to Christ. Nor had you been so convinced of righteousness, of the insufficiency of your own righteousness, as to loath it for its imperfection, and have no dependence thereon for your justification, and of the all-sufficiency of Christ's righteousness, so as to approve of it, and desire to be found in it, as your only justifying dress before God. Nor yet had you been so convinced of judgment, of the wrath to come, (which shall certainly come down upon all the enemies of Christ) as to flee for refuge from it, to lay hold on Him, the mighty Saviour, the only hope which the gospel sets before a perishing sinner. You had not been thus convinced, if the Spirit of Christ had not been sent from the Father and the Son to dwell in your heart. And, as surely as the promised Comforter is come to dwell in you, so surely shall "He abide with you for ever," and perform the begun work of your salvation from all sin and misery, and unto all grace and glory, "until the day of Jesus Christ," or until your conformity to Christ, in soul and body, in grace and glory, is complete; John xiv. 16. Phil. iii. 6. And, as you are blest with the presence of the Comforter, and at times with his consolations, do not refuse to be comforted, lest you grieve the Comforter, and provoke him to withdraw his comforting influence. For, though he will never leave nor forsake you, he may carry it as a grieved friend towards you, and not bring you those stories of Christ's love which you refuse to receive by faith.

I am glad you was enabled to cast yourself, as a perishing sinner, at the feet of Christ the great Saviour, and found rest to your soul in the faith of his precious promise; "Him that cometh unto me I will in no wise cast out." That act of faith was saving, or that unto which the salvation of your soul is inseparably connected. And, as to your fear, when you had lost your comfort, lest that sweet frame, when you was in the exercise of faith, should be nothing but your own attainment by close meditation, be assured that no soul can come to Christ but whom the Father draws; John vi, 44. Meditation was your duty; but it was not your own power in that attempt of duty which brought your soul to Christ; but that fresh display, which the Lord was pleased to give you, of the glorious method of salvation by and through Christ, as every way sufficient to save a sinner. It was this sight, given you from the Father, through Christ, and by the Spirit, that allured you to come to Jesus. It was this that drew your heart, and enabled you by faith to cast your soul at the Saviour's feet for that great salvation which you viewed as every way sufficient to save lost sinners, and to save you as such. And since Jesus, the faithful and true witness, says, in his written word, and by his Spirit to your heart, "Him that cometh unto me I will in no wise cast him out;" will you not count him both able and faithful who has promised? will you not set to your seal that God the Saviour is true, by believing that you shall be saved according to this promise of salvation given you? O give not way to unbelief, which makes God, the God of infinite truth, a liar! Which says of the Rock of ages, whose strength is omnipotent, and whose faithfulness is like the great mountains, yea, firmer than heaven and earth; he is not fit to be trusted; his word is not to be depended on! We should tremble to speak thus with our lips; and yet this is the language of our unbelieving hearts, when we are called to credit our own salvation upon an act of faith. Indeed there is much diffidence and doubting in us whether we do believe truly, and so whether the promise belongs to us. But this is not all; for, when we are comfortably persuaded that we do come to Christ and rest our souls upon him, we cannot tell how to believe steadfastly that we shall be saved; but are apt to waver, perhaps the next moment, upon a glance of the number and strength of our spiritual enemies. And what is this less than making God a liar—than discrediting his word, as if he was not able, or faithful, to fulfil his promise? Instead of that doubting then of the truth of our acts of faith, which souls are put upon by the cunning of Satan and unbelief, let us attempt our duty, to put forth fresh acts of faith, coming unto Christ daily, as unto a living stone, that precious foundation which God hath laid in Sion. And, whenever you are afraid that you have not believed, venture upon Christ afresh; attempt it, and power from God will enable you to do it. Look to him in all your distresses, cast yourself at his feet with all your sins and griefs, and rest your soul upon him with all your burdens; for this is the obedience of faith which the gospel calls for, and that upon which salvation is promised. And let not this direct act of faith suffice you, nor count it enough that you dare not for your life look any where else than to Christ alone for salvation: but, for the Lord's honour and your soul's joy, attempt your duty, to put forth a reflex act of faith, or an act that looks back, as it were, unto the promise of life made to you upon your direct act, and take the Lord at his word, believing you shall be saved, because He hath said it who cannot lie nor repent; who will not, cannot "alter the thing that is gone out of his mouth," and is well able, infinitely able, to perform what he hath promised, as to your eternal life, notwithstanding all that deadness which you feel in yourself, and the utmost efforts of the powers of death and darkness round about you: for to this part of the obedience of faith you are likewise called by the declarations of grace in the gospel; and the stronger you are in faith the more glory you will give unto God; Rom. iv. 20.

I sympathise with you in your distress, because you have not that liberty and joy of faith in receiving the Lord's supper as you could wish, and as others are favoured with. But by no means would I advise you to neglect waiting on the Lord in that ordinance; for, as you are a believer in Jesus, it is undoubtedly your duty to do this in remembrance of him. And, though you have not so much peace and joy as others in breaking of bread, perhaps the Lord may have designed thereby, 1. To humble you more deeply, by letting Satan loose upon you, as it were, in that ordinance, to shew you more of your heart vileness. 2. To exalt your humbled soul more highly when the set time to favour you with his presence therein is fully come; to make you possess the double to that single which others now enjoy. 3. To make your faith in him, and love to him, appear to be both true and eminent in keeping that his commandment in the face of so much opposition and trouble. 4. To baffle and confound the prince of darkness in his attempts to hinder you in that part of your obedience, while the Lord enables you to stand your ground in the hottest battle, and so to bruise the serpent's head through you, a bruised reed. 5. To make your victory over the enemy more glorious, and your joy more full, when the God of peace shall bruise Satan under your feet. 6. To get himself more glory by your obedience, while his own hand upholds, and enables you to wait upon him in a way of duty, without those sweet allurements to it which others receive from his rich bounty. And, 7. To make your crown of glory more exceeding weighty, and your everlasting joy more exceeding great, when the trial of your faith shall be found by his grace, before men and angels, unto your praise, and honour, and glory at his appearing; and you, as an overcomer, shall have the joy of an open grant, to sit with Christ on his throne, even as he also overcame, and is set down with his Father in his throne. And, if the Lord should have designed any, or all, of these by your present exercise, you may well endure the seed-time toil for the harvest-profit, the present sorrow and suffering for the joy and glory which shall follow. And, as you, being a child of God by faith in Christ, have a right to the ordinance, and as the Lord sweetly invited you at first to partake of it, with a 'This is the bread which the Lord hath given you to eat;' despise not your birthright, nor refuse the feast you are called to partake of, for the Lord's heart and word are the same towards you to day as they were yesterday. Wait on him then in this ordinance with all holy, humble boldness, and without slavish bondage fear. And do not be terrified with a fear that you do not discern the Lord's body and blood, through the elements of bread and wine, to your joy of faith; for discern them you do, as represented thereby, or you would not be grieved that you discern them as such no more. It is no wonder that your faith has not that liberty to act as otherwise it would, when your natural spirits, through the suggestions of Satan and the force of unbelief, are all in a hurry.

When you are to approach the Lord's table, therefore, asking help of him, attempt your duty to look afresh to Christ for the whole of his salvation, to take him at his word, that in looking you shall be saved. And, as having a right to the Saviour and his salvation, draw nigh, through his blood and in his righteousness, to receive him afresh as held forth to your faith in an ordinance way. And, when you receive the broken bread, attempt an act of faith that moment, to receive the body of Christ, broken for sinners, and for every one that desires to feed upon him unto life eternal, and so for yourself in particular. And, when you receive the wine, attempt your duty by faith to receive the blood of Christ, who poured out his soul unto death for every poor sinner that desires to drink of his blood unto eternal life, and so for yourself in particular. And leave it entirely with the Lord to give or deny you comfort in the ordinance, just as he pleaseth, who is an absolute Sovereign, and will give or withhold as in his infinite wisdom he sees best for his own glory and your good. The acceptableness of your person and obedience does not depend upon your comfort, but upon Christ's righteousness, while you desire to be found in Him, and to do what he commands in faith. And, though you find much of the working of unbelief in your heart, and of the want of that love to Christ, his people, and ordinance, which you ought to have, remember that the blood of Christ cleanseth you from all sin, and makes you and your service whiter than snow in the sight of God. And, as this full fountain is infinitely free, a fountain set open for sin and for uncleanness, bathe yourself in it when you come from the Lord's table. You shall be no more bold than welcome. It will please your loving Lord to see you come thus to give him the honour of your cleansing, which is his due as the all-sufficient Saviour.

Thus, my dear friend, without confusion of mind and sinful hurry, go on to walk with the Lord in a way of duty, and you shall find him to be a God of infinite bounty, that hath kept the best wine for you till the last; the choicest comforts after sore conflicts. Grace be with you!

I am yours in Christ most tenderly,

LETTER IX.   To --------

Dear and honoured Sir,

I RETURN my humble thanks for your most kind and valuable letter. The Lord made it sweet, very sweet to my taste. I rejoice greatly in those great things which God hath done for you; and feel a springing flow of spiritual love unto you as the Lord's, and as one that is highly favoured of him. But how shall I write to you, Sir? Methinks you need no intimation of the things of God from so weak a creature as myself. And yet I should be guilty of ingratitude if I did not write a line, as a mite of that duty, which, were I able, I would gladly pay. O that the Lord would graciously put a line of his love into my unworthy hand, to comfort your dear heart.

Right glad am I, dear Sir, that, saved by grace, by rich, free, distinguishing grace, you give it all the glory! That you adore the grace of the eternal Father, and of the incarnate Son, the great Saviour! And so begin the work of heaven while on earth. And, as you add, 'Oh, I want both more appropriating and appreciating apprehensions of these sacred things!' You shall have them, Sir. The Lord, who hath begun to love you in a manifestative way, will go on to open his heart to you more and more, to seal you, as a believer, with the Holy Spirit of promise. And the more clearly you view your interest in the grace of God, and of our Lord Jesus Christ, the more highly will you prize, and the more abundantly will you praise, that grace which bringeth salvation.

Now, then, dear Sir, has your mind been illuminated to discern spiritual things in their spiritual glory? Have you seen your own misery, by reason of sin and the law, in a state of nature? That you was utterly undone, self-ruined, and sunk too low for any created arm to raise you? Have you seen the insufficiency of your own righteousness to hide your nakedness from the all-searching eye of a God of infinite purity? Have you felt your own strength to be mere weakness, and all your self-sufficiency to be utter inability? And have you seen Jesus, in his transcendent excellency and infinite all-sufficiency, as the great and only Saviour? Has the Christ of God been made precious to your soul, the chiefest of ten thousand, and altogether lovely on your esteem? Have you been drawn by him to close with him as a complete Saviour; to accept of him, and to rest upon him, for the whole of your salvation, from all misery unto all glory; relying upon him alone, as the sure foundation which God hath laid in Sion? And can you doubt whether this is the Lord's work, a work of his omnipotent and special grace, by which you are raised unto saving faith in Christ, or not? O no, no; "Unto you (saith the Lord) that believe He is precious." And, as surely as God is true, and Christ is precious to your soul, so surely you are a believer, a true believer in Jesus; and you shall be "saved in the Lord with an everlasting salvation; you shall not be ashamed nor confounded world without end!"

And, as a believer in Jesus, Sir, think, O think whence this precious faith was given you! It sprang out of the grace of God in election. "God from the beginning did choose you to salvation, through sanctification of the Spirit and belief of the truth." The Lord, the eternal God, who is an eternal now, before whose vast mind from eternity all things were present at one immense view; all possible worlds with their innumerable inhabitants as they lay in his absolute power, which he could have made, had he pleased; and all the numberless inhabitants of this our earth, as they lay in his ordinate power, in the immutable decree of his omnipotent will: all these lay before our Jehovah at once; and, as an absolute sovereign, for his own glory, he might make or not make, chuse or refuse, as he pleased. And, lo, from an infinity of grace in his heart, He chose a remnant, a small remnant of Adam's race, unto eternal life by Jesus, while multitudes were passed by; the consequence whereof, by reason of their sin, is eternal death! And among the chosen remnant he chose you! You, while he passed by thousands on your right hand and on your left! It was you, Sir, that the great Jehovah set his heart upon in his eternal choice! It was you, as particularly and personally as if he had chosen none but you! It was you, notwithstanding your creature-littleness, your great unworthiness, and foreseen vileness, that Jehovah loved! It was you that he chose in Christ before the foundation of the world! It was you that he blest with all grace in Him, in his well-ordered and sure covenant, before the earth's foundations were laid! And hence it was for you that God the Father delivered up his Son, when none but he could raise you from the depths of your deserved misery, to the heights of your ordained glory! Then, O then, God gave his Son, his only Son, for you! He gave him to be born, to be humbled, in your nature; to sustain your person and law-place; to bear your sin, to obey and die for you! To reconcile you to God, to make you righteous before him, and to bring you to the present and eternal enjoyment of him! And hence, farther, God "sent forth the Spirit of his Son into your heart, crying Abba, Father." He sent the Holy Ghost to convince you of sin, of righteousness, and of judgment;

to shew you the things of Christ and of the Father; to reveal and apply the great salvation of God unto you! To be your sanctifier and comforter, and constant indweller, as the earnest of your vast inheritance in God; until you be taken up to the full possession of his great self, unto light, life, joy, and glory, ineffable and eternal! Was ever grace like this! Adore it, Sir, for you can never comprehend it; but, rejoicing in it and revering of it, to your eternal bliss, you must for ever be comprehended by it in this immense ocean of grace unto ages without end!

Again, Sir, behold with joy and wonder, behold with endless praise, the equal grace of the Son of God! And here I can only point your eye to—the Lord fix it upon—your Saviour's love, which passeth knowledge! See, dear Sir, it was you, it was you, for whom the Son of God came down! It was for you, as really and personally as if he had been incarnate for none but you! And would the Son of God for you vail his infinite glory in the likeness of your frail flesh! Would he take your nature, law-place, sin, curse, wrath and death, that you, who was condemned to die eternally, might live together with him, crowned with immortal glory! O matchless, immeasurable, infinite grace! Begin, begin, to give it the utmost of your creature-praise! And from this infinity of redemption-grace by price, and in pursuit of an immensity of redemption-grace by power, did the exalted Saviour send down the Holy Ghost, the promise of the Father, into your heart; to quicken you when dead in sin; to begin, increase, and perfect your new life; to give you the life of grace, and to ripen it into glory; that, happy, inconceivably happy in him, you might live for ever with him! O what thanks are due from you his redeemed for this unparalleled grace, your Lord-Redeemer!

Once more—behold, with adoring praise, the co-equal, infinite grace of God the Holy Ghost, who, being essentially and eternally God, equal with the Father and the Son, and as sent from both, most freely came, in the immensity of his own grace, to dwell in your heart; to form Christ's image in your soul; to make you an habitation of God through the Spirit here, and an holy temple for the glory of God to dwell in for ever hereafter! It was you, Sir, particularly and individually, that Jehovah the Spirit loved! And would this holy Lord God, in the infinity of his grace, for such ineffably gracious ends, take up his residence in your heart, which before his coming to dwell in it was vile as hell! And, being come, will he abide with you for ever, to answer all the ends of grace in your eternal glory; and this, notwithstanding all the affrontments you give him daily! O unfathomable grace! how doth Jehovah, Father, Son and Spirit, your Three-One God, love you! O man greatly beloved! give God your heart; and in all practical praises declare what great things the Lord hath done for you! Great grace be with you!

I am, dear Sir,
Your most humble servant,

Letter X.   To --------

Dear Sir,

Your most affectionate letter demands my utmost thanks. But why, dear Sir, should you cast your eye upon that which is not? A kind thought upon a creature that least deserves it? Ah, did you know me thoroughly, in all my baseness and ingratitude towards the Lord and his people, surely you could have but little affection, but little value, for a creature so truly little, so greatly vile! Oh, I am the chief of sinners, the most unworthy, the most unlovely! Black, black as hell, in my vile, unregenerate part! Indeed the Lord loves me: his love towards me is great, strong, invincible, all overflowing, unchangeable, and eternal! But he can love sinners, the chief of sinners! and often takes the very worst and vilest, to make them monuments of his choicest favour; and to shew how freely, how greatly, a God can love! Because his love has neither shore, nor bottom, measure, nor end: but is, like his great being, a vast infinity! And, because there is such an infinite abundance in the love of Jehovah, he delights to shew its exceeding riches upon the most undeserving creatures, the most hell-deserving sinners! The Lord can command his loving-kindness: he can love whom he will, and as greatly as he please, notwithstanding the greatest unloveliness in the beloved object. And, if he do but say, "I will be gracious unto whom I will be gracious, and shew mercy on whom I will shew mercy," by way of application to any particular person; thousands of sins, provocations and affrontments, must fall before the majesty of this great resolve. For "Who is a god like unto our God, who pardoneth iniquity, and passeth by the transgression of the remnant of his heritage! He retaineth not his anger for ever: because he delighteth in mercy, he keepeth mercy for thousands;" for thousands of persons, and for thousands of offences. And, when he hath forgiven an innumerable multitude of persons, and in each of them an innumerable multitude of sins, millions and millions of sins, to an infinite amount, which neither men nor angels can number; he is Jehovah, merciful still! He is as ready to pardon and relieve, to love and save, as ever! The mercy of his nature, the mercy of his covenant, is still the same: an immense stock, a fund of grace, that is inexhaustible, undiminishable, all-supplying and everlasting!

And, lo, infinite wisdom hath found out a way in which the love of God's nature, by an immutable resolve of his will, may flow down upon the chief of sinners to an infinite abundance, consistent with the glory of all his divine perfections, with his flaming holiness, eternal truth, and strict justice! He hath smote the rock, his own Son, made sin for us, and smitten him to death in our room and stead: and thence, through the infinite merit of the Father's spotless Lamb, sacrificed for us, the waters of his free grace gush out, and run in dry places like a river4,—a broad river with streams—to the glory of God, Father, Son, and Spirit; and to the joy of saints and angels, through time and to eternity!

This, my Brother, this is the grace that saves me. This is the God that loves and favours me; and that so highly, as to make me a wonder unto many.— And yet, not for my worthiness, not for my loveliness, not for my goodness, have I found this favour in his sight. No: when he passed by me at first he saw me polluted in my own blood, a most loathsome object, deserving of his fierce wrath, and fit fuel for everlasting burnings: and yet, in the infinite freeness of his grace, the sovereignty and immensity of his love, he said unto me "Live." Yea, when I was in my blood, he said unto me "Live." And my time, the time of my loathsomeness, was the time of his love! Then washed he me with water; yea, he thoroughly washed away my blood, my guilt, from me: he clad me with embroidered garments; he adorned me with fair jewels; anointed me with oil, and sware unto me. and entered into a covenant with me, and I became his. Then I said, when he had broke my yoke, and burst my bonds. "I will not transgress;" from henceforth I will be the Lord's. But did I keep my Word? Ah, no! I have not rendered unto the Lord according to the great things which he hath done for me. I have been rebellious against the Lord ever since the day that he knew me. I have dealt very treacherously, and have played the harlot with many lovers under every green tree, and done evil things as I could! My heart-wanderings from God testify to my face. My light esteem of the Rock of my salvation, my little love to him, my ingratitude and unthankfulness, with innumerable evils, which attend me daily—these all speak me still, even still, to be a most unlovely and provoking creature, as a descendant of fallen Adam. And can you love such a one, Brother? such a black sinner? such a mass of sins, weakness, and wants? Oh, look not upon me, because I am black! The sun hath looked upon me. But, though the love of creatures is much too little to delight in me, if they saw my deformity, and especially if I did against any of them in one year but a thousandth part of what I do against my Lord daily; yet the love of Christ, his knowledge-passing-love, forgives all my sins, and remembers them no more! And he remembers me earnestly still as his delight. Oh, my Brother, my Lord is silent because of his love! He does not come with chiding to the streets; but passeth by a thousand affrontments between him and me in secret. He rests in his love, and will never seek another object of it instead of me. Yea, he rejoiceth over me with singing, as if I was a lovely one! O, amazing grace, he looks on me as the fruit of his love and blood, as the joy of his heart! And says of me, as clothed with his beauties, "Thou art all fair, my love, there is no spot in thee! Thou hast ravished my heart, my sister, my spouse, with one of thine eyes, with one chain of thy neck!" And what love and duty, think you now, do I owe to the Prince of Grace? Oh, ten thousand talents! But, ah me! "sold under sin, though to will is present with me, yet how to perform that which is good I find not!" His love humbles me, melts me, draws me! And yet, still, still, my heart hangs behind. I am ungrateful, disingenuous, undutiful, feeble, and what not! Oh, this is my joy, my Lord's love is saving love, transforming love, that will love me into its own image, and shortly make me a perfect beauty, "without blame before him in love!" I long for that time and state when the very being of sin shall be rooted out of my nature; and then not a sinful thought shall pass my heart to a vast eternity! I shall grieve my infinite lover no more; dishonour him no more! But, humbled for ever in the remembrance of all my unkindness, I shall rise in endless praises to give him, in my creature-measure, the full glory of all his immeasurable grace! And shout, with saints and angels, "Salvation unto God and the Lamb, for ever and ever, Amen."

And, since we shall soon meet in heaven, dear Sir, let it not grieve you that we had not the pleasure of meeting on this earth; nor think that you sustained any loss by the disappointment. I am empty now, but shall be full then. We will take the joy of fellowship where the communion of saints will be free, full, and eternal; where we shall all be full of God, as little streams, from that living fountain; and sweet conveyances into that immense ocean of love, life, and glory, to the days of eternity! Mean time let us learn this great truth, that creatures, in this state of imperfection, cannot afford us that full satisfaction which we are apt to promise ourselves from them. They are rather shadows than substance; failing, empty brooks, than rivulets of living water. Again; let us learn to be all submission when God denies us creature satisfaction; and cry unto him continually, "My Father, thou art the guide of my youth; choose thou our inheritance for us!" And let us learn, when our heavenly Father denies us what we desire, to take that denial as a double portion of kindness; for the Lord never denies us what we think would be best for us, but to give us something better, to make us possess the double, that everlasting joy may be unto us. Wherefore in everything let us give thanks. Great grace be with you! I am very affectionately,

Dear Sir, yours in Christ for ever,

Letter XI.   To --------

ON ELECTION.

Dear Sir,

I REJOICE to hear that Mr. S----d's journal hath been of use to your soul; and that therein it hath in some measure answered its end; as I doubt not he wrote it for the glory of God, and the good of souls. And, if you, dear Sir, have heard of God's salvation thereby, so as to be duly affected with your own misery as a sinner, and the excellency of Christ as the Saviour, unto any heart-attraction after him, who is "fairer than the children of men," and soul rest upon him who is "the only foundation which God hath laid in Sion," this is no casual thing, that might or might not have been, or that was dependent only on the will of the creature; but it was matter of divine appointment, and a gracious effect of God's good pleasure, who "worketh all things (in providence and grace) according to the good pleasure of his will," Eph. i. 11. Or, "according to his eternal purpose, which he purposed to Christ Jesus our Lord," ch. iii. 11. You hear, Sir, that I hold election, and ask my reasons for so doing: which please to take as follow.

First. I believe, and hold, the doctrine of God's eternal election of a certain number of persons from among mankind, of his free grace, without respect to their works, unto everlasting life by Jesus Christ, through the sanctifying influences of the Holy Ghost; because it is so abundantly revealed and declared in the Scriptures of truth.

To instance in a few for many: Gen. xxv. 22, 23. "And the children struggled together within her: and she said, If it be so, why am I thus? And she went to inquire of the Lord. And the Lord said unto her, Two nations are in thy womb, and two manner of people shall be separated from thy bowels; and the one people shall be stronger than the other people; and the elder shall serve the younger." Compared with Rom, ix. 10, 11, 12. "And not only this, but when Rebecca also had conceived by one, even by our father Isaac, (for the children being not yet born, neither having done any good or evil, that the purpose of God according to election might stand, not of works, but of him that calleth) it was said unto her, The elder shall serve the younger: as it is written, Jacob have I loved, but Esau have I hated." In this chapter, Sir, ver. 7, Isaac is made a type of the chosen seed, while Ishmael was passed by. And Jacob also is given as an instance of God's special love, of his saving love, while Esau was hated, or less loved, having his portion only in the things of this life. As Ishmael was blessed with external good things, while God's covenant, his everlasting covenant of grace, was established with Isaac. And not the persons only of Isaac and Ishmael, of Jacob and Esau, were types of the election and the rest, but their respective posterities also. As Gen. xxv. 23, "Two nations and two manner of people shall be separated from thy bowels: and the one people shall be stronger than the other people; and the elder shall serve the younger." And Mal. i. 2, "I have loved you, saith the Lord: yet ye say, Wherein hast thou loved us? Was not Esau Jacob's brother? saith the Lord; yet I loved Jacob and I hated Esau, and laid his mountains and his heritage waste for the dragons of the wilderness." And of the seed of Jacob it is said, "Thou art an holy people to the Lord thy God, and the Lord hath chosen thee to be a peculiar people to himself, above all the nations that are upon the earth," Deut. xiv. 2. And "The Lord hath chosen Jacob unto himself, and Israel for his peculiar treasure," Ps. cxxxv. 4. And that the seed of Jacob, the nation of Israel, was typical of the elect of God among all nations, appears; in that when the apostle had proved the doctrine of election, Rom. ix. 6, &c. and answered objections which might be made against it, by asserting God's righteousness, together with his sovereignty over his creatures; and also declared his great design, to make known the riches of his glory on the vessels of mercy; he adds, "Even us, whom he hath called, not of the Jews only, but also of the Gentiles," ver. 24. And of both he says, writing of the converted Jews, and to the Ephesian Gentiles, called to be saints, "Blessed be the God and Father of our Lord Jesus Christ, who hath blessed us with all spiritual blessings in heavenly places in Christ; according as he hath chosen us in him before the foundation of the world, that we should be holy and without blame before him in love," Eph. i. 3, 4. But, as I am obliged to contract, Sir, I will add no more, but only join with this inspired writer to say, "Even so then at this present time also there is a remnant according to the election of grace." And "the election hath obtained it, and the rest were blinded," Rom. xi. 5, 7.

Secondly. I believe and hold the doctrine of election, because it is a part of the word of life—of the faithful word; and of the mystery of the faith; which ministers and private Christians are to hold forth, and to hold fast, Phil. ii. 16. 1 Tim. i. 19. and iii. 9. And a part of that doctrine of faith, of that faith once delivered to the saints, which ministers and Christians, in running their race to the finishing of their course, ought to keep and to contend earnestly for, 2 Tim. iv. 7. Jude ver. 3.

Thirdly. I hold the doctrine of election, because it is a doctrine that gives strong consolation to us miserable sinners, and is a firm ground for our hope of everlasting salvation. For, "Except the Lord of hosts had left us a seed, a remnant, according to the election of grace, we had all been as Sodom, and been made like unto Gomorrah, who suffered the vengeance of eternal fire," Rom. ix. 29. Jude ver. 7.

Fourthly. I hold the doctrine of election, because, through grace, I have experienced the exceeding sweetness thereof on my own soul; I have tasted that therein the Lord hath been gracious to my poor soul. And I am made to cry out, with pleasing wonder and humble adoration, while under the displays of electing love, with Judas, (not Iscariot) "How is it, Lord, that thou wilt manifest thyself unto us (unto me) and not unto the world!" John xiv. 22. And with the apostle John, "Behold, what manner of love the Father hath bestowed upon us, that we should be called the sons of God!" 1 John iii. 1. And with Jesus my Lord; "I thank thee, O Father, Lord of heaven and earth, because thou hast hid these things from the wise and prudent, and hast revealed them unto babes. (The mysteries of salvation-grace by electing love, unto eternal glory, unto me who am a babe!) Even so Father, for so it seemed good in thy sight," Matt. xi. 25, 26.

Fifthly. I hold the doctrine of election, because I feel its sweet and efficacious influence unto all holy conversation and godliness. For, while the love of God, his eternal electing love, is shed abroad in my heart by the Holy Ghost, in this present time, "I love him, because he hath first loved me; and this is the love of God, that we keep his commandments," Rom. v. 5. 1 John iv. 16, 19, and v. 3. And,

Sixthly. I hold election, because otherwise I could not hold fast my confidence of everlasting salvation. As we are commanded to do, Heb. x. 23, "Let us hold fast the profession of our faith without wavering, for He is faithful that promised." And ver. 34, 35, "Knowing in yourselves that ye have in heaven a better and an enduring substance. Cast not away therefore your confidence, which hath great recompense of reward." Cast away election, and we cast away salvation, and the confidence thereof, at once; for nothing less than this can secure both, that "God hath from the beginning chosen his people to salvation, through sanctification of the Spirit and belief of the truth;" and that "He which hath begun this good work in them will perform it until the day of Jesus Christ," 2 Thess. ii. 13, 14. Phil. i. 6. Those, and those only, whom God foreknew, in his eternal electing love, "he predestinated to be conformed to the image of his son. And whom he did predestinate, them he also called; and whom he called, them he also justified; and whom he justified, them he also glorified;" Rom. viii. 29, 30. "What shall we then say to these things? If God be for us, who can be against us? ver. 31.

You see then, dear Sir, that the doctrine of election is a part of God's truth; of that faith which ought to be held fast; that it is full of comfort to poor sinners; that it affords much sweetness to those who know their election of God; that it strongly engageth to holiness of life; and that it strengthens the confidence of believers in their everlasting salvation. And, as it doth not separate the means from the end, but sweetly join them together, from hence I would close with a hint to what you further request—of the way to be finally saved.

And now, dear Sir, as our Lord touched the eyes of the blind man, and he saw men as trees walking; and again touched them, and he saw every man clearly, Mark viii. 24, 25. So, if he hath touched the eyes of your mind and given you some discerning of spiritual things, he will give you another touch, and you shall see them clearly.

Salvation, then, hath two terms, from and to which a person or people is saved; viz. from sin and misery to grace and glory, present and eternal. And the way of salvation is Christ alone; or, the salvation of sinners is alone by the free grace of God in Christ; by the incarnation, life and death, resurrection, ascension and intercession, of the Son of God: in virtue wherof the Holy Ghost is sent from the Father and the Son, to dwell in the hearts of the elect; to quicken them when dead in sin, or to give them the new birth, by forming their souls anew, in the gift of faith, love, hope, and every grace; which he maintains and increaseth in the vessels of mercy, until they are fully prepared for and received up to glory; or, in a word, Christ crucified, and the knowledge of him as such, is the only way to everlasting salvation. For there is salvation in no other; "there is no other name under heaven given among men whereby we must be saved," Acts iv. 12. "For we have all sinned, and come short of the glory of God." But, "are justified freely by his grace, through the redemption that is in Jesus Christ; whom God hath set forth to be a propitiation, through faith in his blood, to declare at this time his righteousness for the remission of sins that are past, through the forebearance of God; that he might be just, and the justifier of him which believeth in Jesus." Rom. iii. 23, &c. "And by him all that believe are justified from all things, from which ye could not be justified by the law of Moses," Acts xiii. 39. Justified unto life eternal, Rom. v. 18.

But, dear Sir, a word to your own soul. What think you of your sad state by nature? We have all destroyed ourselves by sin. We were undone by our first

lover, the Lord your love, is not gone for ever; for, though he hide his face from you at present, whence you now have sorrow, he will see you again, and your heart shall rejoice. Though for a small moment he hath forsaken you, with everlasting kindness will he have mercy on you. And the Lord's forsaking of his people is rather sensible than real. It regards the suspension of the shining of his face in manifestative favour; but does not intimate the least variation of the love of his heart, or remission of the care of his hand. Sion indeed says, when under gloomy dispensations, "The Lord hath forsaken me, and my Lord hath forgotten me." But what saith the answer of God to her? "Can a woman forget her sucking child, that she should not have compassion on the son of her womb? Yea, they may forget, yet will not I forget thee. Behold I have graven thee upon the palms of my hands; thy walls are continually before me." Forsake you, forget you, he doth not, he will not, in your most dark and trying seasons. And, though the Lord doth not shine upon you now, to raise your spiritual joy in him, as your all in all, he may bless you with his gracious influence, unto kindly mourning after him, and a deeper humility before him: and thus in wise grace, by the darkness of the present night, prepare you for the brightness of another day. For, "Blessed are they that mourn, they shall be comforted; and he that humbleth himself shall be exalted."

A mercy it is that you see so much of your heart-vileness, that makes you loath and abominate yourself. This is a precious fruit of God's forgiving love, of his being pacified towards you in Christ for all that you have done. The heart indeed is desperately wicked; who can know it? None, but the Lord alone, can search that depth, that abyss of sin which is in it. And before the eye of his omniscience its most hidden wickedness is naked and bare. And yet, oh amazing grace, with the eye of avenging justice, he sees no iniquity in Jacob, nor perverseness in Israel! "The Lord hath laid on him (the Son of his love, the Man that is his fellow) the iniquity of us all." His sword of justice hath been sheathed in the heart of Christ, unto full satisfaction for all our sins, both of nature and practice: and his hand of favour, of forgiving grace, is turned upon us, the little ones. "There is therefore now no condemnation to them which are in Christ Jesus, who walk not after the flesh, but after the Spirit." Here, my dear Friend, here see your freedom from all sin. Here see yourself a conqueror, and more than a conqueror, through him that hath loved you, and washed you from your sins in his own blood, and hath made you a king and a priest unto God and his Father! You are more than a conqueror over sin, in its guilt, filth and power, already in Christ Jesus, by what he hath done and suffered for you in your room and stead: and you shall be more than a conqueror over sin in all respects shortly, through him that hath loved you; who, having overcome for you, will overcome in you. Your old man was crucified with Christ, that the body of sin might be destroyed in you. Wherefore reckon yourself, by faith, to be dead indeed unto sin, and alive unto God, even now, in Christ Jesus. For this will exceedingly strengthen your hands and animate your heart, in your conflict with the power of sin in yourself under which you groan. You fight against conquered enemies, and under the mighty Conqueror, the Captain of your salvation, who hath gotten the victory for you, and will give it to you. Wherefore "be strong, and fight the battles of the Lord." Watch and oppose all the motions of this deadly enemy sin, since the Lord your God is with you as a mighty, terrible one, and will drive out all your spiritual enemies from before you, and will say, 'Destroy them;' or give you to set your feet upon their necks, with joyful triumph over them.

You think that, if your friends knew one half of your heart-vileness, they would not converse with you. Indeed creature-bowels are too scanty to reach our extensive misery. But one Friend there is, our dear Lord Jesus, who is every way suited to our case, and can have compassion according to the measure of our distress: because his bowels are infinite and never-failing. Unto his bosom let us run, to vent our moan, in whose tender heart we will have always room, and whose tender hand will relieve us under, and deliver us from, our greatest sorrows by reason of indwelling sin.

And, though you are shot at, and hated, and sorely grieved, by that grand enemy Satan, who throws his temptations like fiery darts, to wound and destroy you; get by faith under the shadow of Christ, who is, and will be, a covert from that storm, "For we have not an High-priest that cannot be touched with the feeling of our infirmities, but was in all points tempted like unto us, that he might be able to succour them that are tempted."

As to that temptation to indolence in religious duties,—that, if you are elected you shall be saved, and if not you shall be damned, do what you can—asking help of God, labour to reject it with the utmost abhorrence, as it directly strikes at God's glory and your soul's felicity, and separates the means and end, which God hath joined together. Tell Satan that all, who are elected to salvation, are chosen unto sanctification, as the means unto that end; that holiness is the great work of a Christian, unto which he is called by grace, in order to his eternal glory; that without holiness, in heart, lip and life, no man shall see the Lord. And that, therefore, as a lost sinner, you will comply with the gospel-requirement of faith in the great Saviour, and venture your soul on Christ for all salvation; and, resigning yourself unto him in all holy obedience, make and entire self-dedication to his praise; having this faithful promise given you, that, if you follow on to know the Lord, you shall know him. Thus, my dear Friend, steadfast in the faith, resist the devil, and he will flee from you. And, whenever he tempts you to negligence in any holy duty, let this be rather a spur to you to double your diligence. Reason thus with yourself—Does Satan beat me off from seeking God? It is because he hates God, and hates me: I will go on to seek God, therefore, and seek him more easrnestly, for his glory, yea, and for my own felicity; for God that cannot lie hath said that every one that asketh receiveth; that he that seeketh findeth; and that to him that knocketh it shall be opened. You have not lost your God, but only sensible communion with him. Follow hard after him, and soon you shall be satisfied with his infinite favour. "Commit the keeping of your soul unto him in well doing; and rejoice that he is able and faithful to keep that which you have committed unto him against that day. Great grace be with you.

I am, Madam, with due respect,
Yours in the Lord,

LETTER XIII.   To Mr. L.

My dear Brother in Christ,

I AM sensibly touched with your afflicted state. Remember that, "As a father pitieth his children, so the Lord pitieth them that fear him." And of you, with others of the vessels of mercy, under grieving misery, he saith, "Oh, thou afflicted, tossed with tempest, and not comforted; behold, I will lay stones with fair colours, and will lay thy foundations with sapphires." Are you afflicted? "In all your affliction He is afflicted." "I was an hungered, thirsty, sick, in prison," &c. saith Christ, concerning his afflicted members. Your afflictions are the afflictions of Christ, and you do but thereby fill up that which is behind of his afflictions in your flesh. Christ first suffered, and then entered into his glory; and so must you. And, lo, you are not, shall not be left to suffer without sympathy, without the sympathy of Him whose compassions are infinite! whose bowels are troubled for you, and break out upon you, with an "Oh, thou afflicted!" Are you "tossed with tempest, and not comforted!" Christ knows it, even every circumstance of your distress. Yea, he feels it by an inexpressible pity; whence upon you, in your afflicted state, he will surely have mercy. For "Behold, (says he) I will lay thy stones with fair colours; (thy spiritual building and beauty I will raise out of the blackest, darkest ruins) and lay thy foundations (the foundations of thy present hopes and joys, and future glories) with sapphires;" (which is a precious stone of blue, lasting colour) with the precious promises of my unchangeable grace. For the Lord our infinite lover's pity is, and will be, productive of seasonable relief and gracious supply; yea, of an exalted state, from the depths of grief and misery, unto the heights of joy and glory, of everlasting joy and eternal glory! "Though you have lien among the pots; (as a broken vessel, wherein there is no pleasure) yet shall you be as the wings of a dove, covered with silver, and her feathers of yellow gold." A fresh beauty and glory shall be put upon you, as the Lord's favourite, by his infinite favour. Have you left your first love? Christ remembers you for his first love. Have you broken your covenant to be the Lord's? He will remember for you his covenant, and will establish unto you an everlasting covenant, to be your God. Is your heart cold and dead towards Christ? His heart, even now, is all on flame, of free, great, unchangeable and eternal love unto you; and he is and will be your life. For, lo, this infinite Lover will love you into love, into his own love-image. He will see you again; and your heart shall rejoice, and your joy none shall take from you. The times of refreshing, which await you, will speedily come from the presence of the Lord. You will soon have done with a state of absence, and be with Christ for ever where he is, to behold his glory. His own soft hand will wipe away all your tears, and his sweet mouth will call you, as his mourning servant, to enter into your master's joy. And your present sorrows and afflictions, under the management of almighty love, will serve to make your future joys and glories appear more great and full. "Your light affliction, which is but for a moment, worketh for you a far more exceeding and eternal weight of glory." Your afflictions of every kind were appointed, are measured and bounded; and shall be overruled, for the glory of God and your salvation. In faith and patience, then, continue to be a follower of them who inherit the promises. And "lift up your head; for the day of your redemption draweth nigh." And till you are taken up, to be for ever with the Lord, he will condescend to be always with you, even to the very end of your being in the world. Having loved you as his own, he will love you unto the end; and will never, never leave, nor forsake you. In life with all its trials, and through death with all its sorrows, will your own dear Lord Jesus be with you; to support you under all your burdens, to relieve you in all your necessities, to deliver you from all miseries; and to raise you unto all glories, in and with himself for ever. Unto the boundless love of his gracious heart, and the tender care of his almighty hand, I commit you; and am, with great sympathy,

Dear Sir,
Your affectionate Friend in the Lord, &c.

LETTER XIV. To --------

Reverend Sir,

I AM much concerned about our dear friends at ---- to know how it fared with Mr. F. and his spouse. I pray, with you, that the dispensation may be sanctified. And, blessed be the Lord, who in the midst of judgment remembered mercy, in that, when a tempestuous wind brought in the sea upon them like a mighty torrent, or rather like a destroying deluge, He, who commandeth and raiseth the stormy wind, who gathereth the wind in his fists, and who saith to the raging ocean, "Hitherto shalt thou come, and no farther, and here shall thy proud waves be stayed;" He, this almighty He, as Lord of hosts, of winds and waters, was pleased to command his wind to veer about to a contrary point of the compass; and, blowing strongly, to carry of the rising waters to the fall of five feet in ten minutes (as the account was given here), although it was at a time when the tides was expected to flow three hours longer. "Who is so great a god as our God!" Who is like unto him, "that pardoneth iniquity, and passeth by the transgression of the remnant of his heritage?

Who is like unto his people, "that have God so near unto them in all that they call upon him for!" That have God for their "Refuge and strength, a very present help in trouble!" For I doubt not that this great deliverance wrought for ----, from that utter destruction which was threatened both to place and people, was a signal answer to the earnest prayers of the Lord's remnant there who seek the face of the God of Jacob.

The Lord's giving you a glorious autumn in the N—th, Sir, and to see his stately steps at L—n, rejoiced my heart, and engaged me to give thanks to God, even our Father, who always causes you to triumph in Christ. O, dear Sir, what, not forsaken yet! A favourite of heaven still! Bourne and carried in the arms of everlasting love, safely, sweetly, and triumphantly, as on eagles' wings, through so great a part of your seventy years! Yea, Sir, and he that hath made, borne and carried you hitherto, will yet bear, carry, and deliver you. He will bear you safe through all your labours, difficulties and dangers, until he brings you to himself, and calls you to enter into your Master's joy and rest. Infinite love, grace and mercy, are immutable, inexhaustible, never-failing! Omnipotent strength can never wax weary! And your covenant-interest in God through Christ can never, never be lost! Great and marvellous are the things which God has done hitherto: great have been his appearances to and for you; great have been his operations upon and by you: and greater, and still greater things than these await you in the present and future world! The joys and glories, which are before you, are ineffable and eternal! Run with patience the race that is set before you, in doing and suffering the will of God, that you may glorify him upon the earth; that Christ may be magnified in your body, whether it be by life or by death. For, lo, Jesus hath the crown in his hand, ready to set upon your head, a massy crown of life and glory, unto joy unknown, and ages without end!

I am glad you can say, from experience, Sir, and that you say for my encouragement, 'He is a never-failing God.'—A thousand thanks, that you commend me to his never-failing mercy. There I am, and shall be, for ever safe and happy.— You wish me the choicest blessing in wishing me the gift of the Divine Presence, the presence of his grace, which will fill me with all joy and bliss. And, that the Lord may measure thousand after thousand, and bring you through the waters of life, until, with rising pleasure, you find them a river to swim in that cannot be passed over; is my hearty wish for your dear soul. Great grace be with you! Permit me to be, most affectionately,

Reverend Sir,
Your most obliged humble servant, &c.

Letter XV.   To Mrs. F.

Honoured Madam!

I was much concerned, when I heard of the awful hurricanes at ----, to know if dear Mr. F. and you were preserved alive: and dear Mr. W. informs me that you are safe, and did not sustain so much loss thereby as some others; for which I bless our good God through Jesus Christ.

The great deliverance which the Lord wrought for ----, by commanding such a sudden turn of a strong wind, to carry off the raging waters at a time of imminent danger by the flowing tide, was marvellous in my eyes, and the matter of my joy and praise. And I doubt not but the salvation of the town was granted as an answer to prayer, and in special mercy to the Lord's little remnant there. God's people are the salt of the earth: a preservative to the wicked. And he would have spared Sodom, for their sakes, if there had been but ten righteous in it.

But why, O, why should the God of glory thus greatly regard his own people in misery, when their hearts and lives are so full of iniquity! How is it that they should be the favourites of his tender love, when they are such a provocation of his anger! Oh, not because in themselves they are worthy do they find mercy; but because Jehovah's mercy, his new-covenant mercy in Christ, is absolutely and infinitely free! Because they were chosen and made accepted in the beloved, in a worthy head, in God's first-born, his well-beloved Son, in whom his soul delighteth! Because, being loved with the same love, in their measure, they were to share the same infinite favour, according to the decreed proportion of head and members! Because, being reconciled to God by the Lamb's blood, their sins washed away, their persons justified, and they advanced into a communion with Christ in his dignity, being thus made Kings and Priests unto God and his Father, they have power with God, and with men; and their imperfect prayers, through Christ's perfect sacrifice, are prevalent for the descent of great mercies on themselves and others! and because they have a friend in the court of heaven, a great High Priest, advocate and intercessor with the Father; who presents their prayers in his much incense, pleads their cause in his own righteousness, and by his own merits prevails for favours: therefore it is, for these reasons, that God's people in misery, both for themselves and others, with Him find mercy, notwithstanding all their heart and life-iniquity!—And, O, what thanks are due from us to the God of all grace, who hath so well provided for his own glory and our joy, in and through his dear Son, the given Saviour, for the chief of sinners! Let our language in heart, lip and life be, "Thanks be unto God for his unspeakable gift!"

The gift of the eternal Father's eternal Son, to be incarnate, to be born, to be made under the law, to obey and die, to rise and reign for us, must needs be unspeakable; because his person, his love and grace, his word and works, are unspeakable, and their immense glories unsearchable and eternal! An unspeakable gift that must needs be which comprehends all gifts in itself! All the gifts of nature, grace and glory, respecting our natural, spiritual and eternal life, are comprehended in the unspeakable gift of the Son of God! A gift this is so great, that neither the tongues nor pens of men or angels can set it forth! talk and count they may, they do, they shall, of the riches and greatness of this gift, through all time and unto all eternity: but tongues and sums will fail to give the vast, the immense account of this unspeakable gift! and all, with wonder, joy and praise, will join to say, 'the riches of Christ are unsearchable!' What unsearchable grace, then, must that be, in the Lord the Father, which gave the Lord the Son, this unspeakable gift!

But who is this gift bestowed on? On worthy creatures? No, no; creature-worthiness hath here no place. No creature, though of the greatest excellency, dignity, beauty and duty, ever was, or could be, in the least worthy of so great a gift! No; the great God took all his motives from within himself, from the immense greatness of his love, grace and mercy, from the great good pleasure of his sovereign will, to bestow this great gift upon any of the works of his hands! And, lo, to commend and set off the infinite greatness and sovereignty of his divine love, grace and mercy, God did not give his Son, to take upon him the nature of angels, but the seed of Abraham! not the angelic, but the human nature! not a superior, but an inferior nature! A nature of the lowest rank of rational creatures was the Son of God given to assume, that he might exalt men, while angels sink! And given he was, not only to exalt man from the bliss of an earthly paradise, to the happiness of the heavenly state; but to raise him, even from the depths of hell's deserved misery to the amazing heights of heaven's prepared glory! Men, and not angels, in the Son of God bestowed on; unto guilty, filthy, God-provoking sinners, and not to holy and obedient creatures, is the Son of God given! And not upon all men neither; but upon a remnant, according to the election of grace, is this wondrous gift cast! And not upon that remnant, considered as little, but as great sinners, even the very chief of enemies, and ungodly, is this unspeakable gift of God conferred!

What, then, my dear Sister, shall we say to these things? Verily the Lord herein hath acted like himself; hath given us God, an infinite God! And, since Jesus Christ is God's gift, his free gift to the chief of sinners, what should hinder our receiving of him as such? "For God so (greatly, ineffably, and inconceivably) loved the world, that he gave his only begotten Son; that whosoever believeth in him (or is willing to receive him for all the great ends for which the Father gave him) should not perish, but have everlasting life!" And this life is in his Son. So that God hath given Christ; it is his will to give Christ; and he actually does give him by his great word, for, and to, every soul that is made willing to receive him? May we come, then, and come repeatedly to receive this great gift, as we are invited, freely, "without money and without price." For the royal proclamation of heaven is, unto "whosoever will!" And not a soul that has a will, a desire after Christ, as God's unspeakable gift, but may, and shall, receive him as such, to his full satisfaction, joy and glory, present and eternal! And, having received Christ Jesus the Lord, even so let us walk in him; ever abiding in him, bowing to him, and living upon him, and all his immense fullness, to our rich supply, to his glory, and our joy; until we shall live with him, and be glorified together at God's right hand; where pleasures are new, and plenteous for evermore! And where, with the church triumphant, we shall join our eternal songs in far superior strains than we are capable of in the church militant, and say, to the endless praise of infinite grace, "Thanks be unto God for his unspeakable gift!" Great grace be with you!

  With affectionate esteem, and humble thanks for all favours,

I am, Madam,

Your humble servant, &c.

LETTER XVI. To Mrs. H.

My dear Sister in Christ,

It is well that our salvation is all of grace, from the foundation even to the head-stone thereof, of one pure piece of free, infinite, unmerited favour! That that same grace, which fixt upon us in God's eternal election; which bought us by our Lord's great redemption; which brought us nigh to God by the Holy Ghost's effectual vocation; which blest us with a free and full justification; and which sealed us with the spirit of adoption; will carry us on still, in its own almighty arms, through an increase of grace, into the ineffable bliss of eternal glorification. If God's free, rich, sovereign grace, did not do all for us freely, in the whole of our salvation, we were undone! For of ourselves we deserve nothing, we can do nothing. God's free grace must and will do all for us, in, by and upon us, through all time, to the praise of its own glory, unto all eternity! And, since we are so greatly unworthy, poor and needy, it is well for us that the exceeding riches of God's free grace in Christ are an immense and inexhaustible treasury! For

"God, who is rich in mercy, for his great love wherewith he loved us; even when we were dead in sins, hath quickened us together with Christ; that in the ages to come he might shew the exceeding riches of his grace, in his kindness towards us, through Christ Jesus."

If God, our own God, for us is rich, immensely rich in mercy; O, how well doth this suit our exceeding great misery! If he loves us with such as greatness of love, as brightly displays the glory of his great being; if he loves us with such a greatness of love, that the greatness of our sins, even when we were dead in sins, could never lessen; O, what a firm ground of faith is this to quickened souls; that none of all their sins, under which they groan, shall ever separate them from the love of God's heart! And how great may be our joy, that this great love of God, which freely forgives our great sins, will strongly subdue, and utterly destroy, our great iniquities! It was us, our persons, as chosen and considered mystically in Christ, and not our sins, that God so greatly loved. And the grand design of his great love was to save us from our great sins, by and through Christ influentially, initially, and completely; that it might communicate itself to us delightfully, through time and to eternity! If God, of his great love, hath quickened us together with Christ, mystically and influentially, "That in the ages to come he might shew the exceeding riches of his grace in his kindness towards us through Christ Jesus;" O, what a great salvation may we not, ought we not, to expect for such great grace! Our salvation is of grace; and therefore absolutely free, and of unmerited favour. Of his grace, whose nature and favour are infinite! And for the saved ones, in their salvation, God their Saviour will do such great things, as thereby to shew, to make a shew, before angels and men, before all intelligent beings, of grace, of his grace, of the riches, the exceeding riches of his grace; and this in a way of kindness; of kindness towards us through Christ Jesus: and that not for a few hours, or days, weeks, months, or years only; but for ages, in and through all the ages of time, and unto the innumerable ages of a blest eternity! Hence, then, my dear Sister, we may learn,

1. That God our Saviour hath well provided for our begun and complete, our present and everlasting salvation. There are unsearchable riches, of boundless, bottomless, and endless grace, stored up in Christ, to answer, even to an infinite overplus, all the vast expense of so great a work as that of the salvation of sinners, from all sin and misery, unto all holiness and glory, both present and eternal. Hence also we see,

2. That God's promise of life in Christ, unto all that believe in Jesus, is exceeding sure. "It is of faith, that it might be by grace, that the promise might be sure to all the seed." Had salvation been of works, and for its existence or continuance dependent on our obedience; had the scheme of it been thus laid or proposed; it would have been precarious, nay, impossible! But salvation by grace, unto all the happy heirs of it, stands upon a firm basis, upon an immoveable foundation, that is well able to bear the weight of so vast a superstructure! Again, let us learn from hence,

3. That it is our duty to deal by faith continually with this all-sufficient grace, which hath saved, which doth and will save us, so freely and fully. In every part, and in the whole of our great salvation, let us have recourse by faith to that infinite fund, that immensity of grace, which is provided and engaged to save us, in all respects, unto the uttermost! Once more,

4. "Having access by faith into this grace wherein we stand;" let us rejoice in hope of future glory. In doing and suffering the will of God, let us live to the honour of his grace here, and long for the blissful state hereafter when we shall warble forth the praises of its infinite glory through the circling ages of a vast eternity; while, with the church triumphant, we ascribe, "Salvation, and glory, and blessing, unto Him that sitteth on the throne, and to the Lamb, for ever and ever!" To which all the

adoring angels will say, Amen! Unto the God of all grace in Christ I commit you; and am, most affectionately,

Yours in the Lord, &c.

LETTER XVII.   To Mrs. H.

My dear Sister in Christ,

YOU ask me what I think of a person that can hear God's word with pleasure and delight, and join with others in prayer with much sweetness, and at times with a few friends can pour out his heart; and yet in secret is dead, lifeless and sleepy, and at times doth sleep while upon his knees; and is often so at the Lord's table? You tell me, likewise, that the person who labours under it is greatly distressed, and knows not what judgment to form of himself.—I answer:

As to the state of this person, whether he is a believer or not, it must be judged by his inward experiences, whether they agree with the accounts given in the word of God of those who believe in Christ with a true faith that worketh by love. If that person has been enabled to see himself a lost, miserable sinner, utterly undone by sin, and unable to help himself; if he has been made to loath sin, and himself for all his abominations, and earnestly to desire an interest in God, communion with him, and conformity to him, both in the present and future world; and if he has beheld an infinite all-sufficiency and transcendent excellency in Christ, the only Saviour, together with the exceeding suitableness of Christ's fullness to his every want; which hath made Christ amiable to his eye, altogether lovely in his view, and desirable and precious above all things to his heart; so that, looking unto him alone as the great Saviour, he rests entirely upon him for the whole of his salvation, from all sin and misery unto all holiness and glory; that person is a true believer, and in a safe state for eternity. And, if, when the love of God is shed abroad in his heart, the immediate fruit of it there is love to him again, or a desire to love God, in keeping his commandments, and in all holy obedience, to the praise of the glory of God his Saviour, in the whole of his salvation by grace; his faith is evidently that which worketh by love and evident it is from thence that he hath the glory of God at heart in all his religious appearances and performances. And, though he cannot serve the Lord so perfectly as he would, yet, if he mourns before God sincerely for all his imperfections, forgiving love shall be upon him, and strengthening grace communicated to him, and he may and ought to go on, by faith in Christ, rejoicing in hope of the glory of God, when mortality shall be swallowed up of life, and all natural and sinful weakness of spiritual and immortal strength,

Having given you a hint of the state of this person, if a true believer; I should next give you my thoughts as to his case. And to me it appears as lamentable as it is to himself uncomfortable. It was the saying of a servant of Christ that 'a Christian is what he is between God and his own soul.' Which should humble us in the dust for all our dullness and heaviness before God, and heart-wanderings from him, when we engage with him in secret duties. And, while we daily see and bewail our own impurity, we should be excited hereby to pray for the fresh exercise of faith perpetually, to prize more highly, and wash more frequently, in "the blood of Jesus Christ his Son, which cleanseth us from all sin;" and to draw nigh to God in the Redeemer's perfect righteousness, rejoicing in him as our great High Priest, who now appeareth in the presence of God for us, as holiness to the Lord, for the iniquity (or, to take away the iniquity) of Israel's holy things, that our persons and services may be accepted before the Lord continually.

As to the causes of that person's heaviness in divine service, they may be, 1. A natural disposition to sleep, which prevails in some constitutions more than in others. 2. Want of that sufficient rest which is necessary for the refreshment of nature. 3. Too much bodily labour, which exhausts the animal spirits. And, 4. Natural weakness, illness, or disorder of body. All which, as they are the fruits of sin, and as they unfit us for the service of God, are, and ought to be, matter of our humiliation before him. And, if these are not the principal causes, then weakness of grace, strength of corruption, and Satan's temptation, are the leading causes of this heaviness in divine service; which call for a more deep and solemn humiliation before God.

And, in order thereto, let that person, asking help of God, and as in his presence, set himself frequently and seriously to think what great dishonour he doth to the infinite Majesty of heaven and earth by sleeping before him, when he is and ought to be most intimately and closely engaged with him! Was he but to approach the presence of an earthly king, it would strike such an awe upon his spirits as would keep him from sleeping before him. Was but an holy angel to appear unto him, it would so raise his attention as to prevent his sleeping in his presence. And shall the Lord, the great Jehovah, the eternal I AM, who is Prince of the kings of the earth, and Lord of angels, yea, of all creatures and things in the universe, have less honour given him by us, his dependents, than we should give to his ministering servants, the angels of heaven, or even to his monarch-worms of this earth! Shall we sleep in his presence, before whom the holy angels veil their faces, as unworthy to look upon his infinite glory; and cover their feet, as unworthy to stand in his sacred presence; and stretch out their wings, with the utmost readiness to obey his commands! Shall we sleep in his presence, before whom all heaven adores, and all hell trembles! Shall we thus practically say that he is the basest and most ignoble of all beings! Yea, shall we thus tacitly say that he is not; or at least that he is not our God! or that he hath not done any thing for us which deserves our thanksgiving! or that he will not do any thing for us that is worth our seeking at his hands! And shall we, by sleeping in God's presence, thus provoke the eyes of his glory, and tempt his anger down; who with one look of his wrathful eye, was he to deal with us after our sins, could look us into hell, where sleep is for ever banished by unutterable and eternal torments!

And, as to sleeping at the Lord's table, what shall I say? Jesus did not sleep when he wrought out that great salvation for us which is represented to our faith, yea to our very senses, and sealed up to our persons in and by that solemn ordinance! No; our redemption from sin and hell, our redemption unto God by the Lamb's blood, cost our dear Lord such inexpressible torments in soul and body, as made it impossible for him to sleep in his dying agonies! And shall we sleep while Jesus Christ is set forth evidently crucified, and for us, before our eyes! Was his soul exceeding sorrowful, even unto death, when he bore the ineffable weight of our sins, and of the wrath of God due for them, to deliver us from the bottomless pit of eternal misery, and to raise us to the throne of immortal glory! And shall we be unaffected with his dying love, and unafflicted for our cruel sins, which pierced so deeply our dying Lover! Shall universal nature sympathize with the sufferings of the Son of God, as it did when Jesus died! Shall his great redemption be the wonder and praise of all heaven, the terror of all hell, and the admiration of all the saints on earth; and yet a redeemed sinner sleep when the Redeemer shews before him his redeeming love! Forbid it, mighty God! And never, never, let such monstrous ingratitude be seen or heard of more!

Thus let that person think, and think again, on the exceeding guilt of this great sin of sleep when in the special presence of God; to rouse all the powers of his soul into a detestation of it, and an holy watch against it. But let him not sink into discouragement on account of his sin, as if none of God's people were ever thus guilty. For our Lord's own disciples, Peter, James, and John, his favourites, when their suffering Master was in his agony in the garden, and bade them watch and pray, were so ungrateful, so stupid and senseless, that they fell asleep! They slept when their Lord was suffering, suffering for them, and when he told them that his soul was exceeding sorrowful, even unto death! They slept when they should have been watching and praying, when their Lord had commanded it, and when it is very probable they did really attempt it; and yet they were overcome by sleep! And, though they hereby sinned greatly, such was the boundless compassion of our Lord towards them, that he but gently rebuked them with a "What, could ye not watch with me one hour!" and forgave their iniquity, pitied their frailty, and accepted their desire to serve him as their kindness, notwithstanding their unkindness in neglect of service. "The spirit indeed is willing, says he, but the flesh is weak!"

But, though this may be some support to that person, under that great evil of sleep in divine service; yet let him not be unconcerned at it, nor despair of victory over it, but use all means against it. As, 1. Fasting and prayer; humiliation before God; and earnest petition to him for grace to help against it. 2. In secret prayer let him use his voice, a low voice, if he is in danger of being overheard. 3. Let his secret prayers be short and frequent. Five minutes, well spent in watchful prayer, is better than fifteen ill employed in dull and sleepy prayer; a short, lively prayer, will be more for God's honour, and his advantage, than a long, lazy prayer; by which he affronts the divine Majesty, and wrongs his own soul. And, 4. Let him engage in secret prayer when his stomach is empty, and before his body is weary and sleepy. For it is a matter of great moment that by earnest prayer he should reverently fear this great and dreadful name, "The Lord his God!" And may the Lord send him help from the sanctuary, and strengthen him out of Zion!

Wishing a rich supply of all grace unto all glory,

I am, my dear Sister,

Yours most tenderly, &c.

LETTER XVIII.   To --------

My dear honoured Brother in Christ,

I LONG for the Lord's appearance, and watch for him more than they that watch for the morning. I hope in his word, and wait for his salvation; and firmly believe that I shall not be ashamed. Though I am far from limiting the Lord, as to the way and time of his working; but one way or other, at one time or other, just as he in his infinite wisdom sees best, I believe he will appear, as a prayer-hearing and promise-fulfilling God, for his own glory and our joy. For he hath not said to the seed of Jacob, "Seek ye me in vain." "And this is the confidence that we have in him, that, if we ask any thing according to his will, he heareth us. And, if we know that he hear us, whatsoever we ask, we have the petitions that we asked of him." That is, God hears, receives, approves of, and will answer, every prayer of ours that is offered up unto him by faith in the name of Christ, according to his revealed will. And, if we know that he thus hear us, we have the petitions that we asked of him. We have them in grant, we shall have them in enjoyment, either in kind or in kindness, in the things themselves that we ask, or in things that are better; either in that manner, measure and time, which we desire, or in those that are more for God's honour, his people's good, and our own joy. Away, then, Satan; away, unbelief; be ye far hence, all our soul-enemies, that say to us, in times of providential darkness, "Where is your God?" For the Lord reigneth for ever, as Sion's God; and we that seek the Lord shall praise him. Great grace be with you!

I am very affectionately, dear Sir,

Yours in Christ, &c.

LETTER XIX.   To Mrs. R.

My dear Sister,

As to the words you mention, Rom. x. 13, "For whosoever shall call upon the name of the Lord shall be saved:" they seem to relate to ver. 12, "For there is no difference between the Jew and the Greek; for the same Lord over all is rich unto all that call upon him." Which words do shew the exceeding riches of the grace of God, and of our Lord Jesus Christ, to a remnant among the Gentiles, as well as to a remnant of the Jews; even to as many of both as belong to the election of grace, that were chosen of God in Christ to be vessels of mercy, and thus afore by him prepared unto glory; upon which they are called of God unto faith in Christ, unto their everlasting salvation by him. As ch. ix. 23, 24. "And, that he might make known the riches of his glory on the vessels of mercy, which he had afore prepared unto glory, even us whom he hath called, not of the Jews only, but also of the Gentiles." And thus ch. x. 12, "For there is no difference between the Jew and the Greek; for the same Lord over all is rich unto all that call upon him." That is, unto all those, both Jews and Greeks, that call upon him in faith, he is rich in salvation-grace. And then he gives the proof of it, ver. 13, "For whosoever (of Jews or Gentiles) shall call upon the name of the Lord shall be saved." This verse proves not, as some would have it, that any of the Gentiles have, or can have, salvation in calling upon the name of God, without faith in Christ: but the contrary is evidently intended in this verse, by the apostle's own explanation of it, ver. 14, "How then shall they call on him in whom they have not believed?" It is such a calling on the name of the Lord Jesus as proceeds from faith in him, which he speaks of. And next he shews the necessity of persons' hearing of Christ, in order to their faith in him: "And how shall they believe in him of whom they have not heard?" And then he proceeds to the ordinary way which God hath appointed for persons' hearing of Christ, in order to their faith in him: "And how shall they hear without a preacher?" The preaching of the gospel, then, by Christ's sent servants, is necessary unto persons' hearing of him; and their hearing of him unto faith in him; and their faith in him unto their calling upon him; and all these are necessary unto their salvation by him.

How vain a thing, then, is it for any one to think or say that persons may be saved by the light within, by attending to and improving of that? Which indeed is no other than natural conscience, or the light of the law, in some remains of it, in every man's conscience; which dictates what is moral duty, and reproves for what is sin. The light of reason is indeed from Christ, as head of nature; and so likewise is the light of the law, in that measure of it which illuminates every man's conscience, to direct him, in part, what is his duty, as a creature, towards God his Creator, and towards man his fellow-creature: and with light in these respects Christ, as head of nature, lighteth every man that cometh into this world of nature.

But this light, though it serves to deter persons from gross sins, and is for the preservation of human society; and also is sufficient to leave persons without excuse, that rebel against the dictates of it; yet is it vastly deficient as to directing any man in the way of salvation or as to shewing him the only way in which he can be saved. It is gospel light, from Christ the true light, the sent Saviour, darted into the minds of men by the Spirit of Christ, through the preaching of his sent servants, which alone can direct any man to the only way of salvation by faith in Christ; or it is Christ the true light, as head of grace, of gospel light, that lighteth every man that cometh into the world of grace, with the saving light of God's salvation by faith in him; without which every man by nature is in darkness, and in a perishing condition.

Hence, of the Gentile nations, who had the light of natural conscience, or the light of the law of nature as given to Adam, in some remains of it in their conscience, it is said that they walked in darkness, and dwelt in the region of the shadow of death; until the light (of God's salvation by faith in Christ) shined upon them through the preached gospel, Isa. ix. 1, 2. Matt. iv. 13, &c. And to the Ephesian gentiles the apostle said, "Ye were sometimes darkness, (i. e. before their conversion to Christ) but now (since the gospel hath shined upon you, and into your hearts, unto faith in Christ) are ye light in the Lord," Eph. v. 8.

And not only of the Gentiles, but of the Jews also, who, besides the light of natural conscience, had the light of the moral law, as given at Sinai, even of them it is said that they were in darkness, or ignorant of God's righteousness, Rom. x. 3. The heathens may have, as these Jews had, a zeal of God, but not according to knowledge, ver. 2, "For I bear them record that they have a zeal of God, but not according to knowledge. For they, being ignorant of God's righteousness (of the infinite righteousness of his pure nature, and of the extensive righteousness of his holy law, which reacheth to the inmost soul, and can admit of nothing less than perfect, universal, and perpetual obedience for a justifying righteousness; they, being thus ignorant of God's righteousness) and going about to establish their own righteousness (their good-meanings, well-wishings, and their doing the best they could; this their imperfect obedience they went about to establish, to make it stand as their justifying righteousness before God; and hence it is said, they) have not submitted themselves unto the righteousness of God," ver. 3. That is, they have not bowed themselves, or for their own salvation, to the complete righteousness of the Saviour, which God hath revealed in the gospel, to be received by faith, as the only justifying righteousness of a sinner. "For Christ (in his complete obedience to the law for us) is the end of the law for righteousness to every one that believeth, ver. 4. Whether they be Jews or Gentiles, whoever of both they are, that believe in Jesus, that are light in the Lord, Christ is to them the end of the law for righteousness. They seek no other righteousness for their justifying dress before God, but the complete obedience of his own Son. And, as for all other persons in the world, with all their light of reason, and of the law in the conscience, they are still in gross darkness, in a state of unbelief; and, "being ignorant of God's righteousness, they go about to establish their own righteousness, and have not submitted themselves unto the righteousness of God." They stumble at Christ and his rightcousncss, which is to be received by faith unto eternal salvation; and it proves to them a stumbling-stone, to their utter destruction: but unto them that believe Christ is precious, and his righteousness is submitted to, and received by them, as their only righteousness before God. And upon all them that believe, whether Jew or Gentile, this righteousness is, without difference, by imputaion of God's free grace, unto their everlasting salvation and eternal glory.

This is certain, my dear Sister, that there is salvation in no other—in no other person or thing, but in Christ alone. "For there is no other name given under heaven among men whereby we must (or can) be saved." "If there had been any law given, that could have given life (to fallen man) verily righteousness had been by the law." But, as the eternal, immutable law of God, which is perfectly holy, just and good in its own nature, and which bears upon it the infinite purity of God's nature, can admit of no obedience, for a justifying righteousness before God, but that which is absolutely, universally, and eternally perfect; it is hence impossible that it should ever justify a sinner by his own obedience to it. It is, in this respect, weak through the flesh; weak, as to any power of justification, through man's corruption and imperfection. And, whoever attempts to obey the light within, the light of the law in natural conscience, or the precepts of the law as given at Sinai, which is for substance the same law, to make himself righteous before God, and render himself acceptable to him thereby; instead of his desired salvation, he will bring upon himself swift destruction. The perfect law of God, and God according to his law, will curse him to death for his imperfection; and sink him thereby, as a just punishment, into eternal perdition. "For as many as are of the works of the law are under the curse." But, as "God in the fullness of time sent forth his Son, made of a woman, made under the law, to redeem them that were under the law," by his complete obedience to it, the active part of it, to the law's righteous commands; and, in the passive part of it, in his suffering its just penalty for our sins in the breach of it, in all that curse, wrath and death, which it denounced; by this means Christ hath perfectly redeemed sinners from under the dominion of the law, as a covenant of works, even all those that believe in Jesus; that approve of his blood as a sufficient satisfaction to divine justice for their sins; and that rely upon the merit of it alone for all their pardon and peace with God; and that approve of the righteousness of Christ as infinitely sufficient for their justification before God; that submit to this righteousness, and desire to be found in that alone, for all their acceptance with a God of infinite purity: these, even all these, who thus believe in Jesus, are by him redeemed from the curse of the law unto death, and made righteous in him before God, and accepted with him unto eternal life.

But, though the justification of those that believe in Jesus is perfect, and every way complete before God, as they stand in Christ their head; yet, alas, their sanctification in themselves is very imperfect. Though the dominion of sin is destroyed in their hearts, yet the being of sin remains there, and its mighty working at times is painfully felt by them; and will be so long as their heaven-born souls remain in the earthly tabernacles of their bodies: but he who hath justified believers completely, and hath begun to sanctify them in part, will perform his begun-work, and sanctify them wholly, in spirit, soul and body, by his free grace; and then, having meetened them for, will receive them to, eternal glory.

Meanwhile the just are to live by faith; to come to Christ continually, as miserable sinners in themselves, and to receive him daily, in all his fullness, as the great Saviour; who is held forth by the gospel, to be received by faith, as God's free gift to the chief of sinners, even unto whosoever will. And, thus coming to Christ, and receiving him as sinners, they are to draw nigh to God as believers, with all holy confidence, as being complete in Christ, and made and presented perfect in his spotless, glorious righteousness. And, being made the children of God by faith in Christ Jesus, they are to yield themselves unto God in love as obedient children; and, for the glory of that grace which hath saved them, they ought to direct their conversation as becometh the gospel. And, though they cannot obey perfectly, nor perform any duty without sin; yet they are to walk before God in every known duty, with a childlike liberty, as being heirs of immortal glory; bathing their persons and services by faith continually in the fountain of Christ's blood, which is set open to cleanse them from all impurity. They are to view Christ likewise by faith, not only as their dying sacrifice on the cross, but also as their living High Priest upon the throne; who now appears in the presence of God for us; to present our persons and services, though imperfect as they come from us, complete in his own perfections, as holiness to Jehovah, unto an everlasting acceptance with him. They are likewise to view by faith the Lord Jesus Christ, as their great pattern and glorious exemplar, as their head of representation and communication, in whom they stand, and unto whom they shall be conformed, increasingly and perfectly, both in soul and body, when faith shall be turned into vision, and hope into fruition, and their whole persons complete in bliss, at the morning of the resurrection. Thus the just, in the present state, are to live by faith; their faith to work by love; and in patience of hope they ought to rejoice in the glory of God. For, "as is the heavenly, such are they that are heavenly:" as Christ is, the head of his body the church, such are the members, as they stand in him mystically unto God, even now in this present world; and such they shall be from him shortly in themselves personally. For, "when he shall appear we shall be like him, for we shall see him as he is." We shall be like him in perfect purity; and "When Christ, who is our life, shall appear, we also shall appear with him in glory."

Hence, then, my dear Sister, what reason have we to bless God for his salvation in Christ! That, though we had destroyed ourselves by sin, and could never help nor save ourselves by the law, God, in his infinite wisdom, should contrive, and by his infinite grace provide, such a glorious way of salvation, by Christ crucified, in which all the perfections of God are glorified, and sinners eternally saved!

And what cause have we to bless God for "the gospel of Christ, which is the power of God unto salvation unto every one that believeth; to the Jew first, and also to the Gentile!" And, as faith cometh by hearing, and hearing by the word of God; how greatly should we prize a gospel ministry! And how constantly should we attend that word, by which faith is wrought! How watchful should we be, that we do not lend so much as the ears of our body to a legal ministry, that sets the creature to doing, instead of believing, for life! If the Holy Ghost, by the apostle, said of legal preachers, "If any man preach any other gospel, let him be accursed;" how jealous should we be of harkening unto preachers of the law, lest we ourselves hereby should be drawn aside to the works of the law, which expose all that are of them to the curse of the law!

And, though it is true that we ought to "Prove all things, and hold fast that which is good;" yet ought we not to listen to those teachers who dethrone Christ to exalt the creature; but, from what we have heard of their doctrine, we ought to flee from them as the most dangerous enemies, for God's honour and our souls' safety. Let us not venture to associate ourselves with corrupt teachers, and put the trial of their doctrines upon our weak judgements; and think we have warrant so to do from this scripture: but let us try all doctrines heard, or heard of, by the word of God, which is the only standard of truth, and by which, through earnest care and fervent prayer, with the teachings of the Holy Spirit, we may know certainly if the ministry that we attend is a gospel ministry. And, if we hear the gospel in its purity, let us abide under the sound of it constantly. For the sheep of Christ hear his voice, and know it; and a stranger they will not follow, for they know not, they approve not, the voice of strangers. Grace be with you!

I am, affectionately,

Yours in Christ, &c.

———————

LETTERS

ON

SPIRITUAL SUBJECTS;

SENT TO

RELATIONS AND FRIENDS.

BY THE LATE

MRS. ANNE DUTTON.

--------■-------

PART II.

Wherefore comfort yourselves together, and edify one another, even as
also ye do—I. Thess. v. 11.

SECOND EDITION, REVISED.

--------■-------

𝕷𝖔𝖓𝖉𝖔𝖓:

PRINTED FOR THE EDITOR, BY T. BENSLEY;

AND SOLD BY

R. BAYNES, 28, PATERNOSTER-ROW; J. EEDES, 2, NEWGATE-
STREET, AND OTHER BOOKSELLERS.

1824.

LETTERS, &c.

<hr>

LETTER XX.   To Mr. W.

My very dear Brother,

WE are strangers and pilgrims on the earth, and travelling to the heavenly country: how fare you by the way? Is your way smooth or rough, flowery or thorny, pleasant or grievous? I readily think you will answer, 'It is intermixed with crosses and comforts, joys and sorrows.' And this, my dear brother, is best for us. Was our way to be all delights, we should linger after earth, and loiter in our race to Heaven. And, was our way to be all griefs, our spirits would fail, we could not endure to the end. Therefore our glorious Captain leads us by a right way to the city of habitation. A right way when a rough way, to wean us from the earth, and quicken our desires after heaven. And a right way when a smooth way, to give a little ease to our wearied feet, that we may increase our spiritual strength, to march forward with greater eagerness towards our journey's end, allured by the excellency of God's loving-kindness, which gives us such seasonable reliefs, and ineffable sweets by the way, to hasten us to Immanuel's land, where, present with the Lord, our rest, our joy, our glory, shall be full and eternal. And how great is our privilege, that in all we are the Lord's care, that he always knows and does what is best for us, and will never leave us nor forsake us! How miserable should we be, were we left to our own conduct! How sad would be our case, if life or death, angels or men, things present or things to come, height or depth, or any other creature, could separate us from the love of God which is in Christ Jesus our Lord! But glory to God, enclosed with his inseparable love, and under its overruling influence, all things are ours, and we are Christ's, and Christ is God's. How cheerfully then by faith and love, and how patiently in hope, should we give up ourselves to divine conduct! Let us be careful about our duty, that we do not provoke the Lord to smite us; and then let us leave all things with him, who will overrule them for his glory and our joy.

I am at present, my dear brother, much tried and often cast down; but, blessed be God, I am not forsaken, and I know through grace that I never shall be. In times of providential darkness the enemies of my Lord, the enemies of my soul, frequently say, "Where is now thy God?" And thus at times I go mourning as with a sword in my bones. For nothing pierces a soul that God loves, that loves God, like a representation made to it, that it is an outcast from his special manifestative favour. But, though for a small moment the Lord may seem to forsake us, with great mercies will he gather us. And all his momentary, sensible and partial forsakings, serve as so many foils to illustrate the glory of his everlasting kindness, and make its future displays more bright in our view, and endearing to our hearts. For "the mountains shall depart and the hills be removed, but God's kindness shall not depart from us, nor the covenant of his peace be removed, saith the Lord, that hath mercy on us." Let us therefore make our refuge under the shadow of Jehovah's wings until all our calamities be overpast! Pray and give thanks for me, who have the Lord for my rock, for an house of defence to save me; who is my glory, and will be the lifter of my head. And may the grace of Christ be ever with your spirit!

I am, my dear Brother,

Your's most affectionately,

LETTER XXI.   To --------

My very dear Sister in Christ,

I REJOICE to see that your soul prospers, though (like the palm-tree) under pressing weights. Better is it by far to be exercised with various trials, unto growing spirituality, than to be at ease, and have the greatest flow of earthly pleasures, in carnal security. When things go smoothly with us, we are sadly prone, through the corruption of nature, to backslide from God, and to please ourselves in the creatures. But, when stormy winds blow us into trouble, and the sea of worldly affairs is rough; then, under the sanctifying influences of divine grace, we are brought to "cry unto the Lord in our trouble." And such is his infinite goodness, that, though we forgat him in prosperity, he bows down his gracious ear to our cry in adversity. He sees our sorrows with an infinitely tender eye; his bowels are troubled for us; and with an almighty hand he will surely have mercy upon us.

I rejoice, my dear sister, that you feel the sweet supports of the everlasting arms, and can bless God for Christ under stripping providences. And well you may, for the Lord, the everlasting God, who said unto you, many years ago, "Fear thou not, for I am with thee; be not dismayed, for I am thy God;" he is your God still, and will be your God for ever and ever; and He will be your guide, even unto death. Whatever else he strips you of, he will never strip you of himself, who is your glory. Nor will he take any creature comfort from you, but to give you more of his great and glorious self. And little of God is sweet, ineffable sweet, and far transcends the greatest affluence and confluence of creature delights. Glad may your heart be that He, the great I AM, the self-sufficient and all-sufficient Jehovah, hath said, "I will never leave thee, nor forsake thee." Never, never, never will he leave nor forsake you, in this life with all its trials, in death with all its sorrows, no, nor in life everlasting with all its joys! For sad would be your case even then, when brimful of joy and bliss, if God was to forsake you in the heights of glory; soon you would sink into the depths of misery. But, O, this "never leave thee nor forsake thee" reacheth unto, into, through, and beyond death, even unto life, of an endless duration! So that you may boldly say in faith, "The Lord is my helper, I will not fear what man can do unto me." The God of Jacob is my refuge and strength, a very present help in trouble." "Therefore will I not fear, though the earth be removed, and though the mountains be carried into the midst of the sea. Though the waters thereof roar and be troubled, thou the mountains shake with the swelling thereof. Selah. There is a river, the streams whereof shall made me glad" as a citizen of Zion. For, for ever will the Lord your own God be with you, as your support in trouble, your defence in danger, and your supply in necessity; as the fountain of your life, and the everlasting spring of all your bliss, joy, and glory, through time and to eternity!—Wherefore rejoice in the Lord as your portion, your present and eternal All; for the lines are fallen unto you in pleasant places, and you have a goodly heritage! Not so are the ungodly! Not so highly favoured, not so richly blest, is the greatest monarch on earth that is Christless! You are a child, an heir of God! and what can you desire more? Nothing, I am sure, that is not summarily comprised, and transcendently to be enjoyed, in the Lord your vast inheritance! Wishing the joys of God's salvation unto all increasing grace, and a weighty crown of glory, I am, a dear Sister,

Yours most affectionately in the Lord,

LETTER XXII.   To Mrs. H--------.

My dear Sister in Christ,

Iᴛ is indeed your unspeakable privilege that the fullness of Christ is inexhaustible! we are such empty, needy creatures, that, was there not an infinity of grace in him; it would not be sufficient for us. But, since it hath pleased the Father that all fullness should dwell in Him for us, even the fullness of the Godhead bodily; the fullness of Christ must needs be an immense and eternal ocean of full supply, of all supplies, to the church, which is his body, and to every one of the members related to that glorious Head. It is from hence the church hath been supplied with all grace, with light and life, joy and strength, through all the past ages of time; is now, and shall be supplied unto the end of time, and to a never-ending eternity. And still it is, and ever will be, and inexhaustible stock of grace, an undiminishable ocean of glory!

My dear sister, let us trade with this stock, walk and work in this strength, and come up from the weary wilderness, in every step of it leaning upon our beloved. Our days on earth are as a shadow, and there is none abiding. Time flies; eternity hastens; our Lord comes quickly. Let us watch and pray, and labour to do the work of the day in the day, not knowing but the present day may be our last day. For 'blessed is that servant whom his Lord when he cometh shall find so doing." I am glad that the Lord draws out your desires to glorify him on the earth. In order whereto abide in Christ by faith; and, as you derive strength from him, watch for, and improve all opportunities given you to do any thing for Christ, and for the glory of God in him. Let not any slip, nor say, they were little. For "He that is faithful in few things shall be ruler over many things." Herein in our Father glorified, that we bear much fruit." And there is no time, state, nor case, in which we are not called, some way or other, to glorify God. Let us ask wisdom of him daily, to direct us in and carry us through every duty, as if it were our last. Though we cannot do what we would, let us do what we can. And, though we cannot do so well as we would, let us ask for more grace, and in the Lord's service wait for greater assistance unto better obedience. Our greater Master delights to see us active, not idle, "not slothful in business, but fervent in spirit, serving the Lord." Serving:—it is in the present tense, and denotes the constant work of a Christian; that it should be one continued course of labour. That as soon as one work is done we should begin another, and when that is finished the next. And so pass on, from service to service, as we pass on from day to day, and from hour to hour, until we have "accomplished as an hireling his day;" the day of our life; for the night of death cometh, in which no man can work, in which we can do no more for God in this world. There is no idle time for a Christian. Nor is his constant duty unto him any severity, but is glorious liberty. The soul is an active spirit, and must have some way or other to be employed in service. And, if it serves not God, it serves sin and Satan. The service of Satan is the sorest bondage; and the wages of sin, for its woful service, is death. But the service of God is perfect freedom, and the reward of his work everlasting life! and, that his people might not wax weary, he hath provided strength for them according to their every day's service, and a vast variety, to make their constant employ easy. Nor doth the Lord call his servants to work and not to eat; but, as to work constantly, so to feast continually upon the sacrificed Lamb, and the choicest dainties of free grace in him, that so they may work cheerfully. For his servants shall eat when others are hungry; his servants shall drink when others are thirsty; and his servants shall sing for joy of heart when others howl for vexation of spirit. And, lo, "the way of the Lord is strength to the upright!" Constant work in nature exhausts its strength; but the strength of grace is increased by constant exercise. A spiritual man grows exceedingly weak by indolence and inactivity in spiritual work. If a Christian grows slothful in business, hath his loins ungirt, his shoes off his feet, his staff out of his hand, and begins to sit down at ease, as if there was no present work for him to do; alas for him, he becomes weak as water before he is aware! And, when called to engage afresh in divine service, alas, it seems to be rather a burden than a delight to him, because he feels so little strength, so little fitness for it himself. His harp hangs on the willows, and he is like an instrument that is out of tune; or like a sick man, half dead, that is very unfit for labour; until fresh supplies of grace from Christ renew his strength, to venture again in the way of duty, in faith and holiness, increasing in the fruits of righteousness; in which, under divine influence, he runs and is not weary, and walks and is not faint. A Christian that loves Christ is excited to diligence in his work, when he sees any thing to be done by him for his Lord's glory. And the more he doth for God, the more he may, the more he desires to do, in his delightful, life-giving service. Nothing kills the spirit of a Christian in this regard like a thought that he hath no more to do for Christ. When a Christian, that can say "for me to live is Christ," apprehends that he can do no more for his Lord in the world, the world becomes a darksome place to him, and to die he accounts his gain; that he may see and serve his Saviour in the glories of the upper world, without imperfection or interruption, for ever. But, while it is the Lord's pleasure to continue his people in the world, he hath always something for them to do in it; either actively or passively they are called to glorify his name. And, when we cannot do for Christ according to what, in a strict sense, we call doing, then let us suffer for him. Let us live to the will of God, whether it be in doing or suffering, until our race be run, and our course finished; and thenceforth we may certainly conclude "there is laid up for us a crown of righteousness, which the Lord, the righteous Judge, shall give us at his appearing." The present state is a state of work; but there remaineth a rest unto the people of God. May we then be faithful unto death, and our Lord will give us a crown of life.

I am, with great affection, Yours in Christ,

————

LETTER XXIII.

On the Lord's being the Portion of his People.

Dear Sir,

My heart rejoiceth in your consolation, by that sweet persuasion which the Lord gave you, that he was your portion. And, as to the word you want me to hint something from, alas, I am a child, and cannot speak! nevertheless, if the Lord by unworthy me will please to give you any hints for your furtherance and joy of faith, I would gladly bring what he sends from the words you request my thoughts upon, as they stand recorded, Lam, iii. 24, "The Lord is my portion, saith my soul, therefore will I hope in him."

This book of the Lamentations was written when the church was in great distress, being carried captive from Jerusalem to Babylon. And a most lamentable account of the church's sorrows, by reason of her grievous sins and God's sore chastisements, is herein given by the prophet Jeremiah, who lived to see those great distresses which he had foretold brought upon the Lord's people. And in this third chapter, (personating the church,) how bitterly doth he complain, ver. 1, &c. "I am the man that hath seen affliction by the rod of his wrath." And so deeply was the church humbled in the remembrance of her affliction and misery, the wormwood and the gall, that her faith seemed just ready to fail, ver. 18, "And I said, my strength and my hope is perished from the Lord." And this is often the case with the people of God, when in great distress. But, though Zion said, "The Lord hath forsaken me, and my Lord hath forgotten me." what said the answer of God to her? "Can a woman forget her sucking child, that she should not have compassion on the son of her womb? Yea, they may forget, yet will not I forget thee. Behold, I have graven thee upon the palms of my hands, thy walls are continually before me. Thy children shall make haste; thy destroyers and those that make thee waste shall go forth of thee;" Isa. xlix. 14, &c. And from this boundless compassion of Jehovah his special favour was hinted to his church in sore distress, to revive her faith and hope when just ready to die. Whence, presently after she had said "my strength and my hope is perished from the Lord," she has a turn of thought, and says, "this I recall to mind, therefore have I hope—it is of the Lord's mercies that we are not consumed, because his compassions fail not. They are new every morning, great is his faithfulness;" Lam. iii. 21. &c. It is as if the church should say, Why did I thus give way to unbelief, and as it were despair of seeing light again, because of the darkness which at present covers me? My case is indeed very lamentable by reason of sin, and by reason of chastisement; but it might have been far worse. I might have been utterly destroyed by the fire of God's wrath here, and cast into hell hereafter: this, this my sins have deserved. But "it is of the Lord's mercies that we are not consumed, because his compassions fail not." He hath rebuked us indeed, but not consumed us; in wrath he hath remembered mercy. His dispensations have been terrible; but his compassions never fail. They are new every morning. It is night with me now, as if she should say a night of weeping; but a morning of joy awaits me. "His anger endureth for a moment; in his favour is life." The life of my joy abides in his love, as the stream in the fountain, and shall certainly spring from it. His never-failing compassions will bring a new morning. Brightness upon me, and new displays of his tender mercy, will put a new song in my mouth to his glory. For she rises in faith, and says, "great is his faithfulness." His mercies are not only great; but this merciful Lord is my God, my covenant God; his mercy he keeps for me, and mercy afresh he will bestow upon me, according to the truth of his covenant promises and the greatness of his faithfulness. And thus, having called to mind the mercies of God towards her, with his covenant relation to her, she presently casts her eye upon the great and comprehensive blessing of his covenant, in which all particular blessings are comprised, and from whence they flow; viz. "I will be unto them a God, and they shall be unto me a people." And then breaks out in the triumph of faith, and abundance of hope, "The Lord is my portion, saith my soul, therefore will I hope in him;" ver. 24. It is as if she should say, I have lost my sweet enjoyments in the land of promise, and am cast out, desolate and full of griefs, into an enemy's country; but this is my joy, I have not lost my God; I have him still, I shall have him for ever as my God, and in him I have all things, even now, when I seem to have nothing. In him I have a fullness of mercy, and from him shall have plenteous redemption; an all of deliverances, salvations and enjoyments, that he sees best for me, in time, and a perfection of light, life, joy and glory, to an endless eternity. The Lord is my portion, while others have the creatures for theirs. He is my portion, himself hath said it, and in vain doth my unbelief, or any of my enemies, gainsay it. I believe the word of a God that cannot lie, and therefore my soul saith, as God saith, "The Lord is my portion, therefore will I hope in him" for all the blessings which he hath promised, and all the bliss that my heart desires, both in the present and future state. "The Lord is my portion, saith my soul, therefore will I hope in him."

Thus, Sir, you see how the words are brought in; and from them I would give some hints. 1. Of the portion itself, the Lord. 2. Of the persons interested in him, who may and ought to say, "The Lord is my portion." 3. Of the grounds which they have to hope in him. 4. Of the things which they ought to hope in him for. 5. Of the ends for which they should hope in him. 6. Of the ends for which they should hope in him. And, 7. Of the effects which shall certainly follow their hope in the Lord.—A hint or two,

1. Of the portion itself, the Lord. And oh, who among the sons of men, who among the glorious angels, can tell what this portion is! it is and ineffable portion! What then can a babe lisp out, a child that cannot speak? a child of unclean, of uncircumcised lips? what can a vile, sinful, earth-worm say, of the Lord of glory? what do, in attempting to speak, but darken counsel by words without knowledge? So that, were not God my Father to forgive, Christ my Saviour to sanctify, and the Holy Ghost my comforter to dictate what I may say, I should even sit down in silence. But, depending on the infinite grace of my Three-One God, on the fullness of Him whose grace is sufficient for me, I attempt to lisp a little to his glory.

And this name of God, the Lord, or Jehovah, is a name of essence, which denotes the self-existence, independence, all-sufficiency, immutability, immensity and eternity of the divine Being! it is an awful name, a glorious name, a precious name, as revealed in Christ! a name that displays all the goodness of the divine nature; a name in which sinners may trust. As Exod. xxxiii. 19, "I will make all my goodness to pass before thee, and I will proclaim the name of the Lord before thee, and will be gracious to whom I will be gracious, and will shew mercy on whom I will shew mercy." And xxxiv. 6, "And the Lord passed by before him, and proclaimed, the Lord, the Lord God, (Jehovah, Jehovah El, the strong God) merciful and gracious, long-suffering, and abundant in goodness, and truth, keeping mercy for thousands, forgiving iniquity, and transgression, and sin." Oh the glory of this ineffable name; of this self-existent, independent, all-sufficient, immutable, immense, and eternal Jehovah! angels vail their faces, as unable to behold his infinite brightness; and cover their feet; as unworthy to stand in his glorious presence! how then should sinners glance an eye to this dazzling, inaccessible light!

oh, it is God in Christ that we have to do with, God in our own nature, God in the slain Lamb; and therefore, with holy reverence, and humble boldness, we may draw nigh. We do not approach an absolute God, but God through the Mediator, through Jesus our Saviour! and in him this sacred name Jehovah is a most delightful name.

Let us then, with filial fear and joyful wonder, hear the Lord Jehovah proclaim his self-existence and independence, Exod. iii. 14. "I am that I am." I am! I am in and of myself, and independent of any, and of all my creatures. His all-sufficiency, Gen. xvii. 1, "The Lord (Jehovah) appeared to Abraham, and said unto him, I am the Almighty," or all-sufficient God: Jer. xxxii. 27, "I am the Lord the God of all flesh: is there any thing too hard for me?" His immutability, Mal. iii. 6, "I am the Lord, I change not, therefore ye sons of Jacob are not consumed." His immensity, Jer. xxiii. 24, "Do not I fill heaven and earth? saith the Lord." And his eternity, Isa. vliv. 6, "Thus saith the Lord, the king of Israel, and his Redeemer the Lord of hosts, I am the first, and I am the last; ch. lvii. 15, "the high and lofty One that inhabiteth eternity," (that dwell in my own eternity;) Rev. i. 4, "which is, and which was, and which is to come," the eternal Jehovah.

And, as this great name of God, which is peculiar to him alone, Ps. lxxxiii. 18, is a name of essence, that denotes his eternal self-being and all-sufficiency; so likewise his efficiency, or his giving being and sustentation to all creatures and things; Isa. xlv. 24, "I and the Lord that maketh all things, that stretcheth forth the heavens alone, that spreadeth abroad the earth by myself." Acts xvii. 28, "In him we live, and move, and have our being." Rom. xi. 36, "For of him, and through him, and to him, are all things: to whom be glory for ever; Amen."

And as this glorious name, Jehovah, signifies his giving being to all creatures and things in general, so to his promises to his people, and his threatenings against his enemies in particular, Exod. vi. 3, "And I appeared unto Abraham, and unto Isaac, and unto Jacob, by the name of God Almighty (or allsufficient to perform my promise); but by my name Jehovah (or as a God that had performed, or given being to the bliss I promised) was I not known to them." For it follows, ver. 4, &c., "And I have also established my covenant with them. And I have also heard the groaning of the children of Israel, whom the Egyptians keep in bondage; and I have remembered my covenant. Wherefore say unto the children of Israel, I am the Lord, and I will bring you out from under the burdens of the Egyptians, and I will rid you out of their bondage; and I will redeem you with a stretched-out arm, and with great judgments. And I will take you to me for a people, and I will be to you a God: and ye shall know that I am the Lord your God, which bringeth you out from under the burdens of the Egyptians. And I will bring you into the land concerning the which I did swear to give it to Abraham, to Isaac, and to Jacob; and I will give it you for an heritage: I am the Lord." Thus this name Jehovah signifies his efficiency, to give being to his promises to his people, and his threatenings against his and their enemies; and denotes his eternal truth and covenant-faithfulness, as the all-performing God, according to his covenant engagements. It is security enough to

God's people for all promised bliss, and will be productive of every jot and tittle of it, to a full completion, if he do but say to them concerning it, "I am the Lord."

And, lo, this great Jehovah hath engaged to be a God to his people, or to be their part or portion. As Gen. xvii. 7, "And I will establish my covenant between me and thee, and thy seed and after thee, in their generations, for an everlasting covenant; to be a God unto thee, and to thy seed after thee." 1 Chron. xvii. 22, "For thy people Israel didst thou make thine own people for ever, and thou, Lord, becamest their God." And, as this was the sum and substance of God's covenant with his people of old, which was the covenant of grace in a vailed dispensation of it; so when this same everlasting covenant is promised to be made with God's people under the gospel dispensation of it, in which it shines with an unvailed glory, this likewise is the sum and substance of it, Jer. xxxi. 33, 34, "This shall be the covenant that I will make with the house of Israel; after those days, saith the Lord, I will put my law in their inward parts, and write it in their hearts, and will be their God, and they shall be my people. And they shall teach no more every one his neighbour, and every one his brother, saying, Know the Lord; for they shall all know me, from the least of them unto the greatest of them, for I will forgive their iniquity, and remember their sin no more." And this everlasting covenant, which was to be, and is, new in its dispensation, is recited," Hebrews viii. 10,11,12; and the sum of it is, "I will be to them a God, and they shall be to me a people." Thus "the Lord, the Lord God, merciful and gracious, long-suffering, and abundant in goodness and truth, keeping mercy for thousands, forgiving in quity, and transgression and sin," makes over himself in Christ, in all his persons and perfections, unto his people, to be their God, their part, their portion for ever; so that, whatever God is in himself, that he is and will be to his people in Christ, for their bliss and joy, salvation and glory, both present and eternal! Hence this portion must needs be,

1. A rich portion. For "he that hath the Son hath the Father also," 1 John ii. 23; hath God in Christ. And the riches of Christ, and of God in him are unsearchable! Eph. iii. 9. They that have Christ, and God in him, for their portion, have all things, for time and for eternity, 1 Cor. iii. 21, &c. "All things are yours; whether Paul, or Apollos, or Cephas, or the world, or life, or death, or things present, or things to come; all are yours; and ye are Christ's; and Christ is God's."

2. A soul-satisfying portion. "My people shall be satisfied with my goodness, saith the Lord," Jer. xxxi. 14. "Whom have I in heaven but thee? and there is none upon earth that I desire beside thee," Psalm lxxiii. 25.

3. A present portion. "Thou art my portion, O Lord, in the land of the living; a very present help in trouble," Ps. cxlii. 5, and xliv. 1.

4. A sure portion. "I will make an everlasting covenant with you, even the sure mercies of David," Isa. iv. 3. "For the mountains shall depart, and the hills be removed; but my kindness shall not depart from thee, nor the covenant of my peace be removed, saith the Lord that hath mercy on thee," ch. liv. 10. Thieves cannot

steal this portion, Luke xii. 33. And the title to this is inviolably sure. "For men verily swear by the greater; and an oath for confirmation is to them an end of all strife. Wherein God, willing more abundantly to Shew unto the heirs of promise the immutability of his counsel, confirmed it by an oath; that by two immutable things, wherein it was impossible for God to lie, we might have a strong consolation," Heb. vi. 16, 17, 18.

5. A delightful portion. "Delight thyself in the Lord, and he shall give thee the desires of thine heart," Ps. xxxvii. 4. "I sat down under his shadow with great delight, and his fruit was sweet unto my taste," Song ii. 3.

6. An unfadable portion. "To an inheritance incorruptible, and undefiled, and that fadeth not away," 1 Peter i. 4.

7. A life-giving portion. "He that hath the Son of God (and so God in him) hath life," 1 John v. 12. "Because I live ye shall live also," John xiv. 19. "Your life is hid with Christ in God. When Christ, who is our life, shall appear, then shall ye also appear with him in glory," Col. iii. 3, 4. The life of grace, and the life of glory, is secured in, and communicated by, this portion. "The Lord God will give grace and glory, no good thing will he withhold from them that walk uprightly," Psalm lxxxiv. 11. Once more, this portion is,

8. An eternal portion. "My heart and my flesh faileth; but God is the strength of my heart, and my portion for ever," (or, my eternal lot.) "For this God is our God for ever and ever," Ps. lxxiii. 26, and xlviii. 14. All other portions decay, and end with time; but this is a portion that abides the same through all the successions of time; and, as an inexhaustible, unwasteable stock of life, light, joy, and glory, will endure for ever, to the endless ages of a blessed eternity. Death, which cuts off the enjoyment of all other portions, doth but put thee heirs of God into the full possession of him, their eternal inheritance, reserved for them in heaven. It the Lord, then, is a rich, a soul-satisfying, a present, a sure, a delightful, an unfadable, a life-giving, and an eternal portion; how happy, how ineffably and inconceivably happy, must that people be whose God is the Lord! Whose portion is the self-existent, independent, all-sufficient, immutable and eternal Jehovah! In this all-comprehending and incomprehensible God, the Lord, how great, how full, how glorious, must their inheritance be! But oh, who are they? This brings me to give a hint or two,

II. Of the persons interested in him, who may and ought to say, "The Lord is my portion." And these are all those that believe in Jesus. "For we are all the children of God by faith in Christ Jesus," Gal. Iii. 26. "And, if children, then heirs, heirs of God and joint-heirs with Christ," Rom. viii. 17. And those that truly believe, that have precious faith, the faith of God's elect, are,

1. All those who by the law of God, in the hand of his Spirit, have been convinced of sin, both original and actual; of heart and life-sin; of the guilt, filth, and power of sin; so as to make them cry out "Wo is me, for I am undone, for I am a man of unclean lips!" Isa. vi. 5. The truly convinced soul sees itself by sin to be

utterly undone, guilty and filthy before God, and loathes itself in its own sight for all its abominations. It sees itself by sin to be alienated from the life of God, and without strength to live to him as his law requires; which makes the soul cry out, "O wretched man that I am, who shall deliver me from the body of this death!" Rom. vii. 24. And thence,

2. Those who truly believe have been convinced of their desert, and danger of the wrath to come. As saith the apostle, "When the commandment came (in its revealed purity and spirituality) sin revived, (in its apparent guilt and felt power), and I died," Rom. vii. 9. I became a condemned, a dead man in law. The convinced soul sees that it has deserved all the curses of God's righteous law, and hears its terrible voice, "Cursed is every one that continueth not in all things which are written in the book of the law to do them," Gal. Iii. 10. He sees that all the curses of God's law are denounced against law breakers, against unbelievers; and that, having broken the law, if he abide in a state of unbelief, the curses of the law, in the dreadful execution thereof, will light upon him to his eternal damnation. And yet the soul sees that he is utterly without strength, either to keep the law or obey the gospel, to do any thing that God requires as he should or would," Rom. vii. 18. "How to perform that which is good I find not." And therefore,

3. Those who believe have been convinced of the utter insufficiency of their own righteousness to justify them before God. They see that "by the deeds of the law there shall no flesh be justified in his sight," Rom. iii. 20. That they are "all as an unclean thing, and all their righteousness as filthy rags," Isa. lxiv. 6. Both legal and evangelical, that no righteousness of theirs is perfect, but defiled; and so that nothing which they do, or can do, can be their justifying dress before God. Thus, stript of self-righteousness and strength, guilty and filthy, and in danger of eternal vengeance, their mouth is stopped before God, Rom. iii. 19. They have not a word to say why they should not be sent down to the pit of endless misery. They acknowledge the righteousness of God, and would justify him in his proceedings, if he was to send them down to hell, as to their own place. They admire his infinite patience and forbearance towards them, that they, who have deserved to be the objects of his flaming wrath, should yet be the monuments of his sparing mercy. And, from a quick sense of their having destroyed themselves, and their inability to help themselves, they cry out, "What shall we do? what must we do to be saved?" Acts ii. 37, and xvi. 30. And, when thus convinced of self-misery by sin and the law,

4. Those who truly believe have a revelation of Christ as the glorious remedy, given them by the Holy Spirit in the gospel. As 2 Cor. iv. 6. "For God, who commanded the light to shine out of darkness, hath shined in our hearts, to give the light of the knowledge of the glory of God in the face of Jesus Christ." It pleaseth God to reveal his Son to them. Christ, as the only Saviour, as an all-sufficient, able, and willing Saviour, in all his fullness and suitableness to the soul's case and wants, is set before the eyes of its enlightened mind. Whence Christ, a whole Christ, in his

efficiently. All desirable things for the souls of God's people, for their enjoyment in time and to eternity, are in himself essentially: or God, in his infinite essence, persons, perfections and glories, is an all-sufficient happiness for the souls of his people. And all things that he sees good, and that are really good for their bodies, for the present and future world, are in God efficiently: or, God hath the power in himself of working all things for the good of his people, according to the counsel of his will concerning them. So that in the all-sufficient God his people must needs have an all-sufficient happiness; a fullness, an immensity of goodness, laid up for them, for their full supply through time and to eternity; for their full salvation from all misery, and unto all glory. A small portion of this world's good may be a person's all: but, if there is not enough in it to answer all things, even all the necessities which may come upon him, there is no ground to hope for a full supply from such a portion. And, however large any earthly portion may be, if a man was possessor of the universe, all would be infinitely too little to answer the necessities, and satisfy the desires of an immortal soul; and therefore there is no ground to hope for an adequate bliss from an insufficient portion. But in the Lord, the all-sufficient God, there is enough, and infinitely more than enough, to supply the wants, and satisfy the desires, of every one, of one and all of that happy few, of that innumerable multitude, who have the Lord for their portion, unto all bliss and glory through time and to eternity; and therefore a solid ground have they to hope in him. As Jer. iii. 23, "Truly in vain is salvation hoped for from the hills, and from the multitude of mountains; (from all idol-gods, or creature vanities) truly in the Lord our God is the salvation of Israel." Another ground of hope in the Lord is,

2. Because of the Lord's immutability. For, as he has made over himself to be the God of his people, and hath promised to help and save them, to supply all their wants and fulfil their desires, "he is of one mind, and none can turn him, and what his soul desireth that doth he," Job xxiii. 13. His infinite love, grace and mercy, with his inviolable truth and great faithfulness, bind him in heart and hand to be a God to his people, according to his new covenant promise. And this his covenant he remembers for ever, "the word which he commanded to a thousand generations," Ps. cv. 8. If the Lord's people were entirely interested in his all-sufficiency; yet, if there was but a possibility that he should change his mind towards them, or alter the thing that is gone out of his mouth concerning them, or if their interest in him was precarious, so that any thing, either within or without them, could provoke him to disinherit them; alas! they would want a solid ground to hope in him unto the end. But, as he is the Lord that "changeth not, therefore the sons of Jacob are not consumed," Mal. iii. 6, and therefore they have a firm ground of hope that they shall never be ashamed; for they shall not be ashamed who in patience of hope wait for him, Isaiah xlix. 23. Again,

3. Because of the Lord's eternity. This is a precious ground of his people's hope in him. Was it possible (I speak with reverence) that the great Jehovah, the all-sufficient and immutable God, could cease to be, or to be what he is to his people;

if they could outlive their God, or their interest in him; alas for them! instead of abounding in hope, they might even sink into despair. But, oh, glory be to God in the highest, our Jehovah is the eternal God! and as such the eternal refuge, joy and hope of his people! "The eternal God is thy refuge, and underneath (for thy eternal support) are the everlasting arms," Deut. xxxiii. 27. Our Jehovah, from everlasting to everlasting, is God, Ps. xc. 2. And hence ariseth a strong ground of his people's trust and hope in him for ever, Isa. xxvi. 4. "Trust ye in the Lord for ever; for in the Lord Jehovah is everlasting strength." Or, he is the rock of ages; the support, defence, and supply of his people, through all the ages of time, and to the endless ages of eternity. Well then may they hope in him. Once more, another ground, which God's people have to hope in him, is,

4. Because the Lord has commanded it. And therefore the hope of that happy people in God, who have the Lord for their portion, is not presumption, but obedience; the obedience of faith in him, and love to him. For it is the express word of God, who is the portion of his people, "Let Israel hope in the Lord; for with the Lord there is mercy, and with him is plenteous redemption," Ps. cxxx. 7. And, "Let Israel hope in the Lord, from henceforth and for ever," Ps. cxxxi. 3. A hint or two,

IV. Of the things which the Lord's people ought to hope in him for. And these in general are all the good things which the Lord hath promised, and his people desire. "For the Lord God will give grace and glory; no good thing will he withhold from them that walk uprightly," Ps. lxxxiv. 11. But, more particularly, the Lord's people ought to hope in him,

1. For renewed manifestations and applications of pardoning mercy. For, as God's people sin daily, contract fresh guilt, and deserve fatherly chastisement, so they stand in daily need of fresh extensions of pardoning mercy, and ought to request it of the God of their mercy, and to hope in him for it. "For with the Lord there is mercy," Ps. cxxx. 7. And, if we confess our sins over the head of the great sacrifice, the Lamb that was sacrificed for us, God, even our Father, "is faithful and just to forgive us our sins, and to cleanse us from all unrighteousness," 1 John i, 9,

2. The Lord's people ought to hope in him for the subduing of their iniquities. The power of sin, in the old corrupt heart, is a great grief to those who have a new, a holy heart given them. For, though the Lord at times, for wise and holy ends, is pleased to leave his people to the power of sin, which makes them groan with an "O wretched man that I am, who shall deliver me from the body of this death!" yet "he will turn again, he will have compassion, he will subdue their iniquities," Mic. vii. 19. And has promised that sin shall not have dominion over them, because they are not under the law, but under grace, Rom. vi. 14.

3. The Lord's people ought to hope in him for the graces and comforts of the Holy Ghost; in that God hath promised to give his Holy Spirit to them that ask him, Luke xi. 13. To give him in his illuminating, sanctifying, and comforting influences; to give him as the spirit of grace and supplication, and as the spirit of adoption, to witness with our spirits that we are the children of God; to enable us

to cry, Abba, Father; to give us access through Christ, and fellowship with the Father and with the Son; to seal us to the day of redemption, and to maintain, increase and perfect the work of grace, until it be ripened into glory; or to perfect the good work which he hath begun in us until the day of Christ. For, in all these respects, God, even our Father, hath promised to give his Holy Spirit to them that ask him. And our dear Lord Jesus hath said, "I will pray the Father, and he shall give you another Comforter, even the Spirit of truth." He will send him in my name, and I will send him unto you. John xiv. 16,—26, and xvi. 7. Good reason, then, have the Lord's people to hope in him for his Holy Spirit in every respect for which he is promised.

4. The Lord's people ought to hope in him for his blessing upon all the means of grace, both public and private; in that he hath promised abundantly to bless Zion's provision, and to satisfy her poor with bread; and to draw nigh unto them that draw nigh unto him, Psalm cxxxii. 15, James iv. 8.

5. The Lord's people ought to hope in him for an answer to all their prayers; for the advancement of his kingdom and glory in the earth; for the salvation of the church of God, and of particular saints; for blessings upon all men, upon relations and friends, and upon their own persons; in that manner, measure, and time which God sees best. Because "He hath not said unto the seed of Jacob, Seek ye me in vain," Isa. xlv. 19.

6. The Lord's people ought to hope in him, as for all blessings upon their souls, so for all good things that he sees needful for their bodies; in that the Lord hath promised to supply "all our need according to his riches in glory by Christ Jesus." And that "those that fear him shall not want any good thing," Phil. iv. 19, Ps. xxxiv. 9, 10.

7. The Lord's people ought to hope in him, as for all the great and good things which he hath promised to them in life, so for his presence with them in death, and his reception of their spirits unto glory; because, "This God who is our God, will be our guide even unto death, and afterward receive us unto glory," Ps. xlviii. 14, and lxxiii. 24. And he hath said, "I will never leave thee, nor forsake thee," Heb. xiii. 5. This word "never leave thee," reacheth unto, into, through, and beyond death; and secures the Lord's presence with his people in all their trials, even to the very last, through all time, even to the last moment of it, and to a vast eternity beyond it. Well then may we, ought we, to say with the Psalmist, "Though I walk through the valley of the shadow of death I will fear no evil, for thou art with me: thy rod and thy staff they comfort me," Ps. xxiii. 4. And with our Lord (personated by David) "Thou wilt shew me the path of life; in thy presence there is fullness of joy; at thy right hand there are pleasures for evermore," Ps. xvi. 7.—Once more,

8. The Lord's people ought to hope in him for the resurrection of their bodies unto eternal life and glory at the last day; in that our dear Lord Jesus, the sent Saviour, hath given a promise of the resurrection unto life to every true believer, and that he will raise him up, according to the will of his Father. John vi. 40. "And

this is the will of him that sent me, that every one that seeth the Son, and believeth on him, may have everlasting life, and I will raise him up at the last day." That is, I will raise his dead body, spiritual, glorious, immortal, every way fashioned like unto my glorious body; which being re-united to his soul, and he in his entire person fitted for the enjoyment of glory, I will raise him to the full possession thereof in life eternal, to see and be for ever with the Lord. And this redemption four body the saints groan after, and, in the patience of hope, do and ought to wait for, Rom. viii. 23, &c. For then, O then, "When Christ, who is our life, shall appear, we also shall appear with him in glory," Col. Iii. 4. "We shall be like him, for we shall see him as he is," I John iii. 2. "The Lamb which is in the midst of the throne shall feed us, and lead us to living fountains of waters; and God shall wipe away all tears from our eyes," Rev. vii. 17. "And there shall be no more death, neither sorrow, nor crying, neither shall there be any more pain; for the former things shall be passed away," chap. xxi. 4. For to raised saints, in the new Jerusalem state, there shall be no night, and they need no candle, neither light of the sun; for the Lord God giveth them light; and they shall reign for ever and ever, chap. xxii. 5. But a hint or two,

V. Of the times when the Lord's people are to hope in him.—And they are, in general, all times, as Ps. lxii. 8. "Trust in him at all times; ye people, pour out your heart before him: God is a refuge for us: Selah." As there is no time in which the people of God do not want him to be their refuge and strength; nor any time wherein he is not an house of defence, an house of supply, to save them; so neither is there any time in which they ought not to hope in him: but at all times, whatever is their case, necessity, or distress, their desires or petitions, they ought to hope in the Lord for gracious answers, seasonable relief, and full supplies.—But, in particular, the times that I shall hint in which the Lord's people are to hope in him, are,

1. The time of great dangers; relating to soul, body, or circumstances; to ourselves, friends, or the church of God; in that, whatever are our dangers or distresses, "God is our refuge and strength, a very present help in trouble," Ps. xlvi. 1. And, as God is the Saviour of Israel in time of trouble, he ought therein to be Israel's hope, Jer. xiv. 8. "For the eye of the Lord is upon them that hope in his mercy; to deliver their soul from death, and to keep them alive in famine," Ps. xxxiii. 18, 19. And he hath promised to be with his people when they pass through the waters; that the rivers shall not overflow them; and when they walk through the fires, that the flames kindle not upon them, Isa. xliii. 2. To be a wall of fire round about them, and the glory in the midst of them, Zech. ii. 5. And when enemies are ready to devour them, the Lord of hosts hath engaged to come down to fight for mount Zion, and for the hill thereof. And that, "As birds flying, (hasting to defend their young from imminent danger) so will the Lore of hosts defend Jerusalem; defending also he will deliver it, and passing over he will preserve it," Isa. xxxi. 5, 6. Yea, the Lord saith that he bears his people as on eagle's wings, Exod. xix. 4.

That is, he puts himself between them and danger; as the eagle takes her young, and bears them on her wings, and thereby puts herself between them and their enemies, Deut. xxxii. 11. And a glorious instance of divine care, and an emblem of God's protection of his people when in great danger, he gave to the Israelites when the Egyptians pursued them, in that he caused the pillar of the cloud, that went before them, to remove and come behind them, between Israel and their enemies: which was as if the Lord should say, 'No enemy shall hurt my people, unless they can first destroy me, who am their defence from all danger.' Yea, the Lord keepeth his people as the apple of his eye, Deut xxxii. 10. That is, most speedily, tenderly, and safely. Well then may the Lord's people hope in him when in the greatest dangers, and encourage themselves in the Lord their God, as David did, when the people spake of stoning him, 1 Sam. xxx. 6.

2. The time of great fears: this is a time wherein the Lord's people ought to hope in him; in that, whatever be the object of our fears, there is salvation-help sufficient in the Lord to prevent or deliver us from the things which we fear. And, therefore, when under prevailing fear, we should say with the Psalmist, "What time I am afraid I will trust (and so hope) in thee," Ps. lvi. 3. For, if the things which we fear are not permissively decreed of God, for his glory and our good, he will prevent them; the God of our mercy will prevent us, Ps. lix. 10. And, if they are appointed for us, and the things we fear come upon us, the Lord will be with us in them, and deliver us from them. If he brings us through fire and through water, he will bring us thence into a wealthy place, Ps. lxvi. 12. He will make darkness light before us, and crooked things straight: these things will he do unto us, and not forsake us, Isa. xlii. 16. At what time, therefore, our souls are cast down and disquieted through fear, let us say to ourselves, as the Psalmist, "Hope thou in God, for I shall yet praise him, who is the health of my countenance, and my God:" and he will deliver me from all my fears, Ps. xlii. 11. and xxxiv. 4.

3. The time of great backslidings: this is a time in which the Lord's people ought to hope in him; in that, though God's people are bent to backsliding from him, he hath graciously said, "I will heal their backslidings, and love them freely," Hos. xiv. 4. Prevailing sin is a natural cause of prevailing fear, even in true believers themselves, either that they never had true faith given them, and so that the Lord will utterly forsake them; or, if they had, that the Lord will severely punish them, and cause his wrathful anger to fall upon them, so that they shall never more see good while they are in the world. But even at such a time as this, to help his people against dismaying fear, to encourage their hope in him, and so their return unto him, he saith, "Go and proclaim these words toward the North, and say, Return, thou backsliding Israel, saith the Lord, and I will not cause mine anger to fall upon you; for I am merciful, saith the Lord, and I will not keep anger for ever. Only acknowledge thine iniquity, that thou hast transgressed against the Lord thy God, and hast scattered thy ways unto the strangers under every green tree, and ye have not obeyed my voice, saith the Lord. Turn, O backsliding children, saith the

Lord; for I am married unto you; and I will take you one of a city, and two of a family, and will bring you unto Zion," Jer. iii. 12—14. Hope in the Lord then his people ought to do in times of backsliding. For the Lord will not cast off his people, but heal their diseases, and cause them to return unto him in a way of duty, under fresh displays of his restoring mercy: he will not forsake them for his great name's sake: because it hath pleased the Lord to make them his people, 1 Sam. xii. 22.

4. The time of great desertions. This is a time in which the Lord's people are to hope in him; in that at such a time he saith unto them, "Fear not;" and therein commands them to hope in him; as hope and fear are opposites, Isa. liv. 4. And adds further, to encourage their faith and hope in a time of desertion, "For a small moment have I forsaken thee, but with great mercies will I gather thee: in a little wrath I hid my face from thee for a moment; but with everlasting kindness will I have mercy on thee, saith the Lord thy redeemer," ver. 7, 8. When the Lord forsakes his people for a while, as to his sensible presence, sorrow filleth their hearts, as of he was gone for ever, (for time's ever, at least) and would be favourable no more. But "I will see you again," saith our Lord, "and your heart shall rejoice, and your joy no man taketh from you," John xvi. 22. Great reason then have we to say with David, when under desertion, "Why art thou cast down, O my soul; and why art thou disquieted within me? Hope thou in God, for I shall yet praise him for the help of his countenance," Ps. xlii. 5.

5. The time of divine chastenings. This is a time in which the Lord's people ought to hope in him. The people of God are apt to faint when under divine chastening, though it should be chiefly for the trial of their graces; but more especially when it appears evidently to be a rebuke for their sins. But we ought to "remember the exhortation which speaketh unto us as unto children, My son, despise not thou the chastening of the Lord, nor faint when thou art rebuked of him," Heb. xii. 5. And then follow the choice cordials which are given to raise and support our fainting hope when under the smarting rod, "For whom the Lord loveth he chasteneth, and scourgeth every son whom he receiveth. If ye endure chastening, God dealeth with you as with sons: for what son is he whom the Father chasteneth not?" ver. 6. &c. Here the love of God, as the fountain cause of chastisement to his dear children, with their relation to him as such, and the blessed ends of divine chastening, even their life and holiness, or the further measures of their holiness, unto a rich increase in the life of grace, and preparation for the life of glory; are the rich cordials administered to keep us from fainting under the sharpest rod, and to raise our hope in a chastening God. And it was at a time of great backsliding, of great desertion and great affliction, under divine chastisement, that the church said, "The Lord is my portion, therefore will I hope in him." Hope in him at such a time as this, though backslidden, forsaken, and so greatly chastened. Let us then, when under great chastisements from God, and the insulting triumphs of spiritual enemies, hope in the Lord, and say with the church, "Rejoice not against me, O mine enemy; when I fall I shall arise; when I sit in darkness the Lord will be a light

unto me. I will bear the indignation of the Lord, because I have sinned against him, until he plead my cause, and execute judgment for me: he will bring me forth to the light, and I shall behold his righteousness," Mic. vii. 8, 9.

6. The time of great temptations. This is a time wherein the Lord's people are to hope in him. in that, to strengthen our faith and hope in God, in tempting times, he saith, "There hath no temptation taken you but such as is common to man: but God is faithful, who will not suffer you to be tempted above that ye are able, but will with the temptation also make a way to escape, that ye may be able to bear it," 1 Cor. x. 13. And "we have not an high priest that cannot be touched with the feeling of our infirmities; but was in all points tempted like as we are, yet without sin," Heb. iv. 15. "And in that he himself hath suffered, being tempted, he is able to succour them that are tempted," chap. ii. 18. The infinite mercy and faithfulness of God our Father, and the inexpressible sympathy of the Lord our Redeemer, our High Priest and Advocate with the Father, should engage tempted saints to set their hope in God, who will seasonably succour and graciously deliver. We are, we shall be when tempted, more than conquerors over our grand enemy, Satan, through him that loved us: we shall overcome him by the blood of the Lamb, and by the word of our testimony, Rom. viii. 37. Rev. xii. 11.

7. The time of dark dispensations, when providence seems to thwart promises. This is a time wherein the Lord's people should hope in him; in that all things work together for good, even when they seem to make against us, Gen. xlii. 36. Rom. viii. 28. When the providence of God seems to run counter to what his dear children have apprehended in the promise; they are frequently, through the strength of unbelief and the temptations of Satan, as if they could believe and hope no more, trust in God and hope in him no longer: but are apt to say with the church, "My strength and my hope are perished from the Lord," Lam. iii. 18. "Our bones are dried, and our hope is lost; we are cut off for our parts," Ezek. xxxvii. 11. Until he is pleased afresh by his word and Spirit to strengthen their faith and hope in him, as their all-gracious, all-faithful, and all-performing God. So that, when there is no prospect of supply from any creature or thing round about them, beholding an all-fulness in God through Christ engaged for them, they can say, in the joy of faith and hope, "Although the fig tree shall not blossom, neither shall fruit be in the vines, the labour of the olive shall fail, and the fields shall yield no meat, the flock shall be cut off from the fold, and there shall be no herd in the stalls; yet I will rejoice in the Lord, I will joy in the God of my salvation. The Lord God is my strength, and he will make my feet like hinds' feet, and he will make me to walk upon high places," Hab. iii. 17, &c. For, when every creature-cistern is broken, and death written upon all things round about us, the fountain of living water abides; our life is hid with Christ in God; an all of supplies, deliverances and salvations, are summarily and permanently in the Lord, the living fountain, the boundless ocean of all our bliss; from whence fresh streams of joy and life shall flow abundantly, in manner, in measure, and time, as his infinite wisdom sees best for us, and most for his own

glory. How blessed then is the man whose hope the Lord is! Jer. xvii. 7, 8. And how great is our encouragement, even in the darkest seasons, to believe in hope, even against hope, Rom. iv. 18.

8. The time of pressing necessities. This is a time in which the Lord's people ought to hope in him; in that our extremity is God's opportunity: "In the mount of the Lord it shall be seen," Gen. xxii 14. When Abraham was just ready to slay Isaac, the Lord called unto him out of heaven, and he looked behind him, and, behold, a ram caught in a thicket by his horns, to be offered up for a burnt offering instead of his son! ver. 13. When things are come to the last pinch, as it were, and the people of God are just ready to give up hope; when they are reduced to such extreme necessity, that they must perish if help doth not come speedily; then the Lord will see, and provide. That is the time wherein the Lord chuseth to appear; the more to commend his care for his people, and to exalt his mercy and truth, his faithfulness and power, in their salvation; and to learn them to trust and hope in him for the time to come: as a God that raiseth the dead, that brings life to his people out of providential deaths, that hath delivered, that doth deliver, and that in future straits will yet deliver. For, though the Lord, for wise and holy, great and gracious ends, doth try his people greatly, he will help them, and that right early, Ps. xlvi. 5. Great reason then have we to hope in the Lord in times of pressing necessity, and of the greatest extremity: for "happy is the man that hath the God of Jacob for his help, whose hope the Lord is," Ps. cxlvi. 5. The Lord waiteth to be gracious to his people, as a God of judgment that knows, and will take, the fittest time to help and save them: and, "blessed are all they who" in patience of hope, "wait for him," Isa. xxx. 18.

9. The time of great desires. This is a time in which the Lord's people ought to hope in him; in that he hath said, "Open thy mouth wide, and I will fill it," Ps. lxxxi. 10. When the Lord is about to deliver his people from great distresses unto great enjoyments, he usually works in their hearts great desires after promised mercies: and these are frequently attended, at times, with great fears that we shall not have the desires of our heart granted, by reason of our great unworthiness, vileness, and provocations. But let Israel hope in the Lord at such a time as this: for the Lord, who thus prepares their heart, will cause his ear to hear, to hear the desire of the humble, Ps. x. 17. He will give them, in manner, measure, and time, as he sees best, the desires of their heart, Ps. xxxvii. 4. There is infinitely enough in God to fill, and overflow, the most enlarged desires of his dear children. And he is a God doing wonders, that hath engaged by covenant to work marvels, Exod. xv. 11, and xxxiv. 10. And hath promised to make all his goodness pass before us, chap. xxxiii. 19. That his people shall be satisfied with his goodness, Jer. xxxi. 14. That he will pour water upon him that is thirsty, and floods upon the dry ground, Isa. xliv. 3. That he will open rivers in high places, and fountains in the midst of the vallies; make the wilderness a pool of water, and the dry land springs of water, chap. xli. 18. And that they which hunger and thirst after righteousness shall have the

blessedness to be filled, Matt. v. 6, &c. What abundant reason then have the Lord's people to hope in him in the time of their greatest desires, and, in a word, in all the times of their perplexities, distresses and necessities? in that our God, our prayer-hearing, our promise-performing God, our God who hath all fullness in himself, and will communicate the same unto us through Christ, "is able to do exceeding abundantly above all that we ask or think, according to the power that worketh in us! and, unto him be glory in the church by Christ Jesus, throughout all ages, world without end, Amen." Ephes. iii. 20, 21.—Once more,

10. The whole term of time, from the Lord's giving to the fulfillment of his promise. This is the general time in which the Lord's people ought to hope in him; in that the Lord is a God of judgment, and waits to be gracious in the fulfillment of his promises at the fittest season, at the time which in infinite wisdom he hath appointed, when salvation from all distress, and unto all bliss, shall be most for his glory and praise, and for our good and joy. And, therefore, blessed are all they who thus in hope wait for him, Isa. xxx. 18. For, though the vision should tarry in our apprehension, we are called in patience of hope to wait for it; in that at the end it shall speak, and not lie, it shall surely come, and shall not tarry one moment beyond the time fixed for it in God's counsels, Hab. ii. 3. When the Lord applies promises to our hearts by the Holy Ghost, and faith gets a view, in the glass of the promise, of the promised mercy, in its sureness and nearness, (as faith is the evidence of things not seen, and the substance of things hoped for) love, instantly upon the wings of eager desire, hastes apace to meet it, and, in the sweet expectation of hope, we wait for it for a while. But, if the Lord stays longer than we expected, (as, from our earnest desire after promised mercies, we often fix a time too soon for their birth, before the Lord's time of their full preparation to be brought forth); or if our God do not appear in that way which we thought of and desire, to give us the blessings we seek in the present state; or if, through soul-darkness and distress, a vail is drawn over our interest in the superior blessings of the life to come; alas for us, so weak is our faith that we are ready to give up our hope and expectation of the Lord's promise! and therefore we are exhorted to "gird up the loins of our mind, to be sober, and hope to the end, for the grace that is to be brought unto us at the revelation of Jesus Christ," 1 Pet. i. 13. Which makes it our duty to hope for promised blessings until the time of the promise is fully come, or to hope in the Lord until the morning of deliverance appears. For then, "God will help us, and that right early," Ps. xlvi. 5. When the time, even the set time, to favour us is come, the Lord will arise, and have mercy upon Zion, Ps. cii. 13. And this general time, of hoping to the end, respects all the particular times wherein it is our duty to hope in the Lord; in every of the times of our necessity and distress we should hope to the end, for supplying and delivering grace. Thus in patience of hope we should wait for the Lord, "more than they that watch for the morning, Ps. cxxx. 6. Who never give over looking for day till the dawning light begins to scatter the darkness of the night. For, "then shall we know, if we follow on to know the Lord; his going forth

(to help and save his people) is prepared as the morning (which will certainly appear at the appointed season); and he shall come unto us as the rain; as the latter, and as the former rain, unto the earth," Hos. vi. 3.—But a hint or two,

VI. Of the ends for which the Lord's people ought to hope in him. And these may be considered, 1. With respect to God. And 2. With respect to ourselves.

1st. With respect to God. And the ends for which the Lord's people ought to hope in him, with respect to himself, are,

1. For God's honour. As the Lord is our king and lawgiver, and has commanded his people to hope in him for ever, Ps. cxxxi. 3, it is for his honour as such to be herein obeyed. And as the Lord hath declared that he is a father unto Israel, and has said, "As a father pitieth his hildren, so the Lord pitieth them that fear him, Jer. xxxi. 9, Ps. ciii. 13, it is for his honour, as a compassionate father, that his needy distressed children hope in him as such. Again, as the Lord is an all-sufficient God, and as such the portion of his people, and has promised to help and save them as their God, Gen. xvii. 1, Isa. xli. 10, it is for his honour, as such, that his people set their hope in him in all the times of their necessity and distress. And so far as we give up hope, and yield to fear, we are so far guilty of dishonouring the Lord as our king and lawgiver, as our compassionate father, and as our all-sufficient God and portion. And he may justly reprove us with an "If I be a father, where is mine honour? or if a master, where is my fear?" Mal. i. 6. The Lord our God is an object so worthy of our trust and hope, that we cannot walk worthy of him as God, and our God, if we do not trust and hope in him, even at all times; as we are exhorted to do, 1 Thes. ii. 12. Ps. lxii. 8. And, were there no other motive to hope in the Lord than this, of God's honour, that we thereby give him the glory due unto his name; O how strong a motive should this be, will this be, to a soul that loves the Lord, to put its trust under the shadow of his wings, and to hope in him, even in the darkest times! If we were not to be delivered at last, as all those shall be who continue to the end to hope in the Lord; yet is it not better, far better, to give glory to God by hope in him, than by fear and despair to dishonour him? We so far answer the end of our being, as by hope in God we give glory to him the author of it. And the more we trust and hope in God even in the darkest seasons, and in the greatest difficulties, the more glory we give to his great name, as Abraham, the father of the faithful, "being strong in faith, gave glory to God," Rom. iv. 18—20.

2. For the Lord's pleasure. This is another end, with respect to God, for which his people should hope in him. For, lo, "the Lord taketh pleasure in them that fear him, in those that hope in his mercy," Ps. cxlvii. 11. And how great a motive ought this to be to hope in the Lord, to all those that love him, in that they thereby please and delight him? Oh, a thought of delighting the heart of God our father, of the Lord our redeemer, and of the Holy Ghost our comforter, by hoping in the Lord; how should it engage us to this God-honouring, this God-pleasing duty! Most surely, if we love the Lord, and are in the exercise of that love, we shall hope in

him, that thereby we may walk worthy of God, as our God, unto all pleasing. Col. i. 10.—And,

3. That God may save his people in that way which he hath appointed. This is another end, with respect to God, for which the Lord's people ought to hope in him. Thus the Psalmist, in the name of the Lord, commands us to be of good courage; and gives the promise, "He shall strengthen your heart, all ye that hope in the Lord," Ps. 24. The promise of salvation-strength is given to those that are of good courage, and that hope in the Lord; as this is the way which he hath appointed us to wait for him in, and as this is the way wherein the Lord will communicate saving help unto his people, according to his promise. Just in like manner as of Abraham the Lord said, "For I know him, that he will command his children and his household after him, and they shall keep the way of the Lord, to do justice and judgment; that the Lord may bring upon Abraham that which he hath spoken of him," Gen. xviii. 19. Again, the ends for which the Lord's people ought to hope in him may be considered, 2dly, With respect to ourselves. And these are,

1. For our soul-stay and rest in times of trouble; in that hope is said to be an anchor sure and steadfast, which entereth into that within the veil, Heb. iv. 19. The grace of hope, which lays hold of Christ, and on God in him, the object of hope, is of the same use to the soul in times of trouble as the anchor is to the ship in a storm, which keeps it from being driven away with the tempest, wither wind and water please. Whither, O whither, would the souls of God's people be driven, in times of prevailing corruption, awful desertion, and sore temptation, was it not for hope in the Lord! "I had fainted," says the Psalmist, "unless I had believed to see the goodness of the Lord in the land of the living," Ps. xxvii. 13. "For we are saved by hope (says the apostle:) but hope that is seen is not hope; for what a man seeth, why doth he yet hope for? But, if we hope for that we see not, then do we with patience wait for it," Rom. viii. 24, 25. The whole of that great and eternal salvation, which God hath promised, and which faith beholds afar off, becomes the object of our hope: and so, likewise, all those time-salvations which God works for his people, and which faith beholds in particular promises, before they visibly appear to sense, become the matter of our hope, and are the things which we hope for. And by this hope we are saved; that is, we not only see the promised salvation to be full and sure in the glass of the promise; but the hope of it also brings present salvation to the soul, from that anxiety and distress of mind, whicn would inevitably be caused by the waves of trouble and the winds of temptation, if we had not hope of seasonable relief, and approaching deliverance: "For, if we hope for that we see not, then do we with patience (or sweet quietude of soul) wait for it." Aye, though we are called to have long patience, yet hope, abounding hope, through the power of the Holy Ghost, strongly stays the mind, and stablisheth the heart under a sweet persuasion that the coming of the Lord (to help and save us) draweth nigh, Jam, v. 7, 8.—And,

2. For our deliverance from trouble, and salvation unto all that joy and glory which the Lord hath promised. This is another end, with respect to ourselves, for which the Lord's people ought to hope in him; in that "the eye of the Lord is upon them that hope in his mercy, to deliver their soul from death." And his saving mercy shall be upon them according as they hope in him, Ps. xxxiii. 18, &c.—But a hint or two in the last place,

VII. Of the effects, which shall certainly follow our hope in the Lord. And these in general are as numerous as the good things which God hath promised, and for which we hope; but may be summed up in two particulars. As,

1. All those supports, deliverances, and enjoyments, which we want and wish for, relating to our souls, bodies, or circumstances, ourselves or others, the church of God or the world, in this present state: even all those good things which the Lord hath spoken, and which it is our duty to hope for in him, in this life, shall certainly be given, as the effect of that our hope, in manner, measure and time, as the Lord sees best, most for his glory and our advantage. For 'the hope of the righteous (in these respects, in the enjoyment of the blessings hoped for) shall be gladness," Prov. x. 28.—And,

2. All the blessings of that eternal life which God that cannot lie hath promise, and which believers now live in the hope of, shall certainly follow, as the happy effects of that their hope in the Lord: or, all the blessings of the life and world to come shall be the certain effects of that good hope through grace, which the Lord's people have in him respecting the state of future glory. For, as surely as God, that cannot lie, hath promised eternal life to them that believe in Jesus, so surely shall all the glories thereof be given to believers, as the blessed effects of their hope of eternal life, Tit. i. 1, 2. For unto them who, being justified by grace, are made heirs, according to the hope of eternal life, Titus iii. 7, and in hope thereof are induced to a patient continuance in well-doing, while they seek for glory, honour, and immortality, God will give eternal life, Rom. ii. 7. "The righteous hath hope in his death," Prov. xiv. 32. The hope of immortal glory, as soon as ever his spirit is set free from its mortal flesh. And by the gates of death the spirits of believers enter into life, into all the glories of that perfect and endless life, which respect a separate state, and for which, while in the body, they had so long hoped and waited: their hope then shall be turned into eternal enjoyment.

And O the ineffable glories of that blessed hope which awaits our whole persons at the glorious appearing of the great God and our Saviour Jesus Christ! Tit. ii. 13. Of that eternal life, into which raised saints shall enter when called to inherit the kingdom of glory, to the innumerable ages of a blessed eternity; Matt. xxv. 34, 46. "Eye hath not seen, nor ear heard, neither hath it entered into the heart of man to conceive," fully, no nor a thousandth part, of those great things, which God hath prepared for them then, who now in faith and hope wait for him! Isa. lxiv. 4. Then those happy souls, who by the Father of spirits are begotten again to a lively hope, by the resurrection of Jesus Christ from the dead, shall, in and with him, possess that vast inheritance, incorruptible, undefiled, and that fadeth not away, which is now reserved for them in heaven, who are kept, by the power of God, through faith unto salvation, which is ready to be revealed, 1 Pet. i. 3, &c. To their inheritance in light: in light without darkness, and in life without an end, Col. i. 12. Ps. xvi. 11. Then the children and heirs of God, Rom. viii. 17, as overcomers through the Lamb's love and blood, shall be advanced to inherit all things; yea, to the full possession of the Lord their portion; for he, for their full and eternal enjoyment, will be their God, Rev. xxi. 7. The Lord shall be their everlasting light, and their God their glory! Isa. lx. 19. Then all their sorrows shall be finished, and their desires accomplished. "The ransomed of the Lord shall come to Sion (above) with songs; everlasting joy shall be upon their heads, and sorrow and sighing shall flee away," Isa. xxxv. 10. That hope, which, being long deferred in their apprehension, had used to make their heart sick, in their accomplished desire shall be sweet to their soul, and a tree of life, of life ineffable and eternal! Prov. xiii. 12, 19. If then the hope of the righteous shall be gladness, in such great and blessed effects, in the present time, and in the future state to a glorious eternity, what great cause have we to say, with the church. "It is good for a man that he both hope and quietly wait for the salvation of the Lord!" Lam. iii. 26. And in the words on which you desire my thoughts, "The Lord is my portion, saith my soul, therefore will I hope in him!" ver. 24.

To close the whole, then, dear Sir,—Is the Lord, the self-existent, independent, all-sufficient, immutable, immense, and eternal Jehovah, your portion? And is he mine? O let us admire our portion! The lines are fallen unto us in pleasant places, yea we have a goodly heritage! Let us adore that free, rich grace, that distinguishing infinite favour, which made the Lord our portion while thousands round about us have only the creatures and things of this perishing world for theirs! What are we, or what were our father's house, that the Lord should bring us hitherto!—Let us delight in our portion: it is infinitely excellent, full and eternal! Let us live upon our portion: it will maintain us well, though all things else should fail: for lo, it is an immensity of all fullness, to supply our every want, that is inexhaustible, that can never be drawn dry, lessened, nor sunk one hair's breadth!—Let us hope in our portion; for all desirable things, that we can want to wish for, are comprised in it, and shall richly descend upon us from it!—Let us rejoice in our portion; for an ocean of pleasures it is, and will be to us, through time and to eternity!—Let us walk worthy our portion; for it is so worthy of our whole hearts, that we cannot set our affection of the little trifles of this earth without dishonouring our great and heavenly inheritance!—Let us live to the glory of our portion; for it well deserves our praises, that our language should be continually, in heart, lip, and life, "thanks be to God for the unspeakable gift" of himself in his dear Son! Yea, let us glory in our portion; for whatever we lose, we can never lose our inheritance; whatever the Lord takes from us, he will never take himself away from us; nor will he ever take any thing from us, but to give more of himself unto us, to endear himself the more to us, and our hearts the more to him, who is our all in prosperity, our all in adversity, in life, in death, through time and to eternity!—And since the Lord is our portion, let us follow on to know him; to enjoy him increasingly in this world, and perfectly in the world to come: "rejoicing in hope of the glory of God," Rom. V.2.

In a word, Sir, if the Lord is the portion of his people; if the persons interested in him are true believers; if the grounds which they have to hope in him are so firm; if the things for which they should hope in him are so many; if the times when they are to hope in him are all seasons, even the most trying; if the ends for which they should hope in him are so great, and if the effects which shall certainly follow their hope in the Lord are sl glorious, both for the present and future state, for time and for eternity: O how happy, how ineffably and eternally happy, is that people, is that person, whose God is the Lord! Ps. cxliv. 15. Happy they are in all cases, at all times, and unto all eternity! Happy beyond expression! Happy beyond conception! happy in life! happy at death! happy at judgment! happy, transcendently happy in God, the eternal source, sum, and centre of all their bliss, unto ages without end!

And, on the contrary, what tongue can tell, or heart conceive, the misery, the present and endless misery, of those persons who have not the Lord for their portion! Who are the men of the world, who live and die without faith in Christ, and repentance towards God, and so have their portion only in this life, their good things here, and lift up their eyes in the torments of hell for ever! Ps. xvii. 14. Luke xvi. 23. Mark ix. 43.—And, as our souls are spirits, that must have an eternal existence, either in glory or in misery inexpressible and endless; Oh, of what vast moment are eternal things! and how doth it behove every poor sinner, that hears of the great Saviour, to seek an interest in Christ, and in God through him, without delay! to-day, even while it is called to-day! Heb. iii. 13, 15. To seek the Lord while he may be found, and to call upon him while he is near! Isa. lv. 6. Since, for the encouragement of poor sinners, the Lord says, "Let the wicked forsake his way, and the unrighteous man his thoughts, and let him return unto the Lord, and he will have mercy upon him, and unto our God, for he will abundantly pardon!" ver. 7. And, since our dear Lord Jesus "is able to save to the uttermost all them that come unto God by him," Heb. vii, 25; and hath said, "Come unto me, all ye that labour and are heavy laden, and I will give you rest," Mat. xi. 28; "and him that cometh unto me I will in no wise cast out," John vi. 37;—let us then, dear Sir, who have tasted that the Lord is gracious, who have good hope in the Lord as our portion, endeavour to win other souls to partake with us of the same happiness, that they may be heirs with us of the grace of life: and join with the church and people of God to say in faith, and from blessed experience, "The Lord is my portion, saith my soul, therefore will I hope in him: to whom be glory and dominion for ever and ever." Amen.

Thus, dear Sir, you have my poor thoughts on the words you requested. And, if any hint given is of use to your dear soul, it will be my joy, and to the Lord alone be all the glory; in whom I am very affectionately, dear Sir,

Your sincere friend and servant,

———————

LETTER XXIV.   To --------.

Honoured and very dear Sir,

GREAT is the grace of God, and my joy in him, that he was pleased to make my last of use unto you, to strengthen and encourage you in your great Master's work. I am glad, dear Sir, that you are sometimes pleased with your work, to be employed in the service of the Lord. And likewise that you have a humbling sight of your own insufficiency for it. That is your preparation, by grace, for the glory of your designed service. It is good for the greatest of the Lord's servants to be the least and last in their own esteem. For with the apostle they may truly say, "When I am weak, then am I strong." When the servants of Christ are nothing but weakness and un-worthiness in themselves, discernedly, then his grace is sufficient for them, and his power rests upon them, experimentally. Nothing excludes Christ, and his fullness, like proud self, or the want of a deep sense of our own emptiness. O what a Christ-dishonouring, what a Christ-piercing thing, is the sin of pride; or an high conceit of self-sufficiency, before, in, or after any service! And, on the other hand, when, to shew us our own nothingness, and humble us in the dust, our Lord withdraws from our spirits, and we sadly feel our own insufficiency; then, O then how apt are we to sink into unbelief, as if the grace of Christ was not sufficient for us! And O what a great dishonour doth this great sin reflect upon the infinite glory and immense fullness of our great Lord! And how deeply, by this spear, do we pierce him! Truly our wicked, desperately wicked hearts, dishonour and pierce our great, our kind Lord, every way. And yet, such is the infinity of his love, that the Prince of Peace chuseth such vile creatures to be his own, his dear servants! such is the immensity of his mercy, that he forgives all our sins, and remembers them no more! And such the inexhaustible fullness, the exceeding riches of his grace, that he employs and assists us in his service, and accepts and rewards our little mites of duty, as if we had done worthily! Never was such a master as God our Saviour—as the Lord our Father! he doth all for us, in us and by us, and then accounts us great doers! delights in us as his good and faithful servants now, records our services in the book of his remembrance, and will find and commend them before men and angels, unto our praise and honour and glory, at his appearing! O who would not love, who would not serve, such an infinite lover! such an all-enduring master! O for ravished hearts, captivated souls, with this inscription, "Holiness to the Lord" for ever! But, alas! our coldness, our dullness in divine service! how do we by these, and by our pride and unbelief, and in both by our base selfishness, rob our Lord of his honour, of the glory due to his great name! ah! foolish and unwise, do we thus requite the

Lord!—aye, thus vile, thus ungrateful are we! And yet, it is heaven's wonder, the angels desire to look into the grace; still we are his favourites! O love passing knowledge! And, lo, our loving Lord will pour upon us the Spirit of grace and of supplications, and cause us to look upon him whom we have pierced, and to mourn for our transgressions,—and will fit and prepare us for heaven. And then, as his servants, blest with the vision of his face, we shall love and serve him perfectly and for ever. Meanwhile we are called, and shall be enabled, to live by faith, to derive all supplies from Christ's fullness daily, to quicken our graces, and fit us for our services continually, that the whole glory of our salvation, and of all our usefulness, may be given unto God and the Lamb eternally. Bo on, then, my dear brother, to serve the Lord humbly and cheerfully, earnestly and increasingly. Be free with your own Lord Jesus. His fullness is entirely and for ever yours. God your Saviour is your salvation; therefore with joy shall ye draw water out of the inexhaustible wells of grace and life in him. Attempt your duty, to let down the bucket of faith: you shall draw water, receive supplies for your every time of need: because Christ lives, you shall live also.

And, though at times of suspended influence and great dejections, through corruptions and temptations, you are ready to lay down the Lord's work, and to question whether you ever had any business with it; you have not an High Priest that cannot be touched with a feeling of your infirmities; but one who was in all points tempted like as you are. And, therefore, from an infinite sympathy and an almighty and authoritative power, he is well able to succour you when tempted. Fear not; the Captain of your salvation will not leave you in your conflict with the powers of darkness, but cover your head in the day of battle, and bring you from the field victorious. You must meet with opposition in your work, that you may be crowned as an overcomer. "To him (says our Lord) that overcometh will I grant to sit with me in my throne, even as I also overcame, and am set down with my Father in his throne." Listen not to the suggestion of your soul-enemies, of your Lord's enemies, that you have nothing to do in his service, because of your weakness and unworthiness. For God hath chosen weak and base things, that are so really in themselves, and such in their own esteem, yea, and things that are not, to be his servants, to bring to nought things that are; that his grace and power may be conspicuous, and that no flesh should glory in his presence. And yield not to a thought, no, not for a moment, of laying down your Lord's work when the enemy presseth hard upon you, and you are so weak that you have no might; for you shall be reinforced with strength; "shall run and not be weary, and walk and not faint." Because you shall walk and work in the omnipotence of Jehovah,—in whom for you there is everlasting strength. Wherefore trust you in the Lord for ever; put him for a well, while passing through Baca's vale; and on you shall go from strength to strength, until you appear before God in Zion.

The grace of Christ be with your spirit! In him, with affectionate esteem, I am, dear Sir,

Your obliged friend and servant,

____

LETTER XXV.   To --------

My dear Sister in Christ,

I REJOICE that the Lord hath given a little relief and satisfaction to your troubled spirit by my last letter, and also blesseth you with some refreshing sweetness under the ministry of the word. And in the bowels of Jesus Christ I sympathize with you in your soul-sorrows, pains and fears, through remaining corruptions and Satan's temptations. O that our dear Lord Jesus, the sympathizing head of the church, may send you seasonable succour by unworthy me, the mind of Christ, a word of peace, from the Prince of grace, for the comfort of your dear soul, as one of his suffering members! Jesus hath the tongue of the learned given him of the Father, that he might speak a word in season unto him that is weary: and, if he would graciously send you a word of comfort, a significant line of his heart love, and put it into my unworthy hand; O how gladly would I run, to bring it to your dear soul!

You complain, my dear Sister, that, though the Lord has answered several of your objections, and delivered you in some measure from terrors, yet your heart is not thankful. And whence, think you, doth this complaint arise, but from a thankful heart given you? While you complain of unthankfulness, what is the language of that complaint but—Lord, I would be thankful! And, since to will is present with you, though how to perform as you would and should you find not; your willing mind is accepted. Grace is poured into Christ's lips! there is none can think or speak like him in grace. His love, grace, and mercy, are his own; an immense, all-overflowing, and never-failing ocean! his omniscient and all-gracious eye sees your little thankfulness amidst all your great unthankfulness: he records, and will reward, the one, and forgives, and will remember, the other no more. For "Who is a God like unto our God, that pardoneth iniquity, and passeth by the transgression of the remnant of his heritage!" Believe the free acceptance of your mite of thankfulness, and the free forgiveness of all your unthankfulness; and this will make you more thankful.

I am glad you are thankful that hitherto the Lord hath kept you from fainting, and falling a prey to Satan. And, though you have been brought to the borders of despair, and have not been so remarkably set at liberty from this distress as others have, yield not to those hurries and fears which are apt to seize your mind on account hereof. For the Lord is a sovereign, and may dispense his favours, and display his glories, in delivering his distressed children, just as he pleaseth. What if God breaks in suddenly upon some benighted souls with such bright rays of the light of life, like the sun upon the earth from under an eclipse, that at once raiseth their dejected spirits from the depths of sorrow to the heights of joy, even joy unspeakable and full of glory; and relieves others more gradually, as the dawning light scatters by degrees the darkness of the night, and shineth more and more unto the perfect day! it is the same Sun of righteousness that illuminates both. What, though one enjoys a brighter shine than the other, they are both equally interested in the same glorious sun, and are blest with his light in that manner and measure which infinite wisdom sees best; most for the glory of God in their salvation, and for their advantage as the saved of the Lord. Believe, therefore, that there is no soul that is raised from the depth of dejection, despairing thoughts by reason of sin;—unto believing thoughts and cheerful hopes of the mercy of God in Christ;—so as to attract the eye of the mind after him, the light of life, and fix it on him with relieving expectation of all salvation from him, from him alone as the only Saviour; but that soul that is savingly illuminated, that is delivered from the condemning power of unbelief, and blest with justifying faith in Christ. And though, my dear friend, the Lord has not made such a feast for your faith, or rather for your spiritual sense, as some poor prodigals have found upon their return to their father's house; yet as a son, as a child, you are ever with him, and all that he hath is yours. Then give your father leave to chuse your time-portion of comforts, and to save you in his own way; believing that he will lead you a right way to the city of habitation, and that what you know not now you shall know hereafter.

As to those vain thoughts and imaginations which affright and amaze you; these are to shew you more of your heart's vileness; that you may be glad to receive a salvation that is all of grace; and that the exceeding riches thereof may be the more illustriously displayed in the forgiveness of such innumerable evils, and in the destruction of such potent and prevalent enemies. And you may expect to see, in your depraved nature, greater, and still greater abominations. But "the blood of Jesus Christ his Son cleanseth us from all sin." And "Where sin hath abounded grace doth much more abound; that, as sin hath reigned unto death, even so grace might reign through righteousness unto eternal life, by Jesus Christ our Lord."

And fear not that old things are not passed away, and all things become new, because you see so much vanity remain in your heart; for the being of sin will abide in your soul so long as it remains in the body, and a painful feeling of its prevalent working at times you will find to your grief. And when all things are become new, when the soul is new created in Christ Jesus, "old things are passed away;" not as to the being and working thereof in the heart; but as to that esteem the mind once had of them, that delight the heart had in them, and that pursuit which it made after them as a satisfying good; whence, governed by a carnal mind, the man's life was but one continued course of "fulfilling the desires of the flesh and of the mind." A man that is in the flesh thus walks after the flesh without control; unless it be at times from the light of natural conscience, the terrors of the law, and a fear of God's wrath. But a spiritual man, a man that is a new creature, hath a new nature in him, that discerns the transcendant excellency of spiritual things, that delights in and pursues after them as such; that esteems, delights in, and follows after God in Christ as its chief good; and the laws, ordinances, people and ways of God, for their native excellency, and that exceeding suitableness which is therein, to the appetite of a new creature. Whence the new, the spiritual life in the heart, is the governing principle of such a man's life; old things are not the ruling principle of such a man's life; and, were it possible, he would utterly exclude them out of his heart. But O, to his grief, there they abide, there they work: which makes him cry out, "O wretched man that I am, who shall deliver me from the body of this death!"

Now, then, do you esteem, delight in, and follow after, worldly things, and the pleasures of sin, as a satisfying good? Or do you not rather mourn and lament that you are so much entangled and defiled with these vanities and impurities? If you can say with David, "I hate vain thoughts, but thy law do I love," old things are passed away, and all things are become new in you: partially and initially now, and shall be so completely and totally ere long. Meanwhile you are called by faith to wash in the fountain set open for sin and for uncleanness. Vain thoughts will pass through your heart, but let them not lodge there: pray for divine grace, to oppose their motions and prevent their excursions. For your whole course is to be a conflict: you are called, and shall be influenced, by the grace of God, through faith in Christ and love to him, to go on, "Denying ungodliness and worldly lust; and to live soberly, righteously, and godly in this present world."

As to your terrifying dream—that you deceive yourself with a false hope, and presumed to go among the people of God until the last, and were then sent from them, and the sparks of God's fire issued towards you.—Harken to the word of God rather than to this dream: "Whosoever believeth in Christ shall not perish, but have everlasting life." And whenever it comes into your mind to terrify you, endeavour to look to Christ as the hope set before you, for refuge from the wrath to come: for the arms of Christ are open to receive you, and in no wise will he cast out any poor fearful-hearted sinner; that comes to him the great Saviour. He invites you, when weary and heavy-laden, to come to his bosom, and has promised to give you rest. Jesus will be a strength to your poor and needy soul in its great distress, a refuge from the storm, a covert from the tempest, and a shadow from the heat, when the blast of the terrible one is as a storm against the wall. As rivers of water to refresh you, and an house of defence to save you, will he be to you in the present time, and unto all eternity. Jesus, your rock, is impregnable; get into him by faith, and as an inhabitant of the rock sing.

I rejoice that the preaching of Christ's righteousness hath been sweet and delightful to your soul; that you see the wisdom of God in this way of salvation by Christ. It is sufficient for every soul that ventures upon it, and it is your desire that your own soul may be interested in it.—This, my dear friend, is your heart's discerning and approving of Christ as God's salvation, and your cleaving unto him as such; or this is believing in Christ for righteousness. And upon you, as a believer, this righteousness is; for it is "unto and upon all them that believe," without difference.

And, though you mourn for your unfruitfulncss and unthankfulness when you return from an ordinance, and that so little of the word remains in your memory; whence your fear that you bring forth no fruit to perfection; yet consider, if Christ and you are brought together by the word, if you are brought to desire after and rest upon Christ thereby; this is saving fruit, the fruit of faith, which, more or less, will work by love, and engage you to live unto him who died for you, and rose again. And, as your soul sweetly drinks in the rain of the word, while you are under it you receive blessing from God. And, though your memory doth soon let the words slip, by which the gospel was conveyed to your ears, yet the things of the gospel remain in your heart, and have, and will have, a saving influence upon your life.

You beg me to tell you what difference there is between a child of God's being comforted by the Spirit of God at that very instant when a hypocrite is greatly affected.

I answer: the difference lies, first in the nature of the consolation; and secondly in the effect thereof upon the heart.

A hypocrite, or a stony-ground hearer, may have joy in hearing the word of the gospel: but it flows from, and consists in, some carnal apprehensions of spiritual things. For to discern spiritual things, in their spiritual glory, no natural man can. If a hypocrite hath joy in salvation by Christ, it springs from an apprehension of that salvation's being such as his heart desires; viz. a salvation from wrath hereafter, with liberty to indulge himself in sin here.—And hence the effect of this joy is false peace and carnal ease in sin, or a turning the grace of God, the notions he hath of grace, into lasciviousness. And all that do so are ungodly men; and that joy which they have in the gospel is of a very different kind, and hath a very different effect, from that which is given by the Holy Spirit to the children of God.

Again, a hypocrite may have joy in hearing the word of the gospel, from something that may be communicated to him in the manner of its delivery.—Yea, he may go so far as to have joy from hopes of heaven, as a place of ease and rest from sorrow: but not as it is a state of freedom from all sin, and perfect holiness in the enjoyment of God; for so no natural man has any discerning of, or desire after heaven: but a natural man may desire heaven as a place of ease and rest. And from his joyful hopes thereof he may resolve, in his own strength, to leave some of his sins, and make some external reformation in his pursuits after future happiness; and yet be but a stony-ground hearer, that hath no root of new-creature life in himself; and so in time of temptation he falls away.

But, when the Spirit of God comforts a child of God, he takes of the things of Christ and of the Father, and shews them to the soul in their spiritual glory and excellency, in their connection and dependency: so that the whole of God's salvation in Christ, from sin as well as wrath, unto holiness as well as happiness, appears amiable in the soul's view. Yea, true holiness appears to such a soul to be, as indeed it is, real happiness. Salvation from the torments of wicked men and devils in the state of the damned, and to ease and rest in the company of the blessed, not only appears amiable to such a soul; but also salvation to the enjoyment of God in Christ, conformity to his image, and dedication to his praise, begun here, and complete hereafter: this, O this appears amiable to a child of God, to a spiritual man. It delights such a soul much that the wisdom and grace of God hath found out and provided such a way of salvation by Christ, whereby all his perfections may be glorified, and the sinner saved from his righteous wrath to his infinite favour, from the image of Satan in the deformity of sin to the image of God in the beauty of holiness; or, in a word, from the cruel bondage of sin and Satan into the glorious liberty of the sons of God, begun here, and complete hereafter, to a blest eternity.

Not this or that part only, but the whole of this great salvation, is the consolation which the Spirit of God gives to a child of God by the gospel revelation, while the voice of the Holy Ghost, as the soul's comforter, is, 'See, poor soul, this salvation is free for thee; this great salvation is to be received by thee: therefore pray for power to stretch out the hand of faith to receive it, and you shall live for ever!' And hence, as the effect of this consolation, such a soul approves of Christ, and God's salvation in him in all its parts, and in the whole of its glorious provision opens wide the mouth of its desires after interest in this great salvation, obeys the gospel-call, and looks to the Saviour revealed, and rests upon him alone, as the only and sure foundation which God hath laid in Zion. Then, saith the Spirit, in some or other word of promise, or by some or other sweet intimation to the heart, according to the promise 'Christ is thine, and eternal life in him: follow on to know the Lord, and thou shalt know him: believing on the Lord Jesus Christ, thou shalt be saved.' Which gives the soul good hope through grace; brings some ease and rest to the heart; and engageth the soul's resolution, in the strength of divine grace, to be the Lord's, to oppose and resist all sin, which it hates as sin, and as against a God of infinite goodness, and as destructive to its own happiness: or, in a word, the soul resolves to cleave unto the Lord in a way of duty, in hope of eternal glory. And whenever any soul's comfort by the preached gospel is of this nature, and hath this effect in the main, though it may not be just the same as to the words in which I have hinted it; that soul's consolation is from the Spirit of God, and itself is most certainly a child of God, and saved such a one shall be in the Lord with an everlasting salvation; "he shall not be ashamed nor confounded world without end!"

It is true, my dear friend, that no person can partake of the Lord's supper, (i. e. of the things signified by the signs of the body and blood of Christ, held forth by the elements of bread and wine) without the immediate exercise of faith. But your fear that you do not exercise faith at such seasons is not a sufficient ground for you to neglect the observation of the ordinance. For, as a believer in Christ, you have a right to partake of the external signs; this is your Lord's command, and your reception thereof is obedience. And, as to the exercise of faith therein, believers are not to stay till their faith is in exercise before they receive that ordinance, but to come to the Lord's table at his command, and there wait for the assistance of the Spirit of grace to draw out their faith into exercise while they attempt their duty, to receive a crucified Jesus for their own salvation, which is held forth to be received by them under the forms of bread and wine. And, if when you receive these elements you desire to receive Christ for yourself, as he is then and thereby held forth unto you, you receive in faith, although your faith is not so strong as to say, "My Lord and my God." And, as for your unbelief, unthankfulness, and all manner of apprehended unfitness, Jesus, who bore your sins, takes them all away; none of them shall ever be laid to your charge, who desire to be found in Christ. And your little faith and love, though weak as a bruised reed, and as smoking flax, which make you willing to follow the Lamb whithersoever he goeth, although it be with trembling pace; these the compassionate Saviour will not break nor quench, but bind up and strengthen, until he brings forth for you judgment unto victory; until he sets you free from all the accusations and condemnations of the adversary. And be not hurried at that word, "None of those men that were bidden shall taste of my supper;" for the enemy perverts it in applying it to you: it relates only to those who being called refuse to come, and not to those who come in at the call. Come, then, you shall be welcome to all supplies, prepared on purpose for the full relief of all your necessities.

Thus, as enabled, I have endeavoured to answer your objections, and remove your fears. But such is the vast number and strength of your spiritual enemies, that in various shapes and appearances they will continually terrify you with their innumerable suggestions and false insinuations, unless you take unto you the shield of faith, wherewith you shall be able to quench all the fiery darts of the wicked one; and unless by the sword of the Spirit, the word of God, you hew down temptations, oppositions, and disconsolations by thousands.

And, that you may do so, hear what the God of truth saith, "Believe on the Lord Jesus Christ, and thou shalt be saved." Whenever the enemies put you in fear, then look to Christ, as God's salvation to the ends of the earth, for your own salvation in particular; and believe that you shall be saved in looking, because God that cannot lie hath said it: and you shall find that he is, and will be, both able and faithful that hath promised. Happy then are you, shall you be, that look, that come to Christ for life; "for the eternal God is your refuge, and underneath are the everlasting arms. He shall thrust out the enemy from before you, and shall say, Destroy them. Your enemies shall be found liars unto you, and you shall tread upon their high places!"

I commit you to the tender care of the great Shepherd, and am very affection-ately

Yours in the Lord,

LETTER XXVI.   To Mr. Dutton.

My dear Brother,

I BLESS God I am at this time as well as usual in body, and my soul is held in life: because Christ lives, I live also. I hope you and sister are in health, and wish the best of blessings on you and yours unto life eternal. God grant that you make it your chief concern to be found in Christ, "not having your own righteousness, which is of the law, but that which is through the faith of Christ, the righteousness which is of God by faith:" that you may not be ashamed when the Lord appears! There is no standing with acceptance, for us sinners, before a God of infinite purity, but in the spotless, glorious obedience, the law-fulfilling and everlasting righteousness of his dear Son. O what a contrivance of infinite wisdom, what a provision of infinite grace, is this, for the justification and salvation of law-condemned sinners! what thanks are due to the Lord of heaven and earth that the gospel of the Saviour hath reached our ears! And that we, even we, are not excluded hope in the Redeemer's righteousness; but invited and required, by the gospel declaration of grace for sinners, to accept of, and submit to, this glorious institution of God, for our everlasting salvation by Jesus! and that not a soul shall perish that comes in, at the gospel-call, to shroud itself, for acceptance with God, under the complete obedience of Jesus Christ, that one man by whom all the many that shall be saved are perfectly justified, and shall reign in life unto eternal glory. O, my dear brother, it becomes us to examine whether we are the persons that have bowed to, and put on, that glorious robe, the righteousness of the Son of God, and so by the gospel promise have a declared interest in the Redeemer's merits. And, next to this, if we are blest with his Holy Spirit, and thereby with a new nature, and are earnestly concerned about an increasing conformity to his image in heart and life. As no unrighteous person (and such are all that do not submit to the Saviour's righteousness) shall inherit the kingdom of God, and as without holiness of heart and life no man shall see the Lord: for no unclean thing shall, or can, in any wise enter into the new Jerusalem. And O what tongue can tell, what heart can think, how miserable, and eternally miserable, will be the state of all those who are without!—that after the gospel-day is over shall then be found guilty and filthy, of whom the Lord the judge will say, Let them be so still, or for ever! God grant us grace to improve our present gospel-time, in order to a blest, a glorious eternity. So pray, dear brother,

  Your affectionate Sister and Servant,

LETTER XXVII. To --------.

My dear Friend,

IT is well for you, for me, and for every soul that is enabled to flee for refuge from the wrath to come, unto Christ the great Saviour, the glorious hope set before us in the gospel. It is well for us, that we are Christ's care; that none of all our enemies within or without us shall ever pluck us out of his all-gracious and almighty hands. There, my dear Sister, there, under the shadow of the Saviour's wings, let us make our refuge until all our calamities are overpast. Oh, blessed be God, that time will soon come. We shall soon have done with sin and sorrow, and enter into a state of bliss, of purity and joy, full and eternal! No sin shall enter with us into heaven, none shall we find there, nor shall any impurity ever follow after us, to mar or rob us of that state of glory. No; mortality of every kind, respecting both soul and body, shall then be swallowed up of life, of complete and eternal victory! "Life and immortality are brought to light by the gospel." Not so blest was the first Adam in Paradise. His was a state of perfect natural life and bliss, in which he should have continued, had he not sinned. But it was not a state of happiness into which sin could not enter, and death by sin, to the utter loss of it. No, the first Adam, and all his seed in him, stood upon the uncertain bottom of his own free-will; and thence down he fell, and we in him, from the heights of bliss to the depths of wo! But recovered sinners, by the second Adam, the glorious Saviour, from the depths of misery to the heights of glory, of glory that is and will be of a far superior dignity, shall there live for ever, without fear or danger of the approach of any enemy, of any tempting devil, or defiling sin, to pollute their pure joys, or disrobe them of their bright glories! It is the transcendant excellency of the glory of our Lord Jesus Christ, which all the heirs of grace shall shortly possess, that it is and will be eternal glory! A glory, as of an infinite excellency, so of an infinite duration, that can never, never decay in itself, nor be lost to any of the happy participants of that ineffable bliss! And from hence what an ineffable and eternal joy must needs arise to all the heirs of glory, when once advanced to the full possession of that vast inheritance in light! when once their fears, dangers, and sorrows, are all over and gone; how delightful will they bathe their weary souls, in seas of heavenly rest; while they thus reflect upon all their unspeakable bliss—It shall be ever with me as it is now! while in every ray of their bright glory they see the cheering, the securing word, Eternity! O this word, eternity, will be the joy of joy in glory.

Let this then, my dear sister, be a sweet support; a revising cordial to us, under all our fears, griefs, and dangers, that we shall soon get beyond them, and see them no more for ever, And mean time let us trust our souls, for all salvation, in the almighty Saviour's hands; and fear not but he will keep, to eternal glory, that which we have committed unto him and his grace against that day. And let the joy of faith bear up our spirits against unbelieving fear, until the joy of vision shall exclude it perfectly and for ever. I commit you to the tender care of the great Shepherd of the sheep, to be carried by grace into glory; and am very affectionately,

Yours in our dear Lord Jesus, &c.

LETTER XXVIII.   To Mr. L.

Reverend and dear Sir,

YOUR last, by the account you gave me, that my letter on perseverance had been blest to you, and was a means of exciting you to study and preach that comfortable doctrine, was matter of joy to my poor heart. O how delightful it is to see our labours blest for the good of souls! And it is easy to swim when we are thus held up by the chin; to go on cheerfully in divine service when it is manifest, even to sense, that our labour is not in vain in the Lord. But, on the other hand, when we see but little fruit, how apt are our spirits to die within us! How hard it is for our weak hands to row against both wind and tide! And, if the arms of our hands at such seasons were not made strong by the hands of the almighty God of Jacob, we should soon grow weary of spiritual work, and slide into carnal ease, indolence, and sloth. But whence doth this proceed? doubtless from the weakness of our faith in God and love to him, and the strength of our unbelief and inordinate self-love. When we see but little fruit of our work, alas, for us, we are apt to think that our labour is in vain, and tempted we are to give over. Whereas we are exhorted to go on in the Lord's work, and always to abound therein, as knowing that our labour is not in vain in the Lord. And, if we had strong faith in this firm declaration of grace, O with what giant-like strength should we go on in our work. But, alas, weak in faith, we judge by sense, by the present appearance of things, and so wax weary, and grow lazy. For not only Satan and unbelief, but even spiritual sense also, do greatly misrepresent things to our minds in trying seasons. 'It is in vain to go on in the Lord's work,' say Satan, unbelief, and spiritual sense too, when visible fruit does not speedily appear. But why must it be in vain, if we do not presently see that fruit which we desire? is what we engage in duty? is it obedience to a divine command? If it is, let us go on with our work cheerfully, in the face of all discouragements; for it is and shall be for God's glory. And, therefore, far is the least service we do for him from being in vain. What if we do not see that fruit of our work which we wish to our soul's joy; shall we overlook that precious fruit of it in God's glory, which arises to him even by the very performance of our duty? Surely, if we loved the Lord strongly, and were in the exercise of a superlative love to him, we should do what he bids us cheerfully, and never think that labour lost whereby we render in some measure to the sovereign Lord of all his required and deserved glory. What if it does not please him to grant those happy fruits of our labours we wish to our joy; let us remember that success of our work is a free gift of God's sovereign bounty, which he may bestow or withhold as he pleaseth; and by a humble, cheerful submission to his good pleasure, let us give him the glory of his sovereignty. And, if our hearts seek success for God's praise, the praise of his mercy, and if we would find our own joy in his glory; let us be assured that he, who is infinite in wisdom, best knows when and how to cast abroad the rays of his manifestative glory for his own praise; and that he will glorify his great self, in measure, manner and time, as he sees best; and by a sweet acquiescence with his all-wise disposal, let us labour for God's honour, to lose our own wisdom, as it were, in his infinite understanding! And, if we want to see the success of our labours, the answer of our prayers, and the fulfillment of promises, to our joy, in the glory of divine truth and faithfulness, let us firmly believe that our Jehovah is a God that cannot lie, nor be worse than his word; and for the glory of his infinite truth and faithfulness, which stands for ever, and can never fail, let us cast ourselves and all our desires into their sweet bosom; and there rest entirely, wait patiently, and look earnestly for him, who hideth himself from the house of Jacob. For, though the Lord calls us to go on in a way of duty with a single eye to his glory; to bow to his sovereignty when we want success; to adore his wisdom in delaying what we judge would be for his praise; to believe his truth and faithfulness when providences seem to thwart promises; and, resting in him, to wait patiently and look earnestly for him; yet there are none of those, who thus glorify God by a continuance with him in duty, but shall find him, to their exceeding joy, to be unto them a God of infinite bounty, who, displaying the immense glories of his infinite love, grace, and mercy, his wisdom, power, truth and faithfulness, as a God hearing prayer, and keeping covenant, will appear to their present and eternal joy, to have done for them more exceeding abundantly than they could ask or think! And, "unto him be glory and dominion for ever and ever. Amen!" That the grace of Christ may be with your spirit, and his hand with you in your work; that many may believe and turn unto the Lord, who shall be your joy and crown when Christ appears; is the hearty desire of, dear Sir,

Yours in the Lord for ever, &c.

LETTER XXIX.   To Mrs. H.

My dear Sister in Christ,

As to your late trial in the things of time, you may well endure it, since all the troubles you are to have are limited to your time state, and an eternity of full joy and flowing pleasures await you in immortal glory. Yea, my sister, view all your trials, and this, descending on you from the love of God through the blood of Christ, and under the sanctifying influences of the Holy Ghost, as so many choice blessings, as part of the appointed means of your preparation by grace for your prepared glory; and you will see cause in every thing to give thanks, and to joy and glory even in tribulation. Learn from your present loss the vanity and uncertainty of all earthly enjoyments; and seek more earnestly the heavenly country, where losses and crosses cannot come. You will soon be acvanced to inherit all things, and set for ever out of danger of losing any thing. In the mean time prize more highly your portion in the Lord, which can never be lost. Your interest in Christ, and in God through him, shall be taken from you; nor shall you ever be deprived of any of those spiritual blessings in heavenly places, with which you are blessed in Christ Jesus. Your right to these is unalienable, and your enjoyment thereof inviolably sure. And, as to temporal blessings, you have, you shall have, all of those that God sees best for you. The Lord, who is the portion of your cup, and who maintaineth your lot of spirituals, will also maintain your lot of temporals in such ample manner, that you who seek the Lord shall not want any good thing that is necessary, and really good for you. And, as to those things which are sensibly evil, God will overrule even them for your real advantage. "For we know that all things work together for good to them that love God, to them that are called according to his purpose." All things, both good and evil, to sense and Nature's taste, are and shall be overruled, by infinite wisdom and almighty grace, to work, and work together, as a wisely mixed and kindly operative potion, for good; for that great good of our conformity to Christ in holiness, in order to our conformity to him in glory; to them that love God, as being first loved of him, and to them that are the called according to his purpose.

It is well, my dear sister, that your being obliged at that time to be in vain company was a sore exercise to you. Learn hence to praise that rich, free, and distinguishing grace of God which hath given you a spiritual mind, and which kept you spiritual amidst carnal people and their vain conversation. Whence was it that a spark of love to God of that heavenly fire would then be glowing in your heart, and ascending towards him, when all around you, under the influence of a carnal mind, which in enmity against God, were breathing out nothing but what was contrary to him? Was it not from the great, the special, the distinguishing love of God to you? Oh, praise and adore that infinite love, which in its own infinity is exalted far above all blessing and praise!

Bless the Lord, who by that short confinement with the wicked gave you a more quick and deep sense of the ministry of hell; and made you cry out most earnestly, "Gather not my soul with sinners, nor my life with bloody men!" And hence learn the greatness of your deliverance from hell, with respect to that abominable company of wicked men and devils, who there, when their wickedness is boiled up to its greatest height, and set upon and endless flow, shall, as tormented by and tormentors to each other, be confined together in an amazing gulph of darkness, to a miserable eternity! And know, O you child of light, who cannot endure the darkness of this world, the company of wicked men on earth, that your soul shall not be gathered with sinners into the blackness of darkness, in the wickedness of hell! No; your dear soul, as a believer in Jesus, who bore your sin, and endured your hell, is for ever delivered from the place and state, from the company and misery, of the damned, both as to sin and wrath. Great is the Lord's mercy towards you, for he hath delivered your soul from the lowest hell, and made you meet to be a partaker of the inheritance of the saints in light in the highest heaven! And soon, when your earthly tabernacle is dissolved, your happy spirit shall be gathered to your people, to that general assembly of the spirits of just men made perfect, who, with an innumerable company of glorious angels, shall together live a blest eternity in the immediate vision and fruition, worship and adoration, of God and the Lamb! The present time is a meetening state for an endless eternity, both to the godly and the ungodly: the former, by the grace of God, have their fruit unto holiness, and the end everlasting life; and the latter, under the power of sin and Satan, fill up the measure of their wickedness unto eternal death. And by the disposition of each, and the company which gives them most delight in this present time, it may be certainly known what road they are walking in, and what company they shall be gathered to, if in that state they live and die, for an immeasurable eternity: for every man, every soul, shall be gathered to his own company. They that delight in God and godliness, in holy men and holiness, shall be gathered to the company of the blessed, to inherit with them eternal salvation! And they that delight in the service of sin and Satan, in sinners and their sinful ways, abiding in that condition, shall be gathered to the company of the damned, and sink with them into eternal perdition! What grace then, what amazing grace is this, that laid hold on us, while we lingered in the ways of sin, like Lot in Sodom, and set us without the city of destruction, and led us to Christ, the city of salvation, where we are and shall be for ever safe from endless misery, and advanced with him to inherit immortal glory! And let it be our present, as it will be our future, employ, to ascribe "Salvation, and glory, and blessing, unto him that sitteth on the throne, and to the Lamb, for ever and ever!"

I am, my dear Sister,

Yours most tenderly, &c.

Letter XXX. To --------

Reverend and dear Sir,

As I am informed that the Lord has lately appeared in a remarkable manner for the conversion of souls by your ministry, I beg leave to congratulate your happiness in this regard, and to acquaint you that I rejoice with you for the coming of our Lord's kingdom in your part of his earth, that I pray for its happy progress with you, and its universal spread over the three kingdoms, and over all nations. "Come, Lord Jesus, come quickly!" I know you say, Amen.

How great is the grace, Sir, that made choice of you for this service; that the Gentiles by your mouth should hear the word of the gospel, and believe! was it not enough that God should chuse you in his Son unto eternal life before all worlds! But would he yet further display the exceeding riches of his grace, in his kindness towards you through Christ Jesus, in his chusing and calling you to be a minister of the glorious gospel; and in assisting and succeeding you unto such eminent service! This is grace worthy of a God! of the infinite Jehovah, whose mercy, love and grace, towards you in Christ, are like himself, unsearchable! Grace, Sir, is infinitely free, rich and sovereign; and displays its freedom, riches and sovereignty, in the choice of those instruments it is pleased to work by. And sometimes, to shew its immense glory, it fixes upon the most unworthy!—the least, the last, the worst of all! If God do but say, "I will be gracious unto whom I will be gracious;" unto this or that man, in this or that way; there is such an immensity of grace engaged to fulfill that great resolve, that thousands of provocations, and mountains of oppositions, shall fall down flat before the infinite majesty of its triumphant glory! And, as unworthiness shall not hinder God's working by whom he will, by whom he loves and chuses for temple-service, so neither shall the utmost weakness and unfitness. Grace will give an heart to a heartless dove, a mouth to a man that is not eloquent, and will be with the mouth of its sent servant! It shall be given such a man in the same hour whatever he is to speak for Christ, his royal master. Anointed to preach the gospel of Christ shall his sent servants be; and with the Holy Ghost sent down from heaven shall they publish the glad tidings unto every kind and degree of appointed usefulness, to the glory of God, the edification of the church, and their own joy, present and eternal. And has God's free grace, Sir, thus chosen and called you to, and assisted and owned you in, so great a work as that of the gospel ministry? What glory will you not give to this great grace? And is its omnipotent strength engaged for you in your utmost weakness? With what an holy, humble dependence thereon will you not go forth in all the blest employments it calls you to! Grace will never fail you, nor forsake you, in any of your appointed work; but bear and carry you through it, until you are called to enter into your master's joy and rest; because the riches of grace are inexhaustible, and its arm, its covenant-engaged ability, unweariable! Rejoicing then in the faithful promise of your all-gracious Lord, "Lo, I am with you always, even unto the end of the world," say in faith, though weak in yourself, and you can do nothing, "I can do all things through Christ which strengtheneth me! I commend you to the grace of God for the work whereunto he hath appointed you. Most heartily wishing that great grace may be with you, and that many may be turned to the Lord by your ministry, who shall be your joy and crown in the day of Christ.

I am with all due respect, reverend Sir,
                    Your most humble servant, &c.

LETTER XXXI. To ⸺⸺

Reverend and dear Sir,

As to your inward trials by a hard heart, and heart-wanderings from God, remember, that "the same afflictions are accomplished in your brethren that are in the world." Saints, in this low land, are sinners still; are far from perfection, and groan under their imperfection. And with us all, with all the members of the Lord's body in the church militant, the dear head of the church doth inexpressibly sympathize. His bowels yearn over his pained children; and in all our afflictions, by love-sympathy, he is afflicted. Let us pour out our complaints into his bosom; his ear, his heart, is open to receive them. Nor is his pity weak; but an almighty mercy, that will relieve us under, and deliver us from, all our misery. He bore the weight of our sins and sorrows, to deliver us from the heavy load. And O what grace it is, that, though our sins burden us, they shall not damn us! Our dear, dying Lord, hath borne, and borne away, our guilt, by the sacrifice of his great self. And now, unto us that believe in Jesus there is, there shall be, no condemnation. He hath cleansed us from our filth mystically, and completely in himself, and by his poured-out blood; and cleanse us he will influentially, by fresh applications thereof, until we are personally clean every whit. Sin being vanquished and overcome, atoned for and condemned, by the dying of the Lord Jesus; die it must, it shall, in us. As the dominion of it is already broken, so the power of it shall be further subdued, until at death it will be utterly destroyed, and we shall be made as pure as if sin had never entered; yea, more glorious in holiness, as bearing the complete grace-image of the second Adam, than we were in the first Adam, when he came out of his Maker's hand, in all his nature-purity. And grace, the free grace of our Three-One God, in its exceeding riches, shall have the highest praise of our salvation by Christ, from all sin and misery, unto all holiness and glory, even to the day of eternity!

Meanwhile let us live by faith on the Son of God, who loved us, and gave himself for us, to make us like him, and bring us up to be for ever with him. Let us commit our souls into his hands daily, for the whole of that salvation which he hath promised, and which our hearts desire; and believe that he will perfect that which concerneth us. While in all appointed means we follow on to know him, and the power of his resurrection, and the fellowship of his sufferings, being made comformable to his death; that if by any means we might attain the resurrection of the dead; to be as holy as if we were risen from the dead. Not that we shall be so while in the body: but, forgetting the things which are behind, let our eager souls reach forth towards the mark, for the prize of the high calling of God in Christ; even perfect holiness and eternal glory; that, if it were possible, we might be as holy as we shall be when raised from the dead.

I am glad that you have your encouragements in the Lord's work. And indeed, if gospel ministers saw the greatness of that favour, of that honour, which is put upon them in their being called to make known the mystery of Christ; together with the exceeding greatness of that immortal reward which awaits them; they would rejoice and be exceeding glad, yea, even leap for joy, notwithstanding all their ministerial trials. For even these, as gifts of free grace, are to fit and prepare them for a crown of glory. Were you to have less opposition, less discouragement in your great Master's work, you would have less opportunity to shew your valour, to endure hardness as a good soldier of Jesus Christ; to cut your way through your Lord's enemies; and to appear before all as an overcomer: and so your future crown, your throne, would not appear so glorious. Yea, your Lord's honour and glory by you would be the less. Therefore endure the cross, for the joy (of Christ's glory in and by you, and of your glory in and with him) which is set before you. If you endure the cross you shall wear the crown. What though your occasional discouragements give you a little sorrow now, when Christ's glory shall be revealed you shall rejoice with exceeding joy! Nothing makes the heart of a servant of Christ so sad as his being a coward in the cause, the glorious cause, of his royal Master, Stand your ground for God, and improve the talents he gives you to trade with, amidst a thousand slights and reproaches; for your sorrow shall shortly be turned into joy. One commending word from Christ's mouth, "Well done, thou good and faithful servant; thou hast been faithful over a few things; enter thou into the joy of the Lord:" this, O this will be reward enough for all that you can endure in his sweet service!—I remember you before the Lord. Pray for me. Great grace be with you.

I am, very affectionately, reverend Sir,
Yours in the Lord for ever, &c.

Letter XXXII. To Mrs. T.

My very dear Friend,

May the Lord's loving-kindness in a manifestative way be great to your dear soul, as a rich reward of your abundant love to the meanest worm! Not a favour, the least, even to a cup of cold water, that you ever shewed, or gave to the least of Christ's, as belonging to him, but is recorded in the book of his remembrance for a full reward. And, if our great Lord will reward his servants, he will do it like himself, who is the Lord and King of glory. "Eye hath not seen, nor ear heard, nor has it entered into the heart of man to conceive," the exceeding greatness of that reward which the Prince of grace will confer upon his servants at his glorious appearing and kingdom! O the ineffable greatness of that praise, honour and glory, which their tried faith and labour of love shall be found unto, in that solemn day, before men and angels! With what transports of heavenly pleasure, with what raptures of adoring wonder, shall we receive our great Lord's "Well done, good and faithful servant," when he bids us enter into our master's joy! The infinite grace of the Prince of Peace, in commending the weak services of the meanest of his servants, notwithstanding all the imperfections which attended their works, will strike our strings unto tunes of lofty praise in the blissful state of future glory. Who can tell what it will be to enter into the joy of our Lord! If the joy which the Saviour gives, and which enters into us by faith in this distant state, is at times unspeakable, and full of glory; what a transcendent, super-excellent joy must the joy of vision be, in the state of immediate presence, in the brightest glory, to a blessed eternity, when we shall enter into joy, the joy of our Lord! Into a participation of our Lord's own joy, into that joy wherein he himself is entered; into a sea, an ocean of joy in God, in the vast infinity of the boundless deity, into which all the vessels of mercy shall be cast, with all their various enlarged capacities, for an abundant fill of glory, to the innumerable ages of eternity! How great must the reward of the Lord's servants be, if the Lord himself is, and will be, exceeding great! "I am thy exceeding great reward!" Exceeding expression! exceeding conception! Without bound or end! Exceeding great indeed! O how vast is our inheritance in light! And blessed be God for the earnest of the Spirit, for the light of faith! For,

> "The Word is here the Church's fare,
>   And Faith the Church's light;
> Till shades give way to glory's day,
>   Then she shall live by sight."

My dear sister, I hope you and yours are in some measure of health. O that your souls may prosper exceedingly, and your last days be your best! How great is our privilege, that our Lord, our strength, our light, our life, is and will be with us, as our exceeding joy, even unto death, and afterwards receive us to himself in glory!—"We that are in this tabernacle do groan, being burdened," with a body of sin within, and afflictions without. But our burdens will soon fall off our shoulders. There will be nothing to grieve nor afflict us in our Father's house. O for faith and patience, to do and suffer the will of God, until we inherit the promises! A little glory brought to God by our patient enduring affliction sweetens every bitter, and gives us joy in sorrow. Whereas impatience under afflictions, which way soever they come, in what part soever they touch us, makes every burden heavy, and every cross grievous. Off from our watch against spiritual enemies; out from our work in the service of God, in living to the will of his precept, and the will of his providence: alas, we are wounded presently; we lose our joy and strength, and sink into weakness, sorrow and death! When wisdom's merchants begin to deal in Satan's wares they are instantly great losers. But "The merchandize of wisdom is better than silver, and the gain thereof than fine fold!" And it must needs be so: for what comparison is there between perishing shadows and immortal substance! Between the service of sin, the devil's black drudgery, and the service of God, which is glorious liberty! How happy are we, when enabled to stand fast in the Lord and his work, and not to stir a step at the devil's beck! How bright and glorious do the servants of Christ appear when they wear their Lord's livery, of conversation-holiness! And what shame covers them when they keep not their garments of profession unspotted from the world's pollution! How sad is it with the children of light, who are called to walk in fellowship with God, with saints, with angels; when through the strength of sudden temptations they slip aside from their own company, and associate with any of the powers of darkness! A spiritual man, kept in a good measure spiritual, soon feels the pain and loss of changing his company and employment; and till he returns, washed in his Saviour's blood, and afresh made fruitful unto God by his Spirit, can have no enjoyment. Happy then are the children of light when they have no fellowship with the unfruitful works of darkness, but walk worthy of God, to his glory and their joy!

Great grace be with you! I am most affectionately, dear sister,
Yours in the Lord for ever, &c.

T. BENSLEY, Printer, Crane-court, Fleet-street.

PART THE FIRST OF THESE

LETTERS ON SPIRITUAL SUBJECTS

(Price Eighteen Pence)

WERE LATELY PUBLISHED AS UNDER.

The valuable Writings of the late Mrs. ANNE DUTTON have long since become very scarce, and are therefore comparatively but little known. Their intrinsic excellency, however, induces the present Editor to hope that he may be performing an edifying service to the Church of Christ by bringing them once more into public notice. The reception which the few he has already reprinted have met with, strengthens this hope. It is therefore intended to continue the selections from the most interesting portions of her works (including her MEMOIRS,) and to publish them, by Subscription, in Parts not exceeding 1*s.* 6*d.* each, nor more than four parts in the year. This plan, which it is hoped will prove agreeable to all classes, is more particularly suggested with a view to the accommodation of those to whom it may be more convenient to obtain them by gradual, than by larger or more frequent purchase. In order, therefore, to ascertain, as nearly as may be, the required extent of the impression, it is respectfully requested that those Friends who are disposed to subscribe to the Work, will have the kindness to transmit their names to J. EEDES, Bookseller and Publisher, No. 2, Newgate Street; or to R. BAYNES, No. 28, Paternoster Row.

N. B. A Brief Account of the Gracious Dealings of God with Mrs. DUTTON, written by herself, price 1*s.* 6*d.*; and also her Poem on the Special Work of the Holy Spirit on the Hearts of the Elect, price 9*d.* are already republished, uniform with the above.

A POSTSCRIPT

TO

A LETTER lately published, on the DUTY and PRIVILEGE of a *Believer*, To live by FAITH, and to improve his Faith unto HOLINESS.

DIRECTED
To the Society at the Tabernacle *in* LONDON.

TO MAKE
The Author's SENSE of some WORDS and PHRASES in that LETTER, more *plain* to the Persons to whom *That* was sent, and *This* is addressed.

To which is added,
A CAUTION against ERROR, when it springs up Together with TRUTH.

In a LETTER to a FRIEND.

AS ALSO,
Some of the *Mistakes* of the *MORAVIAN* BRETHREN.

In a LETTER to another FRIEND.

WITH
POSTSCRIPTS to the LETTERS added.

By O N E who has tasted that the LORD *is* GRACIOUS.

LONDON:
Printed by J. HART, in *Popping's-Court, Fleet-Street;* and sold by J. LEWIS, in *Bartholomew-Close,* near *West-Smithfield*; and E. GARDNER, at *Milton's Head,* near *Aldgate.* 1746.
[Price stitch'd Nine-Pence.]

A POSTSCRIPT

TO

A LETTER lately published, on the DUTY and PRIVILEGE of a *Believer*, To live by FAITH, and to improve his Faith unto HOLINESS.

DIRECTED
To the Society at the Tabernacle *in* LONDON.

My dear and honour'd Brethren,

SINCE I writ and sent my *Letter* to the Press, I hear, to my Grief, that there are *some*, who lately were among *you*, that have very different *Thoughts*, from the Ideas of *my* Mind, about a *Life of Faith*, and the *Holiness* of a Believer that flows from it, when they use the same *Words* with *me*. And as I am well satisfy'd, that the Notions which they advance, are Anti-scriptural, and Anti-evangelical, I beg Leave to assure you in this *Postscript*, that when in my letter I use some of the same, or like *Words* with them, I intend no such *Things* as they design thereby. Permit me then, my dear Brethren and Sisters, to prevent Mistakes about some Words and Phrases in my letter, to give you a few Hints.

I. Of my *Intendment* in such Words, as *Sight*, Inward *Feelings*, and Spiritual *Sense.*

II. Of what I *intend* by Believing *without*, and *upon* These.

III. Of some of those *Notions* which have been advanc'd of late, which I take to be *Anti-Scriptural*, and *Anti-evangelical*.

IV. Concerning some *Things* which have been said by Those who advance these Notions. And to close the Whole,

V. With a Word to *you*, my dear Brethren and Sisters, who thro' the *Power of Christ resting upon you*, are enabled to *hold fast the faithful Word as you have been taught.* — A few Hints,

First. Of my *Intendment* in these Words us'd in my letter; *viz.* Sight, Inward *Feelings*, and Spiritual *Sense.* — And you may observe, my dear Friends, that I use these promiscuously, or cast them together without Distinction, and sometimes use one of them, as at other Times another. Because I take them to be much of the same Import. The Word *Sense*, indeed, if taken in its largest Latitude, must include in it all Manner of *Sensation*: As Seeing, Hearing, Smelling, Tasting, and Feeling. And so, the Words *Sight* and *Feeling*, if taken restrictively, must be included in the Word *Sense*. But as they may be taken more largely, I have, as I said, us'd all these

Words promiscuously, for any, and every Part of Sensation. I have added the Words, *Spiritual*, to Sense, and *Inward*, to Feeling; to distinguish the Sensation I intended thereby, from that natural and outward Sensation, of natural and outward Objects, which we have by the Organs of our Body.

By the Words *Sight*, Inward *Feelings*, and Spiritual *Sense*, therr, I *intend*; Those Views and immediate Prospects which the Soul hath by Faith, Of the Glory of God in the Face of Jesus Christ, when it first believes as a perishing Sinner, on CHRIST the might SAVIOUR, thro' the Word of Promise, in general, or particular, apply'd with Power to the Heart; unto a full Persuasion of its Interest in JESUS: Which are attended with all Joy and Peace, even *Joy unspeakable and full of Glory:* And, *Peace which passeth all Understanding:* (of the natural Man) with the *shedding abroad the Love of God in the Heart, by the Holy Ghost*: And the Out-flowing of the Soul's *Love* thereupon, unto *God* in *Christ*, as its *All in All!* — Oh, in those Moments of Revelation, of Application, wherein the Saviour is immedi-ately reveal'd, and his Salvation thro' the Word of Promise powerfully apply'd, whether in first, or After-Displays; the Soul sees, hears, smells, tastes, and feels: Unto demonstrative Evidence, and ineffable joy! The Soul sees JESUS, it sees Him for *itself*; it hears his Voice, smells his Fragancy, *tastes* his sweetness, or that *the Lord is gracious*, and feels his Power: Unto a Clearness of Evidence, a Rapture of Delight, a sweet Satisfaction, a filling Enjoyment! And the Saviour manifesting Himself to the Soul, as its own Lord Jesus: The Soul bosoms itself in Him, receives Him wholly, and gives up itself entirely unto Him. — The Soul also sees, what a glorious Change his Grace hath wrought in it. It hears the Voice of the new Life, in Prayers and Praises, which He hath communicated to it. It smells its Lord's Fragrancy, in the Anointing which he hath given it. It tastes His Sweetness, spread throughout its whole Frame. And feels the lively Exercise of every inwrought Grace. — The Soul also, sees GOD in Christ, as a God of infinite Goodness, it sees Him for *Itself*. It hears his Peace-speaking, and Sin-forgiving Voice. It smells the Saviour of his Grace. It tastes the Sweetness of his Mercy. And it feels the Power of his Love. — And by these Flowings *in* of the Love, Life and Glory of God in Christ upon the Soul, thro' the free and faithful Promise; the Soul flows *out* unto Him again, by Faith and Love, and every other Grace. God manifesting Himself to the Soul, as its own God in Christ; the Soul embraceth him, delights in him, reveres him, and dedicates itself unto Him as such. — And thus, being *called out of Darkness, into God's marvelous Light,* into *Fellowship with the Father, and with his Son Jesus Christ,* by the *Holy Ghost,* unto all *Peace* and *Holiness* thro' the Word of the *Gospel*: The Soul, having every Kind of *Evidence* given, and all *Sensation* afforded, *Believing in Christ, Rejoiceth in Hope of the Glory of God.* — This, my dear Brethren, is my *Intendment*, when I use the Words *Sight*, Inward *Feelings*, and Spiritual *Sense*. — A few Hints,

Secondly. Of what I *intend*, by Believing *without*, and *upon* These. And by Believing *without* Sight, Inward Feelings, and Spiritual Sense; I do *not* intend,

Believing without *ever* having *experienced* these Things: But, without the *present* Experience thereof; or in the same *Degree* that was formerly known. Because the immediate Displays of the Glory of Christ, and the present Application of the precious Promises, are not *always* experienced by Believers, nor the gracious Effects produced thereby. And when God reveals his Son in any Soul, and draws it out as a perishing Sinner, unto Acts of Faith in the Saviour, to look, to come, to trust in Him for Life, and applies the Promise for its strong Consolation: It is the Duty of that Soul for ever after, to believe its Interest in Christ, and in the Promise of Life thro' Him: Even when it don't see, nor feel those blessed Effects, which the immediate Revelation of Christ, and Application of the Promise had upon the Heart. Because God hath said, *That whosoever believeth on* CHRIST, *shall not perish, but have everlasting Life.* That, *This Life is in his Son. That He that hath- the son*; (which is by Believing on him) hath *Life.* — And because the Promise, as it stands in God's Book, and as it was apply'd by his Spirit to the Heart, was made by a GOD *that cannot lie.* The Change in a Believer's Frame, the Want of present Sight of the Glory of Christ, and of God in Him, and of inward Feelings of the Love of God shed abroad in the Heart, unto gracious Out-goings of Soul in Love to Him again; makes no Change in GOD, in CHRIST, nor in the *Promise* of Grace: Nor should it hinder a Believer's *Faith of Interest.* When the Lord hath once manifested Himself unto any Man, as he doth not unto the World: It is the Duty of that Man, and the Excellency of his Faith, forever after, to *believe* his Interest in Christ, and that neither *Things present, nor Things to come, shall be able to separate* him *from the Love of God.* And tho' at present, he feels a sad Decay of his own Love to God, and of the Fruits of the Holy Spirit in his Heart and Life; yet is it his Duty to *believe*, that from the unchangeable Love of God to him, and the over-flowing Fulness of Christ, his Graces shall be again reviv'd and increas'd, and ripen'd into Glory. — This, my dear Brethren, is what I *intend*, by Believing *without* Sight, Inward Feelings, and Spiritual Sense: That is, *without* the immediate *Presence* of These, that was once, and shall be again experienced, and ought to be earnestly fought for.

And by Believing *upon* These, I *intend*, The Soul's Believing its Interest in Christ, as *having* the *Presence* of all Evidences with it. As having, not only once believ'd on Christ unto Interest in him, but also, the Shines of his Face upon it: As having, not only a Right to the Promise of Life in Christ, as formerly apply'd, but also, the present Application thereof, unto all gracious Effects: By which the Soul, in full Sail of Faith, cries out, *My Lord, and my* GOD! — By Believing *upon* Sight, Inward Feelings, and Spiritual Sense, I intend *not*, The Soul's Believing upon These as the *Objects* of Faith: But, that thro' These as *Means*, Faith is brought more fully to its proper Objects; viz. *Christ*, as the only Saviour, and *God* as a Father, in and thro' Him: As declar'd in the Word of the Gospel, and reveal'd and apply'd by the Holy Spirit, in and to the Soul. Spiritual *Sense*, both past and present, is a good Handmaid to *Faith*; and ought to be fought for as a *subordinate* Evidence. But if we make Sense the *prime* Evidence of our Interest in Christ, and will not believe without its immediate Presence and Testimony; we greatly *err*. God's Promise of Life in Christ, made in his blessed Book, and once apply'd to the Heart of a perishing Sinner, that believes on the mighty Saviour; is the *prime*, the *abiding* Evidence of that Soul's Interest in Christ and his Salvation. And this as such, the Soul ought *first* to credit, even when Sense, or gracious Effects of the Promise upon the Heart, as a *subordinate* Evidence, is *present*; and *always* to credit, tho' Sense should be absent; altho' its immediate Presence is not experienc'd, nor its past Testimony now clear and full. And *Believing* thus in *Hope*, in the faithful Promise of God, even *against Hope*, or a Thousand seeming Contradictions in ourselves, is the direct Way to give *Glory to God*, and to see all promis'd and hop'd-for Blessings conferr'd on *us*, both in the present and future World. We ought to believe *upon* Sight, inward Feelings, and Spiritual Sense, as a subordinate Evidence of our Interest in Christ, when the Lord *affords* These; and to believe the Promise of God, as the prime Evidence thereof, *without* These, when the Lord is pleas'd to withhold them. — Having thus, my Brethren, given you a Hint of what I *intend*, by Believing *without*, and *upon* Sight, inward Feelings, and Spiritual Sense; permit me next, to give you a few Hints,

Thirdly. Of some of those *Notions* that have been advanc'd of late, which I take to be *Anti-Scriptural*, and *Anti-evangelical*. And,

1. If there are any who assert, *as I have heard*, That a Person may have *Faith*, without *Sight*, inward *Feelings*, and Spiritual *Sense*, as before describ'd, that is, without *ever* having *experiene'd* these Things; and that these Things ought not to be sought after, as a subordinate *Evidence* of our Interest in Christ, and the *Truth* of our Faith: I take This to be an *Anti-Scriptural*, and *Anti-evangelical Notion*.

I know the Experience of Believers who are blest with the Knowledge of their Interest in Christ, and That of Those who want it, differs much, as to the Degrees of *Sensation* with which they are favour'd. But most certainly, there is no Believer in the World, not one that hath true, living *Faith*; but his Faith is, or has been attended with more or less of Spiritual *Sense*.

To say, That a *rational* Creature, *believes* any Thing, without *Sight*, or a proper *Evidence* to beget Faith, of whatever Kind it be; without *feeling* the Acts of his own Mind; and without any *Sense* of their Effects upon his Heart: Is *irrational*.

And to say, That a *Christian* hath true *Faith* in Christ, or *believes* on Him, without *Sight*, without an internal Revelation of his Glory by the Holy Ghost thro' the Word of the Gospel; without the *Feeling* of the Love and Power of Christ upon his Soul, and of his own Acts of Faith towards this blessed Object; and without any *Sense*, or Experience of his Faith working by Love, unto Holiness of Heart and Life: Is *Anti-Scriptural*, and *Anti-evangelical*. — Our Lord faith, *No Man can* come *to me,* (that is, believe on him) *unless the Father which hath sent Me, draw him,* John vi. 44. And that this Drawing of the Father, which enables the Soul to believe on Christ, is by an inward *Teaching*, an internal Revelation of his Glory, is plain, in that our Lord quotes what is recorded in the Old Testament, *It is written in the*

Prophets, And they shall be all taught *of God.* And then He applies it, *Every one therefore that hath* heard, *and hath* learned *of the Father*, cometh *unto me*, Ver. 45. And the Apostle Paul saith, *It pleased God, who separated me from my Mother's Womb, and called me by his Grace, To* reveal *his Son in me*, that *I might preach Him among the Heathen*, Gal. i. 15, 16. Christ was reveal'd in *Paul*, in order first, to his *Faith* in Him, and next, unto his *Preaching* of Him. He first believed on Christ, and then from his Faith in Christ, he preach'd Him unto all. As *2 Cor.* iv. 5, 13. *For we* (saith he, speaking of HIimself and the other Apostles and Ministers) *preach not ourselves, but* Christ Jesus the Lord. — *We having the same Spirit of Faith, according as it is written, I believed, and therefore have I spoken: We also,* believe, *and therefore* speak. And writing to the *Thessalonians*, he saith, Knowing, *Brethren beloved, your* Election of God. *For our Gospel came not unto you in* Word *only, but also in* Power, *and in the* Holy Ghost, *and in much* Assurance; *as ye know what manner of Men we were among you for your Sake: And ye became Followers of* us, *and of the* Lord, *having receiv'd the Word in much Affliction, with* Joy *of the* Holy Ghost. *So that ye became* Ensamples *to all that believe in* Macedonia *and* Achaia, I. Thes. i. 4, & c. And to the Saints at *Colosse*, He faith, *We give Thanks to God, and the Father of our Lord Jesus Christ, praying always for you: Since we heard of your* Faith *in Christ Jesus, and of the* Love *which ye have to all the Saints: For the Hope which is laid up for you in Heaven, whereof ye heard before in the Word of the Truth of the* Gospel*: Which is come unto you, as it is in all the World, and bringeth forth* Fruit, *as it doth also* in you, *since the Day ye heard of it, and* knew *the Grace of God in Truth*, Col. i. 3, & c. This is the Scripture, the Gospel-Account of Faith in Christ. — And whoever advanceth such a *Faith* that is without *Sight*, Inward *Feelings*, and Spiritual *Sense*, that hath not been, is not, shall not be attended with These, that is without Evidence to the Mind, without the Feeling of powerful Effects on the Heart, and without a Sense of holy Fruit, brought forth in them thereby; and that faith, These Things ought not to be sought for as a subordinate *Evidence* of our Interest in Christ, and of the Truth of our Faith: Most certainly advanceth a *Notion* that is *Anti-Scriptural*, and *Anti-evangelical.*

2. Another *Notion* that I take to be *such,* is, The advancing of *imputed* Holiness, to the Denial of *imparted* Holiness, of representative Holiness in *Christ*, to the Denial of personal Holiness in *us.*

The Word of God acquaints us, That, *If the* Root *be holy, so are the* Branches, Rom. xi. 16. The Branches of any living, flourishing, fruitful Tree, have, not only a Fulness, a Perfection of Life and Sap in their Root; but they also have the Communication thereof to them, to make them green and fruitful in themselves. Not in themselves, as seperate from the Root; but as in Union to, and Communion with it. Our Lord faith, *I am the* Vine, *ye are the* Branches: *He that abideth in Me, and I in him, the same bringeth forth much Fruit: for without* Me, *ye can do Nothing*, John xv. 5. It is plain from hence, that Our Lord asserts, a Communication of his own Life and Fulness, of his Purity and Holiness, to the Branches which are in Him, to make them green and fruitful in themselves. Not to give them a Stock of Life and Strength, of Purity and Holiness in themselves, as seperate from him; but all gracious Supplies from his Fulness, as in Union to, and Communion with Him. In that he saith, The *Branch* that abides in Him, (by faith) and that He abides in (by his Spirit) the *same* bringeth forth much *Fruit*. It is as plain as Words can make it, that the Believer, the Branch that abides in Christ, and that He abides in, the same bringeth forth much Fruit. For without ME, saith our Lord, *Ye* can do Nothing. He speaks of the Fruit produced in, and brought forth by the *Branches*; of the Things which they do: From a derived Sameness of Nature with him, and a communication of Influence from him, as being in Union to, and Communion with Him the *Root*. He speaks not only, nor chiefly, of what he is in *Himself*, and has done for them, as their Representing Head; but of what He is for them, as their Head of Influence, and of what *They* are and do, by and from *Him*, as the communicative Fountain of their Supply. — For Any therefore, to advance *imputed* Holiness, representative Holiness in *Christ*, to the Denial of *imparted* Holiness, of personal Holiness in *ourselves* from Him; it must needs be *contrary* to the *Word* and *Gospel* of Christ.

3. Another *Notion* advanc'd which I take to be *Anti-Scriptural*, and *Anti-evangelical* is, That if any Person looks for Holiness in Himself; He thereby rejects *Christ*, as *his Holiness*.

Nay rather, If any Person looks for Holiness in *Christ*, as *imputed* to Him, so as to disregard Holiness in *himself, imparted* from Christ; He thereby rejects *Christ*, as *his Holiness*, as the communicative *Fountain* thereof, and all that Fulness of Grace, which is treasur'd up in *Him*, to be communicated unto *us*. — *For it pleased the Father that in Him* (in Christ) *should all Fulness dwell*, Col. i. 19. A Fulness of Holiness for Communication, as well as for Representation. *And of his Fulness* (saith the Evangelist *John*) *have all we received, and Grace for Grace*, John i. 16. It is the Fulness of Christ, as our Head of Influence, as the communicative Fountain of all Holiness to us, *that filleth All in All*, Eph. i. 23. In all his Members. That filleth all the Powers of their Souls, and the Members of their Bodies, with Holiness, in a begun Measure now, that will increase their Holiness here, and fill them with perfect Holiness, even brimful hereafter. And who is there that loves and receives Christ, that loves and receives Him as our Holiness, in what He is and will be unto us; that would not cleave unto Him as the Fountain of all Grace, and rejoice to receive from Him continually and increasingly, until He is perfectly conformed unto Christ in Glory?

4. Another *Notion* advanc'd, which I take to be *Anti-Scriptural*, and *Anti-evangelical* is, That if a Person seeks for Holiness in *Himself*, He certainly *depends* upon it.

It is one Thing to seek for *Holiness* in *ourselves*, as a *Fruit* of Faith declar'd in the Gospel; and another Thing to put that Holiness, that Fruit of Faith, in the Place of *Christ*, Faith's Object, to expect our Acceptance with God thereby: It having been said, "That inherent Holiness, is but Self-Righteousness under another Name." Whereas, the Gospel of Christ makes a Distinction between what Christ is made unto us of God in Point of *Righteousness*, and what of him He is made unto us in Point of *Sanctification*, I Cor. i. 30. Our Title to Glory, stands in the complete Obedience of Jesus Christ: Our personal Meetness for Glory, in the Graces of the Holy Spirit wrought in us, in the Sanctification of our Nature, in our inherent Holiness, communicated to us from Christ's Fulness. Upon Christ's Righteousness *alone*, for Acceptance with God, every Believer *depends*. And yet they earnestly *do* and *ought* to seek for personal Holiness, and the Increase of it in *themselves.* — *Thus the* Apostle *Paul, Yea, doubtless, and I count all Things but Loss, for the Excellency of the Knowledge of Christ Jesus my Lord: For whom I have suffer'd the Loss of all Things, and do count them but Dung that I may win Christ, and be found in him, not having on mine own Righteousness, which is of the Law, but that which is thro' the Faith of Christ, the Righteousness which is of God by Faith,* Phil. Iii. 8, 9. There's the Righteousness he desir'd to have *upon* him; there's his *Dependance* for Acceptance with God. Then follows, *That I may know him, and the Power of his Resurrection, and the Fellowship of his Sufferings, being made conformable unto his Death; if by any Means I might attain unto the Resurrection of the Dead: Not as tho' I had already attained, either were already perfect; but I follow after, if that I may apprehend that for which also I am apprehended of Christ Jesus,* Ver. 10, 11, 12. There's his earnest *Pursuit* after inherent and personal Holiness, after Communion with Christ, the *Knowledge* of HIM, in his Fulness of Grace, and in the *Power*, the Virture of his Death and Resurrection, to the Mortification of Sin in him, and quickning of his Soul unto a Life of increasing Holiness, until he arriv'd to an absolute Perfection therein, for which also he was *apprehended of Christ Jesus.* — And thus minded (when in their right Mind) are all Believers. They eagerly seek after *personal* Holiness in Conformity to Christ, *independent* thereon for Acceptance with God: And so far as they see it wrought in them, they rejoice not in *themselves*, but in *Christ Jesus*, their glorious Pattern and Exemplar, to see his Image formed in their Souls: *Giving Thanks unto the* Father, *who hath* thus *made* them meet *to be Partakers of the Inheritance of the Saints in Light*, Col. i. 12. Whoever he be therefore, that saith, If a Person seeks for Holiness in *Himself*, he certainly *depends* upon it; advanceth a *Notion* that is *contrary* to the *Word* and *Gospel* of Christ. For there it is evident, that Believers that seek most earnestly after *personal* Holiness; depend not *thereon*, for their Acceptance with God, nor yet on *themselves* therein, for their Preparation for Glory; but upon *Christ* as their *Righteousness*, and upon *Him* as their *Sanctification*, as their Fountain of Holiness; who hath *begun* this *good Work* in them by his Holy Spirit, and will *perform* it until the Day of his Appearing, *Phil.* i. 6.

5. Another *Notion* advanc'd which I take to be *Anti-Scriptural* and *Anti-evangelical,* is, That the Holy Ghosts's *revealing* of Christ's perfect personal

Holiness, as our Representing-Head, and *shewing* us, our mystical Compleatness in Him; is all that is intended by *that Sanctification of the Spirit.* For,

The *personal* Holiness of God's Chosen, is manifestly intended by *The Sanctification of the Spirit.* As, I. Pet. i. 2. *Elect according to the Forcknowledge of God the Father, thro' Sanctification of the Spirit unto Obedience, and Sprinkling of the Blood of Jesus Christ: Grace unto you, and Peace be multiplied.* Here the People of God are said to be chosen *thro' Sanctification of the Spirit*; viz. *to Salvation*, (as 2 Thess. ii. 13.) *thro'* Sanctification *of the Spirit*, as a Means to that End. And that *personal* Sanctification is hereby intended, is evident, in that it is added, *unto Obedience*,— sanctify'd by the Spirit, unto Obedience, or made holy in Heart by the Spirit, unto Holiness of Life. And to this they are exhorted, Ver. 14, 15, 16. *As obedient Children, not fashioning yourselves according to the former Lusts in your Ignorance: But as He which hath called you is holy, so be ye holy in all Manner of Conversation: Because it is written, be ye holy, for I am holy. Obedience,* respects a *Command.* The Obedience of *Children*, respects the Command of a *Father* given them. The Command here given to the Lord's Children is, *Be ye holy, for I am holy.* The Sense of this Word is not, (as has been suggested) be ye holy by *Imputation*; for I am holy: But be ye holy (as is express'd) *in all Manner of Conversation*; for I am holy: Conform to this my Command given you, as obedient Children; and take ME for the Pattern of your Obedience, of your Holiness in Heart and Life. — This *Obedience* then, this *Holiness* of Conversation, unto which the Children of God are called; being *personal*, or just the Reverse of *fashioning themselves according to the former Lusts in their Ignorance*; their being *sanctify'd by the Spirit*, unto this Obedience, must needs respect *inherent, personal* Sanctification; or, Holiness of Heart, unto Holiness of Life. And whoever teacheth otherwise, must needs advance a *Notion* that is *contrary* to the *Word* and *Gospel* of Christ.

6. Another *Notion* advanc'd, which I take to be *Anti-Scriptural* and *Anti-evangelical* is, That all Holiness which Persons have in *themselves*; is *Pharisaical, Self-Holiness.*

Pharisaical-Holiness, is Holiness in *Shew*, and not in *Reality. Self-Holiness*, is that imperfect Principle of Morality in the Heart, and the Degree of Conformity thereto in the Life, which is in Man by *Nature*: Which hath no higher Spring, than the dim Light of natural *Conscience*, which is in every natural Man; and is under no higher influence, than the *Law* as a Covenant of Works, *Matt.* xxiii. 27. *Rom.* ii. 15. A *Christian's Holiness*, is Holiness in *Reality,* Holiness of *Truth*, and not a mere Shew, and empty Shadow, *Eph.* iv. 24. *2 Cor.* viii. 8. It is *in* Himself; (that is, his personal Holiness) but not *of* Himself. It is *Christ's* Life in *Him*, as his Head of Grace. I *am* crucify'd *with Christ*, says the Apostle; (there's the Mortification of Sin in Him) *nevertheless* I live; (there's his inherent Quiickning to a Life of Holiness) *yet not* I, saith He, (that is, his new Life, his Life of Holiness, his living unto God, was not *of*, or *from* Himself, tho' it was *in* Himself) *but CHRIST liveth in* me, *Gal.* ii. 20. Here the Apostle plainly asserts, that his Life of Holiness, of Sanctification, his living unto God, tho' it was inherent in *Himself*, was not *Self-Holiness*, but the Holiness of *Christ* in *him*. It was *in* Himself: Whence he says, *I live*. But not *of*, or *from* Himself; but communicated to Him from *Christ*: And therefore he saith, CHRIST *liveth in me*. And then in the latter Part of this Verse, and Ver. 23. He also asserts his Life of Righteousness, of Justification, which he possess'd by Faith in Christ: *And the Life* (of Holiness) *which I now live in the Flesh, I live by the* Faith *of the* Son of God, (of that Life of Righteousness which I have in Him) *who loved me, and gave Himself for* me. *I do not* frustrate *the* Grace *of God*: (by putting my own inherent and personal Holiness, in the Place of Christ's Obedience, as my justifying Righteousness) for *if Righteousness come by the Law, Christ is dead in vain.* — And

7. Another *Notion* advanc'd, which I take to be *Anti-Scriptural*, and *Anti-evangelical* is, That a *Believer* in Christ, is not under the *Law of God* as a *Rule of Life*.

It is plain, even from the Scriptures of the New Testament, from the Gospel of Christ, that the Law of God is propos'd to Believers as a Rule of Conduct. Believers are redeem'd by Christ from the *Curse* of the Law: Yea, they are deliver'd from the *Law* itself, as a *Covenant of Works*; that they might serve it as a *Rule of Life*, as Christ's *new Commandment*, from Gospel-Motives, and to Gospel-Ends. *Christ hath redeem'd us* (saith the Apostle) *from the Curse of the Law, being made a Curse for us,* Gal. iii. 13. And, *Rom.* vii. 6. He saith, *But now we are deliver'd from the* Law, *that being dead wherein we were held: That we should serve in Newness of the Spirit, and not in the Oldness of the Letter.* The *Oldness of the Letter,* is the Law in its original Form as a *Covenant of Works. The Newness of the Spirit,* is the *Law* as fulfill'd by Christ in Point of Righteousness, and given by Him under the *Gospel,* to be the *Rule* of his People's Obedience. They are deliver'd from the *Law,* in the Oldness of the Letter, *Do, and live; Sin, and die:* That they might serve the *Law,* in the Newness of the Spirit, *Love the Lord their God, with all their Heart, Soul and Strength, and their Neighbour,* their Brother, *as themselves*; from the Life-giving Influence of the Love of Christ to them, and that all-engaging Motive, *If ye love Me, keep my Commandments,* John xiv. 15. *A new Commandment* (faith our Lord) *I give unto you, that ye love one another, as I have loved you, that ye also love one another,* Chap. xiii. 34. And, *He that hath my Commandments, and keepeth them, he it is that loveth* Me, John xiv. 21. *He that loveth me not, keepeth not my Sayings: And the Word which you hear, is not* mine, *but the* Father's *which sent Me,* Ver. 24. So that in this Command given us by our Lord, *to love one another*, he commands us, to love *Himself*, and the *Father* which sent Him: Inasmuch as in *keeping* this Command, we *love Him* who gave it, and in *keeping* this Command of *love to one another*, as it is the Father's Word, the Father's Command, given us by Christ, we *love* the *Father.* And as this Command of *Love to God*, and our *Brother*, is the *Sum* of God's good old *Law*, that eternal Rule of Righteousness; this being given us by *Christ*, the *whole law*, in both Tables of it, is summarily given us by *Him*; in which all the *Ten Words* are included, and unto which they are reducible. And why should any that profess *Christ* reject his *Law*? Can any *Command* of Christ, by any Man that loves him in Sincerity, be accounted *grievous?* No surely, All that love the Lord, must say, with the Apostle, *His Commandments are* not *grievous*, I John v. 3. Can it be *grievous* to a Soul that loves the Lord its Maker, the Lord its Redeemer, to receive any Thing from *Him* in the Form of a *Command?* No surely, such is the Greatness of his Person, the Goodness of his Nature, and the Glory of his Designs; that they put a native Sweetness into the very *Form* of his Commands; which is well relished therein by Souls that love him. And can the *Matter* of our Lord's Commands be *grievous:* The Sum of which is, *Love to God*, and our *Brother*: Which hath such an ineffable Sweetness in it? Which is the present Holiness and Happiness, and will be the endless Glory of all that obey him! Open your Ears, your Hearts then, all ye that love Christ, to receive his Word of Command: *A new Commandment I give unto you.* And our Lord styles it a *new* Commandment; because given us by *Him,* our Saviour-King, who *fulfill'd* it for us, as an *old* Commandment, in Point of *Righteousness*, and in that Respect is the *End of the Law to every one that believeth.* Further, he stiles it a *new* Commandment; because given us by him as the *Rule* of our Obedience, under this *New* or *Gospel*-Dispensation. He likewise styles it a *new* Commandment; because of the *Newness* of the *End* for which it is to be obey'd; *viz.* not to make ourselves *righteous*, not to obtain Life and eternal Salvation thereby; but to *glorify him* who hath sav'd us from Death to Life, who hath loved us, and washed us from our Sins in his own Blood. Again, our Lord styles the Law, as given by him to Believers under the Gospel, a *new* Commandment; from the *Newness* of the *Strength* in which it is to be obey'd; *viz.* not from the Strength of the first *Adam*, when he was made a *living Soul*, or had a Perfection of moral Rectitude, of Fitness to obey the Law in *Himself*; but from the Strength of the second *Adam*, as a *quickning Spirit*, from his Love and Life, manifested *in,* and communicated *to* regenerate Souls. And of the *Law*, as thus given by Christ unto Christians, the Apostle *Paul* saith, that he was *under* it. *Being not without Law to God, but* under *the Law to Christ*, I. Cor. ix. 21. And writing to the *Galations*, he saith, *Brethren, ye have been call'd unto* Liberty; (from the Law as a Covenant of Works) *only use not Liberty for an Occasion to the Flesh,* (be not careless about your Obedience, your Conformity to the Law as a Rule of Life) *but by* Love *serve one another. For all the* Law *is fulfill'd in one Word, even in This, Thou shalt* love *they Neighbour as Thyself,* Gal. v. 13, 14. Whence it is evident, that these believing *Galations*, of whom he was most jealous, left they should adhere to the Law as a *Covenant of Works*, were under it as a *Rule of Life:* Else, this Motive, of fulfilling the *Law*, which he us'd to excite tehm to brotherly *Love*, had been of no *Force.* They might have reply'd: 'Why do you tell us of the *Law?* Of *fulfilling* the Law? We are under *Grace:* We have nothing to *do* with the Law. Han't you just now bid us *Stand fast in the Liberty wherewith Christ hath made us free?* What have we to do, to attempt to *fulfil the Law?* Han't *Christ fulfill'd* it for us, and become the *End* of it to us? Is it not our *Gospel-Liberty* to be free from the *Law? — 'No*; as if the Apostle should say, you *Believers* in Christ, who are *free* from the *Law,* as a *Covenant of Works,* as a *Yoke of Bondage,* in which Liberty you ought to *stand fast*; are *under* it to Christ, as a *Rule of Life,* as *Christ's Law*, as it is to you thro' him, a *Law of Liberty,* in Conformity whereto, a glorious Part of your *Gospel-Freedom*, from the Servitude of Sin and Satan consisteth. You for whom *Christ* fulfill'd the Law, in Point of Righteousness before God; are to fulfil the *Law yourselves* in Point of Obedience unto him, and for his Glory, and for your own and others Advantage. And therefore, see that you *fulfil the Law,* that you obey your Lord's Command in *loving of the Brethren. "By* Love *serve one another. For all the* Law *is fulfilled in one Word, even in This; Thou shalt* love *they Neighbour as Thyself."* Whoever therefore saith, That a *Believer* in Christ, is not under the *Law of God* as a *Rule of Life:* Advanceth a *Notion* that is *Anti-Scriptural,* and *Anti-evangelical.*

And what now, my dear Brethren, are the *Consequences* of these advanced Notions, unto which they natively tend? And not to mention, Divisions and Discords among Brethren: To the Dishonour of our Lord; to the Grief of those that love Him; to the Stumbling of Souls enquiring after Him; and to the manifest Hindrance of the Progress of the Gospel: Which have sadly appear'd: Permit me to hint the following *Consequences* of these advanced Notions. As,

1. The *Leading* of Persons to take up with such a Faith, as sufficient to Salvation, which is not *Saving.*

2. The *Perverting* of the *Gospel of Christ*, or the *Dividing* of his Salvation declar'd in the *Gospel*; of what he is to, and has done for his People in and by *Himself*; and of what he is to, and doth for his People in *Themselves.*

3. The *Denial* of the *Work* of the *Holy Ghost*, in the Sanctification of our *Nature.*

4. The *Perverting* of the *Judgment* of Believers, and *Overthrowing* of their Faith, in that Part of the Gospel, which respects *personal* Sanctification.

5. The *Drawing* of Believers into a *Denial* of what God hath *wrought in* them.

6. The leading Persons into a *Disregard* of Holiness of Heart. And,

7. The *Opening* the *Sluices* for Ungodliness of *Life.*

If such a *Faith* is advanc'd, which consists in a Person's believing that Christ dy'd for Sinners, for the whole World, for all Men universally; and every Man is thus exhorted to believe that Christ dy'd for him in particular; and to be persuaded that so believing he shall certainly be saved; although this Faith of his be without *Sight* and Inward *Feelings*, without an internal Revelation of the Glory of Christ, and a sweet Sensation of powerful Effects, unto *Holiness* of Heart and Life: Is not this the direct Way to *deceive* Souls? To lead Persons to take up with such a *Faith,* as sufficient to Salvation, which falls far short of the Gospel-Account of *saving* Faith? And is of no other Kind than that of which the Apostle saith, *What doth it profit, my Brethren, though a Man say he hath* Faith, *and have not* Works? *Can* Faith save *him?* Jam. ii. 14.

If such a Notion is advanc'd, That we are to believe in *Christ* as our Holiness, and not to look for Holiness in *ourselves*; that his personal Holiness is *imputed* unto us, and not to seek for Holiness *imparted* from Him, to make us holy in *ourselves*, both in Heart and Life: Is not the *Gospel of Christ* hereby *perverted?* And his Salvation *divided?* Since the Gospel declares, not only what Christ is to, and hath done for his People in *Himself*, as their holy Law-fulfilling Head; but also, what he is to, and doth for them, in *Themselves*, as the Fountain of Holiness in and to them? As a *quickning Spirit*, as our Head of Influence, who communicates his own Life to all his Members, to work in them a Sameness of Nature with Him? I *Cor.* xv. 45.

If such a Notion is advanc'd, That if any Person looks for Holiness in *Himself*, he thereby rejects *Christ* as his Holiness: Is not the *Judgment* of Believers *perverted* hereby, and their Faith *overthrown* in that Part of the Gospel which respects *personal* Sanctification? Doth not the advancing of such a Notion, natively *tend* unto this? And hath not *this* been the sad Consequence thereof?

If such a Notion is advanc'd, That if a Person seeks for Holiness in *Himself*; he certainly *depends* upon it: Are not Believers *drawn* hereby into a *Denial* of what God hath *wrought* in them? Lest they should *depend* upon any Thing short of *Christ*, they are drawn off from *seeking* Holiness in *themselves*, yea, even to *deny* that there is any Holiness in *them*; to the great Dishonour of the God of all Grace, whose *Workmanship* they are, as new Creatures in Christ Jesus, as *created in Him unto good Works;* and whose *Glory* they have frequently beheld in the *Face of Jesus Christ*, unto the *changing* of their Souls into the *same Image*.

If such a Notion is advanc'd, That the Holy Ghost's *revealing* of Christ's perfect, personal Holiness as our representing Head, and *shewing* us our mystical Completeness in him; is all that is intended by *The Sanctification of the Spirit*: Is not the natural Consequence hereof, The *Denial* of the *Work* of the *Holy Ghost*, in the Sanctification of our *Nature?* Are not Persons naturally drawn into this great Error hereby; to the great Dishonour of the *Holy Ghost*, who in his infinite Grace, has undertook the Application of the *Whole* of Salvation unto us, of which The Sanctification of our *Nature*, is so great a *Part*?

If such a Notion is advanc'd, That all Holiness that Persons have in *themselves*, is *Pharisaical, Self-Holiness;* are not Persons *led* hereby into a *Disregard* of Holiness of *Heart*: To the great Hindrance of their *Growth in Grace?*

And if such a Notion is advanced, That a *Believer* in Christ is not under the *Law of God*, as a *Rule of Life*; are not the *Sluices opened* hereby for Ungodliness of *Life?* Doth not the advancing of such a *Notion*, naturally tend to Licentiousness of *Practice?* And sadly heretofore, hath this been found to be the woful *Effect* thereof. — And tho' some Persons, who advance this Notion, that have the Truth of Grace, of Holiness in their Hearts, may be preserv'd from Ungodliness of Life;

yet the Advancement of such a Notion, naturally *tends* to this sad Consequence both in *themselves* and *others*. — I come now to give a few Hints,

Fourthly. Concerning some *Things* which have been said by those who advance these Notions. And it has been said,

1. That they have been *impos'd* upon, in being taught to look for Holiness of *Heart*, a Change of *Nature,* or for their being made *new Creatures.*

2. That the *Effect* of teaching Persons to look for Holiness of *Heart,* spiritual Life, and the Increase of it in *themselves;* is *The bringing of Souls into Bondage.* And,

3. That tho' they *deny* inherent and personal *Holiness*; they do *not* deny the *Fruits of the Spirit,* and a *Conversation becoming the Gospel.* — And to those who have thus said, let me reply,

1. If you say, you have been *impos'd* upon, in being taught to look for Holiness of *Heart*, a Change of *Nature,* or for your being made *new Creatures*: Don't you hereby reproach that Great *Work of God*, in the Awakening and Conversion of Numbers of *Souls,* which hath been amongst us of *late Years?* Was not the Doctrine of the *New* Birth, of Heart-Holiness, of a Change of Nature, or a Man's being a *new Creature* in Christ Jesus; one of the great Doctrines *preach'd* by the Rev. Mr. *Whitefield* and his *Assistants*, as absolutely necessary to be experienc'd by every Man, in order to his spiritual and eternal Happiness, in the present and everlasting Enjoyment of GOD? Was not this a Doctrine that was *own'd* and *blest* of God, for the Awakening and Conversion of Numbers of Souls to Christ? Was not this a Doctrine, the Truth whereof was indeed experienc'd by many? Was not this one of the main Doctrines for which, as an essential Part of the *Faith which was once delivered to the Saints,* the Lord's Wittnesses for some years have been *contending*? Was not this a main Doctrine which their Adversaries *oppos'd* and *reproach'd?* And was not the Advancement hereof by the Lord's Witnesses, one great Cause of their *Sufferings,* of all the *Persecutions* which they have endur'd with much *Patience* and *great Joy?* And must *That* now be taken for *Error,* which was once happily known for *Truth?* And joyfully *felt* and *experienc'd?* And have all the Sufferings of the Lord's Witnesses on Account of this his Truth, been in *vain?* Oh, *Tell it not in* Gath, *publish it not in* Askelon; *lest the Uncircumcised triumph!*

But see now, *you* who think you have been *impos'd* upon; by *whom* the Imposition was made. For most surely by the *Lord of Christians,* is this Doctrine of the *New Birth* impos'd upon *them*, as an Article of their *Faith*: Jesus *answered and said unto him, Verily verily I say unto thee, except a Man be* born again, *he cannot see the Kingdom of God*, John iii. 3. *Verily, verily;* it is a solemn Asseveration, which gives the highest Assurance of the Thing to which it is annexed. *I say unto thee;* I that am *Truth* itself, the *faithful and true Witness,* I say unto thee, *Except a Man be* born again, *he cannot* see (that is, *enjoy) the kingdom of God.* Who then, that professeth himself to be a *Christian*, is not obliged by this Word of CHRIST, to believe the Doctrine of the *New Birth?* Oh my Brethren, *you* to whom these Lines are address'd, are there any among you, or that of late were among you, that have Need to *learn again* this *first Principle of the Doctrine of Christ!* their A, B, C! I call it a *first Principle* of Christian Doctrine: For so it is, as to our *personal* Salvation, or the *Application* of Salvation unto *us*. For not a Man that is not *born of God*, hath true *Faith*; and not a Man that hath not true *Faith*, is in a State of *Salvation*. But perhaps you will say,

This we *allow*; but then by the *New-Birth*, we are *not* to understand, a new, a holy *Nature* produced in the *Man*; but the Man's seeing of himself by Faith, to be a new Creature in *Christ*; or to be what he is as a new Creature, only as he stands *in* Christ, his representing Head, the Holiness of *Christ's* Nature being *imputed* unto him. I reply:

By the *New-Birth*, or a Man's being *born again*, our Lord intends, a new *Nature*, a spiritual *Principle* produced in the *Man*; and don't at all thereby regard what is in *Himself*, and *imputed* unto any Man.

This is evident, in that the Change is said to be in the *Man*: The *Man* is said to be born again; or that except a *Man* is born again, he cannot see the Kingdom of God. And thus Ver. 5. *Jesus answered and said unto him, Verily verily I say unto thee, except a Man be born of Water and of the Spirit,* (of the Word and Spirit of God) *he cannot enter intot he Kingdom of God.* Here again, the Change is said to be in the *Man*, the *Man* is said to be *born again*. And that by his New-Birth is intended a new and spiritual *Nature* produced in the *Man*, further appears from what follows, That *which is born of the Flesh, is Flesh; and* that *which is born of the Spirit, is Spirit,* Ver. 6. Here's a *That* which is born of the *Flesh*, i.e. the Body, is *Flesh*: And a *That* which is born of the *Spirit*, which is said to be *Spirit*. And what is this *That*, which is produced by the New-Birth? It is not the *Soul* of the *Man:* For Body and Soul *united,* constitutes him *such*: And a *Man* he is said to be, before his *New-Birth*. This *That* then, must be something *distinct* from his Soul. And it is said to be *Spirit*, that is, a new, or spiritual *Nature* produced in his Soul, or in other Words, a new, and spiritual *Image* enstampt upon it. For tho' this *That* which is born of the Spirit, or the new Life produced by his creating Power, must be consider'd as *distinct* from the Essence of the *Soul*; (the Soul being *before* this new Life spoken of is *produced*; and wicked Men having *Souls*, who are never *born again*) Yet is the Seat of it *in* the Soul, it being a new Image enstampt upon it. And thence it is the *Soul*, the *Man* that is said to be born again. But tho' this Spirit, or new Life, which is born of the Spirit, or produced by the Holy Ghost in Regeneration; must be consider'd as *distinct* from the Soul; yet is it not *seperable* from the Soul; as hath been objected. — For to enervate any Argument that might be brought for inherent Holiness, for Holiness of Heart wrought in us, it has been said.

That it is a most foolish Thing, for any to think or speak of a new Life produced in Regeneration, that is *distinct* from the Man, that is neither his *Soul*, nor his *Body*: For if any such new and holy Nature was produced in the Soul, that was distinct from the Soul; it must be *seperable:* And so the *Man,* consisting of Soul and Body, might perish at last, notwithstanding this new Life that was wrought in him.

But let such observe: That when I say the new Life produced in the Man by the Holy Ghost at the Time of Regeneration, must be consider'd as *distinct* from the Essence of the Soul; I intend thereby, that it is no otherwise distinct, than as an Accident *in* its Subject, as a Habit or Quality *in* the Mind, or as an *Image,* the Seat of which is *in* the Soul. And thus, when Man was first created, the divine Image imprest upon his Soul, must be consider'd as *distinct* from the Essence of his Soul, as consisting of all its Powers and Faculties; else he could not have *lost* it. The *Soul,* essentially consider'd, being an immortal Spirit, can never die. But when *Adam* sinned, he lost that original Purity and Righteousness in which he was created; he lost the *Image* of his Maker, or that Impress of divine Holiness which was enstampt upon him; he lost his *Likeness* to God, and so his *Communion* with him, which was the *Life* of his Spirit. His *Soul,* the Essence thereof, remain'd; tho' the divine *Image,* the moral *Life* of it, was lost. And another *Image,* black and horrid! *Sin,* the Image of *Satan,* that *Death,* took its Place in that Soul, where *Holiness,* the Image of *God,* was before seated, and brightly shone. And just thus, is the new Life, the Life of Holiness, produced in the Soul by the Holy Ghost in Regeneration, or by his New-Creation-Work upon the Man, to be consider'd as *distinct* from the *Soul* in which it is seated, as being a new and glorious *Image* enstampt upon it. But let it be further observ'd, That tho' *Adam's* Life of Holiness, in which he was created, was *distinct* from his *Soul,* and so may serve to shew, that our Life of Holiness given us by our new Creation, is *distinct* from our *Souls,* essentially consider'd; yet it will not follow from hence, that because *Adam's* Holiness was distinct from his Soul, and was *seperable,* and *seperated* from it; therefore *our* Life of Holiness, if *distinct* from our *Souls,* may be *seperable* from them. For *Adam's* Life of Holiness, as he was the Head of all Mankind, was given him as a *Stock* in *Himself.* Having a Fulness of Life in himself, he was thus made a *living Soul.* And had he stood, the same holy *Image* in which he was created, had been from him convey'd to all his Posterity: As his corrupt *Image* was upon his Fall. But the Case is far otherwise with *us,* as to *our* Life of Holiness, given us in the New-Birth: *That,* tho' inherent *in* ourselves, being not given us as a *Stock* entrusted in our own Hands, for ourselves or others: But communicated from Christ our *Head,* unto us, as *Members* of his Body, from an immense Fulness, a rich Stock residing in *Him,* that can never be *lost,* nor *exhausted.* The *Seed* and Off-spring of *Christ,* the new *Adam,* the *Heavenly Man,* are united to a *Head,* that is infinite, unchangeable, and eternal. Whose Life of Holiness, to communicate to them, is *Yesterday, ToDay, and Forever the same.* And their Union to him being *indissoluble*; their Life of Holiness receiv'd *from* him, by Communion *with* him, being *his* Life *in* them, is not, cannot from them be *seperable,* nor shall be ever *separated,* or *lost.* Because CHRIST *lives,* in this Regard, for and in them; *they* in and with him, *shall live also.* Their *new Life,* their begun Life of Holiness, communicated from Christ to them, extending to all the Powers and Faculties of their Souls, and its Influence unto all the Members of their Bodies, shall by him be maintain'd and increas'd, until it is perfected: Until the utter Extirpation of Sin and Death, the old *Adam's Image*, out of their Souls and Bodies; and they the Seed of the new *Adam*, compleat in Holiness, perfectly conformed unto his bright *Image, shall appear with him in Glory.*

From our Lord's Discourse then with *Nicodemus*, it appears, That by the *New-Birth*, we are to understand, a new, a holy *Nature* produced in the *Man*: And not, the Man's seeing of himself by Faith to be a new Creature in *Christ*; or to be what he is as a new Creature, only as he stands *in* Christ, his representing Head, the Holiness of *Christ's* Nature being *imputed* unto him. Since the Change is said to be in the *Man*: The *Man* is said to be *born again.* And that there is a real *Production* made by the Holy Ghost in the New-Birth, a *That* which is born of the Spirit, which is *Spirit*; or a spiritual, holy *Nature*, in Opposition to that carnal, sinful *Nature*, which wholly over-spreads the Soul of an unregenerate Man. And that by the *New-Birth*, we are to understand, a new, a holy *Nature* produced in the *Man*; and not his seeing of the Holiness of *Christ's* Nature *imputed* unto him; is further evident, in that, this *That* which is born of the Spirit, being a real *Production*, must be produced *somewhere*; either in *Christ*, or in the *Man*. In Christ it is *not*; the Holiness of Christ's Nature, being perfect, unchangeably and eternally the same; it admits, as of no Diminution, so of no Augmentation. No new and spiritual Nature is produc'd in *Christ*, by the Man's *New-Birth.* It remains then, that this holy, spiritual Nature is produced in the *Man*. It is not *Christ* that is born again, but the *Man*. It is not *in* Christ, that this *That*, this Spirit which is born of the Spirit, is produced; but *in* the Man.

And that Holiness of Heart, a Change of Nature, or a new and spiritual Nature, is produced in the Soul at the Time of its New-Birth, may be further proved from the *Parallel* which the Apostle runs betweent he *first Adam*, and the *Second*, and their respective *Seeds*, I Cor. xv. 47, 48, 49. *The* first Man *is of the Earth, Earthy; the* second Man *is the Lord from Heaven.* As *is the* Earthy, such *are they also that are* Earthy: *and as is the* Heavenly, such *are they also that are* Heavenly. *And as we have borne the Image of the Earthy, we shall also bear the* Image *of the Heavenly.* The Scope of the Apostle in these Verses is, to set forth the *first Adam,* and the *Second, as Heads*, to their respective *Seeds*; and the *Influence* which is communicated from each of these Heads, to their respective Seeds, unto their *Conformity* to Them, as their respective Heads. And this he doth to prove the Resurrection of the *Bodies* of the Saints in particular, that they shall be conformed unto the *glorious* Body of Christ. Yet so, that the Words are of a larger Extent, and do also respect the perfect Holiness of their *Souls*, which they shall have in Conformity to the *Soul* of Christ, unto his *holy Image.* — The first Man *Adam*, was the Representative Head of all his *Seed*, of all Mankind: And what *He* was, in his first Make, that *all Men* were, Representatively in Him. Thus, *God made Man upright: All Men* were thus made in *Adam* that *One Man.* And He being constituted of God, their Covenant-Head, while *He* stood, *They* stood; when *He* fell, *They* fell. He being their Representative, what He *was*, and *did*, that They *were,* and *did* in Him. This the Apostle *Rom.* v. proves at large — Now let it be observ'd, That the first *Adam* was not only constituted of God, the *Representative-Head* of all his Seed; but also, the *Fountain* of their *Nature.* So that what He was in *Himself,* Representatively for them, they were to be in *Themselves*, derivatively from Him. He having sinned, and thereby lost the Image of God, and contracted a corrupt Image, the Image of Satan; They having sinned in, and fell with Him their Representative; were to have the same *Image* communicated to *them*, from *Him* the Fountain of their Nature, which He had contracted. — And thus actually it is; *All Men,* all that are *Earthy*, bear the *Image* of their first Father *Adam*, that *One Man,* who was of the *Earth, Earthy.* They bear, not only his *natural* Image, in a Sameness of *Nature* derived from Him, in that they are of the same *Species*, Men, as He was a Man, consisting of Soul and Body: But also his *corrupt* Image, and are Sinful Men, like that first Man: Sin spreads itself throughout their whole Frame, through all the Powers of their Souls, and Members of their Bodies. — And just thus it is between *Christ*, and those that are *His*, between the second *Adam*, and all that are his *Offspring.* The *Lord from Heaven,* this *Heavenly Man,* was constituted of God, the *Representative-Head* of all his *Seed.* What He is in *himself*, as thus their Head, and hath done for them, *They* are reckon'd to be, and to have done in him: His Purity and Righteousness being *imputed* unto them. — And lo, this glorious second *Adam*, was appointed of God, not only to be our *Representing-Head,* but also, to be our *Head of Influence,* the *Fountain* of all *Grace* unto us, to communicate a Sameness of *Nature*, a Likeness of *Image* with him, unto all his *Seed.* He being *holy*, as their Representing-Head; They are *holy,* perfectly so, as they stand before God in *him*: He being *holy*, as their Head of Influence, as thee communicated Fountain of all Holiness to *them*; they are *holy* be Derivation from *Him*: Have a holy *Principle* produced in their Souls by him, which shall be maintain'd and increas'd from him, until it arrives unto a full *Conformity* to him: Until their *Souls* are made perfect in Holiness, compleately *like* unto his holy *Soul,* or *changed* into his *holy Image.* And as his Resurrection-Body, who is the Lord from Heaven, is an *heavenly Body*, a *glorious, immortal Body;* their *Bodies* also, their *vile* Body, by him their Head of Influence, shall be *changed*, and *fashioned like unto his glorious Body.* — Thus the *Offspring* of the second *Adam*, in their entire Persons, shall be wrought up by him, into a full Conformity to *him* their glorious *Head.* For, as the Apostle argues, and the Holy Ghost by him assures, as *is the Earthy, such are they also that are* Heavenly. *And as we have borne the* Image *of the* Earthy, *we shall also bear the* Image *of the* Heavenly.

And that Holiness of Heart, is communicated from Christ to Christians, that a new and spiritual Nature is produced in them at the Time of their New-Birth, in

Conformity to him; may be further proved, by a few more Scriptures, out of many that might be brought. Thus,

Rom. viii. 29. *For whom he did foreknow, he also did predestinate to be* conformed *to the* Image *of his Son, that he might be the first-born among many Brethren.* Those whom God the Father *foreknew*, in all the infinite Grace of his Heart, in his discriminating Love before the World began, he also did *predestinate to be* conformed *to the* Image *of his Son.* To the Image of his *Holiness* in their *Souls*, as the Beauty and Brightness thereof; and to the Image of his *Glory* in their *Bodies*, which will make them bright and glorious. The Conformity of *Christians*, of the *Children* of God the Father's Love, unto *Christ*, his first-born *Son*, consists in their being made *like* unto *him.* And as *real a Change,* passeth upon their *Souls* now, to conform them to the *Image* of his *Holiness*, to make them inherently *holy*; as shall pass upon their *Bodies* at last, to conform them unto his *glorious Image*, to cloath them with his Glory. The Work of *Conformity to Christ,* is but *One,* tho' it hath these *Two* Parts. And whoever denies Holiness of Heart communicated to the Soul now, at the Time of its New-Birth, unto a *real Change*, in Conformity to Christ's holy Image; may as well deny the Glory of the Body at last, or the *real Change*, which shall pass upon that to conform it to his glorious Image. For, as Christ is the Representing-Head of his People, they are now *compleat in Him,* both in Holiness and Glory. *God, who raised Christ from the Dead, being rich in Mercy, for his great Love wherewith he loved* them, *even when dead in Sins,* did *quicken* them *together* mystically *with Christ, hath raised them up together with him, and made them fit together in heavenly Places in Christ Jesus.*

And would those who deny inherent Holiness communicated from Christ, be no otherwise *holy*, than they are in *Him*, their Representing-Head *now*? Would they be no otherwise *glorious,* than they are in *Him* as such, *now?* What, my Friends, is there to be no *real Change* in your *Souls*, nor in your *Bodies* hereafter? Are your *Souls* to go to Heaven, as your profess they now *are*, destitute of all Holiness, and full of Impurity? Are they always to remain under that *Death*, that Deprivation of the divine *Image* which Sin brought up - on them? And are your *Bodies* always to remain *vile* Bodies, and under the Dominion of *Death*? If you say, *"No; our Bodies* are to be rais'd again, and *fashioned like unto the glorious Body of Christ."* And shan't your *Souls* then be chang'd into the *Image* of his *Holiness*, as your *Bodies* into the *Image* of his *Glory?* Oh be assur'd, That *no unclean Thing, shall enter into the New Jerusalem.* No *unholy Soul,* shall have Admittance into *Heaven,* that *holy Place.* And were it possible that an unholy Soul, that hath no inherent Holiness in *itself*, could be admitted into *Heaven,* supposing the Holiness of *Christ's* Nature was *imputed* to it; yet for Want of *imparted Holiness*, it could not *enjoy* Heaven, the *Holiness* of that *State.* No *unregenerate, unholy* Soul, can *see*, can *enjoy* the *Kingdom of God,* a GOD *glorious in* HOLINESS! The bright Displays of infinite, flaming Purity, would rather torment, than delight such a Soul. Because there can be no *Enjoyment*, but what ariseth from an *Agreeableness* between the person or

Thing *enjoying*, and the Person or Thing *enjoyed*. Like loves its Like. Like Things bosom in each other. GOD being the Object of Enjoyment in Heaven, who is infinitely *holy*; if the *Soul*, the *Subject*, be not inherently *holy*, it can have no *Enjoyment* of that *glorious Object*. And if you should say, my dear Friends, "That your *Souls* shall be inherently *holy*, when out of the *Body*." Whence are they to receive that Holiness? If you say, "from *Christ*." Will *he* not then be unto you a *Head of Influence,* a communicative Fountain of Holiness? And if he will be so *then*; why may he not be so *now*, unto *begun* Holiness, unto Holiness of *Truth*, in your *Souls*; as he will be then unto *perfect* Holiness? And if your Souls *are* to be made inherently holy at *last*; will that Holiness you will then have in *yourselves*, be *Self-Holiness?* Or the Holiness of *Christ* in *you?* Will it be your *own* Holiness as *of* and *from* yourselves? Or *Christ's* Holiness communicated to you, as *of* and *from* him? If you say, "It will be *Christ's* Holiness in us, as *of* and *from* him." Why may'nt you thus have Holiness in *yourselves*, communicated from *Christ*, in a begun Measure *now*, as you will *then* have it in Perfection? And if you are to be inherently holy to Perfection at *last*; will you then, think you, *reject Christ*, on account thereof, as *your Holiness*? Or rather bless him forever, that as your Head of Influence, he hath fill'd you from his own Fulness, and wrought you up into a perfect Conformity to his bright Image? And if on account of your perfect inherent Holiness at *last*, you will not reject Christ *then,* as your Holiness; why mayn't you *see*, and *seek* for inherent Holiness, and increasing Degrees thereof, until it arrives unto that Perfection; without rejecting Christ, as your Holiness, *now?* For most certainly, The *Children of God,* are *predestinated* to be thus *conformed* unto his *first born Son.*

Again, That Holiness of Heart, a Change of Nature is communicated to the Soul in its New-Birth, appears, in that this the Lord hath *promis'd* in his New Covenant. As *Ezek.* xxxvi. 25, 26. *Then will I sprinkle clean Water upon you, and ye shall be clean: From all your Filthiness, and from all your Idols will I* cleanse *you. A* new Heart *also will I give you, and a* new Spirit *will I put within you, and I will take away the stony Heart out of your Flesh, and will give you an Heart of Flesh.* In the first of these Verses, the Lord promiseth to *cleanse* the Consciences of his People from all Sin, in its Guilt and Filth, and to subdue its Power, under the *Sprinklings* of the *Blood of Christ*, that *clean* (or cleansing) *Water*: Which was typ'd out by the *Water of Purification for Sin*, that was made of the *Ashes of a burnt red Heifer*; as *Num.* xix. with *Heb.* ix. 13, 14. Then follows the Promise of the *Sanctification* of their Nature, Ver. 26. *A* new Heart *also will I give you, and a* new Spirit *will I put within you, and I will take away the stony Heart out of your Flesh, and will give you an Heart of Flesh.* Is this *new Heart*, and this *new Spirit* which the Lord here promiseth to his People, in *Christ?* or in *Them?* If any say, "It is in *Christ*," the Word of God saith overwise: A new Heart will I give *you*; and a new Spirit will I put *within you.* And I will take away the stony Heart out of *your* Flesh, and will give *you* an Heart of Flesh. What can be plainer, than that a Change of

Nature is here intended, in that a *hard Heart*, the Seat of which is in the *Soul*, is promis'd to be taken *out* of it, and a *tender Heart* given in *Place* thereof? This *new Heart,* and this *new Spirit* which is promis'd, must certainly intend the *Renovation* of the *Soul*, in all its Powers and Faculties, superior and inferior. This new *Spirit*, which the Lord says, I will put *within you*, is not the Spirit of GOD; for the Promise of the *Holy Ghost* as an Indweller, is plainly distinguish'd from this new Spirit, and follows, Ver. 37. And I will put *my Spirit* within you. — This *new Heart*, and this *new Spirit* then, can be no other than that *Spirit*, which our Lord saith is *born of the Spirit*, or that new and holy, that spiritual *Nature*, which is produced in the *Soul* at the Time of its *New-Birth*, John iii.

And thus, when God's new Covenant is recorded, *Jer.* xxxi. 33. He saith, *But this shall be the Covenant that I will make with the House of* Israel, *after those Days, saith the* LORD, *I will put my* Law *in their* inward Parts, *and write it in their* Hearts, *and will be their God, and they shall be my People.* The Sum of God's *Law*, as I before observ'd, consists in *Love* to *God*, and our *Neighbour*. The Law requiring this, is said to be *holy*, Rom. vii. 12. And *Conformity* thereto, is *Holiness*. Heart-Conformity to God's Law, is Holiness of *Heart*; and *Life* Conformity thereto, is Holiness of *Life*. In God's holy Law, the Holiness of his Nature shines. And when Man was made upright, in the Image of his Creator's Holiness, he had a perfect inherent Purity, that was every Way conformable to the Law. But when he fell, he lost the Image of God, his Conformity to the Law, his Love to God and Man. And instead of perfect Purity, of Law-Conformity, of Love to God, the Beauty of Holiness; contracted an Image that was nothing but Deformity, and horrid Enmity against him. *The carnal Mind,* (saith the Apostle) *is Enmity against God: It is not subject to the Law of God, neither indeed can be,* Rom. viii. 7. The *carnal Mind* is the *Corruption*, the *Unholiness* of Nature: This Unholiness is *Enmity* against *God*: And this Enmity consists in a *Non-Subjection* to his *Law*. By the Rule of Contraries then, the *Spiritual Mind* must be the *Renovation* of Nature or a *renewed* Nature, a begun *Holiness* of Nature: This Holiness is *Love to God*; and this Love to God, consists in a *Conformity* to *his Law*. — For any then to say, they have no inherent *Holiness*, no Holiness of Heart in *them*: Is just the same as to say, they have no *Love* to God in their *Hearts*, that there is nothing but *Enmity* against him in their *Souls*. For any to say that they have nothing to do with God's *Law*, that they are not *under* it, nor *subject* to it; Is just the same as to say, they have nothing to do with *God*, that they hate him, and are not *subject* to him. — I am persuaded, that the Case is far otherwise as to the latter, with some of those, who thro' a perverted Judgment have said the former. But however it be with any who advance these Notions; the Word of God assures, That his New-Covenant People shall have his *Law put in their* inward Parts, *and written in their* Hearts, *i.e.* that they shall have the Image of his Holiness imprest upon, and resident in their *Souls*. Can any say, That this New-Covenant Promise, Of God's putting his *Law* in the *inward Parts* of his People, and writing it in their *Hearts*, is his *imputing* the Holiness of *Christ* to *them?* Methinks none can say so. But if any should; God's Word contradicts it, and saith, That he will put his Law in *their* inward Parts, (not in *Christ's* for them) and write it in *their* Hearts. Not in *Christ's* Heart for them, but in *their* Hearts. In their *Hearts*, in the Plural, as respecting all the Members of Christ's Body; and not in his *Heart*, in the Singular, as respecting Him, and what he is for them as the Head of that Body. The Law of God was Indeed written in *Christ's* Heart, and was obey'd by him, as the Representative Head of his People, to give them a Representative Holiness, and a justifying Righteousness before God. But this Promise, Of God's writing his Law in their Hearts, being God's Covenant with *them* respects them personally, and what he doth in them *inherently*, in Conformity to Christ their Head, in conveying unto *them*, the same holy *Image* which is in *him*.

Further, as Holiness of Heart, a Change of Nature, to be communicated to the Soul in its New-Birth, is promis'd in God's new Covenant; so it appears that this is actually *bestow'd* upon the Saved of the Lord; that there is such a new Nature communicated *to* them, such a new Map created *in* them, in Conformity to Christ's Image: In that they are exhorted, To *put on the* new Man, *which after God is created in Righteousness and true Holiness*, Eph. iv. 24. This *new Man* is the same with the *new Heart*, and the *new Spirit* which the Lord promiseth to give to, and put *within* his People. It is said to be *created*, in that it is produc'd by the creating Power of God; and in that the *Man*, the Seat of it, is thereby made a *new Creature*. To be after GOD *created in Righteousness and true Holiness,* in that, it is the *Image* of *God's* Righteousness and Holiness, afresh enstampt upon the *Soul*. And this *new Man*, they are exhorted to *put on*, i.e. In Conversation-Holiness, to walk in their Lives, as such that were holy in their Hearts. And thus also, the Saints are exhorted to walk in Holiness of Life, as such that have *Put on the* new Man, *which is renewed in Knowledge, after the Image of him that created him,* Col. iii. 10. And that this *new Man* is *in* the Soul, is evident, in that it is said to be the *inward Man,* 2 Cor. iv. 16. And, *The hidden Man of the Heart,* I Pet. iii. 4. Will any person say, "That this *inward Man*, which the Apostle speaks of, is *Christ*, or his *Holiness imputed* to them?" IF any should; the Word of God gainsays it. It is *our* inward Man, saith the Apostle, that is *renewed Day by Day.* Is Christ, *our inward Man?* Or doth Christ and his Holiness need, or admit of *renewing Day by Day?* Is not HE in his Person, Is not HE in his Person, *Yesterday, Today, and forever the same?* And doth, or can his personal Holiness, the Holiness of his Nature, want, or admit of any *new Degrees?* Is it not absolutely and unchangeably *perfect?* Yea, surely. It is *our Inward Man,* saith the Apostle, that is *renewed Day by Day.* And that this inward Man, is the *Soul*, as created anew in Christ Jesus, in his holy Image, which daily receives Additions from his Fulness, to the Increase of its new Life; is manifest, in that it is oppos'd to the *outward Man,* the *Body*, which, the Apostle saith, *perisheth*; i.e. decays apace, and hastens to its original Dust. And if any should say, "*The hidden Man of the Heart, is Christ, and his Holiness imputed*:" The sacred Text contradicts it. The Holy Ghost by the Apostle, exhorts *Wives,* holy Women, to

Holiness of Conversation, to adorn themselves with the *hidden Man of the Heart;* or in other Words, to *put on the new Man,* which is not *corruptible*: Which is explain'd by what follows, *Even the Ornament of a meek and quiet Spirit, which in the Sight of God is of great Price. For* (saith the Apostle) *after this Manner in the old Time, the holy Women also who trusted in God adorned themselves, being in Subjection to their own Husbands*, Ver. 5. It was from this *hidden Man of the Heart,* this inherent Heart-Holiness, this Ornament of a *meek and quiet Spirit*, resident *in* the Women that of old trusted in God; *Put on* in Life-Holiness, in *Subjection to their own Husbands*, at God's Command: That they were styled *holy Women*; as appears from the whole Context. And as the Apostle exhorted the holy Women he wrote to, thus to increase in Holiness, to adorn themselves with the Ornament of a *meek and quiet Spirit*; so our Lord Christ also, thus commands Christians: *Learn of* ME, *for I am meek and lowly in Heart*, Matt. xi. 29. which is just the same with, *Be ye holy, for I am holy.* In both the Lord commands holy Obedience, and proposeth his own Holiness as our Example, for our Imitation. *Learn* of ME, for I am meek and lowly in *Heart*; saith our Dear Lord Jesus unto all his Followers. It is as if he should say, "You, my dear Disciples, by having a due Regard unto all my Precepts, *learn* of ME, to be meek and lowly in *Heart*, as I your Lord and Master *am*: Labour after *inherent* Holiness, to have your *Hearts* conformed unto *my Image.*" Our Lord doth not say, "*I* am meek and lowly (holy) in *Heart* for *you*: And you are not to seek for Meekness and Lowliness (Holiness) of *Heart* in *yourselves.*" But "I am meek and lowly (holy) in *Heart*: (as your *Example*) learn to be meek and lowly (holy) like ME, in *your Hearts.*" — And this *hidden Man of the Heart*, this *Ornament of a meek and quiet Spirit*, is said to be *in the Sight of God of great Price!* 1. In that it was *purchas'd* by the *Blood of Christ*: Who *loved the Church, and gave himself for it: That he might sanctify and cleanse it with the washing of Water, by the Word,* Eph. v. 25, 26. And, 2. In that it is of great *Value* in God's Account, or highly *esteem'd* by *him,* as it is the *Image* of *Christ* in his People, or their being *like-minded according to Christ Jesus*, Rom. xv. 5.

And by the Way, if Holiness of Heart, the hidden Man of the Heart, the Ornament of a meek and quiet Spirit, is in the Sign of God of *great Price*, as it is the Purchase of his Son's *Blood,* and as it is his *Image* in the Hearts of his People: How sad is it, that any of the Lamb's *Redeemed*, should *slight* this precious *Fruit* of their Redemption, purchas'd for them by the Lamb's *Blood!* And *disesteem* him *Image* in their Souls, unto which *Conformity* to Christ, they were of old *predestinated!*

But as against inherent Holiness, it has been thus objected,

Object. A Man is said to be a new Creature in *Christ*: Not in *himself.* To clear up the Truth more fully, I answer,

Answ. By Persons being said to be *in Christ*: We are to understand, I. Their being in Christ by *Representative Union.* And so, the Elect of God were *chosen in Christ* (as their Representing Head) *before the Foundation of the World*, Eph. i. 4.

And thus Those for whom Christ dy'd and rose, and for whom he ascended into Heaven as their Representative, are said to be *Raised up together, and made to fit together in heavenly Places* in *Christ Jesus,* Chap. ii. 6. And by Persons being said to be *in Christ:* We are to understand, 2. Their being in Christ by *Influential Union.* And so, *one* is *in* Christ, vitally united *to* him, before *another.* As saith the Apostle, *Salute* Andronicus *and* Junia *my Kinsmen and Fellow-Prisoners, who are of Note among the Apostles, who also were* in Christ *before* me, Rom. xvi. 7. And thus our Lord speaks of Believers, those true Branches of him the true Vine, that are in him by influential and vital Union, *I am the* Vine, *ye are the* Branches: *He that abideth* in Me, *and* I in *him, the same bringeth forth much* Fruit: *for without me ye can do Nothing,* Joh. xv. 5. And when the Apostle saith, *If any Man be* in Christ, *he is a new Creature: old Things are past away, behold, all Things are become new,* 2 Cor. v. 17. It is to be understood in this latter Sense. That if any Man be in Christ by *Influential Union,* if he be vitally united to him as his Root, and Head of Influence; he partakes of Christ's *Life,* hath a Sameness of *Nature* with him, a new Life of *Grace,* from Christ the new *Adam,* communicated to him; or, that by virture of his thus being *in Christ,* he (the Man) is a *new Creature: Old Things are become new* in *him.* — But against Christ's being an Head of Influence, and our receiving all Supplies of Grace from him; it has been objected,

Object. That tho' we are said to receive *of* his Fulness, and *Grace for Grace*: Yet it is thus to be understood; that we receive *of* Christ's Fulness, only as being *in him,* (Representatively) and not *from* it, or *from* him, as our Head of Influence.

Answ. That we receive *of* Christ's Fulness, as being *in him*; I readily grant. But then, it is, as being in him, *influentially*: Or vitally united to him as our Head of Influence; *from* whose Fulness as such, we receive all Grace. And to manifest this Truth, that we receive *from* Christ's Fulness, as our Head of Influence: See what the Holy Ghost by the Apostle saith, Col. ii. 19. *And not holding the* Head, from *which all the Body by Joints and Bands having Nourishment ministred, and knit together, increaseth with the Increase of God.* Evident it is from hence, that there is a real Communication of Grace *from* Christ, to us: That all the *Body* (the Members) of *Christ, from* him their *Head* of Influence, have *Nourishment* ministred unto them, unto their *increasing with the Increase of God.* And this also appears from *Eph.* iv. 15, 16. *But speaking the Truth in Love, may grow up into him in all Things, which is the* Head, *even* Christ: From *whom the whole Body fitly joined together, and compacted by that which every Joint supplieth, according to the effectual Working in the Measure of every Part, maketh Increase of the Body, to the edifying of itself in Love.* Here Christ is expresly said, to be the *Head* of the *whole Body,* (the Church.) And that hereby is intended, his being unto all his Members an Head of *Influence,* is evident, in that the Allusion here, is plainly to a *natural* Head, to the Head of a *natural* Body, which influenceth all the Members; which supplies, directs, and enables them for all their Actions. For every Member of Christ's Body, is said to be a *Joint: Every* Joint. — The *whole Body* fitly joined together, in all its

Members, from Christ, the *Head,* is supply'd with all Grace, communicated to, and thro' every *Joint,* according to his effectual *Working* in the Measure of every *Part*: Whence the Body is increas'd in every Grace, to the *edifying of itself in Love.* This is plainly the Sense of the Words: Whence it is evident, that Christ is indeed to us, an *Head of Influence, from* whom we receve all Grace. — But against our receiving *Grace* from Christ, it has been objected,

Object. That by the Word *Grace,* we are to understand, the free *Favour of God*; and not any Thing that is in *us,* communicated unto us from Christ.

Answ. The free *Favour of God,* is indeed one Sense that the Word *Grace* bears in the Holy Scriptures. And thus we are said to be *saved by* Grace, *Eph.* ii. 5. Divers are the Acceptations of this Word *Grace,* in the sacred Writings; and among them, the *new* Life, the Life of Holiness, communicated unto us from Christ, is stiled *Grace.* Hence our Lord hath promis'd to *pour upon the House of* David, *and upon the Inhabitants of* Jerusalem, *the* Spirit of Grace *and of Supplications,* Zech. xiii. 10. The Holy Ghost is here stiled the *Spirit of Grace*; in that it is his Work, when sent from every *Grace* in the Heart. Whence, as the Effect of our Lord's pouring out the Spirit of Grace upon the House of *David,* he saith, *And they shall* look *upon me whom they have pierced, and they shall mourn for him,*— *Looking* to a crucify'd Jesus; is the Grace of *Faith. Mourning* for the Soul's piercing him by its Sin; is the Grace of *Love,* excercis'd in *Gospel-Repentance.* And where these are, there is every other *Grace,* or *Fruit* of the Spirit. As 2 *Cor.* viii. 7. *Therefore as ye abound in every Thing, in* Faith, *in* Utterance, *and* Knowledge, *and in all* Dillegence, *and in your* Love *to us; see that ye abound in this* Grace *also.* That is, in *Love* to the Saints, shewn by ministring to their Necessities. And speaking of the blessed Fruit of this Minifstration, he saith, *that* the Brethren so supply'd, *Long after you, for the exceeding* Grace *of God* in you, Chap. ix. 14. And thus our Lord said to his Servant *Paul,* when buffeted by a Messenger of Satan, *My* Grace (i.e. to be communicated, to enable thee to endure the Trial) *is sufficient for thee: for my Strength is made perfect in Weakness,* Chap. xii. 9. And to increase our inherent *Grace,* God is said to give Grace, *and* more Grace *to the Humble,* Jam. iv. 6. And thus the Saints are exhorted to *Let their Speech be such that is good to the Use of Edifying, that it may minister* Grace *to the Hearers,* Eph. iv. 29. That thro' them, as Members of Christ's Body, *Grace* from him the Head, might be ministred unto other their Fellow-Members. — And the *Fruit* is said to be *the* Gift *of God,* Eph. ii. 8. And, 2. In that Grace, or Holiness in the Soul, being God's *Image* there; is the *Beauty* of the Soul. For by the Word *Grace,* we are sometimes to understand *Beauty,* or *Ornament.* As *Jam.* i. II. *The* Grace *of the Fashion of it perisheth.* And we are told that Christ's *People shall be willing in the* Beauties *of Holiness,* Psa. cx. 3. — But it may be further objected,

Object. If Holiness of Heart is communicated to a Man in his New-Birth, and the *Image* of God in Righteousness and Holiness is renew'd in *him*: Then the Man must be *perfect* in Holiness; for the first *Adam*, when he bore the *Image of God,* was *perfect.*

Answ. Tho' the first *Adam*, when created in the *Image of God,* was *perfect* in Holiness; it doth not hence follow, that the Soul when new created, *created in Christ Jesus unto good Works,* is *so.*

For, tho' the new Creation Work of God, the renewing of his Image in Man, extends to all the *Powers* of his Soul; so that his whole *Soul* in that Regard, is *renewed:* Yet are not any of the Powers of his Soul *wholly* renewed. The Work of God in renewing his Image in Man, in conforming the Soul to Christ, the second *Adam*; is perfect in respect of *Parts*; but imperfect as to *Degrees*. Hence it is said to be a *Begun Work,* Phil. i. 6. *Being confident of this very Thing, that he which hath* begun *a good* Work *in you, will perform it until the Day of Jesus Christ*. The Work of Sanctification, is said to be in *us*: (in *You*, saith the Apostle) But, it is only *Begun*, not perfected. And therefore we are exhorted to Grow *in Grace, and in the Knowledge* (the Heart-changing Knowledge) *of our Lord and Saviour Jesus Christ,* 2 Pet. iii. 18. And in the Use of all appointed Means, to go on, Perfecting *Holiness in the Fear of God*, 2 Cor. vii. I. *And the very God of peace,* saith the Apostle to the *Thessalonians, sanctify you* wholly*: and I pray God your whole Spirit and Soul and Body be preserved blameless unto the Coming of our Lord Jesus Christ. Faithful is he that calleth you, who also will do it,* I Thes. v. 23, 24. Here the Apostle prays, that the very *God of Peace* would *sanctify* them *wholly*: Whence it's evident, that the Design of God, as the God of peace to his People thro' the Blood of Christ, is their personal *Sanctification*; and that they are at present but in *part* sanctified. To which the Apostle adds; *And your whole Spirit, Soul and Body be preserved* blameless *unto the Coming of our Lord Jesus Christ*. Here he prays for their whole *Persons*, their Spirit, Soul and Body, or their *Souls*, in the superior and inferior Powers thereof, and their *Bodies*, to be preserved *blameless*, in Holiness: Or, unblameable *in Holiness*, as I Thes. iii. 13. And this *Unblameableness* in Holiness which the Apostle pray'd for, is not to be understood of an *absolute* Unblameableness, according to the strict Rule of God's holy *Law*, of a Perfection in Holiness without *Sin*: But of a *comparative* Unblameableness, of a *Gospel*-Unblameableness, in their walking before God in all holy Obedience, in Heart and Life; as having *Respect unto* all *God's Commandments*: In the Observance whereof the Psalmist saith, *I shall not be* ashamed, Psa. cxix. 6. And thus of *Zacharias* and *Elizabeth* it is said, *They were both righteous before God, walking in all the Commandments and Ordinances of the Lord* blameless, *Luke* i. 6. Not *Blameless*, as being without *Sin*: But *Blameless*, as being really, and increasingly *holy* in Heart and Life, as walking before God in *all* his Commandments and Ordinances. Not that they did or could, keep and observe any *one* of them perfectly without *Sin*: But they were unblameable in *Holiness*, in that they had an universal Respect *unto*, and walked *in* them *all*. And thus the Apostle pray'd for these Thessalonians, that they might be *sanctify'd* wholly: Which takes in the highest Degree, even an *absolute*

Perfection in Holiness, which they should attain at last: And that mean Time, their *whole Spirit and Sould and Body* might be *preserved* blameless (that they might be comparatively *blameless*, and increasingly *holy*) *unto the Coming of Christ.* Unto which he adds, *Faithful is* HE *that calleth you, who also* will *do it.* Whence it appears, that the Saints who are made *inherently* holy, are not as yet *perfectly* so: That their increasing Perfection in Holiness, is to be *sought* for; and that this is *engag'd* for by God, until they arrive unto an *absolute* Perfection. — And thus the Apostle prays for the *Hebrews, Now the God of Peace that brought again from the Dead our Lord Jesus, that great Shepherd of the Sheep, thro' the Blood of the everlasting Covenant, make you* perfect *in every good Work, to do his Will, working in* you *that which is well-pleasing in his Sight, thro' Christ Jesus; to whom be Glory forever and ever,* Amen, Heb. xiii. 20, 21. In praying, that God would work in these *Hebrews*, that which is *well-pleasing in his Sight thro' Christ Jesus;* the Apostle prays for the Increase of that Holiness, which was *inherent* in them. And in that he prays that they might be made *perfect* in every *good Work, to do his Will*: It shews, that they were not as then *already* perfect, and that a Perfection in Holiness, is most earnestly to be *sought* for. But to return,

Many are the Texts which might be brought to prove, That Persons *ought* to look for Holiness of Heart, a Change of Nature, or for their being made new Creatures: And that this is no *human* Imposition; but that Those who have advanc'd this Truth, have taught the pure Doctrine of *Christ* and his *Apostles*. But the Texts which I have quoted may suffice, and what I have said thereon, for the Hints which I propos'd to give about this first Thing. IN which I have been larger that I should, had it not been a main Principle of Christian Doctrine, which thro' the Subtilty of Satan, and the Inadvertency of some Men, is struck at. — And now I proceed to give a few Hints to what has been said,

1. That the *Effect* of teaching Persons to look for Holiness of Heart, Spiritual Life, and the Increase of it in *themselves;* is *The bringing of Souls into Bondage.* — I reply,

2. What *Liberty* is it, that you, my Friends, who say thus, would have for yourselves or others? would you be *free* from your own *Salvation?* For Holiness of Heart, spiritual Life, and the Increase of it in *yourselves*; is an essential Part of the *Salvation of your Souls. Sin,* is the *Misery, Holiness*, the *Happiness* of the Soul. Not to *seek* for inherent Holiness, is not to *seek* for inward Happiness. To talk of being inwardly *happy*, without being inherently *holy*, is to advance a Happiness, that is not promis'd in God's Book to any of his People, nor declared there, as experienc'd by them. Nor that is indeed possible to be enjoy'd. For without inherent *Holiness*, no Man shall (or can) *see the Lord.* Let me ask those who say, "They are inwardly happy, but not inherently holy:" What *is* this your Happiness? Wherein doth it consist? If you say,

In seeing ourselves to be *holy* as we stand in *Christ* our Representing-Head, the *Holiness* of his Nature being *imputed* unto us. I reply,

If any of you who say so, are *indeed happy*, in viewing yourselves *holy in Christ*; that inward Happiness of yours, cannot be enjoy'd without *inherent Holiness*, without a *holy Principle* wrought in your Hearts, which desires after, and delights in *Holiness*. For true Happiness consists in the Enjoyment of those Things that are truly excellent, which we desire and delight in. Our *Holiness* in *Christ* is an excellent Thing; but no Man can *see*, can *enjoy* that Holiness, or account himself *happy* in being interested therein: without a *holy Principle* in his Heart, that desires after, and delights in *Holiness*. And wherever such a Desire after, and Delight in Holiness is, in *Representative*-Holiness *in Christ*; there is also in that Man, a Desire after *inherent* and *personal Holiness* in Conformity *to Christ*, even to its highest Perfection, and a Delight in every increasing *Degree* thereof, as his great *Happiness*; and also, a Grief, for Want of greater *Increase* in personal Holiness, for the Prevalence of *Sin*, which that Man accounts his *Misery*. So that there neither is, nor can be *inward* Happiness, without *inherent* Holiness. I know the Apostle *Paul* was very happy by Faith in Christ, when, for Victory over Sin, complete in Christ, begun in himself, he said, *I thank God, through Jesus Christ our Lord.* Although but just before, looking into his own Heart, the corrupt, unrenewed Part of his Nature, he said, *O wretched Man that I am, who shall deliver me from the Body of this Death!* But this Happiness of his, by Faith in Christ, in what he was to him, and had done, and would do for him; was not *without*, but attended *with* Holiness of Heart in *himself*, so far as his Soul was renew'd by Grace: Which he not only saw, but had the Joy of it, as Christ's Salvation begun in him, when he said, in the same Breath that he exprest his Happiness in and thro' Christ, *So then with the Mind I* myself *serve the* Law of God; (or in other Words, am inherently *holy*) *but with the Flesh the* Law of Sin, *Rom.* viii. 24, 25.

And if the *Feeling* of that Misery which the Apostle felt by Reason of Indwelling *Sin*; should be called *Bondage*: Better be in Bondage all one's *Days*, than to have *Sin* remain in the Soul, without such a painful *Sense* of it. For by that *Bondage*, the Soul is further set *free*. That painful *Feeling* of Indwelling Sin, is the Soul's *Hatred* of Evil. Which springs from, and is the Exercise of its *Love* to God. As *Psal.* xcvii. 10. *Ye that* love *the* LORD, hate *Evil.* Love to God, hath in it, not only *Desires* after the Enjoyment of him, and Conformity to him, with an actual *Delight* in him, and *cleaving* to him; but also, *Grief*, for Want of Nearness with, and Conformity to him, and that the Soul can love him no more, and serve him no better. And the more the Soul is in the Exercise of Love to God, in both these Respects, the more it increaseth in Holiness, which is its Happiness. Even *grieving* Love, is not without its *Pleasure*, an holy Freedom of Soul, to pour out its Complaints into the Bosom of God its Father: Whose Ear is open to its Cry, and he gives his Child more Grace. So far as the Soul hath a painful *Sense* of Indwelling *Sin*, of Sin's Being, Usurpation and Tyranny; so far it is deliver'd from Sin's *Dominion*, or made *free* by the *Son of God*, from being a *Servant of Sin*.

at the Time appointed of the Father. That there is a Fulness of all *Grace* in *Christ*, to maintain and increase every *Grace* in *them*, to supply all their Wants, until they are brimful. That there is an Almightiness of *Power* engag'd to keep them through *Faith* unto *Salvation*. And that HE who hath *begun* a good *Work* in them, will *perform* it: That HE who was the *Author*, will be the *Finisher* of their *Faith*: And that HE who hath sanctify'd them in *Part*, will sanctify them *perfectly*, will make them as holy and happy as they can desire; yea, glorious, far above all their present Thought. That mean Time, they are to view themselves by Faith *complete in Christ*; in him as their *Representing-Head*. And to rejoice in Christ as their *Head of Influence*, who hath an immense Fulness in himself for them, to communicate to them, to make them in their own Persons, perfectly like Him. — And that to *receive of his Fulness, and Grace for Grace,* it is their Lord's Will, that they should *abide* in *him*, continually by *Faith*, as being dependent, empty Creatures, and needy Sinners in *themselves*; and be diligent in all appointed *Means*; that so by fresh Supplies of Life and Grace from Him, their personal Holiness may *increase*, until they are made *perfect*, or perfectly conformed to his *holy Image*.

And further, they are to be told, that whenever any Suggestion is cast into their Minds, or any Fear ariseth in their Hearts, that their Faith is not *right*, and their Interest in Christ not *certain*; because they see so little *Increase* of Holiness in *them*: That then it is their Duty to *look to Christ afresh*, as miserable Sinners in *themselves*, for all the *Salvation* they want and desire. And that upon every such fresh Look to Christ by *Faith*; they ought to be *persuaded* of their *Interest* in him, and that they have and shall have all *Life* in and thro' him. They are also to be told, that they ought to be *persuaded* that their *Faith* is true and saving, in the *Kind* of it, in that it *agrees* with the Account given of true and saving *Faith* in the *Word of God*: In that they *look* to Christ the only Saviour, for the *Whole* of his Salvation, to be sav'd from *Sin*, as well as *Wrath*, to be made *holy*, as well as *happy*, yea, in that they esteem *Holiness*, a Likeness unto God, a Fitness for, and an actual Enjoyment of him, and a glorifying of him as God, and their God, to be their *Happiness*. And likewise, that this Persuasion of the Truth of their *Faith*, may and ought to be further *confirmed*, by the experienc'd *Fruits* of it in their Hearts and Lives. They are to be bid to *look*, if they have not found their *Faith* to work by *Love*: Which is the declared *Fruit of Faith* in the *Word of God?* IF when they were in the Exercise of Faith, in its *direct* Act, looking unto Christ for Life; and in its *reflex* Act, taking up all Life in him thereupon, at his great Word; unto a Persuasion of Interest in Christ, and Right to Life in and thro' him; this *Faith* of theirs, did not work in their Hearts, *Love to God;* a *Hatred* of *Sin,* and a *Desire* after *Holiness?* And whether this *Faith* of theirs, when, and so far as they are in the *Exercise* thereof, hath not a proportionable *Influence* upon their Lives; to excite them in *Love to God,* to be *holy in all Manner of Conversation: To deny Ungodliness, and worldly Lusts; and to live soberly, righteously, and godly in this present World?* And if they can't but say, that at those happy *Times*, when theyw ere in the Exercise of *Faith*, they found this blessed *Fruit* of it in the *Love to God*; they are thence to be told, that they ought to be fully *persuaded* of the *Truth* of their *Faith*; and so of their *Interest* in *Christ*, unto their *full Joy*.

And where now is the *Bondage* that was spoken of as an *Effect* of *Teaching* Persons to look for Holiness of Heart, spiritual Life, and the Increase of it in *themselves*? So far as it from bringing Believers into *Bondage*, to teach them to *seek* for personal *Holiness*, that the *Discerning* hereof, adds to their *Freedom*, and increaseth their *Joy*. Since in all true Believers, personal Holiness, is to be *found*, and is *discern'd* by them at one Time or another, if they duly reflect upon their own Experience. And whenever the Fruit of Faith, in Holiness of Heart and Life, *is* discern'd; it *ought* always to be improv'd, as a subordinate *Evidence* of the Soul's *Interest* in *Christ*. Let *Faith* of the right *Kind*, that in its *direct* Act, looks unto Christ for the whole of his Salvation, be the *prime* Evidence: And the *Fruit* of Faith, in *Holiness*, in Love to God, when Faith is in Exercise in its *reflex* Act, unto a Persuasion of Interest in Christ; be the *subordinate* Evidence: And there will be no *Danger* of bringing Souls into *Bondage*, by exhorting them to *look* for Holiness of Heart, spiritual Life, and the Increase of it in *themselves*.

A Believer is never brought into *Bondage*, by looking for *Holiness*, the Fruit of *Faith*; unless he inverts the *Order* which God hath appointed: Unless he seeks that as the *prime* Evidence of his Interest in Christ, which God hath ordain'd as a *subordinate* Evidence. And unless he looks for *Holiness*, the *Fruit* of Faith, in Heart and Life, when his *Faith* is not in *Exercise*. AN din that Case, the *Bondage* that a Believer feels, is not chargeable, and to be charged upon his being *taught* to look for Holiness of Heart, spiritual Life, and the Increase of it in *himself*; but upon his looking for these in an undue *Manner*, and at a *Time* when they are not to be *seen*. This *Bondage*, is indeed the Effect of remaining *Unbelief* in the Heart of a Believer; and not the Effect of this pure *Doctrine* of Christ, and the *Teaching* thereof by any of his Servants: Which if rightly taught, hath no *Tendency* to bring any true *Believer* into *Bondage*; but to increase his *Freedom* and *Joy of Faith* here, and to add to his *Crown of Righteousness* hereafter. — A few Hints next to what has been said by some,

3. That tho' they *deny* inherent and personal *Holiness*; they do *not* deny the *Fruits of the Spirit*, and a *Conversation becoming the Gospel*. — I reply,

3. *What*, my dear Friends, do you *mean* by the *Fruits of the Spirit?* Do you mean those the Apostle mentions, *Gal.* v. 22, 23. *But the Fruit of the Spirit is Love, Joy, Peace, Long-Suffering, Gentleness, Goodness, Faith, Meekness, Temperance?* If you *do*: Is not the *Seat* of these Fruits of the Spirit, in the *Heart?* Are they not resident in the *Soul?* If you say, "They *are* in the Soul, *seated* in the Heart." What are they? *Holiness*, or *Sin? Purity,* or *Impurity? Holiness* is a *Conformity* to God's Holy *Law*, in which the Holiness of his Nature shines. *Sin* is the *Want* of Conformity to, and the *Transgression* of the *Law of God*. There is no Medium between these Two. Unto one of these Heads, you must refer the Fruits of the Spirit. Which

do you *chuse*? Surely you cannot say, They are Sin; because of the Opposition which the Apostle puts between the Fruits of the Spirit in tehse Verses, and the Fruits of the Flesh, Ver. 19, 20. *Now the Works of the Flesh are manifest, which are these, Adultery, Fornication, &c.* And if you say, They are *Holiness*; and that the Fruits of the Spirit have their Seat in the *Heart*: It will necessarily follow from hence, That wherever these Fruits of the Spirit *are; there* is Holiness of *Heart*, inherent in *that Man.* — But if you say, "These Fruits of the Spirit are in the *Life* only, and not in the Heart:" I ask, Is *Faith* an Assent of the *Mind*, or an Action of the *Body* only? Is *Love*, an Affection of the *Soul*, or any Kindness shewn by the *Body* only? Is *Joy*, the Gladness of the *Heart*, in the Hope or Enjoyment of any Thing it desires and delights in, or it any Action of the *Body* only? &c. Surely you cannot affirm the *latter*. And if the *former*, you must acknowledge Holiness of Heart to *be*, where these Fruits of the Spirit *are*. But if you should say, "That the Fruits of the Spirit which you intend, are only Actions of the *Body*:" What are they *worth* in the Sight of *God*? Doth not *he* require the *Heart*, in every outward *Action* that is good? Hath God *made* Soul and Body? And will God be *pleased*, think you, with *bodily Service* only? Is the *Soul* the superior Part of the *Man*? And will *God* who is a *Spirit*, and seeks such to worship to him, who worship in *Spirit* and in *Truth*, be pleased with a little outward Service of the *Body*, the inferior Part of the *Man*? Doth not the Apostle tell us, that *Bodily Exercise profiteth Little*? — And what *mean* you, my Friends, by A *Conversation becoming the Gospel?* Mean ye the same the Apostle speaks of, 2 *Pet.* ii. II. *Seeing then that all these Things shall be dissolved, what manner of Persons ought yet to be in all manner of* holy Conversation and Godliness? If you *do*: Can a Conversation becoming the Gospel, a *holy Conversation*, be without Holiness of *Heart*? Can Godliness be in the *Life*, and not in the *Heart*? Is not *Godliness* oppos'd unto *Bodily Exercise?* I Tim. iv. 8. And don't this shew, that it principally is in the *Heart*? What is *Godliness*? Is it not a being *like God*, according *to God*, or *after* his *Image?* If it *is*; can this be in the *Life*, and not in the *Heart*? Wou'd it be after *God*, or *like God*, if it was? Is not the LORD our Father, *Good* in his *Nature*, as well as *good* in his *Works*? Is it not the Goodness of his *Nature*, that flows out in his *Works*? And can his Children be *Godly*, like *God* in their *Conversation*, if their *Hearts* are not made *good* by his Holy Spirit, as well as t heir Conversation *good*, under the Influence of the same Spirit, drawing out the Goodness which himself hath wrought in their *Hearts*, into Goodness in their *Lives*? Suppose a Person were to observe all the *Commands* of God, and every Rule of Obedience which he hath given, in the *external* Part thereof; and at the same Time was without Holiness in his *Heart*, without *Love* to God and *Man*, without an Aim therein, supremely at the *Glory* of God; and subordinately at the *Good* of his Brother: Wou'd not all the *Goodness*, the *Holiness* of his Life, be a meer *Phantasm*? An Appearance, an empty Shew, in which there was no Reality? Wou'd it not be like a Body without a Soul? Doth not the Apostle say, *Tho' I bestow all my* Goods *to feed the* Poor, *and tho' I give my Body to be* burned, *and have not* Charity,

(Love to God, the Seat of which is in the Heart, and is his Image in the Soul) *it profiteth me* Nothing? I *Cor.* xiii. 3. — If *you* then, my dear Friends, *are* for a *Conversation becoming the Gospel,* and would exhort Persons *thereunto,* you must be *for,* and exhort *to,* a *holy Conversation*: And this holy Conversation, can respect no other than *Holiness of Heart and Life.* What think you of what the Apostle saith, *Phil.* iii. 20. *Our* Conversation *is in Heaven*? Think you not, that he intended thereby, the holy Converse of their *Minds* with *God,* and the holy Behaviour of their *Bodies* before *Men*? Their Converse in both Respects, being such as became *heavenly Men,* the Offspring of *Christ,* the *heavenly Man,* whose *Image* they bore? By his saying, Our *Conversation* is in *Heaven,* the Apostle could not intend the Converse of their *Bodies* there. For they were on *Earth.* The Converse of the *Mind* then, with *God,* Holiness of *Heart,* Conformity to him, and Delight in him; cannot be separated from, but must be included in Holiness of *Life,* or a *Conversation becoming the Gospel,* as is in the Gospel described.

You have no Way left, my Friends, that I know of, to *deny* personal Holiness, of Heart and Life in *us*; unless you were to *say,* "That by the Conversation becoming the Gospel, which you speak of, you *intend,* a Conversation *in Christ*: viz. That was personally in *Christ* for you, or the Conversation that *he* walk'd in, when here on Earth." And were you to advance *such* a Notion, you might bring Scripture (perverted, and not interpreted) for it. For the Apostle, speaking of the Saints, saith, *Your good Conversation* in Christ, I *Pet.* iii. 16. And you must *so* understand this Scripture, if you admit not the Distinction I before hinted, Of Persons being *in Christ Representatively,* and *Influentially,* or *Vitally*: And so, (from what is mention'd in this Verse, which confines the Sense of the Words, to the Conversation of the *Persons* spoken of) refer it to the Saints good Conversation *in Christ,* as being united to him *vitally,* and *influenc'd* by him, unto Holiness of *Heart* and *Life.* And were you *not* to understand, by our *good Conversation in Christ,* that Conversation which is *personal* in *us*: Wou'd there be any Room left for Holiness, for Goodness of Conversation in us, at *all,* either in *Soul* or *Body*? And would not the Floodgates be hereby pulled up to *Christians,* for a Flow of *Vice,* and all *Immorality* in their *Hearts* and *Lives?* — I intreat you to consider these Things: And, Oh that the Lord may convince you of your Mistakes and Inconsistencies. *Restore your Souls, and lead you in the paths of Righteousness for his Name's Sake:* That you may *speak the Things which become sound Doctrine*! For most surely, the *Gospel of Christ,* is an *holy* Gospel; and throughout the *Whole* of it, *Personal Holiness* in Heart and Life, is taught and enjoyn'd upon *Those* who by the Grace of God are called to be *Saints. Taught* and *enjoyn'd,* I say, *Personal Holiness* is, upon *Christians* in the *Gospel of Christ:* By *God,* our *holy* Father, by the *Lord Jesus,* our *holy* elder Brother, and by the *Holy Ghost* our comforter: Whose Work it is in a peculiar Manner, as sent by the Father and the Son to dwell in Believers, to make them *holy Men* unto God through Christ, to begin, maintain and increase their *personal* Holiness here; until they are made perfect, and *personally* presented *holy, and without Blame before God in Love*, hereafter. — How *sad* is it then, my dear Friends, that you, *Christians*, should flight and deny *personal Holiness*, which is such an essential Part of real *Christianity*! God grant you *Grace*, that you may soon *Recover yourselves out of the Snare of the Devil!* — I shall close the Whole, in the last Place,

Fifthly. With a Word to *you*, my dear Brethren and Sisters, who thro' the *Power of Christ resting upon you, are enabled to* hold fast *the faithful* Word, *as you have been* taught. And what shall I say to *you*? Admire the *Grace*, the distinguishing Grace of God to *you*, in that you are made to stand, while others are left to fall! And still cry earnestly to God, as the Psalmist, *Hold* thou *me up*; *and I shall be* safe! Be *strong in the* Grace *that is in* Christ Jesus. *Take unto you the whole* Armour of God: And as good Soldiers *of Jesus Christ,* fight your *Lord's Battles*, for his precious *Truths*, against the Enemy *Satan*, the Father of *Lies*, in all the Falshoods which he advanceth, by whatever Instruments he makes Use of. Contend earnestly *for the* Faith *which was once delivered unto the* Saints: Now it is so much oppos'd and deny'd. Better *die*, fighting for Christ and Truth, than *Coward-like* quit the *Field*, while the Enemy with his Falshoods is *upon it. Peace*, with *Truth*, with *Holiness*, is desirable, and to be follow'd. But without These, *Peace* is far too *dear* bought. I know, my dear Brethren, that for some Time you have been in the *Wars*. And not a contending *Breath* you have ever spent, not a Stroke for *Truth*, you have ever struck against *Error*, with the *Sword of the Spirit*, the *Word of God*; but most kindly is recorded by the Captain of your Salvation, and by his infinite Grace, shall be rewarded with endless Glory. A rich, a weighty *Crown of Righteousness*, is laid up for the faithful Servants of Prince *Emanuel*, who in *keeping the Faith,* have *fought a good Fight*; which shall be *given them at his Appearing*. If Christ hath *A few Names in* Sardis, a few Persons among a backsliding People, at a Time of great Degeneracy, *that have not defiled their Garments*, the Robes of their Gospel-Profession, by Impurity of Doctrine or Conversation: *They shall walk with* Him *in white*, as victorious Princes, and in Grace unknown, by HIM be accounted *worthy!* And fear not, my dear Friends, tho' your Number is lessen'd, and you may be at present but weak-handed; for GOD is able to increase and strengthen you. And I trust, the Cause of Christ and Truth shall be *maintain'd* among the Remnant that abide faithful, in *your Society*, and in *Others*; and that the Lord's Work shall be again *reviv'd* among you, to your great Joy. For it is God's *Promise* to his People, after, *For a Small Moment he hath* forsaken them, to return, *and build* again *the* Tabernacle *of* David, (the Church of Christ in any of its Apartments) *which is fallen* down: *And I* (saith He) *will set it* up: *That the* Residue *of* Men *might* seek *after the* Lord, *Acts* xv. 16, 17. And it is God's usual *Way*, to revive and comfort his People, after Deaths and Conflicts. — And mean Time, this may ease, and rejoice our Hearts: Our Lord's *Work*, is his *own*; and HE will take *Care* of it: His *Truths* are his *own*; and HE will *maintain* them, and bring them forth with an increasing and triumphant *Brightness*, from under every dark, eclipsing *Shade*, which at any Time for wise and holy Ends, he permits for a while to *vail* them. Oh my Brethren, *stand* but with *Christ*, and for his *Truths*; and *fear not*, tho' Men and Devils should stand *against* you. For *mighty* is *Christ* and *Truth,* and shall *prevail* against *Satan* and *Error* in all their Efforts. And, *Blessed* are *they*, who are honour'd of the Lord, to be his faithful *Witnesses*. With HIM, *The faithful and true* Witness, they shall *live and reign forever!* Even so then, *Stand fast in the Lord, my beloved Brethren*; contending *for*, and living up *to* the *Truths* of his *holy Gospel. And the Lord make you to increase and abound in* Love *one towards another, and towards all Men: To the End he may establish your Hearts unblameable in* Holiness *before God even our Father, at the Coming of our Lord Jesus Christ, with all his Saints!* So prays,

My honour'd Friends,

Your most affectionately

In the LAMB's Bowels,

A

CAUTION

AGAINST

ERROR,

When it springs up together with TRUTH.

In a LETTER to a FRIEND.

My very dear Brother in Christ,

I Return you my hearty Thanks for the three Extracts which have lately been drawn from the Works of some that labour'd in the Gospel of Christ about a Hundred Years ago. There was then, a great Revival of the Lord's Work, and of the Truths of the Gospel: Tho' a sad Decay of the one, and Rejection of the other, follow'd, upon the Restoration of King *Charles* the *Second*. But I hope that the Revival which the Lord hath now begun, of his Truth, and Work, will be like the *Morning-Light*, which shineth more and more until the *perfect Day*.

My Concern for *you*, in an especial Manner; for dear Brother *Cennick*, and the rest of the Brethren, which appear on one Side, against Brother *Harris*, and others of the Brethren, since I heard that there was a Division among you; has been great. And now, my Heart as it were *trembles for the Ark*, for the pure Gospel of Christ, and the Work of Conversion amongst you, which for some Time have happily advanced. Left thro' the Malice and Subtilty of the Devil, that old Serpent, the one should be taken from you, and the other hindred. But as the Gospel and its Work, are Christ's *own*; I *hope*, even *against* Hope. — I think you are in Danger, as you seem to adhere to what was taught by some, who were *indistinct* in their Notions about Gospel-Truths, in the last Century.

I like Mr. *Sympson's* Sermon on Justification by Faith alone. He sets the Law, and the Impossibility of being justify'd thereby, or by any of the Works thereof, before or after Conversion, in a clear Light; and also the Fulness and Freeness of the Grace of God in the Gospel, in justifying and saving Sinners, as Sinners, thro' Jesus Christ, and Faith in Him alone. IN these Things he speaks my Heart.

But when he comes to this Sentence: "If thou wilt be a Member of a Church as they speak, that thou mayst be comforted, justified, and saved, thou art bound to fulfil the whole Law." Page 18. I humbly think, that he is *indistinct*. If a Person thinks to join with any Church of Christ, that he may be *justified* and *saved*, or that this his Action will be any Part, more or less, of the Matter of his Righteousness in the Sight of God, or procure his Favour, unto Justification and Salvation: He greatly *errs*, and is upon a legal Bottom, working for Life. But if a Believer that is sav'd by Grace, thro' Faith, gives up himself to a Church of Christ, according to the Will of God, that he may be *comforted*, or fill'd with the Comforts of the Holy Ghost, by the Conduit-Pipes of Ordinances, thro' which the Lord is pleas'd to convey them: He doth *not* err, his Intendment therein, is not legal, but evangelical. What God hath promis'd, Faith should expect, and in the Way which God hath promis'd it. Now God hath promis'd, That his People shall be *comforted* in *Jerusalem,* that they shall be *borne upon her Sides, dandled upon her Knees, and milk out, and be delighted with the Abundance of her Glory,* Isa. lxvi. 11, 12, 13. This is the Promise made unto Gospel-Converts, joining to Gospel-Churches. This therefore they ought to expect. And of the Fulfilment of this Promise, the *three thousand* converted by *Peter's* Sermon, and *added to the Church,* had blest Experience: While *continuing stedfastly in the Apostles Doctrine, in Fellowship, in breaking of Bread, and in Prayers: - They did eat their Meat with* Gladness *and Singleness of Heart,* Acts ii. 41 & c. To join to a Church, that we may be *justify'd,* is one Thing; and that we may be *comforted,* is another. They are Things of a vastly different Consideration; and should not be confusedly cast together. As God hath made no Promise to *justify us,* but thro' the *Obedience of his Son,* imputed to us of his free Grace, and received by Faith alone: We ought to expect *that* Privilege, in no *other Way.* But as of his free Mercy, he hath promis'd to *comfort us* in the *Way of our Duty;* we may and ought *therein,* to expect his Consolations. Accordings to what our Lord hath said, *John* xiv. 21. Thus I think Mr. *Sympson* was wrong, in casting together in the same Sentence, this of *Consolation,* with that of *Justification,* as blameable, legal *Ends,* in the Observation of Ordinances. — There were some at that Time, who were against the *Use of Ordinances,* and call'd 'em *carnal Things.* Whether Mr. *Sympson* was one of them, or not, I can't say. He no where says, That they *ought* to be observ'd by Believers, in Obedience to Christ's Command, or that it is their *Duty* to observe them; but only, "If we *do* submit to outward Ordinances, (leaving it as a Matter of Liberty, whether to do it, or not) we should not do it from legal Principles."

As to the other two little Pieces, I am glad to see the Righteousness of Christ advanced in them both, as the Cause of our Justification in the Sight of God; and also the Duty of our believing our Completeness before God therein. And these indeed are the fundamental Points, that we ought first and principally to be concern'd about.

But when these are advanc'd, to jostle out other dependant Truths, which are closely connected by the Gospel of Christ; it argues *Indistinctness*; may I not say, *Unfoundness*, in any Author? Oh the glorious *Gospel* of Christ! What a Beauty and Excellency is there in all its *Truths*, when they appear in a consistent Light, in that Variety, Harmony and Unity, in that Order and Dependance upon each other, and Connexion with each other, in which the ever-blessed GOD hath plac'd them, to answer all the Ends of his infinite Wisdom and Grace in our Salvation! You will think, my dear Brother, that I apprehend something *wanting* in these little Pieces. To be very free with you, I see no mention made of our *personal, inherent Holiness*, nor is the least Hint, as I perceive, given therein, of its *Necessity*: Nor that it ought to be *look'd after*, as a *Fruit* of Christ's *Death*. There seems to me, to be no other *Sanctification* hinted, in these little Pieces, as needful for the People of God, but that which we had by the *Death of Christ*; as this believ'd, *purgeth the Conscience.*

Indeed our Lord, made an *End of Sin*, perfectly and for ever, and destroy'd it in himself, in all Respects, for all his People, by his one Offering. And now *presents us, in the Body of his Flesh thro' Death, holy and unblameable, and unreproveable* in the Father's *Sight*, Heb. x. 14. Col. i. 22. But when we are said to be sanctify'd *by the Offering of the Body of Christ*, and to be *presented* holy, *unblameable, and unreproveable in the Body of his Flesh thro' Death*: I humbly think, that we are to take Sanctification in a *large Sense*. For our Purgation from all *Sin*, in its Guilt, Filth and Power; and the Induction, or bringing in upon us, all Holiness of *Nature*, and Righteousness of *Practice*: Unto all Acceptance with the Father. And so it takes in, both our *Justification*, and *Sanctification* in Christ. The Sanctification of our *Nature*, in Christ, is perfect: And stands, as I humbly conceive, in God the Father's accounting the perfect Purity and Holiness of *Christ's* human Nature, as fill'd with the Holy Ghost, unto all *those*, whom as a Covenant Head, he represented. And the Justification of our *Persons*, in Christ, as I humbly take it, hath two Parts; *viz.* The Non-imputation of *Sin*, and the Imputation of *Righteousness*. The Imputation of Righteousness, stands in God's accounting of the *active* Obedience of *Christ*, to all the Requirements of his righteous Law, unto *us*, for whom he obey'd, and whose Surety he was. And the Non-imputation of Sin, stands in God's accounting of the *passive* Obedience of *Christ* to the penal Part of his Law, unto *us*, or his enduring all that Curse and Wrath which our Sins deserved, and giving up his Life a Sacrifice for *us*; by which he made full Satisfaction for all our Sin, and for ever made an End of it in *himself.* And as the *Death* of Christ, was the *finishing Part* of that Work which the Father gave him to do on Earth, for the Removal of Sin, for the bringing us unto God, and making us acceptable in his Sight; so, as I humbly conceive, when we are said to be *sanctified*, or *perfected* by the Offering of the Body of Jesus once for all; the *Whole* of his Work which he did for us on Earth, is *included*, imply'd, though not express'd. Even all that he did for us, in representing us in his *holy Person*, from his *Conception* and *Birth*; in all the righteous Obedience of his *Life*; and in his Obedience unto *Death*. By all of which *jointly*, meeting together as it were, in this *last*, he made us, in all Respects, in himself, absolutely *perfect*. As *righteous*, both in the negative and positive Parts of Righteousness, as God's extensive *Law* requir'd; and as *holy*, as his pure *Nature* could desire. — Upon which, God the Father, rais'd him from the Dead, for our Justification: Discharg'd him from all Sin, and justify'd him as righteous, in the Name and Room of all those whom he represented. And advanc'd him to his own Right Hand, as the publick Head of his People: There to present them in *himself*, before him, absolutely *perfect*, compleat, *holy and unblameable, and unreprovable in his Sight*, as the Objects of his eternal Complacence.

This, my Brother, is the Sanctification, the Justification, the Perfection, which we had by the Death, and have by the Life of *Jesus*; who now appears, in the Presence of God for *us*. — But behold, all this is *in Christ*, not *in us*. And it was done in Christ *for us*, that it might be done thro' Christ, *in* and *upon us*.

As Christ was justify'd *for us*, and we *in him*, as our Representative, when he rose from the Dead; so we are justify'd *thro' him*, in our own Persons, and in the Court of Conscience, when *Faith* is wrought in our Hearts, to receive and apply the Righteousness of Christ, and God's justifying Sentence thereby, unto ourselves, according to the Declaration of his Word and Spirit. — And as we receive *Justification* freely by Grace, thro' Faith; so we ought to hold the Faith *of it* stedfastly, in the Face of a thousand Improbabilities that we see and feel in ourselves, or that may be suggested to us by Satan. And this is living by *Faith*, as to *Justification*; to look wholly out of ourselves, unto Christ, for *that*.

But is this *all* the Perfection that we have in Christ, which we ought to look to him for? No, my Brother; we are to live upon Christ by *Faith*, as our complete *Sanctification*: And to believe, that *in him*, we have a perfect Purity of Nature, whatever Impurity we may discover in *ourselves*.

But is this all the *Sanctification*, that we are to look for? Is this all that we are to regard, as to the Life of *Faith* in *Sanctification*? No, my Brother, Christ is made *Sanctification* to us, not only as a *representing Head*, but also, as a *communicative Fountain*, to make us *inherently holy*. And unto *him* daily, for fresh Communications out of his Fulness, we ought to *look*. What we are in *Christ*, is one Thing; what we are in *ourselves*, is another. What we are in Christ *mystically*, in this Regard, we must be in ourselves *personally*; in begun, and increasing Measures now, and in full Perfection erelong. — We are not to look for *Sanctification*, as the *prime Evidence* of our *Justification*; that being *Faith* alone: But a *subordinate Evidence* it is, and ought to be look'd for as *such*. — We are not to look for, and upon our *Sanctification*, as our *Title* to Glory; that stands in an alone, upon the *Righteousness of Christ* without us: But as our inherent, personal *Meetness* for Glory, we ought to look for, and earnestly seek it. And so great is the Necessity of *Holiness*, of that which is personal and inherent in *us*, that *without it*, the Truth of it in the Heart, *no Man shall see the Lord*. It is only "The pure in Heart that shall see GOD." And the *more* Heart, Lip, and Life-Purity we have, the *more* we shall enjoy, and glorify God on Earth; and the *more* are we personally prepar'd for the Glory of the heavenly State, or *made meet for the Inheritance of the Saints in Light*.

Now, my dear Brother, there is not the least Hint given in these little Pieces, about the *Necessity* and *Usefulness*, of inherent, personal *Holiness*; nor of its being a *Fruit*, a blessed Fruit, of the *Death* of Christ, of our complete *Justification*, and mystical *Sanctification* in him. — Mr. *Richardson* says, "Christ by his Death did present all his People to God *without Spot, or Blemish, or Wrinkle*, Page 6." And for Proof, gives *Eph.* v. 25, 26, 27. — But as I humbly think, he mistakes this Text. Christ loved the Church, and *gave himself for it*. And therein and thereby, the Church had *in him*, a complete *mystical Sanctification*. This was the *Root*, as I may say, of that perfect *personal Sanctification*, which as the blessed *Fruit* of it, is after mention'd. Christ gave himself for the Church: That he might *sanctify and cleanse it. How?* by his Blood as *shed?* No, as I humbly think, from what follows, by his Blood *apply'd*, and Grace *communicated. With the Washing of Water* (of the Holy Spirit) *by the Word*: the Word of the Gospel. That he might *present it to himself a glorious Church, — When? Immediately* upon his Death, Resurrection, and Ascension to Heaven? No, as I humbly think, at the *last Day*. When the whole Number of his Chosen are converted by Grace, and perfected into Glory. When the whole Church, shall be made as holy by *Inhesion*, in herself, *thro' Christ*, as she is now by *Representation, in him*. When she shall have on, and in her, the Whole of her Bridegroom's Glory; not only the Glory of his spotless Righteousness *upon her*, but also the Glory of his perfect Purity *within her. Then, then* the entire *Bride*, made *meet* in all Respects, for the Marriage-Glory with her Royal *Bridegroom*; shall be by him, solemnly *presented unto himself, a glorious Church, not having Spot or Wrinkle, or any such Thing, but that it should be holy, and without Blemish!*

That *Sanctification* which we had by the Death of Christ, by his Blood *shed*; and that which we have by his Blood *apply'd*, are distinct Things. The one is *mystical*, the other *personal*: The former was *completed* at *once* in Christ, the latter admits of *Degrees*, and *Repetition* in us, as we contract new Defilement; and it chiefly respects the Purgation of our Consciences from the *Guilt of Sin*.

Again, That *Sanctification* which we have by the *Blood of Christ apply'd*; and that which we have by the *Grace of the Holy Spirit*, are distinct Things. As I *Pet.* i. 2. *Elect according to the Foreknowledge of God the Father, thro' Sanctification of the* Spirit *unto Obedience, and sprinkling of the* Blood *of Jesus Christ*. Our dear Lord came by *Water and Blood*, I John v. 6. By *Blood*, to justify our Persons, and purge our Consciences from the Guilt of Sin. And by *Water*, by the Holy Spirit: To communicate the Spirit of Grace, and all Grace by him, to cleanse us from the Filth, subdue the Power, and destroy the very Being of Sin in us, in his own Time; and to sanctify us throughout in Spirit, Soul and Body, to make us *inherently holy*, truly, and increasingly here, and unto the highest Perfection hereafter.

Now, my dear Brother, as our Sanctification by the Blood of Christ, doth not render *needless* our Sanctification by the Grace of the Holy Spirit, but gloriously *secures* it: So, in our advancing, doctrinally, Sanctification *in Christ*, by his Blood; we ought not to *neglect, disregard*, or draw Persons off from seeking Sanctification, and the Increase of it *in themselves* continually, by the Grace of the Holy Spirit: As a Fruit of Christ's Death, of their Faith, as their inherent Meetness for Glory. Much less ought we to *reject inherent Qualities*, &c. and say, "That we are perfectly holy by "Faith only, *without* these Things." And that *this Sort* of Sanctification, is not to be *sought* after; but that Persons may be at rest, tho' they feel nothing of it in themselves. As is said in the *Preface* to Mr. *Richardson's* little Piece. To exalt the *Blood of Christ*, as the *very Attonement,* is *Truth.* And to say, this Blood *apply'd,* believ'd in, *purgeth the Conscience* from all Sin (in its Guilt) is likewise *Truth.* But to add, in *this* consists true Purity of Soul, and *not* in habitual Qualities, is a very great *Error*; which is subversive of the Truth of the Gospel, and the Honour of God, and likewise destructive to the Souls of Men.

It subverts the Truth of the Gospel, in what it declares concerning the *new Man*, or new Nature in the Soul: Which *after God* (or according to his Image) *is created in Righteousness, and true Holiness*, Eph. iv. 24. It robs God of his Honour. It we ought not to seek inherent Qualities, we are not to regard that holy, reverential *Fear of God*, in our Hearts and Lives, which he calls for, as an *Honour* due to him from his Children, *Mal.* i. 6. Or that great Work and Duty of *Holiness*, unto which we are called by the Gospel, I *Thess.* iv. 7. For, *Having therefore these Promises* (saith the Apostle) *dearly beloved, let us cleanse ourselves from all Filthiness of the Flesh and Spirit, perfecting Holiness in the Fear of God*, 2 Cor. vii. I. But this pernicious Error, subverts the Truth and Fear of *God*, and is most destructive to the Souls of *Men.* It naturally tends to Licentiousness, to lead Men into Looseness and Carelesness, about their Hearts and Lives, or to *turn the Grace of God* (the Notions they have thereof) *into Lasciviousness.* And those that do so, the Apostle *Jude* gives them the Character of *ungodly Men*, and says, they were of Old ordained unto *this Condemnation*, Jude 4. *This Condemnation!* Which denotes the Aggravation of their Sin, in the Abuse of the Gospel, and also the Greatness of that Punishment reserved for them. As Ver. 5, &c.

Some such Men there were, who made this vile Use of the holy Gospel, that crept in *unawares* among the Disciples, even so early as the Apostolick Age. And I fear, my dear Brother, that there are some such crept in among *you*. Who may be suffer'd to overthrow the Faith of many, that only have receiv'd the Notion, and never felt the Power of God's free Grace in Christ, changing their Souls into the Saviour's Image. And sadly, for a Time, may they be suffer'd to shake, even true Believers themselves. But for *these, The God of Peace, after they have suffer'd a-while, will bruise Satan under their Feet, and stablish, strengthen, and settle them. There must be* Heresies *among you*, saith the Apostle, *that they which are approved, may be made* manifest *among you*, I Cor. xi. 19. And, so on the contrary, that unfound Professors may be manifest. As, I *John* ii. 19. *They went out from us, but they were not of us: for if they had been of us* (of the Number of true Believers in Christ, and of his Witnesses) *they would no Doubt have continued with us*: (In advancing the Truths of the Gospel, unto the Ends of the Gospel) *But they went out, that they might be made* manifest, *that they were not all of us.* Thus it was then, and thus I trust in shall be now. That the Lord in suffering Errors, and Divisions thereupon, to prevail among you, will thereby brighten his own People, and purge the Societies of unfound Professors. And I would say to you, my dear Brother, to dear Brother *Cennick*, and to as many as have tasted that the Lord is *gracious*, unto an engaging of your Souls to love *Holiness*; as *Moses* spake to the Congregation of *Israel*, concerning *Korah, Dathan and Abiram, Depart, I pray you, from the Tents of these wicked Men, and touch nothing of theirs, left ye be consumed in all their Sins*, Numb. xvi. 26. For I fear, they are wicked Men, that advance the Errors which appear amongst you: Ad if they are not, their Errors are most pernicious. For God's Honour therefore, for the Love you bear to Christ's Gospel, for your own Soul's Happiness, and for the spiritual and eternal Welfare of Thousands; Oh come not near to these erroneous Men, nor to any of their great Errors!

I can't but fear, that there is a Deceivableness of Unrighteousness in their Words. They assert not Perfection in *Christ*, unto the *Ends* for which it is asserted in the Gospel, *viz.* to encourage our *Faith* in Christ, and to increase our *Conformity* to him. But to exclude the *latter*, as appears from what I have hinted. And as to the *former*, Faith in Christ, I fear, *that* which they speak of, is not true, living Faith, of the Operation of God; but a mere human Fancy, and a Delusion of the Enemy of Souls. True *Faith, purifies the Heart*, Acts xv. 9. But the Faith which they speak of, *excludes* Heart-Purity, that which is inherent in *us: Their Faith*, leads them not to seek *after it*.

But what a contrary Influence, had the *Faith* of the Apostle *Paul?* He exhorts the Saints at *Philippi*, to beware of false Teachers, of those who would rob Christ of the Glory of Salvation, and rival it with him, by joining their own Obedience with his, in the Point of Justification. And says, *Beware of Dogs, beware of evil Workers, beware of the Concision. For we are the Circumcision which worship God in the Spirit, and rejoice in Christ Jesus, and have no Confidence in the Flesh,* Phil. iii. 1, 2. In this second Verse, by his rejoicing in Christ Jesus, and having no Confidence in the Flesh, he professeth his *Faith* in Christ, and his Righteousness alone, for his Justification and Acceptance with God, and his utter Distrust of all his own Obedience, for this great End. He well *knew*, what a Fulness, what a Perfection and Completeness there was in Christ, and in his Righteousness, and that he was every Way complete in him, which fill'd his Soul with *Joy.* But did this take him *off* from a Pursuit after *inherent Holiness?* No, verily. But the Views which he had by *Faith*, of his Perfection in Christ, drew out his Heart into eager *Desires* after Conformity to him. *That I may know him,* saith he, *and the Power of his Resurrection, and the Fellowship of his Sufferings, being made conformable unto his Death; if by any Means I might attain unto the Resurrection of the Dead. Not as tho' I had already attained, either were already perfect; but I follow after, if that I may apprehend that for which also I am apprehended of Christ Jesus*, Ver. 10, 11, 12. It is as if he should say, 'I see what a perfect Beauty I am *in Christ*, what a Fulness of Glory there is in my *Lord*, and in his Obedience for *me*, how righteous, how holy I am *in him*, unto whose bright *Image* I am to be *conformed*, perfectly, at the great *Resurrection-Day*. And the Prospect of that Day's *Glory*, sets my Soul all on a Flame of *Desire* after it; that I may *know my Lord*, more and more, in daily Communion, unto increasing Conformity here; and the *Power*, the Influence, of *his Resurrection*, to quicken me to live to God, and the *Fellowship of his Sufferings*, for the Mortification of Sin in me, being made comfortable unto his Death: If by any Means I might attain *the Resurrection of the Dead*; to be as holy here, if it was possible, as I shall be when raised from the Dead.' — Thus strongly did the Apostle's Faith of *Completeness in Christ*, incline his Heart to *inherent*, and *personal Holiness. This, this* is it, which in its Perfection, he says, he had *not already attained*. The complete Righteousness of Christ, he *had* attained; but a full Conformity to him in Holiness, he had *not* attained. He was *not*, in this Respect, already *perfect*, but follow'd *after it*, most eagerly, if that he might *apprehend*, or lay hold on that, for which glorious End, Christ had *apprehended*, or laid hold on him, by efficacious Grace, to make him thus perfect in Glory. — But, my Brother, what shall we say to the *Faith of those*, that don't engage them to seek after *this Sort* of Sanctification? Have we not Reason to think, that it is only a Counterfeit of true Gospel Faith?

Indeed the *Prefacer* to Mr. *Richardson's* Piece, saith, "That those who are perfectly holy thro' Faith, do bear forth the Fruits of Righteousness, as a *good Tree* cannot bring forth *evil Fruit*." But it is to be fear'd, that he hath another *Meaning*, than his *Words* do seem to import. For as he *rejects* inherent Sanctification, and so the inward Principle of Heart Purity; from whence a Person, according to this Text, is denominated a good Tree: He must have another *Sense*, to supply the Place of it. And I suppose it to be *this*; that he looks upon a Person to be a *good Tree*, merely on Account of that *Goodness* which he hath in *Christ*, by Virtue of the Imputation of his Righteousness. Which is a Goodness *without* the Man, and not the Principle whence his Actions flow. The Root then, of inherent Sanctity, being wanting in the *Man*, which the Prefacer calls a *good Tree*; in saying, that such a Tree, cannot bring forth *evil Fruit*; he cannot intend those holy *Actions* of a Man, which spring from an inward *Principle* of Holiness, whereby the Uprightness of his *Heart*, may be seen in his *Life*, and the Truth of his Heart-purifying Faith, by his Works, by the Goodness of his Conversation. But he must think, as the *Root* of the Man's Goodness, is the *Righteousness of Christ*; so the good *Fruit* that he brings forth, must be from *thence*: And that the Goodness of his *Works*, is wholly *out* of the *Man*, as well as the Goodness of his *Person*. And I suppose, that by the good Fruit, which the good Tree brings forth, he apprehends, that it is the Privilege of a justify'd Man, to have all his Works made *good*, by the *Grace of Justification*.

As saith Mr. *Eaton*; "And mark what I say, not only we our Persons, but also our *Works*, both natural, civil, and religious, which by their Imperfections are in themselves foul and filthy, are by free *Justification* made so pure and clean, yea, so perfectly holy and righteous, and thereby so acceptable and perfectly well-pleasing to God, that they are all (as I said) both natural, civil, and religious Actions, like the excellent Sacrifice of righteous *Abel*, and Works of *Enoch, Noah, Abraham*," &c. Page 4.

And if all the *Works* of a justified Man, universally, are made thus perfectly *good*, even all his natural, civil, and religious Actions, perfectly holy and righteous, by the *Grace of Justification*; he must needs be esteem'd as a Tree that brings forth *good Fruit*. I see not how he can do otherwise. If whatever he doth, however he doth it, is perfectly and perpetually *good*, by justifying Grace without him; he must needs thereby, bring forth perfect and good Fruit *always*; or rather, whatever Fruit a justify'd Man brings forth, it is by Justification made perfectly *good*. And so there can be no Difference or Degrees of Goodness in his Works, but all are equally and alike *good*, and perfectly *so*, by a Goodness *extrinsick*, that is out of the *Man*, and independent on his *Actions*, derived unto them by the *Act* of *God*, in *justifying of him*, and all his *Deeds*. Which he is to *believe*, and so to be at *Rest*; accounting himself perfectly holy and righteous, a *good Tree*, that brings forth *good Fruit*, by what *God* hath done, and doth for him in *Christ*, which is wholly out of *himself*.

This, my dear Brother, I take to be the Notion, which the *Prefacer* to Mr. *Richardson's* Piece, hath, about a justify'd Man's bringing forth Fruits of Righteousness, and a good Tree's bearing of good Fruit. Which I humbly think, doth naturally tend to lead Souls off from the Whole of *personal Sanctification*, in Heart and Life, and to make them careless about the great Work of *Holiness*, which ought to be their chief Care. And therefore it cannot be the *Truth* of God, but a great *Error*.

If *all* the *Works* of justify'd Persons, were good and perfect, and acceptable to God, merely by the Grace of *Justification* without us, and there were no Difference, or Degrees of Goodness, inherent in *them*: Why did our Lord say to the Church of *Ephesus*, who had left her *first Love, Remember therefore from whence thou art fallen, and repent, and do the first Works*, Rev. ii. 5. And to the Church of *Sardis, I know thy Works, that thou hast a Name that thou liveth, and art dead. Be watchful, and strengthen the Things which remain, that are ready to die: for I have not found they Works perfect before God?* Chap. Iii. 1, 2. If the first Works of the Church at *Ephesus*, had not been *better* than her last, why did our Lord say, Remember therefore from whence thou art *fallen*, and *repent*, and do the *first Works?* And what but a Goodness *intrinsick* in her Works, could make her *first* better than her *last?* Ah! She had left her *first Love*. And did not pour forth, such a Heart-full of Love to *God*, in her *last* Works, as she did in her *first*. Whence she is call'd upon to *repent*. And if to the Church of *Sardis*, our Lord said, *I have not found they Works* perfect *before God*; because she had in a great measure lost that Life, Zeal, and holy

Fervour which once fill'd her good Works, and was as it were the very Spirit, or Soul of them: Is it not evident from hence, that there is some other Kind of *Perfection* which the Lord looks for in the Saints Works, and which they ought to regard, than that which is to be found in the Grace of *Justification*? If there had *not*, our Lord would not have said, I have *not* found thy Works *perfect*. For all that is done for the People of God by their free *Justification*, is absolutely and eternally *so*. It admits of no Degrees, Augmentation, nor Diminution. But this Church is call'd upon to be *whatchful, and strengthen the Things which remained*, that is, in her, that were *ready to die*; that so her Works might be more *perfect* before God. Which shews, that there is an inherent *Goodness* in the Saints *Works*, which admits of *Degrees*, and that they ought to press forward after the highest Measures of *Grace*, in the Performance of *Duties*.

An *absolute* Perfection, in any of our *Works*, is not to be attain'd in this Life; but an *increasing* Perfection there is, in *some* of our Works, which is not to be found in *others*. The more inward Life and Spirit for *God*, there is in our outward *Performances*; the more *perfect* they are. The more they flow from a Principle of Love to God in the *Heart*, and from the Exercise thereof; the nearer they come to the Rule of his *Word*; the more extensive they are, with Respect unto all God's *Commandments*; and the more singly and purely they are design'd for his *Glory*; the more *perfect* they are. And this *comparative* Perfection being *wanting* at that Time, in the Works of this Church at *Sardis*; our Lord blames her for, and commands her to seek. To *be watchful*, as to the *Manner*, the inward Frame of her Spirit, in the Performance of *Duties*; and to *strengthen*, in the Use of *Means*, the *Things*, the *Graces*, which *remained* in her, that as to their Actings, were under a sad Decay, even *ready to die*.

Again, if *all* the *Works* of justify'd Persons, were good and perfect, and acceptable to God, merely by the Grace of *Justification* without us, and there were no Difference, or Degrees of Goodness inherent in *them*: How is it that the Apostle speaks of the *Works* of some (and of their religious Works too) that shall be *burnt* at the Day of Judgment, whose Persons shall be *saved*, I Cor. iii. II, &c. There would be *none* of the Saint's Works to be burnt up at that Day, if *all* their Works were good, perfect, and acceptable to God by the Grace of Justification.

That it is the Privilege of justify'd Persons, to have their good Works *accepted* with God; I freely grant. But that *all* their Works, universally, are *good* and *acceptable*; the Word of God doth not assert, but the contrary. — To make a *good Work*, it must slow from Love to God in the *Heart*, be according to the Rule of his *Word*, and directed unto his Glory as its *End*. It must be done in *Faith*: From a Principle of Faith in the Heart, and from some Degree of the Exercise thereof, in the Out-goings of the Soul unto God in Christ. For, *without Faith, it is impossible to please Him*. But, alas, *all* the Works of justify'd Persons, *all* their Actions, natural, civil, and religious, are not *thus* performed. And those which are *not*; are *evil* Works: Which the Grace of Justification, removes the Guilt of, from their Persons.

And tho' those Works of the Saints which are really *good*, and have the greatest Degree of *Goodness* in them, are *acceptable* to God; yet, as they are but *imperfectly* good, I likewise grant, that they are not, cannot be accepted with God, as they are in *themselves*, or as they come from *us*; but are *acceptable to him, only in, and thro' Jesus Christ.*

But, my dear Brother, the Acceptance of our *Works*, as I humbly think, belongs rather to *Sanctification*, than to *Justification*; to that Sanctification of our *Services*, which we have in and thro' Christ, than to the Justification of our *Persons*. Tho' our Purgation from the *Guilt* of Sin, which attends our Services, must be referr'd unto that Head. But as the *Sacrifices* of Old, were to be washed by the Priest at the *Laver*, Exod. xxx. 18. Lev. i. 9. 2 Chron. iv. 6. So our *Services* are purify'd from the *Filth* of Sin, by the *Blood of Christ*. And as the High-Priest of Old, was to have on his Forehead a *Plate of pure Gold*, whereon was engraven HOLINESS TO THE LORD: Which was to be *always* upon his Forehead, when he went in to minister before the LORD; that they might be *accepted*, with Respect to their Services, their holy Gifts, before the LORD continually, *Exod.* xxviii. 36. SO this Type also, is gloriously fulfill'd in *Christ*, our Gospel *High-Priest*. Who not only sanctifies all our *Services*, our good Works, our holy Duties, from all that *Iniquity*, that Defilement of Sin, which cleaves to them, that Imperfection which is in them, by washing them in his own *Blood*, as the Sacrifices were washed at the *Laver*: But also by presenting them in the Perfections of his own *Holiness*, of his own Love to the Father, Zeal for his Service, and Dedication to his Glory, HOLINESS TO THE LORD; unto the highest Acceptance with him. As *Israel's holy Things* were presented before the LORD, unto *Acceptance* with him, by the *High-Priests* appearing in his Presence, as the Representative of the People, with his *holy Crown*.

But tho' all our good Works, our *spiritual Sacrifices,* are thus acceptable to God by *Jesus Christ*, by his presenting them to the Father, in the Perfection of his *own Holiness*: Which fully supplies all that is wanting of Holiness from *us* in them, and brightly clothes our little *Spark*, with his glorious *Flame*: Yet are we not from hence, to be careless about the Truth and Increase of our *inherent Holiness*, in all our Services, in all the good Works that we perform. Inasmuch as the *more* inherent Holiness there is in us, and Goodness in our Works; the *more* we actively glorify God in them; and the *more* we grow up into Conformity to Christ's *Image*, in our silial Obedience, unto *all pleasing*. And as this of our *personal Sanctification*, is the declared *Will of God*, in the Gospel of *Truth*; so whatever is *contrary* to it, or takes Persons *off* from this their great Work, unto which they are called; is a great *Error*. As I take this Notion to be, (which I suppose the *Prefacer* to Mr. *Richardson's* Piece hath) That Persons are said to be *good Trees*, and to bring forth *good Fruit*, merely by the Grace of Justification, which is quite *out* of themselves.

Again, as in this *Preface*, our perfect Holiness in *Christ*, without inherent Qualities in *us*, is asserted, and thereby Persons are deterr'd from seeking after inherent Holiness, as their Meetness for Glory; so likewise, the *Prefacer* doth not seem to have that deep *Sense* of the Depravity and Impurity of our *Nature*, which we all ought to have. He says indeed, " 'Tis true, we have still the vile sinful Body, which continually disposes the Mind to Evil, but the Blood of *Jesus*, by purifying the Conscience, makes *us free from Sin*, and as it were destroys the Connexion." Which last Clause, as I take it, is as much as to say, The Guilt of Sin being taken off the *Conscience*; it is as if we did not *sin* at all. Not the least Hint is here given, of our Duty, of Looking to Christ by Faith, for the daily Pardon of Sin; of Repentance, or Gospel-Mourning for Sin, as a Christ-piercing Thing; nor of Humiliation before God, and Self-loathing for all our Abominations, while we see them in the Light of forgiving Love, of the Lord's being pacify'd towards us for all that we have done. The *Body* is acknowledg'd to be vile and sinful, and that it continually disposed the Mind to Evil. But alas, the principal Seat of *Sin*, is in the *Soul*, in the highest Part of the Man. And there it abides, as an horrid *Mass* of Vileness! A *Fulness* of all Evil! An *Hell* of Iniquity! An unsearchable *Depth* of Wickedness! For the Being and Working of which, in our *inmost Soul*, how *deeply* should we be humbled! Alas! It is from the Heart, the *wicked*, the *desperately* wicked Heart of Man, that the *Members of his Body* are yielded as Instruments of Iniquity, unto Iniquity. Out of the *Heart* proceeds every *evil Thought*, that defiles the Man. And the *Heart* is put for the *Soul* of Man. Out of which proceeds every vile, filthy, abominable Motion, that stirs in, or prevails with him, which is contrary to the holy, righteous, and good Law of *God*. Which a true Believer, with his *Mind*, or the new Nature in his Soul, *loves and serves*. And for all his Non-conformity to God's holy *Law*, and to every of its *Commandments*, as given from Christ the King of *Sion*, to be the *Rule* of his Gospel-Obedience; he *mourns*, and is *deeply* humbled. But I see nothing of this Spirit, appear in that Preface.

And in *The Steps of Abraham's Faith,* by Mr. *Eaton*, it is said, "That the Children of *Abraham*, walk holily, soberly, and righteously in all God's Command- ments declaratively to Man-ward, *without* the Law of the Ten Commandments." And this also, my dear Brother, I take to be an *Error*. That by the *Grace* of the Gospel which bringeth *Salvation* to a true Believer, he is efficaciously *taught*, to walk *soberly, righteously, and godly in this present World*; is a great *Truth*. And to say, that he walks thus, *without the Law* of the Ten Commandments, as a *Covenant of Works*, is likewise *Truth*. But to say, that a Believer walks thus, *without* the Law of the Ten Commandments, in a *large, undistinguish'd* Sense; is a great *Error*. For hereby the *Law of God*, as a *Rule of Life* to a Believer, is *rejected*. And what saith the Apostle *Paul* of himself? *Being* not *without* Law *to God, but* under *the* Law *to Christ*, I Cor. ix. 21. And evident it is, that he exhorts Believers under the Gospel, to *obey* the Law of the Ten Commandments, *Rom.* xiii. 8, 9. *Owe no Man any Thing, but to* love *one another: For he hath loveth another, hath fulfilled the* Law. *For this, Thou shalt not commit Adultery, Thou shalt not kill, Thou shalt not Steal, Thou shalt not bear false Witness, Thou shalt not covet; and if there be any other* Commandments, *it is briefly comprehended in this Saying, namely, Thou shalt* love *they Neighbour as thyself.* For any therefore to assert, That a Believer doth walk holily, *without* the *Law* of the Ten Commandments, as the *Rule* of his Obedience, whereby he is to glorify God, and the Grace which hath saved him; is a great *Error.*

Surely I may say, *An Enemy hath done this.* Hath sown the *Tares* of false Doctrine, which thus spring up together with the precious *Wheat* of Gospel-Truth. And the Design of the Enemy herein, is, to pervert, and destroy the Gospel of Christ, and the glorious End of it, and to ruin Souls. — Oh the *Subtilty* of this *old Serpent!* If he can't destroy and devour *Souls,* by advancing the *Law,* and a Sinner's Obedience to it, into the *Place* of the Righteousness of *Christ;* he will try what he can do, by setting up the *Gospel,* one *Part* of it, to pull down *another,* the *Foundation* of it, to destroy the *End* of it; to set aside the *Superstructure,* which is and ought to be laid upon it: The Righteousness of *Christ,* reveal'd in the *Gospel,* to destroy Heart-Conformity to the *Law,* to be begun, increas'd and perfected by the Holy Spirit in *us.* Which is the glorious *Fruit* of Forgiveness of Sins thro' the Lamb's *Blood,* and a Joint-*Branch* with it, of God's *New-Covenant.* — Oh my dear Brother, the Lord deliver *you,* dear Brother *Cennick,* and all the Brethren and Sinners, from this Adversary and Enemy which is come out against you! The Lord grant you may see his pernicious Deisgn, recover yourselves out of his Snare, and stand to your Arms. *Having on the whole Armour of God,* and in particular, *your Loins girt about with Truth,* on every Side; and that you may *resist him stedfast in the Faith,* as valiant Soldiers of Jesus Christ, and *Warriors* for the *Cause and Gospel of God!*

Oh my Brother, as I think this letter will grieve *your Heart,* it paineth *mine.* But Love to Christ and his Truth, to you and the Brethren, constrains me to be *faithful.* What can I *do?* Here is a *Wound* made upon the Souls I *love.* — *Lord Jesus, take it into thine own tender, skilful, almighty Hand, search it thoroughly, and heal it perfectly; for the Glory of thy Name, and the saving Health of they People! Even so,* Amen.

In no wise, my dear Brother, would I by what I have written, weaken your Faith in, and Testimony for any Truth of the *Gospel.* But I earnestly desire, that you may receive *all* the Truths of Christ in a consistent Light, and hold them forth in your Testimony for the same, in that Order and Dependance *on* each other, and Connexion *with* each other, in which they *stand* in the glorious Gospel. And with the greatest Love and Tenderness, would I intreat you to *beware,* of receiving every Thing as *Truth,* which you find in the Works of *indistinct* Authors. Ask Wisdom of God; and search the Scriptures daily, to see whether the Things which may be asserted, are the *Truths of God,* or *not.* It is a great Advantage to a *Believer,* to have his *Judgment* well inform'd in the *Truths of the Gospel;* and is a Thing of vast Moment to a *Minister.* If a Minister is *unfound* in any Point; not only is it a Wrong to his *own* Soul, but what Injury thereby may he do to *Thousands!* What Numbers of Souls, at this Time, may *suffer,* if dear Brother *Cennick,* and others of the Teaching Brethren, should give into any *Error?* I beseech you *all* therefore, for the

Honour of God and Truth, by the Love you bear to the Gospel and its Work, and the Concern you have for the present and eternal Welfare of precious Souls; that you will make a *Stand*, and *weigh* the Notions which are at present advanc'd, before you assert them as Truths. — Oh be not hasty, to receive any Thing *contrary* to the Doctrine which you have been *taught*. It is very evident, that it was not the Design of the dear Mr. *Whitefield*, (that eminent Instrument in this glorious Work of Reformation) in exalting the Righteousness of *Christ* alone, for *Justification*; to deter Souls thereby, from seeking after inherent *Sanctification*, and personal *Holiness*, as their *Meetness* for Glory. The *latter* shone as *bright*, in his Preaching, as the *former*. And *both*, in their due Place, do shine in his printed *Sermons*. — I hope, my dear Brother, that the Differences which of late have appear'd among the Brethren, might be well *adjusted*, if the Truths which are asserted on either Side, in the Spirit of Christ, and by his Word, were duly *weigh'd*: And that the *Wheat of Truth*, as precious to you all, would be you jointly be *preserved*; and that the *Chass* of *Error*, as light and unprofitable, hurtful and offensive, would be by you all as jointly *rejected*. Oh may the Lord direct you, and by his own appointed *Means*, effect so great an *End*! You have the Help of my poor Prayers. And to the Love, Care and Guidance, of *Israel's* tender, watchful *Shepherd*, I commit you. — *In the Bowels of Jesus Christ*, I remain,

> Dear Sir,
> Your most affectionate Friend and Servant,

--- ---

P O S T S C R I P T.

My dear Brother, The unpurpos'd Length, and especially the Contents of this letter, with some Fears which I had about the Effect of it; very much try'd me as to sending it to you. By several Scriptures the Lord encouraged me. And yet I was so try'd about it at last, that I knew not what to do. To appear thus *against* you, as it were, went very *near me*, and especially as I knew not but it might be more than you could well *bear*. Upon which, I sought the *Lord*, to know if he would have me send you the *Whole*, or only a *Part* of what I had written. And by these Scriptures, brought to my Mind, he fully satisfy'd me, that I ought to send the *Whole: Thou shalt not* hate *thy Brother in thine Heart: thou shalt in any wise* rebuke *they Neighbour, and not suffer* Sin *upon him*, Lev. xix. 17. By this I saw, that it was my Duty to send you the *Whole* of what I had written, which seem'd to be a Rebuke of *Error*, and not *hate* you, by keeping back a *Part*, but in *Love* to tell you *every Whit*. And while I was thinking, that *Error* was *Sin*, this Scripture dropt into my Mind with some Encouragement: *He that converteth a Sinner from the* Error *of his Way, shall save a Soul from Death, and shall hide a Multitude of Sins*, Jam. v. 20. And when I look'd it, the 19th Verse was very sweet to me, and encourag'd me to attempt my Duty, as it exactly refers to the Case: *Brethren, if any of you do* err *from the* Truth, *and one convert him; let him know*, &c. as in the next Verse. This Word also, to shew me my Duty, was brought to my Mind: *But exhorting one another; and so much the more as ye see the Day approaching*, Heb. x. 25. And again, this Word, to strike me with a holy Awe, and to silence all Gainsayings: *If the Watchman see the* Sword *come, and blow not the* Trumpet, *and the People be not* warned: *If the Sword come, and take any Person from among them, he is taken away in his Iniquity, but his Blood will I require at the Watchman's Hand*, Ezek. xxxiii. 6. And as it is the Duty of all the *Saints* to *watch* over one another, (as well as it is eminently the Duty of *Ministers*, to *watch* over the People) and if they *see the Sword* of Error *come*, to *blow the Trumpet*, that every man may be *warned* of his Danger: I dare not but send you what I have written. I pray you receive it in *Love*; as I only aim'd at the *Glory of God*, and the *Good of Souls*, in writing it. May the Lord make it a *Blessing* to you and others! My beloved Brother, *Adieu*.

Some of the

MISTAKES

OF THE

Moravian BRETHREN.

In a LETTER to a FRIEND.

My dear Friend,

YOURS I receiv'd by Mr. *F______o*, in which you desir'd me tow rite a Line to inform you, wherein the *Moravian Brethren* are *mistaken*. And in brief, I take the *Moravian Brethren* to be mistaken in the four following Points: In that,

I. They assert *Universal Redemption*.

II. They are against a *Doctrinal Knowledge* of the *Truths of God in his Word*.

III. Are against the *Use* of the *Means of Grace*, by *converted Sinners*, and *weak Believers*. And

IV. Against the *Law of God*, as to its being a *Rule of Life* to a *Believer* under the *Gospel*.

First. In that they assert *Universal Redemption*: Or, the Redemption of all, and every Individual of the Human Race. Whereas our Lord saith, That he laid down his Life for *his Sheep*, John x. 15. For the Elect of God, appointed to Salvation thro' Jesus Christ, before the World began. For these, given by God the Father to Christ, to be his *Sheep*, did HE as the *good Shepherd*, lay down his *Life*. And not for the *Goats*, who shall stand at the last Day on his *Left-Hand*, and be sent away from him, as *cursed*, into *everlasting Fire, prepar'd for the Devil and his Angels*, Mat. xxv. 33, 41. Our dear Lord shall see his *Seed*, shall see *of the Travel of his Soul, and shall be* satisfied, *Isa*. liii. 10, 11. He shall see to his endless Joy, all those *saved* to *eternal Life* with him, for whom his Soul *traveled*, for whom he *died*. And for the *rest*, for the *World*, he did not *pray*, and therefore did not *die*: His Intercession, being founded upon his Oblation, or his attoning Sacrifice. *I pray not for the* World, saith he, *but for* them *which thou hast* given me, *for they are thine. And all mine are thine, and thine are mine, and I am glorified in them*, John xvii. 9, 10. Here our Lord pray'd for the whole Number of God's Chosen, for all that were given Him of the Father, to be saved by Him. Not only for those who were given Him in the New-Birth, and to be his Apostles and Ministers; but for all them who were given Him in the Everlasting Covenant, between the Father and the Son before the World was; and who should in After-Times, even to the World's End, *believe on Him thro' their Word*, or thro' the Word of the Gospel, by his Apostles and Ministers. As, Ver. 20. But for the rest, the World, they stand excluded from Christ's Prayer; and therefore had no special, saving Interest in his Death. His Life not being given as a Ransom for their Souls. Altho' by Virtue of Christ's dying for his Sheep, and so to uphold the Frame of Nature, till they are all brought in by his efficacious Grace, or made to hear his Voice, and also brought safe Home to Glory; every Man in the World, hath common Mercies, and temporal Favours bestow'd on him. And so our Lord is the Saviour of *all Men*, in general. But as to special and eternal Salvation, He is the Saviour of none but them that *believe*. And the Reason why *they* believe, while *others* believe not; is, because they are of the Number of Christ's *Sheep*, for whom Jesus *dy'd*: And the Efficacy of his *Death*, produceth their *Faith*. But as to others, as our Lord saith, they believe *not*; because they are not of his *Sheep*, John x. 26. Mark this Text. Our Lord doth not say, Ye are none of my Sheep, because he *believe not*; but ye believe not, because ye are *not* of my *Sheep*. For as to those for whom Jesus dy'd, He calls them *His Sheep*, even while they abide in *Unbelief*. And says concerning them, *And other* Sheep *I have, which are not of this Fold; them also I must bring, and they shall hear my Voice*, Ver. 16. Their being Christ's *Sheep*, secures their *Faith*, as the Fruit of his *Death*. But as to others, that live and die in *Unbelief*, they must bear their own Sins, in the Torments of Hell for ever. Whereby it will be manifest, that they were none of Christ's Sheep, for whom Jesus dy'd. The meritorious Cause of the Salvation of Christ's *Sheep*, is the *Death* of Him their *good Shepherd*. And the meritorious Cause of the Damnation of the *Goats*, is their own *Sin*. Sovereign *Grace* is display'd in the one; and strict *Justice* in the other. And therefore the Lamb's Redeemed, in their Song to the Redeemer, do shout the Glories of his distinguishing Grace to *them*, while *others* were left. *For thou wast slain*, say they, *and hast redeem'd* us *to God by thy Blood*, out *of every Kindred, and Tongue, and People, and Nation*, Rev. v. 9. mark it; they don't say, Thou hast redeem'd every *Kindred, Tongue, People and Nation*: But *us*, *out* of all these. And it is not Redemption by *Power*, by the Power of efficacious Grace, that is spoken of; but Redemption by *Price*, by the Lamb's *Blood*. Which notes, the *Speciality* of Christ's Redemption by *Price*, by his *Blood*: That it is not *all Kindreds, Tongues, People and Nations*, that were redeemed by his Blood: But *some*, out of *all these*. Who as as an Effect thereof, are redeemed by the Power of his Arm, or rescu'd from the Power of Sin and Satan, and brought unto God. The *Moravians* therefore, do greatly *err*, in that they assert *Universal Redemption*. And mistaken they are, in that,

Secondly, They are against a *Doctrinal Knowledge* of the *Truths of God in his Word*. This they slight, as if it was nothing Worth. Whereas, one great Design of

God, in the Revelation of his Truths in the Holy Scriptures, is, that we should *acquaint ourselves* therewith. And a *Head-Knowledge* thereof, the Lord hath appointed, in order to an *Heart-Acquaintance* therewith. Hence the LORD commanded his People of Old, and in them He commands his People now, to *teach his Words*, his *Truths* unto their *Children*, Deut. vi. 6, 7. *And these* Words *which I command thee this Day, shall be in thine Heart. And thou shalt* teach them *diligently unto they* Children*, and thou shalt* talk of them *as thou sittest in thine House, and when thou walkest by the Way, and when thou liest down, and when thou risest up.* And we are told, That, *Whose loveth* Instruction*, loveth* Knowledge*, Prov.* xii. I. That *The Heart of the Prudent, getteth* Knowledge*; and the Ear of the Wise, seeketh* Knowledge, Chap. xviii. 15. And we are told*, also, that the Soul be without* Knowledge*, it is not* good, Chap. xix. 2. *Thro'* they Precepts, saith the Psalmist, I *get* Understanding: *therefore I* hate every false Way, *Psal.* cxix. 104. By a diligent Acquaintance with God's Precepts, He is pleas'd to give his People an Understanding of his Truths, both what they are to believe, and what to do. By which, as they receive the Truth in the Love of it, so they are excited to hate every false Way. A Head-Knowledge of the Truths of God in his Word, is a good and desirable Thing,, a Blessing in itself. And tho' of itself, it is not sufficient to save the Soul; yet is it God's Way, whereby He brings Salvation to his People. It is thro' the Truths we know in our *Heads*, that the Holy Ghost affects and attracts the *Heart*, and changeth the *Soul* into the same Image, from Glory to Glory. The *Moravian Brethren*, constantly commend *Simplicity.* By which they mean, *Childishness* in Knowledge, an affected Ignorance of the Doctrines and Truths of God's Word. But the Lord's Voice to us is, *Be not* Children *in* Understanding: *Howbeit, in Malice be ye Children, but in* Understanding *be* Men, I *Cor.* xiv. 20. And we are commanded to *let the* Word of Christ *dwell in us richly in all* Wisdom, *Col.* iii. 16. *And this I pray,* saith the Apostle, *that your Love may abound yet more and more in* Knowledge*, and in all* Judgment, *Phil.* i. 9. And thus he pray'd for the Saints, *Col.* i. 9. *For this Cause we also, since the Day we heard it, cease not to pray for you, and to desire that ye might be filled with the* Knowledge *of his* Will, *in all* Wisdom *and Spiritual* Understanding. And for this he gave Thanks concerning the Saints at *Corinth. I thank my God always on your Behalf, for the Grace of God which is given you by Jesus Christ; that in every Thing you are enriched by Him, in Utterance, and in all* Knowledge, I *Cor.* i. 4, 5. And thus the Apostle *Peter* exhorts the Saints, *Giving all Diligence, add to your Faith, Virtue; and to Virture,* Knowledge, 2 *Pet.* i. 5. — Many are the Texts that might be brought to prove, That the *Knowledge* of the *Truths of God*, of the Doctrines reveal'd in his *Word*, is highly commended to us, as an exceeding great Privilege, and Matter of Thanksgiving; and that our utmost Diligence to attain the same, is requir'd, and strictly enjoin'd, as the Duty of all Men, as rational Creatures, and especially of such that are born again. But these may suffice, to shew how much the *Moravian Brethren* are *mistaken* in this Point, and how great an Advantage Satan hath gain'd over them. In that he makes them his Instruments, to dissuade Men from their Duty, of reading, and meditating on the Scriptures of Truth. And whoever they be, that neglect the Reading and Study of the Holy Scriptures; they practically say unto God, with the *Wicked, Depart from us; for we desire not the* Knowledge *of thy Ways*, Job. xxi. 14. These poor Souls think it their Wisdom to be *Simple*, to neglect the *Search*, the *Knowledge* of the *Scriptures*. This you yourself have asserted. And I suppose you know from whom you received this Notion. But oh see with your own Eyes, how contrary it is to the Truth of God in his Word! See what the Holy Ghost saith by the Apostle *Paul, 2 Tim.* iii. 15, 16. *And that from a* Child *thou hast* known the Holy Scriptures, *which are able to make thee wise unto Salvation, thro' Faith which is in Christ Jesus. All* Scripture *is given by Inspiration of God, and is profitable for* Doctrine, *for Reproof, for Correction, for Instruction in Righteousness; that the Man of God may be perfect, thoroughly furnished unto all good Works*. Consider, I pray, that the Holy Ghost doth not say, the *Moravian Brethren*, That a Head-Knowledge of the Truths of God in his Word, is nothing Worth, a mere useless unprofitable Thing. But commends *Timothy*, that from a *Child* he had *known the Holy Scriptures*. And adds, which are able to make thee *wise unto Salvation, thro' Faith which is in Christ Jesus*. As CHRIST is the Sum and Substance of the *Holy Scriptures*: So the *Knowledge* of Him, and *Faith* in Him, is communicated thereby. And if the *Scriptures* are able to make us *wise unto Salvation*; is it not our *Duty* to *read* and *meditate* therein? And thus to wait upon God, to illuminate our Minds in the Knowledge of CHRIST, whom to *know*, is *Life eternal?* Attend further, I pray you, to what the Holy Spirit saith. That the Scripture is profitable for *Doctrine*. The *Moravians* say, that doctrinal Knowledge is *unprofitable*. The Holy Ghost saith, that *Doctrine* is *unprofitable*; and that the *Scripture* and the *Knowledge* thereof, is profitable for Doctrine. And adds, for *Reproof, for Correction, for Instruction in Righteousness; that the Man of God may be perfect, thoroughly furnished utno all good Works*. Which shews, that the *Scripture* is a rich Treasury of all *profitable Things*; that all its Parts, richly serve to the various Uses for which they were given; and jointly answer this great End, to *make the Man of God perfect, thoroughly furnished unto all good Works*. Whence every Man, whose Duty it is, to seek the Glory of God and his own Advantage, is oblig'd to read, and study the Holy Scriptures. And with great Joy and Thankfulness ought he to esteem it an unspeakable Privilege. But alas, for the *Moravian Brethren!* they have in this Regard, *Rejected the* Word *of the* LORD: *And what* Wisdom *is in them?* Jer. viii. 9. Again, they are *mistaken*,

Thirdly, In that they are against the *Use* of the *Means of Grace*, by *unconverted Sinners*, and *weak Believers*. That they are against the Use of the *Scriptures*, I have already hinted, and need say the less here. But only you may observe, that while they assert, that unconverted Men, and such that have not receiv'd the full Assurance of Faith; ought not to read the Scriptures: Our Lord's Command, even to Unbelievers, is, *Search the Scriptures*: for in them ye think ye have eternal Life, and they are they which testify of ME, *John* v. 39. And there is a *Blessedness* pronounc'd upon *that Man*, whose *Delight* is in the *Law of the* LORD, and who makes it his *Meditation* Day and Night, *Psal.* i. I, &c. But, The *Ungodly*, the Holy Ghost saith, are not *so*, ver. 4. That is, they are not so *employ'd*, in reading and meditating in the Word of God, their Delight is not in the Law of the LORD: And therefore they are not so *blessed* as the righteous Man; who makes it his daily Practice. But they (as in the After-Part of the Verse) are like the *Chass*, which the Wind driveth away. Not to *read the Scriptures* then, is a Part of *Ungodliness*, and a Character of the *Ungodly*.

And some of the *Moravians* have asserted, That it is not the Duty of Unbelievers to *pray*. Whereas the Holy Ghost said by the Apostle *Peter*, even to a *Simon Magus*, who was apparently in the *Gall of Bitterness, and in the Bond of Iniquity: Repent therefore of this thy Wickedness, and* pray God, *if perhaps the Thought of thine Heart may be forgiven thee*, Acts viii. 22.

Again, the *Moravians* say, That it is not the Duty of weak Believers, of such that have not the full Assurance of Faith, to partake of the *Lord's Supper*. Whereas the weakest Believer, hath an equal Interest in Christ, and Right to this Ordinance, with the strongest. And the Voice of Christ to every one of them is, whether weak or strong, This do *in Remembrance of Me*, Luke xxii. 19. And one great End of the Institution of this Ordinance is, to strengthen the weak Faith of Believers, and raise it into full Assurance. The *Moravians* therefore, by saying that those who have not the full Assurance of Faith, ought not to partake of the Lord's Supper: Do *err* from the Truth, and hinder the Faith of weak Believers.

Once more, under this Head, the *Moravian Brethren*, are against *preaching*, or *expounding* of the Word of God. They are against preaching of the *Law*, to shew Sinners their Misery by Nature: And say, we have nothing to do with the *Law*, in this Regard, under the *Gospel*. Whereas, the Lord hath made the Law *subservient* to the Gospel. And though the Apostle *Paul*, writing to the *Corinthians*, saith, *I determined not to know any Thing among you, save* Jesus Christ, and him crucified, I *Cor.* ii. 2. Yet did he not thereby exclude the preaching of the *Law*, but rather necessarily include it. Inasmuch as, *By the* Law, *is the Knowledge of* Sin, *Rom.* iii. 20. Of Sin in its Guilt, Desert, and Punishment; which being transferr'd from the Sinner to the SAVIOUR, was the Cause of the Crucifixion and Death of JESUS. And to convince Sinners of their extreme Misery by Sin, of their being Helpless and Hopeless, as in and from themselves and the Works of their own Hands, their own Obedience to the Law; how doth this Apostle in this Chapter preach the *Law*? See what he saith from Ver. 10. to Ver. 21. And evident it is, that he shews poor Sinners their Misery by the *Law*, in order to prepare their Hearts to receive the glorious Remedy, which God had provided for them in the *Gospel*. And that he takes Occasion from this his preaching of the *Law*, the more to commend and exalt the infinite Freeness of the Grace of God in the *Gospel*, in justifying and saving Sinners through Jesus Christ, even *all them that believe, from all Things, from which they could not be justified by the Law of* Moses: See, Ver. 21, &c. And concerning *Himself* he says, *I had not known* Sin, *but by the* Law. *But when the* Commandment *came*, Sin *revived, and I died*, Chap. vii. 7,—9. That is, when the Commandment came to his *View*, in its Strictness and Spirituality, as extending to the inmost Thoughts and Motions of the Heart; then Sin *revived* in its extensive Guilt, and appeared in its own Colours, as *exceeding sinful*. Upon which he *died*, became guilty, and expecting nothing but *Death* from the *Law*: And was hereby prepar'd to receive *Life* by the *Gospel*. — The *Moravians* therefore do *err*, in that they are against preaching the *Law*, as a Means to awaken Sinners to a Sense of their Misery; which is God's Way to prepare them to receive the Remedy.

And as they are against preaching of the Law to Sinners, so against the *expounding*, or *opening* of the Scriptures: As by the Expressions of several of them hath been hinted: Whatever their Practice may be in some Places. They speak as if they would have the Word of God *read* to the People, and left with them, just as it lies in the *Text*, without giving any *Sense*, or *Comment* upon it. Which is in Effect, being against the *Scriptures* themselves; and doing what in them lies, to keep the People in Ignorance of the Mind of God therein. When *Philip* was sent to the *Eunuch*, who was reading in the Prophecy of *Esaias*, he put this Question to him, Understandest *thou what thou* readest? *Acts* viii. 30. And if to such Hearers, that have the Word of God barely *read* to them, a like Question was put, *Understand* ye what ye *hear*? Each one for himself might reply with the *Eunuch, How can I, except some Man should* guide me? Ver. 31. Upon which, and his Desire to be taught, *Philip began at the same* Scripture, *and* preached *unto him* JESUS, Ver. 35. And well would it be for the *Moravian Hearers*, if their Ministers *preached* from the Scripture, and not barely *read it* to the People, or said *little* to them from it. *Ezra*, and the Servants of God that were with him, not only *read* in the Book, in the Law of God distinctly, but they also gave the *Sense*, and caused the People to *understand the Reading*, Nehe. viii. 8. And our Lord, *beginning at* Moses *and all the Prophets*, expounded *unto* his Disciples *in all the* Scriptures, *the Things concerning himself*, Luke xxiv. 27. And those that preach the Gospel, are commanded to speak as *the* Oracles of God, I *Pet.* iv. 11. Not only to *read* the Oracles of God, but to *speak*, in their Exposition thereof, *as*, or according to the Oracles of God; to see that what they advance from thence, be agreeable wherewith. And of the Apostle *Paul* it is said, That he reasoned *with the Jews out of the* Scriptures, opening *and* alledging *that Christ must needs have suffered, and risen again from the Dead; and that this* JESUS *whom he preach'd unto them, is* CHRIST, *Acts* xvii. 2, 3. And thus of him it is said, *he* expounded *and testified the Kingdom of God, persuading the* Jews *concerning* JESUS, *both out of the Law of* Moses, *and out of the Prophets, from Morning till Evening*, Chap. xxviii. 23. And for this End, of *expounding*, or *opening* of the *Scriptures*, and the Things therein that concern JESUS, the ascended SAVIOUR gave *Gifts* unto Men. *And he gave, some, Apostles: and some, Prophets: and some, Evangelists: and some, Pastors and Teachers: For the perfecting of the*

Saints, for the Work of the Ministry, *for the* edifying *of the Body of Christ*, Eph. iv. 8,—11, 12. But the *Works of the Ministry*, among the *Moravian Brethren*, is almost laid aside. Little or nothing do they say in their short Discourses to the People, by way of *Explanation* of the Word of God, or of *Exhortation* from it. And therefore the *Edification* of the Hearers, must be much hindred. Satan has got an Advantage against them. And by suggesting to them, that they must use no *Words*, but *Scripture-Words*, nor give into the *Sense* of any Expositor on a Text, &c. He has drawn them off from the Use of those *Means* of Increase in the Knowledge of Christ, which the Lord hath appointed, both for Ministers and People.

And thus the old Enemy, has drawn them off from reading *good and useful Books*, that are wrote by Men, and thereby renders many of the precious Gifts given to the People of God, useless to Souls. We are commanded to *Follow after the Things whereby one may* edify *another*, Rom. xiv. 19. And this takes in, not only teaching and exhorting one another by *Word of Mouth*; but also by *Writing*, and in *Print*. It is the Duty of the Saints to communicate the Light they receive from Christ, to their Brethren, by Writing and in Print: *That*, as the Apostle saith, they may have those Things always in *Remembrance*, after their *Decease*, 2 *Pet*. i. 15. And therefore it is our Duty to *read* such Books, and therein to wait for the Spirit of Christ, to illuminate our Minds in the Knowledge of HIM. We are commanded to be Followers *of them, who through* Faith *and* Patience *inherit the Promises*, Heb. vi. 12. And therefore we should use all the Means which the Lord gives us, to be acquainted with the *Faith* of his People. Not only of those who are gone before us out of the World; but also of those who are gone before us out of the World; but also of those that are with us in it; who may justly be esteemed *Fathers* in Christ; and who ought as such, in what they teach, to be regarded by us their *Children*. We are to follow *them*, as they follow *Christ*; and their *Faith*, just so far as they *keep the Faith, that was once deliver'd to the Saints*, I Cor. iv. 16. and xi. I. with *Jude*, Ver. 3. But the *Moravian Brethren* do *err*, in that being against the Use of *Means* in this Respect, in the Perusal of *Books*, they are against our being *Followers* of the *Faith* of the Saints; and so they hinder the People of God, from *running the Race that is set before them*. And *mistaken* they are,

Fourthly. In that they are against the *Law of God*, as to its being a *Rule of Life* to a *Believer* under the *Gospel*. That Believers are deliver'd from the Law as a *Covenant of Works*, is a certain Truth, and an unspeakable Privilege. It is in this Respect that the Apostle speaks of our Deliverance from the *Law*, Rom. vii. 4. *Wherefore my Brethren, ye also are become* dead *to the* Law *by the Body of Christ, that ye should be married unto another, even to him who is raised from the Dead, that we should bring forth Fruit unto God. Believers* are here said to be *dead* to the Law; and the *Law* is likewise said to be *dead* to them, Ver. 6. That *being* dead *wherein we were held*. But then observe, the Law is dead to *us*, and we to *it*, only as a *Covenant of Works*; that requires *Doing, for Life*. In this Respect, since Christ was made under it, and has fulfill'd it for his People, He is become the End *of the*

Law *for Righteousness, unto every one that* believeth, *Rom.* x. 4. Christ is the *perfecting* End of the Law, as a Covenant of Works; he having fulfill'd it in Point of *Righteousness*, and given it all that it could demand, the Law hath nothing more to require of us, or to say to a Believer in *that* Respect. A Believer, in this Regard, is as *free* from any Obligation to the *Law*, as a Woman is *free* from the Law of her *Husband*, when he is *dead*. And as the Law is become dead to *us*, by the *Body of Christ*; so we likewise become dead to *it*, when the Holy Spirit works *Faith* in our Hearts, to receive for *ourselves*, for our own Justification in the Sight of God, the complete Obedience of Jesus Christ; which God hath revealed in the Gospel, as the only justifying Righteousness of a Sinner. Thus, *To every one that* believeth, *Christ is the* End of the Law. That Soul, receiving and possessing the perfect Righteousness of Christ, for his complete Justification before God; *ceaseth* for ever from his *own Works*, from his own Obedience to the Law, to make himself righteous, and give him a Title to Life.

And Believers are thus *loosed* from their former Obligation to the Law as a Covenant of Works; that they should be *married* unto another; even to CHRIST, who is *raised from the Dead. Who was deliver'd for our* Offenses, *and raised again for our* Justification: *That we should bring forth* Fruit unto God. That henceforth, we should perform good Works, not to *ourselves*, under the Influence of the Law of Works, for our Justification; but unto GOD, under the Influence of the Love of Christ, and for the Glory of Him who hath saved us. Being freed from our old Obligation to the *Law*, which was *slavish*, and only suited a Bondage-State, while we were *Children of the Bond-Woman*, of the first Covenant; we are laid under a new, a higher, a stronger Obligation to Obedience, by *Christ's Love*, which renders it *free and generous*, and every Way becomes the Liberty, the *glorious Liberty of the Sons of God*, or the Freedom of our State, as *Children of the New-Covenant*.

And that same JESUS, who fulfill'd the Law, and thereby wrought out a Righteousness for us, and is become the End of it to us, as a Covenant of Works; hath took the *Law*, this fulfilled Law, in Point of Righteousness before God, into his own Hand, as our SAVIOUR-King, and gives it to us from his Throne in *Sion*, as the *Rule of our new Obedience*, of that Obedience, whereby as saved Souls, we are to glorify our SAVIOUR. We have the *Law* given us, not now from *Sinai*, but from *Sion*; not as the Law of *Moses*, the Voice of which was, *Do*, and *Live*; *Sin*, and *Die*: But as the Law of CHRIST, the Voice of which to us, thro' the Lamb's Love and Blood, is, *Live*, and *Do*; blessed are ye in *Christ's Deed*; bless him now in *your Deeds*. The moral *Law*, which for *Substance* was given to *Adam* in Paradise, and in him, unto all Mankind, *Gen.* ii. 16, 17. Which oblig'd him to *love the* LORD *his God, with all his Heart, Soul and Strength,* as a glorious Creator, and rich Benefactor: The moral *Law*, which in *Ten Commandments*, was given to the *Jews* at Mount *Sinai*, which oblig'd them to *love the* LORD *their God, with all their Heart, Soul and Strength*, as a Creator, and Benefactor, and also as their Redeemer from *Egypt's* Bondage: This *same* moral *Law*, is given to us *Christians*, to us *Believers*, that are Christians *indeed*, from Mount *Sion*: And obligeth us to *love the* LORD *our God, with all our Heart, Soul, and Strength*, as our great Creator and kind Bene-factor, and especially as our SAVIOUR and Redeemer, who hath redeemed us from Sin, Death and Hell, and deliver'd us out of the Hands of all our spiritual Enemies. And by this *royal Law* of King JESUS, by this *perfect Law of Liberty,* we are obliged to *love our Neighbour,* our Brother, *as ourselves.* And in this, of *Love to God*, and our *Neighbour*, the whole *Law*, in all the *Ten Words*, is *fulfilled.* Every of which, for the Sake of CHRIST, *Christians* should have *Respect* to.

And that Believers, who are deliver'd from the Law as a *Covenant of Works*; are under it to Christ, as a *Rule of Life*; is evident: In that the Apostle *Paul* expresly asserts it, I *Cor*. ix. 21. *To them that are* without Law, (that is, the *Gentiles*, who were not under the *Law*, as given at *Sinai*) *as without Law, being* not without Law to God, *but* under the Law to Christ. And after he had shew'd our *Deliverance* from the Law, as a *Covenant of Works*, Rom. vii. 6. He adds, our being *under it*, as a *Rule of Life*: And gives our Deliverance from it in the *former Sense*, as the Ground of our serving it in the *latter Sense. But now we are* deliver'd *from the* Law, *that being* dead *wherein we were held, that we should* serve *in the* Newness of the Spirit, *and not in the* Oldness of the letter. The plain Sense of the Holy Ghost by the Apostle *Paul*, in this Text is, That Believers are deliver'd from the Law as a *killing letter*, that requir'd Duty for Life, and curs'd to Death for Disobedience; and set free from their former Service to it thus, in the *Oldness of the Letter*: That henceforth they should serve the *Law*, or serve GOD according to this Rule of Life given them under the *Gospel*, in the *Newness of the Spirit*; from Gospel-Motives, under Gospel-Influence, and unto Gospel-Ends. And thus the Apostle saith, *I* consent *unto the* Law, *that it is* good, Ver. 16. *I* delight *in the* Law of God, *after the inward Man*, Ver. 22. And when he draws up the Conclusion, from that Conflict which he found in his Soul, between Sin and Grace, between his spiritual Part, with which he desir'd to serve God according to his *Law*; and his carnal part, which was *Enmity*, against God, and not *subject* to his Law: He saith, *so then with the* Mind (or new Nature) I myself serve the Law of God; *but with the* Flesh (or corrupt Nature) *the Law of Sin*, Ver. 25.

And as here the Apostle saith, that he himself *Served the Law of God*; so he commends this unto the Saints, *Rom*. xiii. 8, 9, 10. *Owe no Man any Thing, but to* love one another; *for he that* loveth *another, hath* fulfilled the Law. *For this, Thou shalt not commit Adultery, Thou shalt not kill, Thou shalt not steal, Thou shalt not bear false Witness, Thou shalt not covet; and if there be any other* Commandment, *it is briefly comprehended in this Saying, namely*, Thou shalt love they Neighbour as thyself. Love *worketh no Ill to his Neighbour; therefore Love is the* fulfilling of the Law. How clear is it from hence, that Believers are *under the Law?* And ought, in their good Conversation in Christ, according to the *Gospel*, to have Regard to the *Law*, as the *Rule* of their Obedience?

Hence also, *Children* are commanded to be *obedient to their Parents*, Eph. vi. 1, 2, 3. *Children obey your Parents in the Lord; for this is right. Honour thy Father and thy Mother, (which is the first* Commandment *with Promise) that it may be well with thee, and thou mayst live long on the Earth.* It is observable, that the Apostle here speaks of *believing Children*, and of their Obedience, that are *in the Lord*. And yet to these *Believers*, he gives the *fifth Commandment* of God's *Law*, as the *Rule* of their *Gospel-Obedience*, in this Branch of it. Which shews us, That Believers by the *Gospel*, are laid under the strongest Obligations to regard the *Law*, as the *Rule* of their Gospel-Obedience.

The Apostle *James* also, commends to Believers under the *Gospel*, a constant Regard to the *Law*, as a *Rule of Life*, Jam. i. 25. *But whoso looketh into the perfect* Law of Liberty, *and continueth therein, he being not a forgetful Hearer, but a Doer of the Work; this Man shall be blessed in his Dead.* And again he saith, *If ye fulfil the* royal Law, *according to the Scripture, Thou shalt love they Neighbour as Thyself, ye do* well. *But if ye have Respect to Persons, ye* commit Sin, *and are convinced by the* Law as Transgressors. *For whosoever shall keep the whole Law, and yet offend in* one Point, *he is* guilty of all. *For he that said, Do not commit Adultery, said also, Do not kill. Now if thou commit no Adultery, yet if thou kill, thou art become a* Transgressor of the Law. *So speak ye, and so do, as they that shall be judg'd by the Law of Liberty*, Chap. ii. 8, &c. The Apostle here styles the Law of God, *The Law of Liberty*: Because, as given to Believers under the Gospel, as Christ has fulfill'd it for them in Point of Righteousness, and redeem'd them from the Curse of it; it is indeed *so*; while it becomes to them, the *Rule* of their Obedience, and cannot *curse* them for their Disobedience. He likewise styles it, *The Royal Law*; because given from CHRIST the King of *Sion*; to *Believers*, his royal Off-spring; who obey this royal Law, as royal Princes, in a Royalty of Spirit, that every Way becomes their Freedom, their Dignity, their Glory, as *washed from all their Sins, and made kings and Priests unto* GOD, *by the* LAMB'S *Blood*. And that Gospel-Believers, or true *Christians*, are thus under the Law to *Christ*, this Law of Liberty, this royal Law, is evident, in that the Apostle says, *If ye fulfil the Royal Law, according to the Scripture*, (or according to this Rule given you) *ye do* well. If they had not been *under the Law*, and oblig'd to obey it; in attempting Obedience to it, or to *fulfil it*, they would not have done *well*, but *ill*: In doing that which was *not* requir'd. And in that the Apostle commends to them a due Regard to *all* the Commandments of God, and tells them, if they offended in *one Point*, they were *guilty of all*, and became *Transgressors of the Law*: It plainly shews us, that they were *under it. For where* no Law is, *there is* no Transgression. *For* Sin *is the* Transgression *of the* Law. What the *Law of Moses* saith, as a Covenant of Works, in requiring Obedience for Life, and cursing to Death for Disobedience; it saith to them that are *under it*. And what the same Law saith, as the *Law of Christ*, as the Law of Liberty, in requiring Obedience of saved Souls, to glorify their SAVIOUR; it saith to them that are *under it*. Whence upon the *Breach* of it, Believers become *guilty*. Were they not under its *Requirements*; they could not commit *Sin*. But this they *do*, when they act *contrary* to it; and therefore must needs be *under it*. And tho' they are deliver'd from the just *Desert* of their Sin, which is, the Law's *Curse*, and God's *Wrath*, by Christ's enduring it for them; yet the Lord their King and Lawgiver, for their Breach of his Law, from his infinite Love to their Persons, will visit them with the *Rod* of his fatherly *Chastisements*. And therefore the Apostle saith, *So speak ye, and so do, as they that shall be* judged *by the* Law of Liberty, *viz.* as such whose every Action, the Law of Christ takes *Cognizance* of; and who, if you break his *Law*, by the LORD your *Lawgiver*, will be adjudg'd *guilty* of the Breach thereof, and accordingly *rebuked* of Him. As Ver. 13. *For He shall have* Judgment *without* Mercy, *that hath shewed no Mercy.* Or, *Chastisement*, the Lord will not *spare him*, tho' he be a *Son*, a *dear* Son, but bring his *Rod* upon him for his rebellious Behaviour. *And* Mercy (as the Apostle adds) *rejoyceth against* Judgment. As if he should say, 'It is more delightful to the Prince of Peace, to the Lord your Father, to *spare* his Children, and to exercise *Loving-Kindness* towards them, in the pure and native Displays thereof, than to lay them under his severe *Rebukes: He doth not afflict willingly, nor grieve the Children of Men.* And therefore provoke him not by your Disobedience to his *Law*, which he hath given you as a *Rule of Life* to walk by.

And thus the Apostle *Paul*, exhorts the Saints to *fulfil the Law*, in bearing one another's *Burdens*, Gal. vi. 2. *Bear ye one another's* Burdens, *and so* fulfil the Law of Christ. Which was, to *love one another*, John xiii. 34. *A new Commandment I give unto you, that ye* love one another; *as I have loved you, that ye also* love one another. And he puts this their *Obedience*, upon their *Love to him*, Chap. xiv. 15. *If ye* love me, *keep my* Commandments. Which carries in it the Force of a *Command to love him*, and is *descriptive* of the Persons that *obey it*. For this is not to be understood, as if they were left at their Liberty, whether to *love him*, or *not*; but as that which laid them under *Obligation* to love him, and to shew their *Love* to him, in keeping his *Commandments*. As Ver. 21. *He that hath* my Command-ments, *and* keepeth them, *he it is that* loveth me. And Ver. 23, 24. *If a Man* love me, *he will* keep my Words. — *He that loveth me* not, *keepeth* not *my Sayings: and the Word which you hear is not* mine, (only, and originally) *but the* Father's *which sent me.* And so, in their being commanded to *love the Father also.* Inasmuch as the *Word* which Christ gave them, was not *his only*, but the *Father's also. For this is the* Love of God, *that we* keep his Commandments, I *John* v. 3. Our Lord therefore, in laying his Disciples under Obligation to keep *his Commandments*, as they were his, and the Father's *Word*; commanded them to *love God*, and their *Brother*, and to shew it by their *Obedience.* for their Encouragment, he adds, in this *John* xiv. 21,—23. *And he that loveth me shall be* loved *of my* Father, *and I will* love him, *and will* manifest myself to him.—*And we will come unto him, and make our* Abode *with him.* Happy then are the Souls, that in obeying Christ's Commandments, *love God*, and are thus *loved of him!* — This Command of *Love* to *God* and our

Neighbour, our *Brother*, is the Sum of *God's Law*: And as given to Believers from Christ, it is the Sum of *Christ's Law*. Believers therefore, are *not without Law to God*; but *under the Law to Christ*. Who has fulfill'd it *for them*, in point of *justifying Righteousness*; and given it as a fulfill'd Law *by him*, to be fulfill'd *by them*, in point of *Filial Obedience*. As this perfect *Law*, is made by him, the *Rule* of their Conduct, unto which their Actions are to be *conformed*.

And thus the Apostle *John, He that saith he abideth in him, ought himself also so to walk, even as he walked*, I John ii. 6. And Ver. 7, 8. *Brethren, I write* no new Commandment *unto you*, (of my own devising, that ye have not received from the *Lord Jesus*, and been long acquainted with) *but an* old Commandment *which he have heard from the Beginning. Again, a* new Commandment *I write unto you, which* Thing *is true in* him, *and in* you: *because the Darkness is past, and the true Light now shineth*. This Commandment which the Apostle wrote to them that believed on the Son of God, was *Love*: As Ver. 10. *He that* loveth his Brother, *abideth in the Light*. Love being the Substance of what was commanded in God's *old Law*; the Apostle stiles it an *old Commandment*. This good old Law of God, being fulfill'd by Christ; he saith, this Thing is true in *him*; that *he loved perfectly*, according to the utmost of the Law's *Requirement*. And as the Darkness of Curse and Death, which attended the Law as a Covenant of Works, was thereby chased away from Christ's People; and as the Darkness of Unregeneracy, and of a carnal Mind, which is Enmity against God, and his Law, was in part driven away from the Hearts of these Believers; and God's old Law, which commanded Love, given to them by Christ, as his *new Commandment*, and thereby highly commended and exceedingly endear'd to their Souls, and they drawn out by his Love, and in his Strength to obey it: He saith, This Thing is also true in *you*. That is, *they* obey'd the *Law*, as Christ's *new Commandment*, (for as given them by *him*, the Apostle so stiles it) in their Measure, so far as they were renew'd by Grace, and enabled to act graciously, as Members of his Body, in Conformity to him their glorious Head: Who obey'd the *Law* perfectly, as his *Father's Commandment*. And therefore it is evident that they were *under it*.

Once more, As our Lord fulfill'd the Law for us in Point of justifying Righteousness; and gave it to us to obey for Him, or to regard it for his Glory, as the *Rule* of our filial Obedience; so he saith, *Whosoever therefore shall* break *one of these* least Commandments, *and shall teach Men* so, *he shall be called the* least *in the Kingdom of Heaven: But whosoever shall* do *and* teach them, *the same shall be called* great *in the Kingdom of Heaven*, Matt. v. 19.

See then, my Friend, how much the *Moravian Brethren* are *mistaken* in this Point (as in the three former) in that they are against the *Law of God*, as to its being a *Rule of Life* to a *Believer* under the *Gospel!* Alas, poor Souls! they do, tho' not knowingly and designedly, despise the Authority of CHRIST, as the crowned *King of Sion*; while they advance this Position: "That Believers under the *Gospel*, are not to regard the *Law*, to do any Thing as *Duty*, or as *commanded*." And so far as they refuse *Subjection* to the *Law of Christ*, by breaking the *Authority* of the Lawgiver from off any of his *Commands*, and teach others *doctrinally so* to *do,* whereby their Obedience to our Lord and King is *hindred*; so far they shall be called the *Least* in the Kingdom of Heaven. And tho' those among them who are true *Believers* in *Christ*, shall be *saved* at last, upon the Bottom of his perfect Righteousness and infinite Grace; yet they shall *suffer Loss*, the Loss of all that Praise, Honour and Glory, which otherwise they would have had in the Day of Christ. Their *Works*, their *Doctrines*, this and others, that they have advanc'd, wherein they are *mistaken*, which are not *Gold, Silver, precious Stones*; which are not according to the Purity of *God's Word*, nor agree with the *Glory of Christ*, the *Foundation laid in Sion;* but are *Wood, Hay, and Stubble,* shall be *burnt up*, tho' they *themselves shall be saved; yet so, as by Fire:* Or as a Person that escapes the Flames, and hath his Goods consumed, I *Cor*. iii. I I &c.

You may think, Sir, my Answer to your Request *long*; and indeed it is much longer that I design'd. But if the Lord will please to make any Thing of Use to your Soul, for your Instruction and Edification in the Knowledge of CHRIST, and to promote your Obedience to Him: I shall rejoice with you, and give all the Glory to GOD. — Wishing sincerely your Soul's Prosperity: I remain,

Sir,
Your affectionate Friend and Servant,

A POSTSCRIPT *to the last* LETTER *added.*

AS since I writ and sent this letter, I have been inform'd by a worthy Friend, of what the *Moravians* say against the Use of the Means of Grace by *unconverted Sinners*, and *weak Believers*; I thought it best to acquaint the Reader, and to give a Word of Reply. They thus object,

Obj. No Means can be effectual, but by the Operation of the *Holy Ghost*; Men are strongly inclin'd to think, that of *themselves* they can do something, and that by the *Use* of Means they may spiritually *profit*: The *Uncoverted* not having the Spirit, by the *Use* of Means in their own Strength, are brought to fancy that they become *Spiritual* and *please God*; whence they become mere *Pharisees*, further from the Kingdom of Christ, and harder to be persuaded to enter into it than before: And therefore it is *best* for them not to use the Means at *all*.

Ans. It is a daring Thing for Men to pretend to be wiser than God. If God commands *unconverted* Sinners the *Use* of Means: Who is he that dares say, "It is not *best* for them?" *Let* GOD *be true; and every Man* (that says thus) *a Liar*. Shall God command a *Simon Magus* to *pray* to him, *if peradventure the Thought of his Heart may be forgiven*: And shall any Man say, "It is not *best* for him so to do?" Shall God command *unconverted* Sinners to *search the Scriptures*, which testify of

Christ the Saviour, that so their Minds may be enlightned in the Knowledge of Him: And shall any Man say, "It is not *best* for them so to do?" *He that reproveth* GOD, *let him answer it.*

But farther, Tho' no Means can be effectual, but by the Operation of the *Holy Ghost*; yet unconverted Sinners in the *Use* of Means, are to wait for this *Blessing*; as the *impotent* Folk at *Bethesda's Pool, for the Moving of the Water.* Tho' Men are strongly inclin'd to think, that of *themselves* they can do something, and that by the *Use* of Means, they may spiritually *profit*: Yet are they not to *neglect* the Use of Means; since God therein is pleas'd to shew Persons their own *Inability*, and his *All-Sufficiency.* And tho' unconverted Men, by the *Use* of Means in their own Strength, do often fancy that they become *Spiritual* and *please God*; whence they become mere *Pharisees*, further from the Kingdom of Christ, and harder to be persuaded to enter into it than ever: Yet ought they not to *neglect* the *Means* which God has commanded, because their unbelieving Hearts *pervert* them. And blessed be God, *all* unconverted Sinners, that use the Means, are not left thus to pervert them, but soon find the Grace of them. And where some of God's Chosen, remaining in Unbelief, for a while may be thus suffer'd to pervert the Means of Grace; yet even this shall be overrul'd by the Grace that saves them, for the further Advancement of its infinite Riches in their Salvation. If any of the Souls which the Lord designs Mercy for, should for a while please themselves with the Performance of Duties, and thence become beautiful Creatures in their own Conceit: *The Spirit of the* LORD for them, shall *blow* upon all this *Glory*, and make it *wither* like the mown *Grass* in their Sight. When irresistible Grace takes them in Hand, and reveals the *Glory of the* LORD, *and the Excellency of our God:* Down all their *Idols* shall fall, before the Majesty thereof. And they, sweetly drawn in the Day of Christ's *Power*, shall become his *willing* Subjects, and gladly enter into his Kingdom, adoring the Grace, that did not suffer them to perish in open Prophaneness, nor yet in their *Pharisaical* Righteousness; which as they once admir'd, they shall then abhor, and loath themselves in their own Sight for all their Abominations, and for this, of their setting up their *own* Righteousness, in the Room of *Christ's*. And sovereign Grace, shall have the eternal Glory, that brought *near* the Redeemer's *Righteousness* to them, who were thus *stout-hearted, and far from Righteousness.* And if any Person in the Observance of religious Duties, remains a *Pharisee*; the Evil of his trusting to his Duties, is not to be charg'd upon his Performance of them, upon his *Use* of the Means of Grace; but upons his *Abuse* of them, his using them for, and improving them to a wrong End. And most certain it is, that since God hath reveal'd himself to be the *God of all Grace* towards Sinners to his *Son*, and commandeth all Men every where to *repent*, and *believe the Gospel*, and so to use the *Means* thro' which Faith and Repentance is given: No Man can *neglect* any of the Means of *Grace*, without *neglecting this great Salvation* which is proclaim'd in the *Gospel*; nor yet without the *Breach* of God's righteous *Law*; which obligeth him to *love the Lord his God*, and so to use the *Means* which he hath appointed, as conducive to that *End. The Sacrifice* (the Prayer, the Performance) *of the Wicked,* we are told, *is an Abomination to the* LORD. And that, *Without Faith it is impossible to please Him:* But since Unbelievers can't *pray*, without *sinning* therein; must they therefore *neglect* Prayer? Most surely, tho' they can't *pray* without Sin; it is a much greater Sin, *not* to pray. And the Lord hath threatened to *pour out* his *Fury upon the Families that call* not *upon* his *Name.* And so, tho' an Unbeliever can't *read*, nor *meditate* on the Word of God, without *Sin*; it is a much greater Sin, *not* to search the Scriptures. For let it be observ'd, that the Sin which attends an Unbeliever in the *Use* of the Means of Grace, is *accidental* to his Duty; but his Sin in the *Neglect* thereof, is *formal.* And if for Fear of Persons trusting to the Performance of Duties, they are to be deterr'd therefrom; what a wide Door would be open'd hereby for all Immorality and Irreligion? — Again, they thus object against the Use of Means by weak Believers,

Obj. Weak Believers, by *using* the Means of *Grace*, are brought to *trust* in them, and in their own Working, and not in JESUS alone; which *overturns* their Faith, instead of *building* them up in it: And therefore it is *best* for them that han't receiv'd the full Assurance of Faith, not to use the Means at *all.*

Answ. That the *weakest Believer* on Earth, *trusts* in the Righteousness of Christ alone, for his Acceptance with God, and not in his *own* Performances for this End; is an undoubted *Truth*: Whatever may be suggested to the *contrary*: And therefore there is no *Danger* of overturning his Faith, by his Performance of Duty. His *Faith* is kept by the *Power of God*, and he through it, resting upon *Christ* the sure *Foundation* laid in *Sion*, while working by *Love*, in the Performance of Duties, he waits on God, and is bless'd by him, with all Increase of Grace here, utno he's crown'd with Glory hereafter; or until he receives the *End* of his *Faith*, the complete *Salvation* of his *Soul.* And if God commands weak Believers to *desire the sincere Milk of the Word*; to pray, and search the Scriptures, and for this End, *that* they *may grow thereby*: Is it not a daring Affront to infinite Wisdom and Goodness, for any Man to say, "It is not *best* "for them so to do." And were any weak Believers to *regard* such Persons that would thus deter them from their Duty: Would not the Authority of Christ, through their Neglect of his appointed Means, be hereby *despised?* And their Growth in Grace by *hindred?* Oh that none of them that fear God, that believe in Christ, even to the weakest in Faith, may be *ignorant* of this *Device* of *Satan*!

And as there are some Persons that perplex Believers in some Places, by telling them, "That there are *no Degrees* in Faith; that they have no true *Faith*, if they have any *Doubt* or *Fear*, if they have not *full Assurance:*" I beg the Reader's patient Attention to a Hint on this Head. And,

If there are *no Degrees* in Faith; why is one Person said to be *strong*, and another *weak* in Faith? As, *Rom.* iv. 20. and xiv. I. If there was no true *Faith*, where there was any *Doubt* or *Fear*; why did our Lord say to *Peter, O thou of* little Faith, *wherefore didst thou* doubt? *Matt.* xiv. 31. And to the Disciples, *Why are ye* fearful,

O ye of little Faith? Chap. viii. 26. Our Lord did not say to *Peter, O thou of no* Faith; *but O thou of little* Faith, *wherefore didst thou* doubt? Nor to the Disciples, here, *Why are ye* fearful, *O ye of no* Faith? but *O ye of little* Faith? Indeed our Lord said unto them, *Why are ye so* fearful? *how is it that ye have* no Faith? *Mark* iv. 40. But this is to be understood of the present *Exercise* of their Faith, and not of the *Principle* thereof in their Hearts. And must be taken *comparatively*, and not *absolutely*, even as to the *Exercise* of their Faith. For it was from the Exercise of their Faith in their Lord's Power, that they said unto him, *Master, carest thou not that we perish?* Ver. 38. But as they *fear'd* perishing, when their Lord was with them; he thus rebuk'd their *Unbelief*, by saying, *How is it that ye have* no Faith? That is, no Faith as it were in *Exercise?* And thus he said unto them, *Where is* your Faith? *Luke* viii. 25. q.d. Where is the *Exercise* of that Principle of *Faith* which is in *your Hearts?* And that they had true Faith, and the Actings thereof on him as the great Saviour, is evident, by what he said concerning them to his Father, John xvii. 8. *I have given them the Words which thou gavest me; and they have received them, and have known surely that I came out from thee, and they have* believed *that thou didst send me.* And if our Lord's Disciples *then*, had true Faith in him, and yet at Times had but little Faith in Exercise, and were subject to Doubts and Fears: It shews that Persons *now*, may have true Faith in Christ, and yet at Times have but little Faith in Exercise, and be attended with Doubts and Fears. — Again, if there were *no Degrees* in Faith: What room would there have been for the Apostle to distinguish between *Faith*, and the *full Assurance* thereof? As he manifestly doth, when he saith, *Let us draw near with a true Heart, in* full Assurance *of* Faith, *Heb.* x. 22. If nothing less than *full Assurance*, had been *true Faith*; he need have said no more than, *Let us draw near with a true Heart, in* Faith. But as he adds *full Assurance* to Faith: *In* full Assurance *of* Faith: It shews, that *Faith*, and the *full Assurance* of it, are *distinct* Things: Or, that there *are Degrees* in Faith, that there *may* be true Faith, where there is *not* full Assurance. And also, that Believers ought not to *indulge* Doubts and Fears, but to *labour* after full Assurance. And thus the Apostle speaks in the next Verse, *Let us hold* fast *the Profession of our* Faith *without* wavering, *for he is faithful that promised*, Ver. 23. If Believers had not been subject to *wavering*, and to *let go* their Confidence; he would not have said, *Let us hold* fast *the Profession of our* Faith *without* wavering: Nor yet would he have spoken thus, if it had not been their Duty, to *seek* the full Assurance of Faith, a Steadiness in Faith, in the faithful Promise of God, amidst a thousand seeming Contradictions.

True *Faith* consists, in the Soul's *discerning* of the Excellence of *Christ*, as the only and all-sufficient *Saviour*, and in its *approving* of, and *cleaving* to him as such. Thus, I Pet. ii. 6, 7. *Wherefore also it is contained in the Scripture, Behold, I lay in* Sion, *a chief Corner-Stone, Elect, Precious: and he that* believeth *on him shall not be confounded. Unto* you *therefore which* believe, *he is* precious. If *Christ* is made *precious* unto any Soul: God's Word assures, that that Soul hath true *Faith*:

Whatever *Doubts* and *Fears*, as to its own Salvation by him, may at Times attend. If any Soul *discerns* the Excellency of *Christ*, as the chief *Corner-Stone*, the *Foundation-Stone*, which God hath laid in *Sion*; if the Soul *approves* of, and *cleaves* unto him as such: That Soul hath true *Faith*: However *weak* its Persuasion may be, of the Truth of its Faith, of the Reality of its Interest in Christ, and of its Salvation by him. That Soul hath a full Persuasion, an Assurance, a Sight of the Excellency and Glory of *Christ*, as the only and all-sufficient *Saviour*: Fully doth that Soul, approve of *him*, as such; the *one Thing needful*, and *altogether lovely is Christ*, in that Soul's Esteem: And wholly doth that Soul, as a perishing Sinner, *rest* upon *him*, the might *Saviour*, for its *own* Salvation; or lay the whole *Stress* of all its Hope of *Life*, upon *Christ*; as the whole *Weight* of the Building, *lies*, or *rests* upon the Foundation. And wherever *Christi is* thus *precious* unto any Soul: The Word of a GOD that cannot *lie*, assures, that that Soul hath true *Faith*: And likewise, that thus *believing* on Christ, that Soul shall *not be confounded*; but be *saved in the* LORD *with an everlasting Salvation.* And that Soul's Duty and Privilege it is, to take GOD at his *Word:* That thus *believing* on Christ, it *shall not perish, but have everlasting Life.* And to hold this Confidence *fast*, in the Face of a thousand Difficulties, and Doubts and Fears, that may at Times be suggested to, or arise within its own Mind.

With one Text more, I close this. The Apostle *John* saith, *These Things have I written unto you that* believe *on the Name of the Son of God, that ye may* know *that ye have eternal Life, and that ye* may *believe on the Name of the Son of God*, I John v. 13. It is evident from hence, that there *are Degrees* in Faith. The Apostle writes to those who *believ'd* on Christ; that they *might* believe; or that they might *advance* in Faith, unto higher Degrees. It is likewise clear from hence, that saving Faith may *be*, where full Assurance is *not*. If all saving *Faith*, was full *Assurance*, or the *Knowledge* of a Person's having eternal Life in Christ: There would have been no room to *distinguish* between their *Believing*, and their *Knowing* that they had eternal Life; as here the Apostle manifestly doth: Nor yet to have made this *latter*, their *knowing* that they had eternal Life, his *End* in writing to those Persons who had the *former Faith* in Christ. But the Apostle here shews his Concern for Believers, that they might *increase* in Faith; and herein speaks his Lord's Heart: Whose Will it is, that the weakest Souls who *believe* on him, should press *forward* in Faith, unto the *Knowledge* of their having eternal Life in him, and that they might still advance in Faith, unto a *Settled* Assurance, in their Further *believing on the Name of the Son of God.*

Another great *Mistake*, which some of the *Moravian Brethren* are fallen into, is this; *Universal Salvation*; or, the Salvation of *all*, wicked Men and Devils, at last. Unto this I would give a Hint.

And if we believe what our Lord saith, is Truth, infallible, unchangeable and eternal *Truth*: We must believe, that the Notion of Universal Salvation, is a very great *Error*. For when our Lord declares to us, the final State of *all Men*, good and bad, and also, the last State of *Devils*: He assures us, that he will say unto the

Righteous, Come ye blessed *of my Father, inherit the* Kingdom, *prepared for you from the Foundation of the World*: — And unto the *Wicked, Depart from* Me, *ye cursed, into* everlasting Fire, *prepared for the Devil and his Angels*, Matt. xxv. 34,—41. And as an Effect of this solemn Pronunciation of Blessing upon the Righteous, and efficacious Call given them, to inherit eternal Life; and this dreadful Sentence pronounc'd upon the Wicked, at the great Day of Judgment: Our Lord saith, *And* these (the Wicked) *shall go away into* everlasting Punishment: *but the* Righteous *into* Life eternal, Ver. 46. This is the *last State of all*, Men and Devils, which our Lord here presents us with.—And how bold a Thing is it, for any Man that professeth himself to be a *Christian*, to pretend to talk of *another State*, a State of Happiness, for wicked Men and Devils; after the *Lord* of Christians hath thus declar'd, that they shall be sent away from him as *cursed*, into *Everlasting Fire, Everlasting Punishment*? But against everlasting Punishment, as denoting eternal Torment, it has been objected,

Obj. That by the Word *Everlasting*, we are not to understand, an *eternal Duration*; but, a certain long *Period*, that shall have an *End*; as *Aaron's* Priesthood was said to be an *everlasting* Priesthood, which yet had an *End*.

Ans. That by the Word *Everlasting* in Scripture, we are sometimes to understand, a long Period of *Time*, which hath an *End*; I allow. But whenever this Word is us'd in this Sense, in the sacred Writings; the Thing to which it is annexed, is likewise there declar'd to have *ceased*; which necessarily restrains the Sense of the Word *Everlasting*, to a long *Time* that hath had an *End*. But the Word *Everlasting*, as us'd by our Lord, *Matt*. xxv. 46. cannot be *thus* understood; because it refers to what shall be just at the *closing up of Time*, or the two great Events of Sin and Grace, in the Salvation of the Righteous, and the Damnation of the Wicked: Which shall appear at the *Close of Time*, as Time wasts both into a vast *Eternity,* the Righteous, into an eternal State of Glory, and the Wicked, into an eternal State of Misery. — And that the Word *Everlasting*, as us'd here, must be taken, as denoting an *endless Duration*; is further evident, in that in the same Verse, it stands annexed to the Punishment of the Wicked, as the Word *Eternal* doth to the Glory of the Righteous: Which two *States*, are just the *Reverse* of each other, and of an equal *Extent* in Duration. — And that the Word *Everlasting*, as annexed to that *Fire*, which wicked *Men* shall *depart into*, prepared for the *Devil* and his *Angels*, and to that *Punishment*, which wicked *Men* shall *go away into*, must be understood of an *endless Duration*; may be further proved from other Scriptures.

Thus, *Mark* ix. 43, 44. *And if thy Hand offend thee, cut it off; it is better for thee to enter into Life maimed, than having two Hands, to go into* Hell, *into the* Fire *that* never *shall be* quenched; *where their Worm dieth* not, *and the* Fire *is* not quenched. Here again, our Lord tells us of the final State of wicked *Men*, as also of the State of *Devils*; of all those that are *now* in Hell, and of all those that shall *go* into Hell: And of this *Hell*, of this State of Torment, in which wicked Men and Devils are, and into which all Men that live and die wicked, shall enter; our Lord saith, *The* Fire never *shall be* quenched: And repeats it again, to give the greater Assurance to his Assertion, and to demand the greater Attention from us: *The* Fire *that is* not (i.e. never shall be) quenched. Which fully expresseth an *Eternity* of Misery, an *Everlastingness* of Torment, in which wicked Men and Devils are, that are now in Hell, and into which all men that live and die wicked, shall enter. — And weak enough is this, which some vain Men have said,

That tho' the Fire of Hell is *not quenched*, yet Persons may be taken *out* of it.

For, if this was *true*; our Lord's Dissuasion of Persons from *Sin*, by presenting this to their View, of their going into *Hell*, into the *Fire* that is *not quenched*; would have no *Force*. "What, might a stout-hearted Sinner reply, if I *shou'd* go into Hell, into the Fire that is not quenched; if I am to be taken *out* of it, what wou'd the Fire that is not quenched, be to *me?*" But evident it is, that when our Lord saith, *The* Fire never *shall be* quenched, that He intends it, of *theiri Fire,* of the Eternity of *their* Torment, who go into Hell, that *they* shall never be taken *out* of that Misery. And therefore he saith in the next Verse, Their *Worm dieth* not: A guilty Conscience, shall *gnaw*, and torment them *forever*; and the Fire (of God's Wrath into which they are cast) *is* not *quenched*: That is, never *shall be quenched*. And thus we are told, that our Lord will *burn up the* Chaff (the Wicked) *with* unquenchable Fire, *Matt.* iii. 12. Which denotes the *Eternity* of their Torment. And thus, *Rev.* xx. 10. *And the* Devil *that deceived* them, (i.e. the Wicked, who compass'd the Camp of the Saints about) *was cast into the* Lake of Fire *and* Brimstone, *where the Beast and the false Prophets are, and shall be tormented Day and Night,* forever and ever. And after the general Judgment, Ver. 13. it is said, Ver. 15. *And* whosoever *was not found written in the* Book of Life, *was cast into the* Lake of Fire. Into this *Lake*, then, all wicked *Men* and *Devils* shall be *cast*, as *surely* as the Word of God is *true*, which burneth with *Fire* and *Brimstone*, and the *Smoke of their Torment*, who are cast into it, *shall ascend up* forever and ever, Chap. xiv. 11. But lo, such hath been the Boldness of some Men, that they have said,

This *forever and ever*, is to be understood only of two certain *Periods*, which shall have an *End*.

But that by the Words *forever and ever*, we are to understand an *eternal Duration*, is evident, in that they are us'd to set for the *Eternity* of GOD'S *Life*. As in several Places in this Book. Thus Chap. xv. 7. *And one of the four Beasts gave unto the Seven Angels, Seven golden Vials full of the Wrath of* God, *who* liveth forever and ever. Will any vain Man be so bold to assert, from these Words, *Forever and ever*, as annex'd to the *Life of* GOD, that GOD'S Life is to be but for two certain *Periods*, that shall have an *End?* If such a Thought would strike any Person with Awe, who affirms, That the Torments of the Damned shall have an *End*: Let him from the Words, *forever and ever*, as annex'd to those *Torments*, be deterr'd from so bold an Assertion. And observable it is, that the *Eternity of* GOD'S *Life*, who is here said to *live forever and ever*; hath a Connexion with his *Wrath*, and denotes the *Eternity* of his Wrath, from the *Eternity* of his Life. *Full of the*

Wrath *of* GOD, *who* liveth forever and ever. *Forever*, thro' Time, and *Ever*, to Eternity beyond it. — And thus the Apostle saith, *It is a fearful Thing to fall into the Hands of the* living GOD, *Heb.* x. 31. He speaks of the *Eternity of* GOD'S *Life*, in Relation to his *Wrath*; that the *Vengeance* of GOD, must needs be most *fearful*; since his *Life* to perpetuate it, is *eternal*; that as there will be no *End* of his *Life*; so nor of his *Wrath*.

And that the Word *Everlasting*, as annexed to the *Fire of Hell*, and the *Punishment* of the Damned, must be understood of an *endless Duration*; doth likewise appear from *Dan.* xii. 2. *And many of them that sleep in the Dust of the Earth shall awake, some to* everlasting Life, *and some to* Shame *and* everlasting Contempt. Here the *final State* of the Righteous, and of the Wicked, after the Resurrection of the Just, and of the Unjust, and the Judgment of both, is spoken of: And the Word, *Everlasting*, equally annexed unto the State of the one, and of the other, to the *Life*, the Glory of the Righteous, and to the *Shame and Contempt*, the Misery of the Wicked. Which shews, that both *States*, are of an *equal*, and *eternal Duration*. — And thus the Word, *Everlasting*, is us'd, as denoting an *endless Duration*, Deut. xxxiii. 27. *The Eternal* GOD *is they Refuge, and underneath are the* everlasting *Arms*. The Word *Everlasting*, here, as annex'd to *Arms*, signifies the *Eternity* of GOD'S *Power*, to support his People; as the Word *Eternal*, annex'd to GOD, denotes the *Eternity* of his *Life*, of that great BEING, who is the *Refuge* of *Israel*. Both these Words, as here us'd, are evidently of an *equal Extent*, and intend an *endless Duration*. And in divers Places of Scripture, the Word *Everlasting*, is annexed to GOD, to shew the *Eternity* of his *Being*. Thus, *Isa.* xl. 28. *The* Everlasting GOD, *the* LORD, *the Creator of the Ends of the Earth sainteth not.* — But I need add no more as to this; only I would just observe, that the Word *Eternal*, as annex'd to the *Life* of the Righteous, when they *enter* into it, *Matt.* xxv. 46. is of no *larger Extent*, than the Word *Everlasting* was, in the *Promise* of that Life, *John* iii. 16. *For God so loved the World, that he gave his only begotten Son, that whosoever believeth in Him, should not perish, but have* everlasting Life. The Encouragement to *Faith* in Christ, is God's Promise of *everlasting Life* to every Believer; the *End* of Faith, in the Fulfilment of that Promise, or Declaration of Grace, in the Salvation of Believers, is said to be *eternal Life*. Which shews, that the Words *Everlasting* and *Eternal*, as annex'd to the *Life* of Believers, promis'd and posses'd, are of an *equal Extent*, and that the *former*, as well as the *latter*, denotes an *endless Duration*. — By the Word *Everlasting*, then, as annexed to the *Punishment* of the Wicked, as the Word *Eternal*, is to the *Life* of the Righteous, when the *final State* of both is spoken of, which two States, are just the *Reverse* of each other; we must needs understand, an *endless Duration*, an *Eternity* of Torment, which the Wicked shall *enter into.* — And evident this also is, in that the great Day of Judgment, in which the Righteous shall be call'd to enter into *Life*, and the Wicked sent away into *Punishment*, is stiled *eternal Judgment*, Heb. vi. 2. Which denotes, the *Irreversibleness* of what is then done, that the *State* of both the

Righteous and the Wicked, shall then be *decided*, or unchangeably *fix'd* for *Eternity*.

I might also prove the *Eternity* of *Hell-Torments*, 1. From the *Being* of them: Which would have no *Existence*, if Men and Devils there, did not abide under the *Guilt* of their own *Sins*. 2. From the *Impossibility* of any finite Being's making Satisfaction for *Sin*: Which is of an infinite *Guilt*, as against an infinite GOD. And 3. From the full and proper *Sanctification* made by the Death of JESUS, for Those, whose Sins he bore, and that full and *eternal Redemption* which he obtain'd for them thereby. Whence it appears, that those who go to Hell at *all*, must *for ever* abide there, under the Guilt and Punishment of their *own Sins*. CHRIST being a *complete Saviour*, unto all those whom *he Saves*, from the Guilt of Sin, from the Law's Curse, and from the fierce Wrath of a Sin-revenging God: There can be no *halving it*, between the *Sinner* and the *Saviour*, Christ to bear *one Part*, and the Sinner *another Part* of the vindictive *Wrath* of *God*, of the *Punishment* due to the Sinner for his *Sin*: But all those, who are sent to Hell at *all*, to bear the *Punishment* of their own *Sins*; must themselves bear the *Whole* of that Weight, in *Misery* inexpressible, *forever and ever!* — But the Scriptures quoted, and what I have hinted may suffice, to prove this awful Truth: *That the Torments of Men and Devils in Hell, will be eternal.*

From what hath been said then, on this Head, see, dear Reader, how *contrary* the Notion of *Universal Salvation* is, to the *Truth* of *God* in his *Word*! And learn hence, if thou be an *unconverted Sinner*, the absolute *Necessity* there is, of they *fleeing* unto *Christ* by *Faith*, for *Refuge from the Wrath to come*, while it is called *To-day*, before that Wrath overtake thee, from which there will be no escaping, nor Recovery!

And learn hence, you that have *believed in Jesus*, to admire that *great Salvation* you have by him, *from the Wrath to come*, from that *Eternity* of Misery, in that *Wrath*, which *ever, ever* will be Wrath to *come*; which your Sins have *deserved*, and which all Men that die in Unbelief, must *endure*! And *forever* adore the *Grace*, that fav'd you from the *bottomless Pit!* Look frequently to those Depths of endless Misery, you were redeemed *from*; as well as to those Heights of eternal Glory you are redeemed *to*: And in all holy Obedience, love and bless the LORD your *Redeemer*! GOD your *Saviour*! Begin the Work of Heaven now, and say, *Salvation and Glory, and Honour and Blessing be unto Him that sitteth upon the Throne, and to the* LAMB, forever and ever, *Amen*. And again say, *Hallelujah*!

And let us *all*, Believers, and Unbelievers, learn from the *Eternity of Hell-Tormens*, the *Greatness of Sin's Guilt!* For lo, the *eternal* Wrath of GOD Almighty, will be a *righteous* Wrath! *The Judge of all the Earth, will do* right. *He will not lay upon* Men nor Devils for their Sins, *more than is* meet. And however any vain Man, may *reply* against his Maker *now*; *every Mouth will be* stopped *hereafter*. God will be *clear* from any Injustice, and appear to be strictly *righteous*, in adjudging of wicked Men and Devils unto *endless Punishment* for their *Sins*, the *Guilt* whereof, as not satisfy'd for by *Christ*, and as remaining upon *them*, is endless. The *transient*; and *righteous* therefore it will be, that *eternal* should be the *Punishment*. The Glory of GOD, his Holiness, Justice, Power and Truth, will *forever* shine, in the *eternal Punishment* of the *Damned*.

And as to the Atribute of Divine *Mercy*, that is and will be glorify'd in a Way of absolute *Sovereignty*. The LORD will *have* Mercy, *on whom he* will *have* Mercy. And not a *Dram* of Mercy, will the *God* of Mercy, shew unto *any out* of *Christ*. There is no *Salvation* by *Christ* for *any*, but for those who *believe* in him. And *All* will be found *out* of Christ at last, who don't enter *into him* by Faith now. *If ye* believe not *that I am* HE, saith our Lord, *ye shall* die *in your* Sins, *John* viii. 24. And those who *die* in their *Sins*, must be forever *damned* for their Sins. God *spared* not his *Son*, from the utmost of Sin's *Punishment*, when *Sin* was charged upon *him*: Altho' with respect to *him*, it was soon over. For HE being an infinite and eternal Person, soon made an infinite and eternal Satisfaction: Which was the Reason why the Punishment of Sin which fell on Christ, was *not* eternal. And if God spared not his *own Son*, from the just *Punishment* due to *Sin*, when Sin was charged upon *him*: He will not *spare* either *Men* or *Devils*, from the righteous *Punishment* of their *Sins*, which shall at last be charged upon *them*: Altho' the *Punishment* of their Guilt, with respect to *them*, must needs be *eternal*.

What a glorious Project of infinite *Wisdom*, then is it, what a Provision of infinite *Grace, That Mercy and Truth should* meet together, *that Righteousness and Peace should kiss each other!* That all the divine Perfections should *harmonize* in the *Salvation of Sinners*, thro' the *crucify'd Saviour*; as is declar'd in the glorious *Gospel*! And how worthy *of all* Acceptation, is this *faithful Saying, That* Jesus Christ *came into the World to save* Sinners, even the very Chief! — *To-day* then, you *Sinners*, that hear this *joyful Sound, To-day*, if you will *hear God's Voice*, which calls you unto *Faith in Christ*, that you may *escape the Damnation of Hell*, even while it is called *To-day, Harden not your Hearts*. For he *that* believeth on CHRIST, *and is baptized, shall be* saved: *but* he *that believeth* not, *shall be* damned, *Mark* xvi. 16.

F I N I S.

[Errata corrected in text.]

INDEX

Baptists
History, Literature, Theology, Hymns

[Available (and forthcoming) titles in order of publication.]

John Taylor. *Baptists on the American Frontier: A History of Ten Baptist Churches.* Edited by Chester Young (1985).

Thomas Helwys. *A Short Declaration of the Mystery of Iniquity (1611/1612).* Edited by Richard Groves (1998).

Roger Williams. *The Bloody Tenant of Persecution for Cause of Conscience.* Historical introduction by Edwin Gaustad. Edited by Richard Groves (2001).

James A. Rogers. *Richard Furman: Life and Legacy* (1985; reprint with new forewords, 2002).

Lottie Moon. *Send the Light: Lottie Moon's Letters and Other Writings.* Edited by Keith Harper (2002).

James P. Byrd, Jr. *The Challenges of Roger Williams: Religious Liberty, Violent Persecution, and the Bible* (2002).

Anne Dutton. *Selected Spiritual Writings of Anne Dutton, Eighteenth-Century, British-Baptist, Woman Theologian.* In six volumes. Edited by JoAnn Ford Watson. 1. *Letters* (fall 2003). 2. *Discourses, Poetry, Hymns, Memoir* (fall 2004). 3. *The Autobiography* (summer 2006). 4. *Theological Works* (spring 2007). 5. *Miscellaneous Correspondence* (winter 2008). 6. *Various Works* (winter 2009).

David T. Morgan. *Southern Baptist Sisters: In Search of Status, 1845–2000* (fall 2003).

William E. Ellis. *"A Man of Books and a Man of the People": E. Y. Mullins and the Crisis of Moderate Southern Baptist Leadership* (1985; reprint, fall 2003).

Jarrett Burch. *Adiel Sherwood: Baptist Antebellum Pioneer in Georgia* (winter 2003).

Anthony Chute. *A Piety above the Common Standard: Jesse Mercer and the Defense of Evangelistic Calvinism* (spring 2004).

William H. Brackney. *A Genetic History of Baptist Thought* (September 2004).

Henlee Hulix Barnette. *A Pilgrimage of Faith: My Story* (November 2004).

Walter B. Shurden. *Not an Easy Journey: Some Transitions in Baptist Life* (Spring 2005).

Marc A. Jolley, editor. *Distinctively Baptist: Essays on Baptist History: Festschrift Walter B. Shurden* (Spring 2005).

Keith Harper and C. Martin Jacumin. *Esteemed Reproach: The Lives of Rev. James Ireland and Rev. Joseph Craig* (2005).

Charles Deweese. *Women Deacons and Deaconesses: 400 Years of Baptist Service* (BH&HS, 2005).

Pam Durso and Keith Durso. *Courage and Hope: The Stories of Ten Baptist Women Ministers* (BH&HS, 2005).